SAGE was founded in 1965 by Sara Miller McCune to support the dissemination of usable knowledge by publishing innovative and high-quality research and teaching content. Today, we publish more than 750 journals, including those of more than 300 learned societies, more than 800 new books per year, and a growing range of library products including archives, data, case studies, reports, conference highlights, and video. SAGE remains majority-owned by our founder, and on her passing will become owned by a charitable trust that secures our continued independence.

Los Angeles | London | Washington DC | New Delhi | Singapore

Sayyid Ahmad Barailvi

Sayyid Ahmad Barailvi

His Movement and Legacy from the Pukhtun Perspective

Altaf Qadir

www.sagepublications.com
Los Angeles • London • New Delhi • Singapore • Washington DC

First published in 2015 by

SAGE Publications India Pvt Ltd
B1/I-1 Mohan Cooperative Industrial Area
Mathura Road, New Delhi 110 044, India
www.sagepub.in

SAGE Publications Inc
2455 Teller Road
Thousand Oaks, California 91320, USA

SAGE Publications Ltd
1 Oliver's Yard, 55 City Road
London EC1Y 1SP, United Kingdom

SAGE Publications Asia-Pacific Pte Ltd
3 Church Street
#10-04 Samsung Hub
Singapore 049483

Published by Vivek Mehra for SAGE Publications India Pvt Ltd, typeset in 10/12 Minion Pro by RECTO Graphics, Delhi and printed at Saurabh Printers Pvt Ltd, New Delhi.

Library of Congress Cataloging-in-Publication Data

Qadir, Altaf, author.
Sayyid Ahmad Barailvi : his movement and legacy from the Pukhtun perspective / Altaf Qadir.
    pages cm
  Includes bibliographical references and index.
  1. Sayyid Ahmad Shahid, 1786–1831. 2. Khyber Pakhtunkhwa (Pakistan)—History—19th century. 3. Islamic renewal—Pakistan—Khyber Pakhtunkhwa—History—19th century. 4. Jihad. 5. Islam and politics—Pakistan—Khyber Pakhtunkhwa—History—19th century. I. Title.
  DS392.N67Q23   322'.1095491209034—dc23   2015   2014040210

ISBN: 978-93-515-0072-8 (HB)

The SAGE Team: Supriya Das, Vandana Gupta, Rajib Chatterjee and Rajinder Kaur

To

My parents

Thank you for choosing a SAGE product! If you have any comment, observation or feedback, I would like to personally hear from you. Please write to me at <u>contactceo@sagepub.in</u>

—Vivek Mehra, Managing Director and CEO,
SAGE Publications India Pvt Ltd, New Delhi

Bulk Sales

SAGE India offers special discounts for purchase of books in bulk. We also make available special imprints and excerpts from our books on demand.

For orders and enquiries, write to us at

Marketing Department
SAGE Publications India Pvt Ltd
B1/I-1, Mohan Cooperative Industrial Area
Mathura Road, Post Bag 7
New Delhi 110044, India
E-mail us at <u>marketing@sagepub.in</u>

Get to know more about SAGE, be invited to SAGE events, get on our mailing list. Write today to <u>marketing@sagepub.in</u>

This book is also available as an e-book.

Contents

Preface

The Mujahidin Movement of Sayyid Ahmad Barailvi has been taught in courses during the British colonial period and in today's nation-states from a specific perspective, as an ideologically inspired movement. The majority of earlier narratives have blamed the inhabitants of the trans-Indus areas, the British North-West Frontier, and today's Khyber Pakhtunkhwa Province of Pakistan, for the failure of the Jihad Movement. The present book analyses the reform and jihad activities of the period based on indigenous narratives. An attempt has been made to understand the different phases as well as factors responsible for failure of the Jihad Movement. Issues include the selection of the North-West Frontier region for the 'jihad' programme, the Mujahidin's failure to understand the socio-economic dimensions of Pukhtun community life, and the limited financial and material resources available to the Mujahidin that were never sufficient to defeat the Sikhs.

Importantly, the so-called *charisma* of Sayyid Ahmad was not decisively effective in Pukhtun society. For several Pukhtuns he lacked the virtues and qualities of a traditional leader, one always seen in the forefront and prepared to lay down his life for the sake of his people and movement. The actions and personality of Sayyid Ahmad did not resonate or correspond to this leadership model, and in the end he could not mobilize a majority of the Pukhtun population to support his movement. Nevertheless, the impact of the Jihad Movement on the North-West Frontier, ignored by the earlier ideologically inspired writers, had long-term consequences. These will be discussed.

The majority of the previous writers on Sayyid Ahmad were not familiar with Pukhtun cultural dynamics, and many commentators have misinterpreted parts of the history. Some were too biased against the Mujahidin, such as the British, and others were too sympathetic, including Indians in the colonial period ideologically inspired by the Jihad Movement. British colonial administrators and writers have attributed most of the disturbances in the North-West Frontier to the Mujahidin. Indian Muslim writers have accused the local population for the 'betrayal', as is commonly called, of Sayyid Ahmad. The purpose of the present book is to analyse the reform and Jihad Movement of Sayyid Ahmad Barailvi from the immediate sources to avoid misinterpretation of intentions or events.

The present-day Khyber Pakhtunkhwa and adjacent tribal areas of Pakistan are passing through a critical phase due to years of militancy. Local, regional, and foreign actors are competing at the cost of the Pukhtuns. Sayyid Ahmad's Jihad Movement has been claimed by some as an inspiration or cause for the present-day jihadi mentality in the region. This book attempts to present a balanced view of such different claims and influences that have often justified continued war and violence.

The book is based on my PhD dissertation submitted to Quaid-i-Azam University, Islamabad, in 2012, which was revised, improved, and turned into a book. Many people have been sources of encouragement and inspiration in the completion of this work. I am thankful to my mentor Professor Sayed Wiqar Ali Shah for his encouragement and support. I am also thankful to my teachers and friends in the Department of History, Quaid-i-Azam University, who have always remained a source of encouragement throughout the study.

Dr Sultan-i-Rome needs to be thanked for being a constant source of encouragement and support. Professor Abdul Rauf, Department of Political Science, University of Peshawar, provided some material for this study. I am indebted to my students Gulzar Ali, Nasir Amin (a descendent of Sayyid Akbar Shah of Sithana), and Mr Javed Ali (Lecturer in History, Government College Gulabad, Dir Lower) for identifying places which otherwise were very difficult to discern. I am also thankful to Sayyid Mahboob Shah, son of Sayyid Abdul Jabbar Shah of Sithana, for providing some rare material for this study and for access to his father's manuscripts. Special thanks is due to my teacher and colleague Dr Salman Bangash, who took the burden and brought a good collection of Sayyid Ahmad's letters from London. I had lost hope after a road accident, but Rizwan Khattak (PhD Candidate, Department of Botany, University of Peshawar) came to my rescue and followed the process of my treatment. I owe much to her for my recovery and consequent completion of this work.

I am thankful to the management of Higher Education Commission, Islamabad, Pakistan, for financing my study at the Department of History, South Asia Institute (SAI), Heidelberg, Germany, in 2008. I am indebted to Professor Gita Dharmpal Frik, my supervisor at SAI, for the cooperation she extended. Dr Inayatullah Baloch, my teacher at SAI, was always available to discuss different aspects of this project. Long settings with him broadened my vision to explore new aspects of the movement. The list is long, but I would like to record my thanks to Ejaz Bhatti, Nitin Varma, Soumen Mukherji, Prabhat Kumar, Chaiti Basu, Vera Hoke, Lenita Cuhna E. Silva, Luzia Savary, Katia Rosttete, and Katja Phonekg of SAI. Special thanks is due to Muhammad Ali Usman Qasmi (now LUMS, Pakistan) for facilitating and making the initial arrangements at Heidelberg.

I would like to record my thanks to Dr Sana Haroon (Assistant Professor, College of Liberal Arts, University of Massachusetts) for providing some important manuscripts. I am also thankful to the staff of different libraries in Peshawar, Islamabad, Lahore, Swabi, Dhaka (Bangladesh), and Heidelberg (Germany). Thanks is due to Robert Nichols, Richard Stockton College, for his support.

Lastly, I am greatly indebted to my parents and especially my father, who always remained a source of inspiration, and to Dr Muhammad Farooq, my elder brother for sending very important documents from the United Kingdom. I am thankful to my wife for taking on the burden of my responsibilities at home and sparing me to complete this work.

Introduction

After the death of the Mughal Emperor Aurangzeb in 1707, the central authority in India started weakening and led to the emergence of provincial governors as independent rulers in different regions. Eighteenth-century politics in India was a continuous struggle among various factions for political supremacy in Delhi and the provinces. The Indian rulers of different regions were busy in faction fighting with no realization of the expanding power of the East India Company. The states of southern India were the first to feel the might of the Company. The Marathas, who could have checked or halted expansion of the East India Company, remained busy in internal conflicts and the struggle for occupying the throne of Delhi. The Sikhs of the Punjab organized themselves in bands; and after a long struggle with the Mughal forces and faction fighting, Ranjit Singh (d. 1839) occupied Lahore in 1799 and founded the Sikh kingdom. This coincided with the victory of the Company's forces in Sarangapatam against Tipu Sultan, the ruler of Mysore.

The dawn of the nineteenth century did not bring positive changes for Indian Muslims. The English had controlled the economy of the country for a generation but in 1803 they occupied Delhi, a symbol of their suzerainty in India. The Anglo-Sikh Treaty of Amritsar (1809) resulted in collaboration between the two emerging powers, which continued until the death of Ranjit Singh in 1839. This treaty defined the directions of expansion for both the powers. There were Muslim nobles and princes who fought against the enemies of the Muslims and the Mughals. Besides the nobles, some *ulama* endeavoured to reform the lives of the Indian nobility. But their activities remained limited to a specific circle.

This book aims to analyse Sayyid Ahmad Barailvi's movement in its different stages and legacies. He was born in Raebareli in 1786, a small town of the then Oudh state. Though not interested in education, he studied a few basic books of religion. At a very early age, he visited various cities in search of employment, including Delhi, where he stayed for four years with the family of Shah Waliullah, a Muslim scholar. Later he remained for seven years with Amir Khan (d. 1834), who later became Nawab of Tonk.

He left Nawab Amir Khan following the truce between the Nawab and the English. Sayyid Ahmad then began his reform movement, intended to purify Muslims of the Indian subcontinent.

The movement was his personal initiative, though Shah Waliullah's teaching partially moulded his thought. He drew his two main disciples, Shah Ismail (d. 1831) and Abdul Hai (d. 1828), from Shah Waliullah's family. In the course of his reform movement, he travelled various districts of northern India and afterwards proceeded overseas for the Haj. After his return from the Hijaz, he started preparations for jihad. He, along with his associates, left for the North-West Frontier and arrived in the Peshawar Valley in October 1826. The North-West Frontier was selected for various reasons: it had a favourable geographical and strategic location, it allowed the confronting of the newly expanding Sikh rule in that area, and the egalitarian nature of its inhabitants might serve a common purpose.

Sayyid Ahmad was warmly received by the Pukhtun communities and their chiefs, including Said Muhammad Khan and Yar Muhammad Khan, the Barakzai brothers, in command of Hashtnagar (Ashnaghar) and Peshawar, respectively. They had previously agreed to pay annual tribute to Ranjit Singh. Sayyid Ahmad and his followers left Peshawar after a brief stay. Their first encounter with the Sikhs happened as a sudden attack on the night of 21 December 1826 at Akora Khattak, near Nowshera. Shortly after, Khadi Khan of Hund joined Sayyid Ahmad and invited him to establish his centre at Hund, an invitation he accepted. The mismanagement by the Pukhtuns accompanying Mujahidin during the attack on Hazro was taken as an excuse for Sayyid Ahmad to establish his own authority. This was an early indication of his lack of knowledge of the religious sensibility and social and political dynamics of the area.

His declaration of *imarat* in January 1827 at Hund created multiple problems, and the Mujahidin had to face related repercussions until the final Balakot episode. In the next fight with the Sikhs at Shaidu, a small village near Nowshera, the desertion of the Barakzai chiefs resulted in the defeat of the Mujahidin. Feeling endangered, they took refuge in Panjtar, a mountainous village in Buner and stronghold of the Khudu Khel chief Fateh Khan, who had joined the movement. Sayyid Ahmad and the Mujahidin toured in Buner, Swat, and Mandanr area, and the subsequent ascendancy of Sayyid Ahmad's authority led to the development of differences between him and the Pukhtuns. Khadi Khan of Hund, one of the first supporters of the Mujahidin, turned against them. This resulted in his assassination in 1829. Amir Khan, brother of Khadi Khan, persuaded Yar Muhammad Khan to march against the Mujahidin. In the battle of Zaida (September 1829), Yar Muhammad was defeated and killed. Ahmad Khan Kamalzai of Hoti, Mardan, was also amongst those who resisted the new system. He was joined by Sultan Muhammad Khan and in the ensuing battle of Mayar (October 1830), Ahmad Khan and Sultan Muhammad Khan were defeated. Peshawar was taken by Sayyid Ahmad after the defeat of his opponents but then the city was restored to Sultan Muhammad Khan.

Restoring Peshawar to the Barakzais was one of the major blunders of Sayyid Ahmad. Some of his associates did not endorse this decision, but Sayyid Ahmad overruled their view. Sayyid Ahmad appointed his Indian deputies to various posts to enforce *sharia* and collect revenue in the recently conquered areas of Peshawar Valley. The replacement of old practices and institutions with new ones affected the local political economy and society and these changes were soon resisted by the locals.

Apart from his struggle in Peshawar Valley, Swat, and Buner, Sayyid Ahmad also sent forces to occupy Kashmir. The Mujahidin wanted to make Kashmir the centre of their activities. It was one of the richest provinces of the Mughal and Durrani kingdoms. Sayyid Akbar Shah of Sithana and Painda Khan of Amb agreed to assist the Mujahidin. In various attempts, the Mujahidin failed to take Kashmir. Differences with Painda Khan of Amb emerged which resulted in the occupation of some of Painda Khan's areas by Sayyid Ahmad's followers. The skirmishes were still underway when Sayyid Ahmad received his most severe setback in the Peshawar Valley. Unhappy Pukhtuns assassinated the small bands of Mujahidin posted in various stations by Sayyid Ahmad. Disappointed, Sayyid Ahmad left Panjtar for Nandihar Valley. The assassination of the Mujahidin by the local population is discussed with due care in this book. The last fight between the Sikhs and Sayyid Ahmad took place in May 1831. His forces were defeated and he was killed by the Sikhs. Many of his prominent disciples including Shah Ismail and Arbab Bahram Khan were also killed in the battle.

While the story of Sayyid Ahmad has been told in earlier narratives, this study discusses the movement at the very local level while also examining elements of the overall political, social, religious and economic impact of the Jihad Movement on the North-West Frontier. This book is perhaps the first academic attempt to analyse the Jihad Movement of Sayyid Ahmad from perspectives drawn from the immediate localities involved. One contribution is the recovery and interpretation of minute details of the movement, neglected or ignored by earlier writers. Earlier commentators and historians have blamed the inhabitants of the North-West Frontier region for the failure of the Jihad Movement. We have attempted to illuminate the quite complicated factors responsible for the failure of the Jihad Movement. These include the original selection of the North-West Frontier region for the 'jihad' purpose, the Mujahidin's failure to understand the sensitivity of the many socio-economic dimensions of Pukhtun society, and the ultimately meagre financial resources of the Mujahidin movement that were insufficient to counter the Sikhs. Moreover, the so-called *charisma* of Sayyid Ahmad did not work well in the Pukhtun society. He lacked, did not understand, or chose not to project the virtues and qualities respected in a Pukhtun leader; one always seen at the forefront and prepared to lay down his life for the sake of his people and movement. Though having limited knowledge of the religion, local poets had long contributed lengthy *na'at*, a form of poetry, that discussed the life and achievements of the Prophet Muhammad (Peace Be Upon Him) and provided the Pukhtuns a model of *charismatic* leadership in the personality of the Prophet Muhammad (Peace Be Upon Him). He had often been seen in the forefront in the battles fought in the early days of Islam. The required model of legitimacy was missing in the personality of Sayyid Ahmad and he did not attract a majority of the Pukhtun population. Nevertheless, the impact of the Jihad Movement on the North-West Frontier was substantial and has received serious attention in this study.

In preparation, we considered how potential theoretical frameworks might apply to discussion of the movement of Sayyid Ahmad. The movement at its initial stage was a reform movement named *Rah-e-Suluk-e-Nabuwat*, though at times it turned sectarian. The focus of the movement remained on the reformation of society, ideally to replicate early Muslim society. In the second phase, it turned into a resistance movement and armed struggle was initiated against the Sikhs. It took yet another turn when the focus of the Mujahidin turned to subduing their local opponents and expanding their authority in the North-West Frontier region. Applying resistance and millenarianism theories as discussed by Adas[1] has limits. Adas' case studies were the movements initiated by locals against the colonial order. The case of Sayyid Ahmad was different. No doubt, Sayyid Ahmad knew grievances of Indians due to the establishment of the English colonial order.[2] Many old aristocratic and religious families were deprived of their previous positions including his own. But his armed struggle in the Frontier was directed against the Sikhs and his local opponents. Furthermore, support of the Pukhtuns may be considered a case of 'millenarianism', and in Weber's words *charisma*, and the locals' resistance against the Mujahidin may be put in the category of 'neo-institutionalism' to follow North.[3] Yet applying 'neo-institutionalism' to the Jihad Movement would lead to confusion, as many aristocratic families among the Pukhtuns adopted themselves according to the requirements of the time, and indeed took advantage from such institutions. Moreover, the Mujahidin rose against the Sikhs though new institutions were introduced by the East India Company. Application of 'Messianic' theory as discussed by Shaukat Ali[4] also bears problems. All components of the movements discussed in his work were not found in the Jihad Movement. The problem with the application of any theoretical framework is due to the peculiar situation of the North-West Frontier on one hand and the movement, itself, on the other. How will one explain the support and resistance of the Pukhtuns if it is taken as a resistance movement and yet explain why the *charisma* of Sayyid Ahmad failed to attract Pukhtun support after he introduced his system of administration?

We have preferred to focus on an analytical method instead of directly applying any specific theoretical framework. These frameworks, developed in different environments, at times are difficult to apply to historical phenomenon and may lead to distortion of fact-based analysis. The book is aimed at analysing and interpreting minute details of the Jihad Movement and to clarify related myths. It focuses on explaining the movement of Sayyid Ahmad Barailvi and drawing inferences from details of his journeys and personal interactions. Themes include the various phases of the movement, its achievements and setbacks, the initial support of the Pukhtuns and their final opposition, the establishment of the *khilafat* and resulting opposition from the learned, the organizational structure of the Mujahidin and their supplies, and the overall impact of the movement. Several sources that have been consulted may be classified into four major categories though a few sources may not fit any of them. First are sources on the *ulama*'s role in Indian politics or exclusively on the Jihad Movement and Sayyid Ahmad. Second are sources on the North-West Frontier by the foreign visitors, colonial administrators, and people of the region. Third, are academic works on the North-West Frontier and fourth are Sikh sources.

The first category of such literature has been produced either by the associates or by ideological followers of Sayyid Ahmad, and by a few academics. The first source of foremost importance is Khan's *Waqai*.[5] The whole *Waqai* is based on the events of Sayyid Ahmad's life, narrated by those Mujahidin who had settled in Tonk after the battle of Balakot (1831). The beauty of the *Waqai* is its narrators' style. It has been compiled in a simple tone without interpretation. The events of the *Waqai*, however, were narrated by the Mujahidin with an emotional attachment that avoided discussion of the shortcomings of the Mujahidin. Mihr[6] has written a detailed account of the Jihad Movement, analysed according to the writer's own understanding and inspiration. He blamed the Pukhtuns for the failure of the movement, avoiding any discussion of mistakes by the Mujahidin. He justified every action of Sayyid Ahmad and his associates, making them almost supernatural. He has not discussed the dynamics of the tribal structure or clan-to-clan and clan–state relations. Mihr had extensively travelled in the places where the Mujahidin stayed and fought, and he identified most of the places correctly. Nadvi's[7] two volumes are a useful narration of the Jihad Movement of Sayyid Ahmad. His analysis is not better than Mihr's in discussing the failure of the movement.

Abdullah Butt[8] discusses some aspects of the services and personality of Shah Ismail in the Jihad Movement. Abdullah Butt, however, also belongs to the group of writers who has overly elevated the leaders of the movement. Zahur-ud-Din Butt[9] has written from the perspective of Indian nationalism. He has interpreted the events to support his ideology. Khan[10] informs about the locals who had joined the Mujahidin, especially from the Hazara belt. This work covers a long period, mainly focusing on the aftermath of the battle of Balakot. Nasiri's[11] two volumes are a detailed poetic version of the Jihad Movement. His sources are those which have typically been consulted by authors on the subject. There is no difference between his work and that of other ideologically inspired writers about the Jihad Movement.

The major academic work exclusively on the Jihad is written by Qeyamuddin Ahmad.[12] Ahmad was perhaps the first academician who conducted a doctorate-level research on the subject. However, his main focus remained on the aftermath of the Balakot episode (1831). His analysis is important but his discussion lacks knowledge of Pukhtun social dynamics. Mohiuddin Ahmad[13] has worked extensively on the movement of Sayyid Ahmad. He has consulted numerous sources for his work. However, there is little difference between his narration and Nadvi's. Hedayatullah's[14] is one of the best works, especially for those researchers studying the first phase of Sayyid Ahmad's movement, before his migration to the North-West Frontier. Masud Nadvi's[15] book was written before Partition. His tone is flawed as he has mainly answered the objections about the personality and movement of Sayyid Ahmad raised by movement's opponents. Husain's[16] edited work contains two articles by the editor. The content and analysis of the author is hardly different from that of Mihr and Nadvi.

Qureshi[17] has allotted considerable space to Sayyid Ahmad and his Mujahidin Movement. He has given a detailed account of the Mujahidin activities after the battle of Balakot and a very good account of the role of the Mujahidin in the First Anglo-Afghan War (1839). Ikram[18] has written an excellent account of services of the Muslim intelligentsia in the nineteenth and twentieth centuries. The author, despite his respect for Sayyid Ahmad, has discussed the grievances of the Pukhtuns during the Mujahidin sojourn. Madani's[19] is perhaps the first work to suggest that Sayyid Ahmad's movement was a continuation of Shah Waliullah's efforts. Furthermore, he discusses the movement in the context of Indian nationalism, followed by Sindhi[20] and Sayyid Muhammad Mian.[21]

The nationalistic interpretation of the Jihad Movement has linked Sayyid Ahmad with Shah Waliullah's followers and has minimized his role as a pioneer. The nationalist views have one more thing in common. They blame the British for the failure of the movement. Sindhi, however, has referred specifically to the high handedness of the Mujahidin and blamed Sayyid Ahmad for not taking into consideration the socio-political dynamics of the Pukhtuns. Shahjahanpuri[22] has also written from an ideologically inspired point of view. The argument is to prove that Sayyid Ahmad's movement was the unanimous consensus of Indian Muslims, though the title suggests that the only focus is the battlefield of Balakot. Thanesari's[23] book was written to divert the attention of colonial administrators from the 'Wahabis'. Thanesari intentionally altered parts of Sayyid Ahmad's letters to show he was 'friendly' to the British. This point has also long been stressed by Punjabi 'nationalist' writers, some of whom consider Sayyid Ahmad a British agent and try to prove that the Jihad Movement was engineered by the English to counter the Sikhs and check Ranjit Singh's forward moves in the North-West Frontier. This claim remains unsupported by evidence. Thanesari's *Tawarikh-e-Ajiba*, later published with the titles of *Sawanih-e-Ahmadi* and *Hayat-e-Sayyid Ahmad Shahid*, was the first Urdu work on the subject. The publication of *Waqai Sayyid Ahmad Shahid* has minimized the importance of Thanesari's work. Details of many other sources consulted in this category are present in the bibliography.

The second category of sources for this study includes works of foreign visitors, colonial agents, and inhabitants of the area writing contemporary with the events or later. Masson's[24] three volumes have priority as he visited the area when Sayyid Ahmad was in Peshawar Valley. Apart

from narrating the social geography of the area, Masson briefly referred
to Sayyid Ahmad's movement and his relation with the Barakzai brothers.
The *James Settlement Report 1853*[25] and its *Supplement* prepared in 1865
are good sources of information about the Pukhtun tribes, their ethno-
graphic composition, and inter-clan and state-clan relations. These reports
also shed some light on the Sayyid's movement and Pukhtun opposition.

Among the colonial officials, Bellew's *Report*[26] and *Races*[27] are useful.
Bellew has discussed the Jihad Movement in some detail. All his narratives cannot be trusted but he provides some information. The *Gazetteer
of Hazara*[28] and *Peshawar*[29] are also sources for basic information. The
present study, however, has serious reservations about the colonial documents produced after the *James Settlement Report*. Colonial administrators
of the area distorted facts to influence policy makers in London and to
justify their actions. Plowden[30] has given a detailed account of Akhund
Abdul Ghafur of Swat, Sayyid Akbar Shah of Sithana, and other leading
men in the region. The description of the tribes in Swat is mostly accurate
though there is misinformation. Caroe[31] has also written a chapter on the
Mujahidin Movement. Joseph Davey Cunningham's,[32] one of the earliest
colonial sources on the Sikhs' history, is another useful account. While the
rule of Ranjit Singh was discussed in detail, Sayyid Ahmad is discussed
in a few pages. Elphinnstone[33] has discussed the tribal composition and
past history of the Pukhtuns in Afghanistan until the first decade of the
nineteenth century. Raverty's *Notes*[34] helps to understand the Pukhtuns
and different routes in the region. Ibbeston[35] gives details of the composition and culture of the local inhabitants.

Latif's[36] work is one of the most detailed studies on the history of the
Punjab. The writer, a British employee in the colonial period, not only
had access to information, but also knew the mindset of the colonial
administrators. Das[37] prepared his report for the permanent settlement
of the Peshawar Valley and there is very useful information about the
inhabitants of different villages and towns, the numerical and economic
strength of clans, the number of male and female residents, and the followers of different religions. This comprehensive settlement report meant
that few villages escaped mention in this work.

Kakakhel[38] deals with question of the Pukhtun origin and their history through the ages. His analysis of the failure of the Jihad Movement
is significant. Panni[39] highlights that every clan cared for their own
interests when invasions took place from different corners. This includes
a useful narration of the Mujahidin struggle for supremacy in Hazara.
Quddusi's[40] title suggests that only those Sufis who originally belonged to

the North-West Frontier are discussed, but the volume also covers those who migrated to the region. Moreover, Sayyid Ahmad is rarely known to the Pukhtuns as a Sufi, rather he is famous as the leader of the Jihad Movement. Yusafi[41] has discussed the Jihad Movement as his focus was on Yusafzais and the Mujahidin lived in their midst for most of the time during their stay in the North-West Frontier region. He tried to dig out the causes of Pukhtuns' grievances against the Mujahidin though he committed blunders at times especially when he referred to the opposition of the local *ulama*.

Sithanavi[42] discusses the history of the area and ethnic composition of the North-West Frontier. The movement of Sayyid Ahmad is also discussed thoroughly. A descendant of the Sayyid Akbar Shah of Sithana, ruler of Swat (1915–17), and close to colonial administrators, he had insight into the dimensions of the area and the Jihad Movement. Sabir[43] draws upon many sources though these are not properly cited. Abdul Ghaffar,[44] in his autobiography, has dealt in detail with the socio-political situation of the North-West Frontier of that time. He has also referred to the Jihad Movement briefly. Khalil's work,[45] though not a history book, is very useful as the *charbitah*—a form of Pukhtu poetry in which four stanzas complete an expression—expresses sentiments about historical events. Asar's[46] is a different collection of *charbitay*. There are few historical essays related to the Jihad Movement. But Shaheen's[47] collection is very useful for understanding the Pukhtun culture through the study of poetic, two-line verse, *tapah*. The present work has cited such sources, perhaps for the first time in discussion of the Jihad Movement of Sayyid Ahmad. The poetry of Pukhtun tribal people, living at the peripheries, presents itself as more authentic than that of the urban centres. Mahsud's[48] analysis might not be fully objective, but his work contains a good understanding of the dynamics of the Pukhtun culture. He has referred to the factors responsible for the failure of the Jihad Movement.

The third category of sources consulted includes works written on the area that apply different theoretical frameworks. Nichols'[49] arguments might not be agreed with in totality but still are thought-provoking. He considers the resistance movement in the North-West Frontier as a historical phenomenon. Resistance might be historical continuation, but the Pukhtuns had always provided mercenaries, and history is replete with ample evidence that they did so for sustenance. A polarization involving 'jihad' developed with Sayyid Ahmad, but its precedents were found in the times of Akhun Darwizah and Bayazid Ansari, as Nichols argues. Pearson[50] has discussed the movement in northern India, but rarely referred to the jihad in the North-West Frontier. Jafri and Reifeld[51] focus on the Sufi cult instead of the jihad and its various aspects. Haroon's[52] work is a good analytical study, covering first half of the twentieth century. She argues that formation of tribal areas by colonial administrators empowered the religious class to assert authority. Importantly, those who asserted authority were Pukhtuns, stakeholders in the Pukhtun social order.

Jalal's[53] is a substantial work, though with some misinterpretation of events of the Jihad Movement. Allen[54] has wrongly attributed the origin of Wahabism in India to Shah Abdul Rahim, father of Shah Waliullah.

A good account of the Sikh sources that were consulted include Kohli,[55] Sethi,[56] Ganda Singh,[57] Harbans Singh,[58] Lal,[59] and many others, discussed in the text at relevant places. Apart from books, many articles from Pukhtun writers as well as academics from across the globe have been consulted and are included in the bibliography.

The majority of the previous works on Sayyid Ahmad were written by those who were not familiar with Pukhtun cultural dynamics and who misinterpreted parts of the phenomenon. Some were too biased against the Mujahidin, and others too sympathetic, including Indians ideologically inspired by the Jihad Movement. British colonial administrators and writers attributed most of the disturbances in the North-West Frontier to the Mujahidin, and Indian Muslim writers accused the local population of the 'betrayal', as is commonly called, of Sayyid Ahmad. The purpose of this study is to analyse the Jihad Movement of Sayyid Ahmad Barailvi from an objective distance, and to understand the goals of the movement from the evidence of its own statements and actions.

Presently Pukhtun region is passing through a critical phase amidst an increasing tide of militancy. Local, regional, and foreign state and non-state actors have played their hands at the cost of Pukhtuns. To what extent has Sayyid Ahmad's Jihad Movement been responsible for an enduring jihadi mindset, as some writers have tried to prove? How might the movement be understood in historical perspective?

The book pursues descriptive and analytical methods. It not only records the minute details of the movement, but also focuses on the proper interpretation of such instances as allowed by sources. Sayyid Ahmad and his Mujahidin have been presented by many as pious souls. Is it possible to compare the goals and deeds of these Mujahidin with the acts of earlier Muslims with similar goals? A study has been made of the declaration of *imarat* by Sayyid Ahmad and its role in the failure of the 'movement'.

This work is divided into seven chapters. Chapter 1 offers an account of Mughal India and the North-West Frontier after the death of Emperor Aurangzeb in 1707. Traced is the emergence of the East India Company as a major stakeholder in Indian politics and the role of local rulers in this process. The dynamics of the political, socio-religious, and economic situation of the North-West Frontier region are outlined.

Chapter 2 discusses the biography and thoughts of Sayyid Ahmad Barailvi. A brief account is given of the role played by Sayyid Ahmad's family in the preceding generations. The life sketch of Sayyid Ahmad is followed by a study of the evolution of his thought under the influence of Shah Abdul Aziz within the socio-political situation of India after the occupation of Delhi by East India Company.

Chapter 3 surveys Sayyid Ahmad's call for jihad, the Mujahidin's migration to the North-West Frontier, and subsequent events up to his defeat in the battle of Shaidu. Sayyid Ahmad's selection of the North-West Frontier region for jihad is discussed in detail as well as the route of his migration. Also analysed are the few writers who claimed that Sayyid Ahmad was financed by the British. Full space is allocated to Sayyid Ahmad's declaration of *imarat*, one of the most important events of the Jihad Movement.

Chapter 4 outlines in detail the situation after Sayyid Ahmad's defeat in the battle of Shaidu (1827). Sayyid Ahmad attempted to find a sanctuary for his activities. Sayyid Ahmad toured Swat and Buner. He then entered Hazara with the aim of finding a safe place for his activities. The chapter studies his failure to get practical assistance.

Chapters 5 and 6 deal with the Mujahidin's rise and fall in parts of the North-West Frontier region. Events include the second moment of *bai'at* at Panjtar and the imposition of *sharia* in the Khudu Khel, Mandanr, and Yusafzai areas. The Mujahidin struggled for supremacy in Hazara and Kashmir. Chapter 7 examines the impact of the Mujahidin Movement on the North-West Frontier and is followed by Conclusion.

Notes and References

1. Adas, Michael. 1979. *Prophets of Rebellion: Millenarian Protest Movements against the European Colonial Order.* New York: Cambridge University Press.
2. We have used the term English colonial order and not the British as India was ruled by English East India Company until 1858.

3. North, Douglass C. 1990. *Institutions, Institutional Change and Economic Performance.* New York: Cambridge University Press.

4. Ali, Shaukat. 1993. *Millenarian and Messianic Tendencies in Islamic History.* Lahore: Publishers United.

5. Khan, Nawab Muhammad Wazir. 2007. *Waqai Sayyid Ahmad Shahid.* Lahore: Sayyid Ahmad Shahid Academy.

6. Mihr, Ghulam Rasul. nd. *Sayyid Ahmad Shahid.* Lahore: Sheikh Ghulam Ali and Sons.

7. Nadvi, Sayyid Abu Al-Hassan Ali. nd. *Tarikh-e-Dawat wa Azimat: Sirat-e-Sayyid Ahmad.* Karachi: Majlas Nashriyat.

8. Butt, Abdullah. 1999. *Shah Isma'il Shahid: Majmu'a-e-Muqalat.* Lahore: Makki Dar-ul-Kutub.

9. Butt, Zahur-ud-Din. nd. *Shah Waliullah ka Qafila.* Lahore: Idara Adab-e-Atfal.

10. Khan, Khawas. 1983. *Roidad Mujahidin-e-Hind.* Lahore: Maktaba Rashidiah.

11. Nasiri, Alim. 1995. *Shahnama Balakot: Tahrik-e-Jihad ki Manzoom Dastan,* vols. I–II. Lahore: Idara Matbu'at-e-Sulaimani.

12. Ahmad, Qeyamuddin. 1979. *The Wahabi Movement in India.* Islamabad: National Book Foundation.

13. Ahmad, Mohiuddin. 1975. *Saiyid Ahmad Shahid: His Life and Mission.* Lucknow: Academy of Islamic Research and Publications.

14. Hedayatullah, Muhammad. nd. *Sayyid Ahmad: A Study of the Religious Reform Movement of Sayyid Ahmad of Ra'e Bareli.* Lahore: Sh. Muhammad Ashraf.

15. Nadvi, Masud Alam. 1979. *Hindustan ki Pehli Islami Tahrik.* Lahore: Idara Matbu'at-e-Sulaimani.

16. Husain, Mahmud et al. (eds). 2008. *A History of the Freedom Movement, 1707–1831.* Karachi: Royal Book Company.

17. Qureshi, Ishtiaq Hussain. nd. *Ulema in Politics.* Karachi: Ma'arif.

18. Ikram, Shaikh Muhammad. 2000. *Mauj-e-Kausar.* Lahore: Idara Saqafat-e-Islamia.

19. Madani, Hussain Ahmad. nd. *Naqsh-e-Hayat.* Karachi: Dar-ul-Isha'at.

20. Sindhi, Obaidullah. nd. *Shah Waliullah aur un ki Siyasi Tahrik: Yaney Hizbi Waliullah Delhlvi ki Ijmali Tarikh ka Muqadimma.* Lahore: al-Mahmud Academy.

21. Mian, Sayyid Muhammad. 1977. *Ulama-e-Hind ka Shandar Mazi.* Lahore: Maktaba Mahmudiya.

22. Shahjahanpuri, Payam. 1971. *Shahdatgah-e-Balakot.* Lahore: Idara Tarikh wa Tahqiq.

23. Thanesari, Muhammad Jaffar. 1969. *Maktubat Sayyid Ahmad Shahid aur Kala Pani.* Lahore: Nafees Academy.

24. Masson, Charles. 1974. *Narrative of Various Journeys in Balochistan, Afghanistan and the Panjab,* I–III. Karachi: Oxford University Press. Charles Masson (1800–1853) was the pseudonym of James Lewis, a British East India Company soldier.

25. *James Settlement Report 1853,* Khyber Pakhtunkhwa Provincial Archives, Peshawar.

26. Bellew, H. W. 2001. *A General Report on the Yusufzais.* Lahore: Sang-e-Meel Publications.

27. Bellew, H. W. nd. *The Races of Afghanistan.* Lahore: Sang-e-Meel Publications.

28. *Gazetteer of Hazara District 1883–84.* 2000. Lahore: Sang-e-Meel Publications.

29. *Gazetteer of the Peshawar District 1897–98.* 1989. Lahore: Sang-e-Meel Publications.

30. Plowden, T. J. C. 1932. *Report on the Leading Persons and State of Factions in Swat.* Simla: Government of India.

31. Caroe, Olaf. 1965. *The Pathans, 550 BC–AD 1957.* London: Macmillan & Co Ltd.

32. Cunningham, Joseph Davey. 1849. *A History of the Sikhs: From the Origin of the Nation to the Battle of the Sutlej.* London: John Murray.
33. Elphinstone, Mountstuart. 1990. *An Account of the Kingdom of Caubul.* Quetta: Gosha-e-Adab.
34. Raverty, Henry George. 1982. *Notes on Afghanistan and Baluchistan.* Quetta: Nisa Traders.
35. Ibbeston, Denzil. 1993. *Punjab Castes.* Delhi: Low Price Publications.
36. Latif, Sayyid Muhammad. 1964. *History of the Panjab: From the Remotest Antiquity to the Present Time.* Delhi: Eurasia Publishing House.
37. Das, Gopal. 1878. *Tarikh-e-Peshawar.* Lahore: Koh-e-Noor Press.
38. Kakakhel, Sayyid Bahadar Shah Zafar. nd. *Pukhtanah da Tarikh pah Ranra Kay, 550 BC–1964 AD.* Peshawar: University Book Agency.
39. Panni, Sher Bahadar Khan. 2006. *Tarikh-e-Hazara.* Lahore: Maktaba Jamal.
40. Quddusi, Ijaz-ul-Haq. 1966. *Tazkirah Sufia-e-Sarhad.* Lahore: Markazi Urdu Board.
41. Yusafi, Allah Bakhsh. 1973. *Yusafzai Afghan.* Karachi: Sharif Arta Press.
42. Sithanvi, Sayyid Abdul Jabbar Shah. 2011. *Kitab-ul-Ibrat,* vol. I. Islamabad: Porab Academy.
43. Sabir, Muhammad Shafi. 1986. *Tarikh-e-Subah Sarhad.* Peshawar: University Book Agency.
44. Ghaffar, Abdul. 1983. *Zama Jwand aw Jadujahd.* Kabul: Dawlati Matba'.
45. Khalil, Hamesh. 2008. *Da Charbitay Pakhwani Shairan.* Peshawar: Pashto Academy.
46. Salarzai, Qazi Abdul Halim Asar Afghani. 2006. *Da Pukhtu Charbitay: Bagh wa Bahar.* Peshawar: Pashto Academy.
47. Shaheen, Salma. 1994. *Rohi Sandaray: Tapay.* Peshawar: Pashto Academy.
48. Mahsud, Ali Khan. nd. *La Pir Rokhana tar Bacha Khan Porey: Da Pukhtanu Milli Mubarezay ta Katanah.* Peshawar: Danish Khparandwa Tolanay Takhniki Sanga.
49. Nichols, Robert. 2001. *Settling the Frontier: Land, Law, and Society in the Peshawar Valley, 1500–1900.* Karachi: Oxford University Press.
50. Pearson, Harlon O. 2008. *Islamic Reform and Revival in Nineteenth-century India: The Tariqah-e-Muhammadiyah.* Delhi: Yoda Press.
51. Jafri, Saiyid Zaheer Husain and Helmut Reifeld. 2006. *The Islamic Path: Sufism, Politics and Society in India.* Delhi: Rainbow Publishers Limited.
52. Haroon, Sana. 2011. *Frontier of Faith: A History of Religious Mobilisation in the Pakhtun Tribal Areas c. 1890–1950.* Karachi: Oxford University Press.
53. Jalal, Ayesha. 2008. *Partisans of Allah: Jihad in South Asia.* Massachusetts: Harvard University Press.
54. Allen, Charles. 2007. *God's Terrorists: The Wahabi Cult and the Hidden Roots of Modern Jihad.* Massachusetts: Da Capo Press.
55. Kohli, S. R. 2004. *Maharaja Ranjit Singh.* Lahore: Sang-e-Meel Publications.
56. Sethi, R. R. 1950. *The Lahore Darbar: Punjab Government Record Office Publications Monograph No. 1.* Delhi: Gulab Chand Kapur and Sons.
57. Singh, Ganda. 1977. *Ahmad Shah Durrani: Father of Modern Afghanistan.* Quetta: Gosha-e-Adab.
58. Singh, Harbans. 1964. *The Heritage of the Sikhs.* Bombay: Asia Publishing House.
59. Lal, Kanhia. 2002. *Tarikh-e-Punjab.* Mirpur, Azad Kashmir: Arsalan Books.

1

Mughal India and the Frontier at the Dawn of Nineteenth Century

Mughal India After the Death of Aurangzeb

The war of succession[1] that ensued after the death of Aurangzeb on 2 March 1707 (28th Dhul Qa'idah 1118 A.H.) culminated in the victory of Muhammad Muazzam Shah,[2] popularly known as Bahadur Shah I. He had good qualities but lacked the political ambition that a successor of Aurangzeb needed to keep the vast empire intact.[3]

Aurangzeb's absence from northern India during his reign had encouraged the Rajputs[4] to hold their territory independently.[5] Mughal forces subdued them during the time of Bahadur Shah I,[6] but complete order was not achieved as Bahadur Shah marched to the Deccan to deal with his brother Kam Bakhsh. The return of Bahadur Shah terrified the Rajput chiefs and Jai Singh started negotiations. The news of the Sikhs revolt in Sirhind hastened the peace process and a nominal submission of the Rajputs was accepted.[7]

The Sikhs[8] were active in Mughal politics for many years but they resorted to vigorous armed struggle under the leadership of Banda Bairagi, popularly known as Banda Bahadur, during Bahadur Shah's reign. By May 1710 Banda Bahadur conquered Shahabad, Sadhaura, Sirhind and all the area between the rivers Sutlej and Yamuna. He appointed officers and struck a new coin in the names of Guru Nanak and Guru Govind Singh.[9] He plundered all the Mughal-administered towns in the Doab area and villages around Lahore, but the city was defended by its governor Sayyid Aslam. Banda left Mukhlispur and went in hiding after finding it difficult to defend himself.[10] Bahadur Shah moved to Lahore where he died on 27 February 1712, after a brief illness.[11]

Muezzuddin Jahandar Shah ascended the throne on 29 March 1712, after killing his brothers in war of succession.[12] Jahandar Shah was deposed by his nephew Muhammad Farrukh Siyyar after his defeat near the walls of Agra on 10 January 1713[13] with the help of Sayyid brothers, Hassan Ali Khan, commonly known as Abdullah Khan, and Hussain Ali Khan.[14]

Taking advantage of the war of succession, Banda Bahadur rose again, and defeated the Mughal officers of Jammu and Sultanpur (Jalandhar Doab). Abdul Samad Khan, the governor of Punjab, then defeated and expelled Banda from Sirhind in 1713.[15] Banda reappeared and plundered many towns. Farrukh Siyyar ordered the Imperial army to join Abdul Samad Khan in crushing the Sikhs. The Imperial forces besieged the Sikhs in Gurdaspur and captured Banda. He was executed in Delhi on an Imperial order.[16]

Farrukh Siyyar was suspicious of the Sayyid brothers and wanted to get rid of them. Intrigues and counter intrigues on the part of the emperor and the Sayyid brothers resulted in an agreement between Hussain Ali Khan and the Marathas.[17] Sayyid Hussain dethroned Farrukh Siyyar in February 1719, and then blinded and murdered him.[18] Shams-ud-Din Abu-al Barakat Rafi-ud-Darajat, a grandson of Bahadur Shah I, was proclaimed the new emperor on 18 February 1719. The Sayyid brothers ran the administration and established law and order in the empire. Rafi-ud-Darajat died of tuberculosis and Rafi-ud-Daula was enthroned with the title of Shah Jahan II on 27 May 1719.[19] Shah Jahan II[20] died soon and Roshan Akhtar, son of Khujista Akhtar and grandson of Bahadur Shah I, was enthroned with the title of Abul Fath Nasir-ud-Din Muhammad Shah Badshah Ghazi on 26 September 1719.[21]

The Turani party was not happy over this state of affairs at the court. Therefore, they killed the Sayyid brothers.[22] Muhammad Shah rewarded Muhammad Amin Khan with *wazirat*, but he died soon. Nizam-ul-Mulk was called from Deccan and appointed *wazir* on 8 February 1722.[23] Nizam-ul-Mulk tried to manage the administration, but courtiers and the emperor equally obstructed his way. Court intrigues against Nizam-ul-Mulk motivated his move to take firm control over the Deccan in an independent capacity, though the provinces of Gujarat[24] and Malwa[25] were taken of him and conferred upon others.[26]

The subsequent competition for power in the South gave immense importance to the Marathas,[27] who took Malwa in 1736. Gujarat and then Bundelkhand were soon taken over by them.[28] The Marathas crossed the Yamuna River under Mulhar Rao Holker in 1736, and entered northern India for the first time, but were repulsed by Sa'adat Khan, the *subedar* of Oudh. Another force of the Marathas under Baji Rao was defeated by the Mughal force near Delhi. But Baji Rao's complete sovereignty was accepted over all territories between the Narmada and Chambal Rivers in addition to the Mughal payment of ₹50 lakh for war expenses.[29]

The Sikhs found a new leader in the person of Kapur Singh, founder of the *Dal Khalsa*. Zakriya Khan, the governor of Punjab, tried to check the Sikhs but failed. In 1733, the Mughal government offered peace to the *Khalsa*, left the sanctions imposed on them, and entitled one nominee of the *Khalsa* to serve as Nawab. Kapur Singh was elected as the Nawab by the *Khalsa*.[30] Zakriya Khan, an able administrator, kept the Sikhs in order by various means. The brief period of peace, however, was disturbed by the invasion of Nadir Shah.

Nadir Shah, the Persian king, after establishing himself on the throne and defeating his local opponents, conquered Qandahar and then turned his attention towards India. The Persians conquered Kabul and Punjab, defeated the Mughal army near Karnal, and forced a peace treaty signed by the two parties that bound the Mughals to pay ₹2 million indemnity. Sa'adat Khan persuaded Nadir Shah to demand more than the ₹2 million offered.[31] At this time Nadir Shah entered Delhi and lodged in the Royal Palace. A rumour of Nadir Shah's assassination resulted in the cold blooded killing of many Persian troops by the inhabitants of Delhi. In retaliation, Nadir Shah ordered a massacre in Delhi. The Persians plundered Delhi and the Royal Palace including the famous Peacock Throne.[32] Nadir Shah enthroned Muhammad Shah in Delhi, but annexed all territory to the west of the Indus to his domain. He marched back on 5 May 1739.[33]

Nadir Shah's invasion further weakened the Imperial authority on distant provinces such as Bengal, Oudh,[34] Maharashtra, the Deccan, and other minor principalities which became virtually independent. Their governors acted like independent princes not only in internal affairs but also in dealing with foreign trading companies. European traders and settlers gained firm footings.[35]

The Marathas turned towards Bengal, but were pushed back by Ali Vardi Khan,[36] the governor of Bengal. The revenue of the empire was reduced due to the loss of the provinces.[37] Apart from the internal disorder which the turbulent elements had created, the Mughal Empire faced another danger in the shape of Afghan invasion from the North-West under Ahmad Shah Abdali[38] in 1748. Ahmad Shah captured Kabul, Punjab, and Sirhind, but Mughal forces finally defeated the Afghans. Muin-ul-Mulk was appointed to govern the Punjab while Safdar Jang returned to Delhi. Muhammad Shah died soon after on 26 April, and Prince Ahmad Shah was enthroned on 29 April 1748.[39]

Ahmad Shah, the new Mughal ruler, promoted Javid Khan, an eunuch, to manage the affairs of the state which signalled weakness in the existing Imperial authority. To counter Abdali's invasion, Safdar Jang, the *wazir* and *subedar* of Oudh, negotiated with the Marathas and arranged for a 'defensive subsidiary treaty'. Although Abdali was defeated, the late arrival[40] of Safdar Jang along with his allies resulted in the ceding of the provinces of Sindh and Punjab to Abdali control. A Mughal failure to pay the Marathas a promised ₹50 lakh resulted in the plunder of villages around Delhi.[41] Safdar Jang's, *subedar* of Oudh, disliking the Ruhillas,[42] sparked a war[43] between them with the active assistance of allied Marathas. Shortly after, the eunuch Javid Khan was murdered by Safdar Jang. This resulted in the dismissal of Safdar Jang from the post of *wazir*. Defeated by Imperial forces, he retired to Lucknow and was succeeded by his son, Shuja-ud-Daulah, at his death in 1756.[44]

In the meantime, Imad-ul-Mulk, the *wazir*, imprisoned and blinded Ahmad Shah. Muhammad Aziz-ud-Daulah, son of Jahandar Shah and grandson of Bahadur Shah I, was proclaimed emperor with the title of Alamgir II in June 1754.[45] Ghazi-ud-Din recovered Punjab and Adina Beg[46] was appointed governor. In the Punjab, Mughlani Begum was appointed regent of her infant son after the death of her husband Muin-ul-Mulk.[47] Abdali re-entered India and reached near Delhi in January 1757.[48] Imad-ul-Mulk agreed to Abdali's demands of ₹2 crore in cash, the cession of the territory west of Sirhind and the emperor's daughter. The *khutba* in the name of Abdali was read in Delhi. Abdali married Hazrat Begum, the daughter of Muhamamd Shah, and his son Taimur married Zahra Begum, the emperor's daughter. Prince Ali Gauhar was appointed *wazir*.[49]

The Afghans and the Marathas first encountered each other during Ahmad Shah Abdali's occupation of Delhi. Before his return to Qandahar, Abdali appointed Prince Taimur to the government of the Punjab in May 1757. The Sikhs revolted against the government and Taimur summoned Adina Beg to Lahore to suppress them. His refusal culminated in a battle between Adina Beg and the Afghans. The Marathas came to Punjab at Adina Beg's request and installed him as governor after taking Lahore from Taimur in April 1758. Adina Beg died on 13 October 1758.[50] The capture of Punjab by the Marathas intensified enmity between them and the Afghans due to their previous clashes.[51] The fringes of the empire were now increasingly lost to the central authority. The political turmoil generated social and religious responses.

The teaching of Shah Waliullah was to convince the Muslim nobility that the Marathas were a force of darkness and that opposing them was a religious duty. Shah Waliullah wrote a detailed letter to Abdali containing a comprehensive account of the political and economic situation of India. He invited him to save Muslim India and advised that his invasion should be different from Nadir Shah's which had weakened the Mughals, but left the Jats and Sikhs unmolested.[52] Apart from writing to Ahmad Shah Abdali directly, Shah Waliullah also tried to influence Najib-ul-Daulah, inviting him as well to destroy the forces of 'darkness'.[53] Some sources have stated that Hindu *rajas* of northern India also wrote to Abdali to save them from Maratha and Sikh tyranny.[54]

Ahmad Shah Abdali invaded India in 1759, and the combined forces of the Abdali and the Ruhillas routed the Marathas and threw them back across the Narmada River.[55] In the meanwhile, the emperor, Alamgir II, was murdered by Imad's agent on 29 November 1759 and a grandson of Prince Kam Bakhsh was enthroned with the title of Shah Jahan III.

To avenge their defeat, a huge Maratha force marched out of Patdur in March 1760 under the command of Sadashiv Rao Bhau and arrived outside Agra in the middle of July. On 21 July, the Marathas captured the city of Delhi and attacked the fort. Bhao captured the fort on 3 August 1760 after a severe fight. In the meanwhile, Shuja-ud-Daulah, Nawab Wazir of Oudh, proposed peace between the Abdali and the Peshwa,[56] which could not succeed owing to strong opposition of Najib-ud-Dawla.[57] After some skirmishes between the two forces at different places and after uncertainty of ten months, Bhao encamped at Panipat on 29 October 1760 while Ahmad Shah Abdali encamped at Sonipat.[58]

The famous battle culminated in Marathas' defeat and the deaths of their leaders except Malhar.[59] The victory of Abdali and his supporters at Panipat, on 14 January 1761, shattered the Maratha might, and though they were able to come to Delhi in 1771, they could not control northern India.[60] Shah Alam was installed emperor with Najib-ud-Daulah his Mir Bakhshi and Imad as *wazir*. Abdali came to India five times after Panipat but dealt only with local issues and forces of disruption. Abdali's last invasion of the subcontinent was in January 1770 to tackle the Sikh uprising but this time he failed even to cross the Indus and returned Qandahar due to his deteriorating health.[61]

Najib-ud-Daulah was summoned to Delhi to manage the affairs of the empire. Shuja-ud-Daulah was appointed *wazir* next year. Najib was able to uphold the prestige of the empire despite Sikh and Jat revolts. Suraj Mal took the fort of Agra in 1761 by giving bribes and plundered ₹50 lakh in addition to looting military stores and royal wardrobe.[62] Najib, avoiding battle, offered a peace treaty, but Suraj Mal did not accept and war with the Jats broke out.[63] Suraj Mal was defeated and killed in the battle of Hindan on 25 December 1763. Jawahir Singh continued the fight against Najib, and invited Marathas and the Sikhs to his assistance. The Sikhs joined him and the combined force laid siege to Delhi. This culminated in a peace agreement between the two sides, an ultimately fruitless venture of Jawahir, costing ₹16 million for nothing in return.[64]

The death of Najib-ud-Daulah in October 1770 frustrated Shah Alam who wanted to return to Delhi at the earliest. The Marathas took Delhi on 9 February 1771 from Zabita Khan, Najib's son, who managed affairs of the state after the death of his father. The Marathas handed over the city to the emperor's heir on 13 April 1771. Shah Alam entered the city on 6 January 1772, ending his long exile.[65] He was warmly received by the people and nobles alike hoping that he would bring stability to the empire. He, however, had neither resources nor the capacity to restore the lost territories and prestige of the empire. His treasury was empty; troops were not paid and his capital was surrounded by hostile forces. He also owed a huge amount to the Marathas who helped him return to Delhi.[66]

Shah Alam's return to Delhi neither improved the political situation nor changed the attitude of the nobility. There was constant struggle for power among the nobility and the English and the Marathas also vied for supreme influence. After the death of Najaf Khan in 1782, there were palace intrigues for several years. Ghulam Qadir Khan, son and successor of Zabita Khan, wanted to muster army to fight the Marathas. But the treasury was empty and Emperor Shah Alam refused to assist him. Ghulam Qadir Khan became so furious that he blinded Shah Alam and was about to replace him with another prince. His scheme was foiled by Rana Khan who rushed to the capital leading a Maratha force. Ghulam Qadir Khan fled the capital, was caught, and sent to Sindhia, who killed him on the orders of Emperor Shah Alam. Ghulam Qadir Khan was the last Muslim chief who had influence in the court of Delhi.[67]

The Maratha supremacy caused many hardships for Shah Alam and his family as the pension fixed for his maintenance was never realized fully from the lands assigned for the purpose.[68] The Marathas did not control Delhi for long. In 1803, they were defeated by the English outside the walls of Delhi. Shah Alam became a pensioner of the English and his authority did not exist beyond the four walls of the Red Fort. Three years later Shah Alam died, after occupying the throne for thirty-six eventful years. He was succeeded by his eldest surviving son, who became Akbar Shah II.[69]

Taking advantage of the turmoil during the Abdali invasions, the Sikhs had erected forts in different places as the Mughals concentrated on the

Abdali army. At times Sikhs besieged the governors of Lahore, Sirhind and Dinapur in their capitals.[70] After the Abdali's return from India, the Sikhs defeated Zain Khan, governor of Sirhind and Hangam Khan, *faujdar* of Malir Kotla. When the Abdali army returned to India in 1762, fifteen thousand Sikhs were killed in the field of Ghora Ghara some twenty miles from Ludhiana; and their temple at Amritsar was destroyed.[71] But in January 1764, the Sikhs attacked Sirhind, killed Zain Khan, captured and distributed the province among their chiefs. Sardar Charat Singh, a Sikh chief, took possession of the area to the Jhelum River including the fort of Rohtas.[72] After another Abdali campaign in 1765, the Sikhs struck coins in their name, after the occupation of Lahore by the three Sikh chiefs.[73] The Sikhs reoccupied their vacated territories after every Abdali return to Afghanistan from the Punjab. During Ahmad Shah Abdali's invasion in 1769,[74] he returned before reaching the Punjab due to disturbances at home and his falling health.[75]

Taimur Shah, son of Ahmad Shah, succeeded to the Afghan leadership after his father's death in 1773. Taimur came to the Punjab in January 1775 and defeated a Sikh contingent. He, however, did not proceed further. He sent a force to capture Multan that defeated the Sikhs in 1778, but the force retired to Peshawar.[76] Taimur Shah defeated the Sikhs in several battles in 1780. He came to the subcontinent several times until his death in 1793, but these campaigns never established stable political administration.[77]

Zaman Shah, the new ruler of Afghanistan, crossed the Indus near Khairabad and sent a force to capture Rohtas in 1795. The Sikhs left the fort and fled to mountains. They returned as soon as Zaman Shah hastened back to Afghanistan on the eve of a Persian invasion.[78] Zaman Shah came to the Punjab for the last time in 1798–99. The Sikhs had vacated Lahore before his arrival. Not yet decided whether to destroy the Sikhs once and for all or make peace with them, he hastened back to Afghanistan due to the revolt of his brother Mahmud. He was assisted by a young Sikh chief Ranjit Singh[79] in crossing the Jhelum. Zaman Shah appointed Ranjit Singh governor of Lahore in lieu of his services.[80]

The occupation of Lahore, the traditional capital of the Punjab, strengthened Ranjit Singh's position. He proclaimed himself Maharaja and minted coins in his name. He won victories against his opponents and in the Treaty of Amritsar, the English granted recognition to Ranjit Singh. The areas of the Rajput chiefs of Jammu and Kangra, Khari Khariali, Akhnur, Bhimber, Lakhanour, Nurpur, Guler, Siba, Kotla, Jaswan and Datarpur were annexed by Ranjit Singh. Attock was taken from the Afghans. The Awan, Gakkhar and the Tiwana chiefs were overpowered and their possessions were annexed. The Baloch chiefs of Khushab and Sahiwal in the Chaj Doab, and the Sial chief of Jhang lost their territories to Ranjit Singh before 1818. Multan was finally occupied in 1818, Kashmir in 1819, Dera Ghazi Khan in 1831, Peshawar in 1834; Bannu and Kohat were annexed to the Sikh domain in 1836.[81] The diminished court in Delhi, symbolic of lost Muslim leadership and authority, now was also subordinated to European power.

The Portuguese first came to the subcontinent by sea for trade purposes. They were followed by the Dutch, the French, and finally the English.[82] Like other Europeans, the English East India Company was merely a trading agency that changed its nature with the passage of time. By the last two decades of the seventeenth century, the Company potential to rule India was hinted at in a dispatch sent in 1687, by the directors mentioning the thought to, 'establish such a Politie of civil and military power and create and secure such a large revenue ... as may be the foundation of a large, well grounded sure English Domination in India for all the times to come.'[83]

The political competition and endless infighting among Indian rulers allowed the Company to embark upon a policy of political alliance and territorial annexation. The Mughals were busy either in palace intrigues or in controlling regional uprisings. This provided the Company an opportunity to seize territories and strengthen its position. The Carnatic Wars of the 1740s and 1750s gave an opportunity to the English to show their strength and skills in military affairs. In 1751, Clive defended Trichinopoly and seized the fort of Arcot, the political capital of the Carnatic.[84]

Bengal[85] was the first province of Mughal India to experience English conquest under the East India Company. Ali Vardi Khan (1741–56) was wise enough to save his dominion from the English domination despite different attempts, but his successor Siraj-ud-Daulah[86] failed and was defeated by the English in the battle of Plassey on 23 June 1757.[87] The battle of Plassey laid the foundation of British rule not only in Bengal but also in rest of the subcontinent. The battle was won by the English due to their military superiority and political skills in fragmenting opposition. The victory strengthened Clive's position and earned him rapid promotion, culminating in his governorship of Bengal and becoming one of the wealthiest persons in England within a few years.[88]

Mir Jafar was appointed Nawab of Bengal on 25 June 1757, but the real authority rested in Clive. In 1760, Mir Jafar was replaced by Mir Qasim.[89] The new *nawab* had the capability, courage, and potential to work out a plan and establish a strong rule over Bengal. All his efforts failed, mainly due to the non-cooperative attitude of his officers. He fled from Bengal and entered Oudh's territory in December 1763. Mir Jafar was reinstated to the *nawabi* on 7 July 1763. Mir Qasim, Shuja-ud-Daulah, and Shah Alam II made a collective attempt to counter the English activities. The defeat of the Indian forces at the hand of the Company force in the battle of Buxar in September 1764 further transformed the political scene of the subcontinent. Mir Qasim fled from the battle field, followed by Shuja-ud-Daulah. Shah Alam II was arrested. The English invaded Oudh, defeated the forces of Shuja in different places, and at last a treaty was signed which gave monetary and political supremacy to the Company in northern India. Clive received the *Diwani* of Bengal for the Company from Shah Alam in 1765. The province belonged to the emperor but was administered by the Company on his behalf.[90] After Buxar, Shuja-ud-Daulah twice attempted to resist the English but failed. He tried to form a coalition of the Indian chiefs, but to no avail. He was defeated at Kora in May 1765 as the Marathas, his allies, fled from the battlefield. A treaty was signed between him and the English on 16 August 1765, which further strengthened the English position. The English emerged the most powerful actor in the politics of the subcontinent and the Nawab of Oudh became a mere vassal. A series of treaties deprived Oudh of the little independence it held and of its taxable resources. Still the Company was not content and gradually annexed more territories to its dominion. By the treaty of Lucknow, on 10 November 1801, the Company acquired the territories of Allahabad, Doab, Rohilkhand, Azamgarh and Gorakhpur that generated an annual revenue of ₹13,523,374.[91]

The Company expanded territorially to the north during the time of Wellesley, Hastings, and Dalhousie.[92] The system of subsidiary alliance was the most dangerous for the independence of Indian rulers. The objective of the alliance was to crush the opponents of the English with the assistance and resources of other Indian princes. This subsidiary alliance worked well against Tipu Sultan of Mysore.[93] Through the treaty of Bassein, 31 December 1802, the Peshwa, head of Maratha confederacy in exile, joined the subsidiary alliance. According to the terms of the treaty he agreed to keep the Company troops at Poona, to give the English control over his foreign policy, and to cede different territories to meet the expenses of the occupational army. His claims on the Nizam's territories and Baroda were subjected to English arbitration.[94] This was most humiliating for the Marathas and the Peshwa called Bhonsla and Sindhia to Poona. The subsequent series of battles fought in Deccan and northern

India proved disastrous for the Marathas. They were defeated everywhere by the Company's troops and Gerard Lake moved into northern India. In August 1803, Aligarh was taken by Gerard Lake. He advanced towards Delhi, which was taken in a short time as the only resistance was offered by Sindhia's troops.[95] With Gerard Lake's entry into the Mughal capital, the Emperor came under the protection of the East India Company. The Emperor conferred a title upon the victor, Samsam al-Dawalah 'Ashjai' al-Mulk, Khan Dawran Khan Sipah Salar Fath Jang.[96]

The conquest of Delhi by the English in 1803 was one of the most important events of the nineteenth century. It initiated a process of replacing old policies and institutions and marked the cultural and religious moment when an Indian scholar issued a *fatwa* declaring India Dar-ul-Harb. The shattering of old hierarchies led eventually to the movement of Sayyid Ahmad.

The Frontier at the Dawn of the Nineteenth Century

The North-West Frontier Province of British India, now Khyber Pakhtunkhwa province of Pakistan, is situated between 31° and 36° North latitude and between 69° and 74° East longitude.[97] For many centuries it was a gateway to India and Central Asia alike.[98] During recorded history, the country of the Afghans, Afghanistan, and Khyber Pakhtunkhwa witnessed invasions by the Persians, Greeks, Mauryans, Huns, Mongols, Mughals, British, Soviets, and, most recently, Americans.[99] Khyber Pakhtunkhwa was not only a highway to the Indian subcontinent, but also from the Indian subcontinent to Central Asia.[100] The Peshawar Valley remained part of the *Subah-e-Kabul wa Peshawar* of Mughal India until its occupation by Nadir Shah Afshar of Persia in 1738.[101]

Ahmad Khan, popularly known as Ahmad Shah Abdali, was elected king of the Afghans by the tribal *jargah* in October 1747, after the murder of Nadir Shah by his Persian troops in June 1747.[102] After consolidating his authority at Qandahar and Ghazna, Ahmad Shah marched on Kabul. Naseer Khan, the governor of Kabul, fled to Peshawar, leaving the city to his deputy. Ahmad Shah occupied the city and sent Sardar Jahan Khan, his *sipah salar*, to Peshawar, followed by the king in person. Naseer Khan evacuated Peshawar, as he was unable to oppose Ahmad Shah Abdali's army, and fled to Punjab.[103] At the Abdali's occupation of Peshawar in 1749, all the clan nobility of the valley submitted to him. They included

Abdul Samad Khan, chief of the Muhammadzai of Hashtnagar;[104] Fateh Khan, chief of the Mandanr clan; the khans of Toru and Babozai, and chief of the Khattaks.[105] These tribes of the valley were knitted in a loose confederacy, independent to manage their internal affairs according to their traditions. Many of them served in Ahmad Shah's army during his Indian campaigns.[106] Ahmad Shah had divided his dominion into eight *Vilayat*—larger provinces and fifteen *Hakumat-e-'Ala*—smaller provinces.[107] Although details of the pattern of his rule are scanty, there is a hint that Ahmad Shah's rule was a sort of tribal confederacy—the tribes being independent in their internal affairs. The governor of a province was required to keep the peace in his province, to pay annual tribute, and to join the king with his troops when required.[108] Taimur Shah, son and successor of Ahmad Shah Abdali, shifted his capital to Kabul from Qandahar due to his fear of the influence of the Pukhtun tribes over Qandahar, including the power of the Barakzai clan in particular. Due to the proximity of the new capital with Peshawar, Taimur Shah used to spend his winters in Peshawar and it emerged as the second capital of the empire. During the reign of Taimur Shah the tribes of Peshawar Valley remained quiet and all tribes, especially the Yusafzais, contributed their due share in revenue to the state treasury.[109] The only disturbance in Peshawar during Taimur Shah's reign was a coup attempt by Faizullah Khan Khalil, a tribal chief, living in Tahkal. Faizullah Khan had sought the permission of the king to enlist troops for invading Punjab. In the year 1779, when the preparations were complete, Faizullah Khan rushed to the Peshawar fort along with his troops, killed the guards on duty, and entered the citadel. The disturbance was suppressed by Taimur Shah's troops and the conspirators were killed. Sahibzada Muhammadi, son of Mian Umar of Chamkani, was behind the conspiracy. He fled to Buner after the failure but was allowed to return due to the fear of a tribal uprising against the king.[110] Prince Abbas Mirza was appointed governor by his father after his accession and it seems that he retained the position till the death of his father.[111]

Zaman Mirza,[112] popularly known as Zaman Shah, ascended the Afghan throne after the death of his father in 1793. Mahmud, his brother, contested the seat, but peace was restored after his defeat, and he was allowed to rule Herat. Shuja-ul-Mulk, his brother, was the governor of Peshawar during the reign of Zaman Shah. The Shah lost his throne to his brother Mahmud in 1800, due to his policy of alienating the tribal chiefs, especially the Sadduzais and Barakzais, who were the strength of the empire.[113] Mahmud[114] ascended the throne at Kabul after defeating his brother Zaman Shah. Shuja was in Peshawar by that time with a huge sum in his hands. He sought the allegiance of the tribes of the Peshawar Valley and marched towards Kabul, but was defeated by Mahmud's troops. He took refuge with the Afridis of the Khyber. His second attempt for Peshawar also failed and Fateh Khan, the *wazir* of Mahmud, came to Peshawar and collected the revenue. Later, Shuja took possession of Peshawar with the help of the tribes and he received the English envoy Elphinstone there.[115] In 1803, Shuja-ul-Mulk took power in Kabul after defeating Fateh Khan, the *wazir*, and ruled till 1809, when he was replaced by his brother Mahmud. Gulistan Khan Achakzai was appointed governor of Peshawar by Shuja, who remained on the post for some time.[116] Information about the governor of Peshawar during the second term of Mahmud's rule is not available. Comparative peace prevailed due to Shuja's ties with the tribes of Khyber. He paid them generously during his sojourn in Peshawar and had close ties with the people of Peshawar Valley. Shuja's mother was a Yusafzai. The Barakzai brothers espoused Mahmud's cause and Shuja was defeated by Fateh Khan near Tahkal. Mahmud was proclaimed king. Shuja fled across the Indus, occupied Peshawar again in March 1810, but was ousted by Muhammad Azeem Khan, brother of Fateh Khan.[117]

Out of jealousy, Kamran, son of Mahmud, blinded and murdered Fateh Khan, an act which changed the power politics in Afghanistan. The numerous Barakzai brothers had been appointed in various provinces and all of them revolted to avenge the murder of their brother. They each acquired independent rule over their respective governments to which they were appointed; subsequently Peshawar was taken by Yar Muhammad Khan.[118]

Swat lies in a strategic region north of the Peshawar Valley. For most of known history it was a witness to the fusion of many civilizations. It retained its independent status until the 1969.[119] Zahiruddin Babar had mentioned his meeting with Sultan Ala-ud-Din and Sultan Awais of Swat and with Shah Mansur, a leading man of the Yusafzai tribe.[120] The Mughal emperors, except Akbar, neither attempted to occupy Swat nor sought its submission.[121]

After leaving Kabul[122] in the fifteenth century, the Yusafzais, came to Peshawar, moved forward to Mardan and later occupied Swat.[123] Shortly afterwards, Buner, the Chamla Valley, the Khudukhel area and Swabi were occupied and different clans of the Yusafzais settled there. Malak Ahmad, chief of the Mandanr and Yusafzai and his trusted friend Sheikh Malli introduced a *wesh* system among the Yusafzais. Instead of founding a state structure for a government; they lived in a tribal system that divided into two opposite blocks.[124] Each clan was independent in running their affairs. Disputes were settled by the chiefs of the clan and referred to a grand council or *jargah* only in the case of a greater emergency or danger.[125]

Hazara, directly east of the Indus, came under Mughal influence during Akbar's bid for Kashmir. Nadir Shah and later Ahmad Shah invaded India and the territories to the west of Indus as well as Hazara and Kashmir were ceded to the Afghan kingdom in 1752. The Afghans were not interested in extracting much revenue from the region. Rather huge allowances were granted to the tribal chiefs to serve two objectives: the chiefs always provided good fighting forces from this area on the ruler's call, and they guarded the road to Kashmir, one of the richest provinces of the Afghan Empire.[126] During the reign of Taimur Shah, an Afghan force came to the area under the command of Painda Khan and Madad Khan to suppress the revolt of Azad Khan, governor of Kashmir.[127] Another Afghan force came to the area under Akram Khan against Ata Muhammad Khan to subdue Kashmir for Shuja.[128]

The rest of the Durrani period was full of struggle for Kashmir among various factions of the Empire and the Sikhs of Punjab. The Hazara tract was divided among different *sardars*, who administered their areas according to their tribal traditions. There were small tribal states in the region on the eve of Sayyid Ahmad's migration. There were intrigues and counter intrigues among the tribal chiefs and states.[129] Taimur Shah appointed Ali Mardan Khan to the government of Chach Hazara, which he governed from Attock. He divided Hazara into four divisions for revenue administration. Himmat Khan Tarin, one of the leading chiefs of the time, managed most parts of the area on behalf of the Durranis and paid annual tribute regularly as well as recruited troops for the governor when required.[130]

The Durranis did not disturb the internal management of the area and kept a loose control of the Swatis, Tanawal, Karral, and Gakhar hills through their respective chiefs. The plain of Hazara was either managed by a *kardar* from Attock or the respective Tarin chief.[131] Tanawal was further divided into two tribal states or as kind of *jagirs*, namely Palal and Hindwal. The latter was also known as Amb,[132] and was ruled by Painda Khan when Sayyid Ahmad migrated to the Peshawar Valley. Apart from the Tanawal states or *jagirs*, there was another small principality, Pakhli, established by the Swatis that included the areas from Mansehra to the vicinity of Balakot. The chief of the state was Habibullah Khan when Sayyid Ahmad came to the area.[133]

Hazara remained an integral part of the Afghan kingdom for a considerable time but the Durrani rule over the area was decentralized. The political disturbance in Afghanistan paved the way for rejecting the nominal submission. The prominent local chiefs who overthrew the Afghan authority were Najibullah Khan Tarin, Jaffar Khan Gakhar, Gul Sher Khan Tanawli, Hashim Khan Turk, Sa'adat Khan Swati, and his son Habibullah Khan.[134] At the beginning of the nineteenth century both local politics and Punjab provincial politics were transformed. The Sikhs had embarked upon an expansionist policy soon after their occupation of Lahore (1799) and civil war in Hazara paved the way for Sikh success there. The struggle for independence by the local chiefs and Sikh attempts to control the region continued for years. Both sides used all possible means to achieve their goals.[135] But before Sayyid Ahmad arrived in the Frontier, Hazara was subjugated by the Sikhs, who occupied most of the Kashmir as well, except few places such as Muzaffarabad, which was in nominal control of local chiefs. Some of the Hazara and Kashmir chiefs contacted Sayyid Ahmad soon after his arrival in the Frontier and expressed their willingness to join him provided he would help them in liberating their country. These included Sarbuland Khan Tanawli, Habibullah Khan Swati, Zabardast Khan and Najaf Khan of Muzaffarabad, Abdul Ghafur Khan of Agror, Amanullah Khan and his son Inayatullah Khan,[136] Nasir Khan of Battagram, and Painda Khan Tanawli of Amb.[137]

Social and Religious Life of the Frontier Pukhtuns

Social Structure: *Pukhtu* and Sharia

Historically, Pukhtuns are egalitarian by nature and tribal in outlook, individualistic to some extent, but with lives regulated by unwritten yet well-defined rules and norms. Those codes, called Pukhtu (also Pukhtunwali and Pashtoonwali), emerged over centuries and were acted upon and preserved by the community. Spain wrote:

> Nonetheless, there are important traditional and social factors which guide community life and in many cases influence or even determine the actions of individuals. These norms vary considerably in different parts of the

Pathan area, and codification of them is virtually impossible. However, certain of them are almost universal, and some knowledge of these is essential to an understanding of what the Pathan is and how he got that way.[138]

A brief account of those norms is given below which is essential for proper understanding of this work. *Badal* was one of the most important components of Pukhtu. It is commonly seen in the meaning of revenge, as defined by Ibbeston[139] but it has other meanings as well. *Badal* is taken by an aggrieved party to damage the offender, his family member, or sometimes a related clan or tribe. It depended upon the nature of the wrong done and the reaction of the aggrieved party. The most influential person of the offender's family might be murdered when murder was avenged. *Badal* had a positive aspect as it ensured peace in a tribal society where there was no law enforcement agency or government.[140]

Melmastya was the second important component of Pukhtu, which means offering hospitality to guests. It is not only offered to relatives, friends, and fellow tribesmen but to any person, known or stranger. Hospitality included food, boarding and lodging and it depended upon the social and economic status of the host. The significant thing counted in *melmastya* was not the food served but the warmth with which the guest was received and the food served. There is a Pukhtu proverb:

پیاز دِ وی خو په نیاز دِ وی

Pyaz di wi kho pah nyaz di wi

Meaning: No matter, the food may be coarse but it
needs to be served with love and honour.

Jargah or consultative body or assembly was a forum of tribal elders. All the issues of common interests and community affairs were brought to this body, discussed and decision were taken in unanimity. Every stakeholder was free to express his view and put forward his suggestions irrespective of the age and economic status of the person concerned.[141]

Panah, an important commandment of Pukhtu, meant asylum and sanctuary. Asylum was granted even to an enemy when it was sought. The obligations of *panah* were very difficult to observe and at times caused great troubles for the Pukhtuns, including during the time of British and recently when the Taliban could not deny asylum to Osama bin Laden though it caused their fall. There is famous Pukhtu *tapah*:

پښتو اسانه نۀ ده خلقه

څوک چي پښتو کړي پښتی ماتې ګرځوينه

Pukhtu asanah nah dah khalqah,
Sok che Pukhtu kri pukhtai matay garzavinah

Meaning: Listen! O people! Pukhtu is not easy to observe
Those who abide by Pukhtu get around with broken ribs.

The *Hujrah* was a community-owned property. It served as a meeting place of a village and sometimes the clan or tribe. Guests were entertained in the *hujrah* that also served as a sleeping place for the unmarried men of the village. It was a community centre but with a much broader meaning and purpose.[142]

Riwaj meant customs, prevalence, and customary law. Pukhtuns' lives were regulated mainly by *riwaj* and followed more closely than *sharia* itself. Traditionally, a Pukhtun preferred *riwaj* as compared to *sharia* or laws imposed by government machinery. There were certain customs which Pukhtuns observe in general. Official, state-sanctioned marriage is not acceptable, and women are not given their due share in inheritance, especially in land. The many other components of Pukhtu are less relevant for this work. Importantly, a Pukhtun remained a staunch Muslim until his Pukhtu was at stake. Many preferred Pukhtu when decisions came into conflict with the norms of any other system—religious, judicial, or administrative. Pukhtu was not a judicial or administrative rule, but a code of social conduct which regulated an individual from cradle to grave.[143] It is pertinent to note that most of the tribal entities, across the globe, were regulated by their respective code of conduct which have been evolved over the centuries and have many components in common. It would not be right to attribute such features to Pukhtun society only.

Spiritual and Religious Dimensions

Pukhtuns as a community had and have an emotional attachment with Islam whether or not they strictly abided by it in their personal, social, and economic practices. Interestingly, instead of Islam in general, they often owed much attachment to their sectarian identity within Islam, and often preferred dealing with a non-Muslim than a person of another sect within the fold of Islam. They had great regard for religious figures of varying status, including Mullas, Sayyids, Pirs, and Akhuns, whose blessings were sought in time of difficulties. People turned towards them for guidance and also acted upon their calls for a cause.[144] In normal situations, the *mulla* was expected to lead prayers and funeral congregations, read the *nikah* at the time of marriages, and issue decrees for a particular issue when needed. A *mulla* or Sayyid was influential, but this depended on the degree of his social status and knowledge. An ordinary *mulla's* decree would not be respected or acted upon, but a learned *alim* would be followed by a larger portion of the population due to his knowledge. History is full of instances in which a king or tribal chief was the follower of a *mulla* or *pir* and with this tie was followed by the vast majority of the people or tribe. This class has been the most influential among the Pukhtun society through ages. Bayazid Ansari (1525–72) gained great popularity among many Pukhtuns due to the religious blend of his views, but he also faced opposition from other Pukhtuns. He was declared a heretic by his most vocal opponents, Pir Baba and Akhun Darwezah. Many Pukhtuns were alienated from Bayazid Ansari's ideology and his movement failed.[145] Importantly, one of the factors generating opposition from Pukhtuns was his attempt to assert authority as preeminent over the tribal chiefs.

The prestige of the religious class helped maintain peace. At times the humiliation of a religious man led to war. The famous *jargah* of Pukhtun chiefs at Qandahar to select an Afghan ruler after the death of Nadir Shah was a leading example of the influence of a *mulla's* decree. It is said that the *jargah* continued for several days, when at last Pir Sabir Shah rose and announced Ahmad Khan's suitability for selection as king of the Pukhtuns.[146] In the same manner, the role of *mulla* and Sayyid was important during negotiations for peace. The *mulla* and Sayyid, respected by both the aggrieved and aggressor, had his role honoured in negotiations due to his impartiality being recognized by both sides. There are instances when the *nanawatay*—begging of pardon—by these people was accepted and offenders were pardoned.[147] In some instances, *pirs*, Sayyids and religious men were even appointed to govern. In Swat, first Sayyid Akbar Shah, then Sayyid Abdul Jabbar Shah of Sithana, both descendents of Sayyid Ali Tirmizi, were called by the Yusafzais of Swat to become their ruler. Later Miangul Abdul Wadud, a descendant of Abdul Ghafur, the Saidu Baba, ruled in Swat.[148]

There were examples of wars being declared at the call of a religious man. For our study, one example was the opposition to the Sikhs in 1823 by the Pukhtun tribesmen under Sayyid Akbar Shah of Sithana at Pir Sabaq.[149] The same Sayyid remained popular his whole life, and was the most prominent figure in the Jihad Movement of Sayyid Ahmad, as well as being ruler in Swat from 1850 to 1857. The Sayyid family of Sithana played a crucial role in the later Mujahidin Movement and never stepped back despite the destruction of their homes by the British on several occasions.

Equally, *pirs* were respected by all sections of the population. One such saint was visited by Elphinstone during his visit to the kingdom of Afghanistan in 1809. Even the king and chiefs would not sit unless ordered by the *pir* repeatedly.[150] There are instances that a son has been disinherited due to the decree of a *mulla*. The history of Hoti family recorded that Ahmad Khan was disinherited by his father Nazar Bahadar Khan when Qazi Muhammad Akbar Hoti issued a *fatwa* against him due to his drinking, adultery and other un-Islamic practices.[151]

The sources are silent as to whether there were formal *madaris*, religious schools, in the area. However, historically in every village where an *alim* was living, a considerable number of *Taliban*, seekers of religious knowledge or students, would live in mosques and come to the *alim* during specific hours to learn Islamic knowledge. The presence of *taliban* in Pukhtun society was evident from the Pukhtu *tapah*:

طالبان ډلي ډلي راغلل

زما د يار ډله روستۍ ده راﺑﻪ شينه

Taliban dalay dalay raghlal,
Zama da yar dalah rostai da ra ba shinah

Meaning: Taliban arrived in groups
My beloved's group is at the tail but will arrive!

طالب ده بل وطن سرے دي

ﭘﻪ تش ديدن يي زړګے څﻪ ﻟﻪ بد ومه

Talib da bal watan saray day,
Pa tash didun ye zargay sa la badawoma[152]

Meaning: *Talib* basically lives abroad, why should I make
him unhappy just for sightseeing!

Very famous religious shrines were located in the Pukhtun areas. In
Buner, there was the shrine of Pir Baba. In Nowshera was that of Sheikh
Rahamkar, popularly known as Kaka Sahib. The area is known as Ziarat
Kaka Sahib due to his shrine. In Chamkani, near Peshawar, the shrine of
Mian Umar remains most popular. There is Pukhtu proverb:

الحمدُ هغه الحمدُ ده خوخله د ميا عمر نه ده

Alhamdu haghah alhamdu dah kho khulah dah Mian Umar nah dah

Meaning: Words are the same but mouth is other than Mian Umar!

People visited these shrines at times and on specific days for specific
purposes. The majority of Pukhtuns both educated and illiterate held high
regard for saints and disregard for any of them was might cause enmity
and hatred from the society at large and result in violence.

The political, social, economic, and religious situations of the former
Mughal Indian possessions on the eve of nineteenth century were alarming for the Muslim intelligentsia. Many tried to serve their community
in different ways. The movements of Shah Waliullah and then Sayyid
Ahmad gained much popularity due to their active responses to issues
related to the perceived crisis. The son and successor of Shah Waliullah
declared India as *dar-ul-harb*. This was a place where living for Muslims
was not allowed according to the Islamic law. This statement provided
the ideological basis for the forthcoming Jihad Movement. Sayyid Ahmad
would be one person who responded to the chaotic dynamics of the era
with a plan of action. He developed a whole strategy of jihad that remained
influential for decades to come.

Notes and References

1. Keene thought that intermarriage with other stocks added to the prolonged succession
   of able rulers. Second, he thought that war of succession was a 'Natural Selection' which
   resulted in the 'survival of the fittest'. At the same time he agreed that both these factors contributed to the downfall of the monarchy as dissatisfaction among the Hindus

added their strength either to one rival or the other. Keene, Henry George. 1999. *The Moghul Empire: From the Death of Aurungzeb to the Overthrow of the Mahratta Power 1866.* Lahore: Sang-e-Meel Publications. pp. 23–24. Henceforth, Keene, *The Moghul Empire.*

2.   Muhammad Muazzam became heir-apparent after the imprisonment and death of his eldest brother Muhammad Sultan and was active in expeditions especially in Deccan. At the time of his father's death, he was governor of Kabul. Irvine, William. 2007. *Later Mughals, 1707–1739.* Lahore: Sang-e-Meel Publications. pp. 28–29. Henceforth, Irvine, *Later Mughals.*

3.   Zaheer, Muhammad. 2006. *Alamgir aur Sultanat-e-Mughlia ka Zawal.* Karachi: Educational Press. pp. 435–36. Henceforth, Zaheer, *Alamgir.*

4.   Rashid, Sh. Abdul. 1975. *History of the Muslims of Indo-Pakistan Subcontinent, 1707–1806,* vol. I. Lahore: Research Society of Pakistan. pp. 4–5. Henceforth, Rashid, *History of the Muslims of Indo-Pak.*

5.   Haq, S. Moinul. 2007. 'Successors of Aurangzeb', in Mahmud Husain et al. (eds), *A History of Freedom Movement, 1707–1831,* vol. I. Karachi: Royal Book Company. p. 83. Henceforth, Haq, 'Successors of Aurangzeb'.

6.   Khan, Seid Gholam Hossein. 1975. *The Seir-Mutaqherin,* vol. I. Lahore: Sheikh Mubarak. p. 13. Henceforth, Khan, *The Seir-Mutaqherin,* vol. I. Also Haq, 'Successors of Aurangzeb', pp. 83–84.

7.   Irvine, *Later Mughals,* pp. 78–79; Haq, 'Successors of Aurangzeb', pp. 84–85.

8.   Rashid, *History of the Muslims of Indo-Pakistan,* pp. 23–27.

9.   Grewal, J. S. 2002. *The New Cambridge History of India: The Sikhs of the Punjab.* New Delhi: Foundation Books. pp. 82–83. Henceforth, Grewal, *The Sikhs.*

10. Lal, Kanhia. 2002. *Tarikh-e-Punjab.* Mirpur, Azad Kashmir: Arsalan Books. pp. 69–70. Henceforth, Lal, *Tarikh-e-Punjab.*

11. Irvine, *Later Mughals,* p. 123; Lahori, Muhammad Qasim Ibrat. 1977. *Ibrat Nama.* Lahore: Research Society of Pakistan. p. 60. Henceforth, Lahori, *Ibrat Nama.* Khan, *The Seir Mutaqherin.* vol. I, pp. 20–21.

12. Irvine, *Later Mughals,* pp. 179–87; Lahori, *Ibrat Nama,* pp. 62–63; Khan, *The Seir Mutaqherin.* vol. I, p. 30.

13. Farrukh Siyyar, great grandson of Aurangzeb, born in Aurangabad (Deccan) on 11 September 1683, was left in Bengal by the order of Aurangzeb, when Azim-ul-Shan was recalled from that province. He was in Bengal when was called to the court by his father Azim-ul-Shan. He was near Azeemabad (Patna), when he heard the news of the death of Bahadur Shah I. He proclaimed his father's accession to the throne but within few days received news of his father's death. Lahori, *Ibrat Nama.* p. 63; Irvine, *Later Mughals,* p. 188.

14. Irvine, *Later Mughal,* p. 189.

15. Grewal, *The Sikhs,* p. 83.

16. Lal, *Tarikh-e-Punjab,* pp. 71–73.

17. Khan, *The Seir Mutaqherin,* pp. 107–12.

18. Lahori, *Ibrat Nama,* pp. 75–76.

19. Ibid., pp. 92–93.

20. Shah Jahan II died on 18 or 19 September but his death was kept secret for a few days to install a new monarch.

21. Lahori, *Ibrat Nama,* p. 80; Irvine, *Later Mughals,* pp. 385–86.

22. Lahori, *Ibrat Nama*, pp. 82–90; Irvine, *Later Mughals*, pp. 412–54. Sayyid Abdullah died of poison on 30 September, 1722. Khan, Muhammad Hashim Khafi. 1952. *The Later Moghuls*. Calcutta: Susil Gupta. p. 128. Henceforth, Khan, *The Later Moghuls*.
23. Irvine, *Later Mughals*, pp. 469–70.
24. Sarbuland Khan was appointed the governor of Gujrat to replace Hamid Khan, Nizam-ul-Mulk's uncle.
25. Raja Girdhar Bahadur was appointed the governor of Malwa to replace Azimullah Khan, cousin of Nizam-ul-Mulk.
26. Irvine, *Later Mughals*, pp. 505–6.
27. Ibid., pp. 509–13.
28. Rashid, *History of the Muslims of Indo-Pakistan*, pp. 76–77.
29. Keene, *The Moghul Empire*, pp. 35–36; Irvine, *Later Mughals*, pp. 612–30.
30. Singh, Harbans. 1964. *The Heritage of the Sikhs*. Bombay: Asia Publishing House. pp. 52–53. Henceforth, Singh, *The Heritage of the Sikhs*.
31. Nizam-ul-Mulk was entitled *Amir-ul-Umara* by the emperor after the conclusion of the treaty but Sa'adat Khan was not happy as he wanted to secure the title for himself.
32. Haq, 'Successors of Aurangzeb', pp. 103–5. The estimated value of all the property in grand total was 70 Krors. Irvine, *Later Mughals*, p. 687.
33. Irvine, *Later Mughals*, pp. 689–90.
34. Azhar, Mirza Ali. 2008. 'The Nawab Wazirs of Oudh', in Mahmud Husain et al. (eds), *A History of Freedom Movement, 1707–1831*, vol. I. Karachi: Royal Book Company. pp. 210–33. Henceforth, Azhar, 'The Nawab Wazirs of Oudh'.
35. Haq, 'Successors of Aurangzeb', pp. 103–4.
36. Ali Vardi Khan (1671–1756) was the Nawab Nazim (governor) of Bengal, Bihar and Orissa. He was recognized *subedar* of Bengal by the Mughal Emperor Muhammad Shah in 1740. He thus signed a peace treaty for war-indemnity with the Marathas in 1751. He appointed his grandson Siraj-ud-Daulah, (his daughter Amina Begum's son) as the *subedar* of Bihar on the eve of the Afghan invasion of Bihar. Ali Vardi Khan passed away on 9 April 1756, and was succeeded by Siraj-ud-Daulah.
37. Rashid, *History of the Muslims of Indo-Pakistan*, p. 85.
38. Parts of modern Afghanistan, including Herat and Qandahar, were ruled for long periods by Persians, Turks, and dynasties based in India and Persia. The rise of Mirwais Hotak in Qandahar (1709) established an independent first Afghan state, followed by a struggle for power between his surviving brother Abdul Aziz and his son Mahmud after his death in 1715. The years of attacks and counter attacks between the Qandaharis and Persians was followed by Sadduzais' reign and the consolidation of modern Afghanistan under Ahmad Khan, popularly known as Ahmad Shah Abdali. Ahmad Khan was elected the Afghan king by Afghan *jargah* at the age of twenty-four. Caroe, Olaf. 1965. *The Pathans, 550 BC–AD 1957*. London: Macmillan & Co Ltd. pp. 250–55. Henceforth, Caroe, *The Pathans*. Also Singh, Ganda. 2003. *Ahmad Shah Abdali*. Lahore: Takhleeqat. Henceforth, Singh, *Ahmad Shah Abdali*.
39. Sarkar, Jadunath. 1949. *Fall of the Mughal Empire, 1939–1954*, vol. I. Calcutta: M. C. Sarkar & Sons Ltd. pp. 3–4. Henceforth, Sarkar, *Fall of the Mughal Empire*. Also Rashid, *History of the Muslims of Indo-Pakistan*, pp. 87–89.
40. The terrified emperor has given up Sindh and the Punjab before Safdar Jang's arrival at Delhi on 25 April 1752.
41. The terms agreed upon were, payment of ₹50 lakh to Peshwa for his armed assistance, the right to collect *chauth* from Punjab, Sindh and the four *mahals* of Sialkot, Pasrur,

Aurangabad and Gujarat was recognized. The districts of Hisar, Sambhal, Muradabad and Badayun were also assigned to the Marathas. The Peshwa was appointed governor of Ajmer and Agra. The Peshwa's help was also sought to bring under control and hand over the lands which were usurped by the local Rajas and *zamindars*. Rashid, *History of the Muslims of Indo-Pakistan*, pp. 96–97.

42. Rashid, Abdul. 2008. 'The Ruhillas', in Mahmud Husain et al. (eds), *A History of Freedom Movement, 1707–1831*, vol. I. Karachi: Royal Book Company. pp. 303–36. Henceforth, Rashid, 'The Ruhillas'. Also Sarkar, *Fall of the Mughal Empire*, vol. I, pp. 24–37.
43. The war ended in February 1752 but created a permanent hatred between the Ruhillas and Nawab Wazir of Oudh.
44. Rashid, 'The Ruhillas', pp. 311–14.
45. Rashid, *History of the Muslims of Indo-Pakistan*, p. 102.
46. Adina Beg (d. 1758), governor of the Punjab for a few months before his death, was born at the village of Sharakpur, near Lahore, now in Sheikhupura district of Pakistan.
47. Abdali had invaded India several times before in 1747–48, 1749 and 1751–52.
48. Haq, S. Moinul. 2008. 'Ahmad Shah', Alamgir II and Shah 'Alam', in Mahmud Husain et al. (eds). *A History of Freedom Movement, 1707–1831*, vol. I. Karachi: Royal Book Company. p. 109. Henceforth, Haq, 'Ahmad Shah', Alamgir II and Shah 'Alam'.
49. Haq, S. Moinul. 2008. 'Shah Abdali and the Third Battle of Panipat', in Mahmud Husain et al. (eds), *A History of Freedom Movement, 1707–1831*, vol. I. Karachi: Royal Book Company. pp. 271–72. Henceforth, Haq, 'Shah Abdali and the Third Battle of Panipat'.
50. Rashid, *History of the Muslims of Indo-Pakistan*, p. 107.
51. Keene, *The Mogul Empire*, p. 52.
52. Nizami, Khaliq Ahmad. 1978. *Shah Waliullah kay Siyasi Maktubat*. Lahore: Idara Islamiyat. pp. 83–98. Henceforth, Nizami, *Shah Waliullah kay Siyasi Maktub*.
53. The Marathas were rapists and Muslims and Hindus alike were targeted in this. Sarkar, *Fall of the Mughal Empire*, vol. I, p. 87; Nizami, *Shah Waliullah kay Siyasi Maktubat*, pp. 173–74.
54. Nizami, *Shah Waliullah kay Siyasi Maktubat*, pp. 279–80.
55. Rashid, *History of the Muslims of Indo-Pakistan*, pp. 108–9; Haq, 'Shah Abdali and the Third Battle of Panipat', pp. 281–83.
56. The terms presented for peace were: Recognition of Prince Ali Gauhar as Emperor, his eldest son Jawan Bakht as his heir apparent, and Shuja as the Imperial *wazir*, and that the Abdali should return to Afghanistan and the Marathas to Deccan. Sarkar, *Fall of the Mughal Empire*, vol. I, p. 182.
57. Rashid, *History of the Muslims of Indo-Pakistan*, pp. 109–10.
58. Haq, 'Shah Abdali and the Third Battle of Panipat', pp. 285–87.
59. Ibid., pp. 289–95; Singh, *Ahmad Shah Abdali*, pp. 227–68.
60. Sarkar, *Fall of the Mughal Empire*, vol. I., pp. 260–62.
61. Haq, 'Shah Abdali and the Third Battle of Panipat', pp. 297–301.
62. Haq, 'Ahmad Shah, 'Alamgir II and Shah 'Alam', pp. 114–15.
63. Sarkar, *Fall of the Mughal Empire*, vol. I, pp. 283–84.
64. Rashid, *History of the Muslims of Indo-Pakistan*, pp. 112–13.
65. Ibid., pp. 117–18.
66. Haq, 'Ahmad Shah, 'Alamgir II and Shah 'Alam', p. 126.
67. Ibid., pp. 133 36.
68. Rashid, *History of the Muslims of Indo-Pakistan*, p. 135.

69. Haq, 'Ahmad Shah, 'Alamgir II and Shah 'Alam', pp. 136–37.

70. Sarkar, S. C. and K. K. Datta. 1959. *Modern Indian History*, Vol. II. Allahabad: The Indian Press. pp. 230–31. Henceforth, Datta, *Modern Indian History*.

71. Kohli, S. R. 2004. *Maharaja Ranjit Singh*. Lahore: Sang-e-Meel Publications. pp. 29–30. Henceforth, Kohli, *Maharaja Ranjit Singh*.

72. Malik, Ikram Ali. 1990. *Tarikh-e-Punjab: Qadeem Zamana ta 1857*. Lahore: Salman Matbu'at. p. 139. Henceforth, Malik, *Tarikh-e-Punjab*.

73. Grewal, *The Sikhs*, p. 92.

74. According to another source his last attack was in 1770. Haq, 'Shah Abdali and the Third Battle of Panipat', pp. 297–301.

75. Singh, *Ahmad Shah Abdali*, pp. 310–13.

76. Two instances coincided with the event of the Durrani force return to Peshawar. One is the disturbance in Khurasan where the Persians had revolted and the other was a secret plan to kill Taimur Shah and enthrone his brother Prince Sikandar. Arbab Faizullah Khan Khalil, Sahibzada Muhammadi Sahib Chamkani and Arsala Khan Mohmand were among the intriguers. The planning was revealed to Taimur Shah and he was able to save himself and arrest the trouble makers. Kakakhel, Sayyid Bahadar Shah Zafar. nd. *Pushtun: Tarikh kay Ayenay Main 550 AC–1964 AD*. Peshawar: University Book Agency. pp. 641–42. Henceforth, Kakakhel, *Pushtun*.

77. Nadvi, M. Rashid Akhtar. 2008. 'The Sikhs', in Mahmud Husain et al. (eds), *A History of Freedom Movement, 1707–1831*, vol. I. Karachi: Royal Book Company. pp. 154–55. Henceforth, Nadvi, 'The Sikhs'.

78. Elphinstone, Mountstuart. 1990. *An Account of the Kingdom of Caubul*, vol. II. Quetta: Gosha-e-Adab. pp. 313–14. Henceforth, Elphinstone, *An Account of Caubul*, Vol. II.

79. Ranjit Singh was born on 13 November 1780 at Gujranwala in the house of Mahan Singh of *Sukerchakia misl* of the Sikh. At the death of his father he was accepted chief of the *misl* but being too young he was unable to manage the affairs of the *misl*. He was assisted by his mother, mother-in-law Sada Kaur and Dewan Lakhpat Roy, the aged assistant of his father Mahan Singh. Ranjit Singh took the control of his *misl* in his hands after the killing of the Dewan in 1798. Some sources say the Dewan was killed for having illicit relations with his mother. Latif, Sayyid Muhammad. 1982. *Tarikh-e-Punjab*. Lahore: Sang-e-Meel Publications. pp. 97–98. Henceforth, Latif, *Tarikh-e-Punjab*.

80. Malik, *Tarikh-e-Punjab*, vol. I, pp. 141–42.

81. Grewal, *The Sikhs*, pp. 101–3.

82. Khan, Namdar. 2008. 'The East India Company', in Mahmud Husain et al. (eds), *A History of Freedom Movement, 1707–1831*, vol. I. Karachi: Royal Book Company. pp. 380–81. Henceforth, Khan, 'The East India Company'.

83. Ibid., p. 384.

84. Roberts, P. E. 2006. *British Rule in India: Rule of East India Company 1600–1857*. Dehradun: Reprint Publications. pp. xi–xii. Henceforth, Roberts, *British Rule in India*.

85. Rashid, *History of Muslims of the Indo-Pakistan*, pp. 141–61.

86. Siraj-ud-Daulah succeeded Ali Vardi Khan to the *nizamat* of Bengal in April 1756. He was hot tempered which alienated many of the old chiefs of Ali Vardi Khan. Jagat Seth, one of them, applied to the Company for a change of the Nawab. For a comprehensive study, see Khan, *The Seir Mutaqherin*, vol. II.

87. Torrens, W. M. 1938. *Empires in Asia: How We Came by It; A Book of Confessions*. Calcutta: Lakshami Narayan Nath. p. 31. Henceforth, Torrens, *Empires in Asia*.

88. Gopal, Ram. nd. *How the British Occupied Bengal: A Corrected Account of the 1756–1765 Events.* Lahore: Book Traders. p. 215. Henceforth, Gopal, *How the British Occupied Bengal.*

89. Rashid, *History of Muslims of the Indo-Pakistan*, pp. 186–89.

90. Bari. 1976. *Company ki Hukumat.* Lahore: National Book Foundation. pp. 122–31. Henceforth, Bari, *Company ki Hukumat.*

91. Azhar, 'The Nawab-Wazirs of Oudh', pp. 228–30.

92. Khan, 'The East India Company', p. 397.

93. Tipu Sultan (November 1750–99) was the son of Hyder Ali. During Tipu's childhood, his father rose to take power in Mysore, and Tipu took over rule of the kingdom at his father's death. For detail see Habib, Irfan. 2001. *Confronting Colonialism: Resistance and Modernization under Haidar Ali and Tipu Sultan.* Delhi: Manohar; Habib, Irfan. 2002. *State and Diplomacy under Tipu Sultan: Documents and Essays.* Delhi: Manohar.

94. Roberts, *British Rule in India*, p. 255.

95. Bari, *Company ki Hukumat*, pp. 242–43.

96. Haq, S. Moinul. 1958. *The Great Revolution of 1857.* Karachi: Pakistan Historical Society. p. 5.

97. Baha, Lal. 1978. *N-W.F.P. Administration Under British Rule, 1901–1919.* Islamabad: National Commission on Historical and Cultural Research. p. 1. Henceforth, Baha, *NWFP Administration.*

98. Qadir, Altaf. 2008. 'Anti-Colonial Movement: The Struggle of Haji Sahib Turangzai to do away with the Authority of the British *Raj*'. *Journal of the Pakistan Historical Society.* Karachi, vol. 56, no. 2, p. 111.

99. Tanner, Stephen. 2002. *Afghanistan: A Military History from Alexander the Great to the Fall of the Taliban.* Karachi: Oxford University Press. p. 2. Henceforth, Tanner, *Afghanistan.*

100. Sultan-e-Rome. 2006. 'Geography of the North-West Frontier Province'. *Pakistan Perspectives.* Karachi, vol. 11, no. 1, p. 1.

101. Shah, Ibrahim. 1998. 'Governors of Peshawar: Post-Mughul Period (1738–1997)'. *Journal of the Pakistan Historical Society.* Karachi, vol. 46, no. 3, p. 81. Henceforth, Shah, 'Governors of Peshawar'.

102. Elphinstone, *An Account of Caubul*, vol. II, p. 281.

103. Singh, Ganda. 1977. *Ahmad Shah Durrani: Father of Modern Afghanistan.* Quetta: Gosha-e-Adab. p. 38. Henceforth, Singh, *Ahmad Shah.*

104. Abdul Samad Khan had fled to Jalalabad out of the fear of Naseer Khan, the governor of the Province. The latter sacked his fortress at Hashtnagar (Ashnaghar) and murdered his relatives.

105. Bellew, H. W. 2001. *A General Report on the Yusufzais.* Lahore: Sang-e-Meel Publications. p. 77. Henceforth, Bellew, *A General Report.* Singh, *Ahmad Shah*, pp. 38–39. Kakakhel, *Pushtun*, pp. 632–33. Another source says that Fateh Khan had joined Nadir Shah's troops and was present at the latter's camp when he was assassinated. He brought together the Afghan troops around Ahmad Shah Abdali and accompanied him to Qandahar, Ghazni, Kabul and later to Peshawar. *History of the Hoti Family*, p. 16. His services were recognized and was rewarded a *Jagir.* See Appendix A for Abdali's *farman.*

106. Singh, *Ahmad Shah Durrani*, p. 39; Kakakhel, *Pushtun*, pp. 632–33. It is prudent to note here that in this study we have not used *tribe* in colonial context and meaning rather for *Qaum*-Pukhtun ethnic group.

107. The *Vilayat* were Qandahar, Herat, Kabul, Mazar-e-Sharif, Khurasan, Badakhshan, Punjab and Kashmir while *Hakumat-e-Ala* were Farah, Maimnah, Baluchistan, Ghazni, Laghman, Peshawar, Dera Ismail Khan, Dera Ghazi Khan, Shikarpur, Siwi (Sibi), Sindh, Chhachh Hazara, Leih, Multan and Sirhind. Singh, *Ahmad Shah*, pp. 353–54.
108. Ibid.
109. Bellew, *A General Report*, p. 78; *History of the Hoti Family*, p. 16.
110. Elphinstone, *An Account of Caubul*, vol. II, pp. 302–3; *Gazetteer of the Peshawar District 1897–98*. 1989. Lahore: Sang-e-Meel Publications. pp. 63–64. Henceforth, *Gazetteer of Peshawar*.
111. Bellew, H. W. nd. *The Races of Afghanistan*. Lahore: Sang-e-Meel Publications. p. 33. Henceforth, Bellew, *The Races*.
112. The sons of Taimur Shah might have adopted the title Mirza under the influence of the Mughals as one of Taimur wives was daughter of Mughal Emperor Ahmad Shah.
113. Elphinstone, *An Account of Caubul*, vol. II, pp. 319–25.
114. Mahmud's cause was espoused by Fateh Khan Barakzai, son of Muhammad Azeem, the major conspirators to replace Zaman Shah with his brother Shuja.
115. *Gazetteer of Peshawar*, p. 64.
116. Shah, 'Governors of Peshawar', p. 82.
117. Rashid, Haroon. 2002. *History of the Pathans: The Sarabani Pathans*, vol. I. Bannu: Author. pp. 188–89. Henceforth, Rashid, *History of the Pathans*.
118. Kakakhel, *Pushtun*, pp. 673–77. There is another version that Muhammad Azeem Khan appointed Yar Muhammad Khan to the government of Peshawar. Shah, 'Governors of Peshawar', p. 83.
119. Sultan-i-Rome. 2002. 'Mughuls and Swat', *Journal of the Pakistan Historical Society*. Karachi, vol. 50, no. 4, pp. 39–50. Henceforth, Rome, 'Mughuls and Swat'.
120. Babar has written that he wanted to invade Yusafzais of Swat but Sultan Awais, Sultan Ala-ud-Din and Shah Mansoor offered their submission to him. He married Bibi Mubaraka, daughter of Shah Mansur. Babar, Zaheer-ud-Din Muhammad. 2007. *Waqai Babar*. UK: Shahar Bano Publishers. pp. 192–93. Babar's own narrative has rejected the version of some writers who have claimed that Babar marched to the vicinity of Manglawar. For Babar's claimed march to Manglawar see Khan, Roshan. 1986. *Yusafzai Qaum ki Sarguzasht*. Karachi: Roshan Khan and Co. pp. 109–19. Henceforth, Khan, *Yusafzai Qaum*. Pir Muazam Shah, *Tawarikh Hafiz Rahmat Khani*, pp. 92–103.
121. Akbar sent a strong force to capture the valley but was defeated and repulsed with heavy loses including the killing of Raja Birbal, one of his close associates. Rome, 'Mughuls and Swat', pp. 41–42.
122. Khan, Muhammad Asif. 1958. *Tarikh Riyasat-e-Swat wa Sawanih-e-Hayat Bani-e-Riyasat-e-Swat Hazrat Miangul Shahzada Abdul Wadud Khan Bacha Sahib*. NP. pp. 39–40. Henceforth, Khan, *Tarikh Riyasat-e-Swat*.
123. Sayyid Ahmad Barailvi visited and stayed in lower Swat for a year. The Swat Valley includes Abazai, Baizai, Ranizai, Khadakzai and Adinzai, Nikpi Khel, Shamozai, Babuzai, Maturizai, Sebjuni, Shamizai, Aba Khel, Musa Khel, Azi Khel and Jinki Khel. Plowden, T. J. C. 1932. *Report on the Leading Persons and State of Factions in Swat*. Simla: Government Press of India. p. 1. Tribal Research Cell, Government of Khyber Pakhtunkhwa, Peshawar. Also Sultan-e-Rome. 2004. *Forestry in the Princely State of Swat and Kalam (North-West Pakistan: A Historical Perspective on Norms and*

Practices, IP6 Working Paper No. 6, p. 18. www.nccr-north-south.unibe.ch [accessed on 26 March 2009]).

124.   Sultan-i-Rome. 2009. 'Swat: A Critical Analysis'. *IPCS Research Papers*, no. 18, p. 2. http://ipcs.org/pdf_file/issue/1542140255RP18-Rome-Swat.pdf (accessed on 2 February 2009).

125.   Khan, *Tarikh Riyasat-e-Swat*, pp. 42–44.

126.   *Gazetteer of Hazara District 1883–84*. nd. Lahore: Sang-e-Meel Publications. pp. 21–22. Henceforth, *Gazetteer of Hazara*.

127.   Kakakhel, *Pushtun*, p. 644.

128.   Ibid.

129.   Hussain, Fida. 1992. *Tarikh-e-Tanawal*. Rawalpindi: Asad Mahmud Printing Press. pp. 103–4. Henceforth, Hussain, *Tarikh-e-Tanawal*.

130.   Panni, Sher Bahadur Khan. 2006. *Tarikh-e-Hazara*. Lahore: Maktaba Jamal. pp. 89–90. Henceforth, Panni, *Tarikh-e-Hazara*.

131.   *Gazetteer of Hazara*, p. 22.

132.   Panni, *Tarikh-e-Hazara*, pp. 94–95.

133.   Khan, Nawab Muhammad Wazir. 2007. *Waqai Sayyid Ahmad Shahid*. Lahore: Sayyid Ahmad Shahid Academy. p. 1192. Henceforth, Khan, *Waqai Sayyid Ahmad*.

134.   Mihr, Ghulam Rasul. nd. *Sayyid Ahmad Shahid*. Lahore: Sheikh Ghulam Ali & Sons. p. 411. Henceforth, Mihr, *Sayyid Ahmad*.

135.   Nadvi, Sayyid Abu al-Hassan Ali. nd. *Tarikh Dawat wa Azeemat: Seerat-e-Sayyid Ahmad*, vol. II. Karachi: Majlas Nashriyat. pp. 28–29. Henceforth, Nadvi, *Seerat-e-Sayyid Ahmad*.

136.   Both the father and the son were residing in exile at Amb.

137.   Mihr, *Sayyid Ahmad*, p. 413.

138.   Spain, James W. 1985. *The Pathan Borderland*. Karachi: Indus Publications. p. 63. Henceforth, Spain, *The Pathan Borderland*. The word tribe should not be confused in the context used by the colonial/western perspective. We have used it for the Pukhtun ethnic group-*qaum* in the entire work.

139.   Ibbeston, Denzil. 1993. *Punjab Castes*. Delhi: Low Price Publications. p. 58. Henceforth, Ibbeston, *Punjab Castes*.

140.   On the whole, our summary of Pukhtu is based on Sultan-e-Rome. 2006. 'Pukhtu: The Pukhtun Code of Life'. *Pakistan Vision*. Lahore, vol. 7, no. 2, pp. 1–30. Henceforth, Rome, 'Pukhtu'.

141.   Yunas, S. Fida. nd. *Afghanistan: Jirgahs and Loya Jirgahs, The Afghan Tradition (977 A.D. to 1992 A.D.)*. Peshawar: Area Study Centre. pp. 1–2. Henceforth, Yunas, *Afghanistan*.

142.   Rome, 'Pukhtu', pp. 1–30.

143.   Yousafzai, Hassan M. and Ali Gohar. 2005. *Towards Understanding Pukhtoon Jirga: An Indigenous way of Peace building and more ...* Peshawar: Just Peace International. p. 43.

144.   Assertion of political authority by the religious class is, however, rare in Pukhtun society. The religious class usually played a major role when they cooperated with the political figures. One may see the example of Ahmad Shah Abdali, who, along with other factors, faced the Marathas in the battle of Panipat (1761) upon the invitation of Shah Waliullah (1704–63).

145.   Mahsud, Ali Khan. nd. *La Pir Rokhana tar Bacha Khan Poray: Da Pukhtanu Milli Mubarizay ta Katana*. Peshawar: Danish Khparwanay Tolanay Tekhniki Sanga.

pp. 41–50. Henceforth, Mahsud, *Pir Rokhana tar Bacha Khan.* Nichols, Robert. 2001. *Settling the Frontier: Land, Law, and Society in the Peshawar Valley, 1500–1900.* Karachi: Oxford University Press. p. 32. Henceforth, Nichols, *Settling the Frontier.* Bayazid had named himself *Pir Rokhan* or *Pir Roshan,* apostle of light while Sayyid Ali Tirmizi, popularly known as Pir Baba named him *Pir-e-Tarik,* apostle of Darkness. Caroe, *The Pathans.* p. 198.

146. No doubt there were other considerations for the selection of Ahmad Khan as Shah but the role of a religious person was not less important. Mahsud, *Pir Rokhana tar Bacha Khan,* pp. 112–13.

147. Elphinstone, Mountstuart. 1990. *An Account of the Kingdom of Caubul,* vol. I. Quetta: Gosha-e-Adab. pp. 226–27. Henceforth, Elphinstone, *An Account of Caubul,* vol. I.

148. For a detailed study of Swat State, see Sultan-i-Rome. 2008. *Swat State (1915–1969): From Genesis to Merger; An Analysis of Political, Administrative, Socio-Political, and Economic Developments.* Karachi: Oxford University Press.

149. Nichols, *Settling the Frontier,* p. 91.

150. Elphinstone, *An Account of Caubul,* vol. II, pp. 83–84. There is a very interesting narration attached to Elphinstone. Mulla Jafar told him that if 10,000 French were in each of the cities of Kabul, Herat, Qandahar, and Peshawar, nevertheless the word of one *mulla* would be sufficient to destroy them with the assistance of a single soldier. Macmunn, George Fletcher. 1977. *Afghanistan: From Darius to Amanullah.* Quetta: Gosha Adab. p. 84.

151. *Family History of Hoti Family,* pp. 14–15.

152. Shaheen, Salma. 1994. *Rohay Sandaray: Tapay,* vol. II. Peshawar: Pashto Academy, University of Peshawar. p. 205.

2

Sayyid Ahmad Barailvi: Biography and Thoughts

Family Background

Sayyid Ahmad Barailvi[1] was born on 27 November 1786 (6 Safar 1201 A.H.) at Raibaraili,[2] in Oudh state. His family was known for its piety. Sayyid Qutb-ud-Din, ancestor of Sayyid Ahmad, migrated to India during the reign of Shams-ud-Din Iltutmish in AD 1210–11, and settled in Karra. He was appointed Shaikh-ul-Islam[3] by Sultan Shams-ud-Din Iltutmish, who gave his daughter, Fatiha, in marriage to Sayyid Qawam-ud-Din, son of Sayyid Qutb-ud-Din.[4] The family migrated to Badayun after several generations. Some of them were appointed *quza* in different locations, including Oudh and Badayun. One of them, Sayyid Ahmad was appointed at Nasirabad, where he lived for a considerable time. Family dispute caused his second migration to Raibaraili. Sayyid Fateh Alam was appointed *qazi* of Nasirabad after Sayyid Ahmad's migration. Abu Muhammad, son of Sayyid Fateh Alam, was appointed to the *diwani* by Prince Murad Bakhsh, son of Shah Jahan.[5] The most important among the family in the Mughal era was Shah Ilmullah (1623–85). There are traditions that he had joined the Mughal service and became a Sufi, yet another story is that he had travelled to Lahore to join the service but instead preferred mysticism and became a disciple of Sheikh Adam Binori.[6] Shah Ilmullah died during Aurangzeb's reign.[7] Sayyid Muhammad Huda, one of Shah Ilmullah's sons, was famous for his piety. He lived a very simple life despite having a *jagir*. He died in May/June 1708 in Burhanpur while on his way to the Deccan to meet Bahadur Shah I. His son Sayyid Muhammad Noor also served with Prince Azam Jah but later left his service. Sayyid Muhammad Noor was devoted to mysticism and died in Nasirabad. Among his four sons and two daughters, one was Sayyid Muhammad Irfan, father of Sayyid Ahmad, who served in

Lucknow and died in 1800.[8] It is quite interesting that the family lineage of Sayyid Ahmad served the rulers ever since the migration of his distant ancestor and later served those princes and nobles who had established independent principalities during the weakening of Mughal Imperial authority. Sayyid Ahmad also rendered services for Amir Khan (d. 1834) at Rajputana, but quit the service when Amir Khan signed a peace treaty with the English.

Early Life, Education, and Career

At the age of four, Sayyid Ahmad was sent to a *madrassah*. Unlike other children of his family, he was more interested in outdoor activities[9] than books.[10] In three years he learned some chapters of the Qur'an and basic writing skills. His elder brothers Sayyid Ibrahim and Sayyid Ishaq were worried about his lack of interest in education, but their father told them to leave the matter to Providence.[11] Sources agree that he was pious in his personal life from childhood and never indulged in any vice. He always extended a helping hand to widows, the needy, and wayfarers.[12]

No biographer of Sayyid Ahmad has told details of his family's economic status and resources. Only mentioned is that his father lived in Lucknow and one of his brothers was in the service of Amir Khan in Rajputana. Some sources have recorded that because he belonged to a saintly family he was little interested in worldly affairs.[13] However, as a young man, Sayyid Ahmad along with few friends travelled to Lucknow in search of a job.[14] His companions found service, while Sayyid Ahmad, not finding any employment, left for Delhi. After his arrival at Delhi, he visited Shah Abdul Aziz, who entrusted him to the care of his brother, Shah Abdul Qadir. Sayyid Ahmad studied under Shah Abdul Aziz, Shah Abdul Qadir, Shah Rafi-ud-Din, and perhaps even Shah Ismail. However, his spiritual guide remained Shah Abdul Aziz.[15] He studied the Qur'an, exegesis and *ahadith* but did not attain excellence in the standard education of the day.[16] He was not an *alim* in the technical meaning of the term, but could not be considered illiterate either. Several instances showed that he possessed a good knowledge of Islam. He wrote letters in Arabic and Persian. Later, during his stay in the North-West Frontier region he studied the *Mishkat-ul-Masabih*.[17]

After several years in Delhi, he returned to Raibaraili and married Bibi Zahra, who gave birth to Bibi Sara.[18] Sayyid Ahmad lived in his hometown for few years and then joined Amir Khan (1768–1834), popularly known as the Nawab of Tonk.[19] He served for seven years in Amir Khan's army and was held in high esteem by Amir Khan and his troops. No doubt, he was a common trooper initially, but due to his gallant performance on the battlefield he was promoted to command the personal bodyguards of Amir Khan.[20] He gave valuable counsel to Amir Khan on different occasions,[21] though one scholar, Peter Hardy, believed that he remained a common trooper in Amir Khan's army and any importance given to his time in Tonk was a later fiction of his followers.[22] Hardy's contention is against the *Waqai Sayyid Ahmad Shahid,* which tells about the close association of Amir Khan and Sayyid Ahmad. Moreover, Amir Khan sent his son to Delhi[23] under Sayyid Ahmad's supervision, following a clause in the treaty with the East India Company. Other events indicating a close relationship include Sayyid Ahmad's visit to Amir Khan's principality during the former's migration to the North-West Frontier; the care of Sayyid Ahmad's family by Amir Khan and his son; the gathering of desperate Mujahidin in Tonk after the Balakot setback (1831), and other stories are testaments that Sayyid Ahmad was not simply an ordinary soldier in Amir Khan's army. The peace treaty of 9 November 1817, between the English and Amir Khan, did result in the breakup of the direct association between Sayyid Ahmad and Amir Khan. Long pages in the *Waqai Sayyid Ahmad* detail that Sayyid Ahmad tried to convince Amir Khan to avoid the peace agreement.[24] Perhaps the English expansionist policies or fear of losing his job set Sayyid Ahmad in opposition to the peace treaty. At the conclusion of the treaty, Sayyid Ahmad left for Delhi[25] after Amir Khan's army was disbanded and he, along with many other soldiers, lost their places.

Sayyid Ahmad's service in Amir Khan's army has been discussed by every writer according to his interpretation of events. Interestingly, the *Waqai* is silent about his objective in joining Amir Khan's service. The only narrative is that he joined his army when Amir Khan was besieging a town.[26] Indian nationalists like Hussain Ahmad Madani[27] and Ubaidullah Sindhi suggest that he was sent to Amir Khan's army by Shah Abdul Aziz to acquire military skills. This version suggests that Shah Abdul Aziz was running a revolutionary organization[28] divided into two sections, one under the leadership of Shah Muhammad Ishaq, doing scholastic and academic activities, and the other under Sayyid Ahmad, with Shah Ismail and Maulana Abdul Hai as his councilors.[29] Notably, Madani, Sindhi and Sayyid Muhammad Mian[30] wrote from their background in Indian nationalist though and interpreted these events from that particular framework. Other sources, including by Ghulam Rasul Mihr and Abu Al Hassan Ali Nadavi, have contended that Sayyid Ahmad joined Amir Khan in a plan to use his forces against the English to restore Muslim rule.[31] However, it simply appears that he joined Amir Khan's troops because he did not get employment in Lucknow.[32] No doubt, he learnt a lot during his service with Amir Khan, but using the Khan's military to restore Muslim rule in India is unlikely. Amir Khan had a tribal outlook and narrow vision. He never utilized his capacity for constructive work. Sayyid Ahmad could not rely on such people for restoring Muslim rule since they were partially responsible for its downfall. Despite his theoretical approach to 'destruction of all the existing system',[33] Shah Waliullah relied on the Muslim nobility to restore Muslim rule in India.[34] Sayyid Ahmad could not repeat the failed strategy. He was very close to Shah Waliullah's family and must have studied their strategy. Sayyid Ahmad's Jihad Movement was therefore a later initiative developed when he realized the strength of the colonial power.

Concept of Sufism and *Rah-e-Suluk-e-Nabuwat*

Sayyid Ahmad met Shah Abdul Aziz during his first visit to Delhi and took *bai'at* at his hand in 1806[35] into the *Naqshbandiya* order.[36] There is a claim that Shah Abdul Aziz initiated him into four orders, the *Chishtiah, Qadiriyah, Suhurawardiyah,* and *Naqashbandiyah* in 1807,[37] and according to another source also the *Mujaddidiyah* in addition to the earlier four orders.[38] It is worth mentioning that though he was initiated by Shah Abdul Aziz into Sufi order, his main training along spiritual lines was by Shah Abdul Qadir[39] during his first stay in Delhi. As mentioned, Sayyid Ahmad returned to Delhi[40] in 1818[41] following the peace treaty between Amir Khan and East India Company. Sayyid Ahmad's second stay at Delhi was different from his previous time. Then, he had attained spiritual distinction but was far from choosing a line of action. His previous training in Amir Khan's army, the association with Shah Abdul Aziz, and the prevailing political, socio-economic and religious crisis shaped his evolving religio-political thought.

Sayyid Ahmad introduced a new order in Sufism,[42] the *Rah-e-Suluk-e-Nabuwat* at Delhi in 1818. According to Ahmad Khan this was the culmination or fulfilment of the *Mujaddidiyah* order of Sheikh Ahmad Sirhindi (1564–1624), popularly known as Mujaddid Alf Sani or Imam-e-Rabbani. Ahmad Khan further asserted that the initiative was taken with the blessing of Shah Abdul Aziz.[43] It is important to note that like other religious personalities of the time, Sayyid Ahmad followed the traditional Sufi order as it fit into the South Asian environment; yet he was different in many ways. Sources suggest that when during Sayyid Ahmad's spiritual training Shah Abdul Aziz asked him for *tasawwur-e-sheikh*, he did not obey on the ground that it was *shirk*.[44] Likewise, his emphasis was on *zahiri* instead of *batini*. Sayyid Ahmad did not sit idle to wait for the seekers of salvation, he visited them in person. He followed the way of the Prophet Muhammad (Peace Be Upon Him), who always preferred visiting people for preaching.

Sayyid Ahmad began taking *bai'at* from his adherents in the way done by other spiritual preceptors of the time. His popularity was evident from the fact that within a short period of time the number of his adherents grew tremendously. His first support from among the *ulama* was received from the close relatives and associates of Shah Abdul Aziz. These especially included Shah Ismail and Maulana Abdul Hai, nephew and son-in-law of Shah Abdul Aziz respectively; Maulvi Muhammad Yusaf of Phulat, the grandson of Shah Waliullah's elder brother Shah Ahlullah; Maulana Wajih-ud-Din, Hakim Mughid-ud-Din, and Hafiz Muin-ud-Din, who all took *bai'at* at his hands. The early association of such persons was a signal spurring other learned people to join Sayyid Ahmad's movement.[45] Their *bai'at* elevated the status and increased the reputation of Sayyid Ahmad. He received invitations from all segments of society to visit their respective areas. Sayyid Ahmad, along with his companions, toured many towns and villages including Saharanpur, Muzaffarnagar, Deoband, Rampur, Baraili and Shahjahanpur.[46]

As he thought uneducated Muslims in general and the residents of rural areas in particular practiced superstitious acts, social vices, and were victims of heretic Sufis, Sayyid Ahmad addressed these people in particular, but not at the cost of other groups. Though initially he received support from the elite of the society, he did not confine himself to the spiritual or learned elite, but concentrated on the masses. The rural areas had the bulk of the population who had converted to Islam from Hinduism in earlier generations but was not properly educated in religion.[47]

Aziz Ahmad writes:

> He tried to eliminate three kinds of excesses: those encouraged by heterodox Sufis such as the neglect of or opposition to the external tenets of Islam, 'poetic license' in one's attitude to God or his Prophet, idolization of one's spiritual preceptor, and homage to saints' tomb; secondly, those of popular Shi'i origin such as the celebration of Muharram as a public festival; and thirdly, those borrowed from Hindus.[48]

He faced opposition from many 'heretics' and 'worldly preceptors' due to his teaching, and at times he and his companions would receive threats from different quarters. They included those whose earning was affected by his teaching.[49]

The mystic practices of Sayyid Ahmad consisted of *dhikar, tawajuh* and *bai'at*.[50] However, as stated earlier, his emphasis remained on strict observance of *sharia*. His order was also named *Tariqah-e-Muhammadiyah* which attracted criticism for its name.[51] His *tariqah*, being a claimed culmination of the *Mujaddidiyah*, the youngest of all Sufi orders in India, stressed following the *sunnah* in day to day life to achieve all successes in this life and the life hereafter. In the same way Sayyid Ahmad stressed following *sharia* as there was no salvation without it. The *tariqat* which is not subject to *sharia* would not help an individual for salvation in eternity.[52] The *Rah-e-Suluk-e-Nabuwat* was not merely a mystic order but a framework of life. He stressed upon his followers to spend each moment in seeking the pleasure of Allah. Sayyid Ahmad urged his disciples to follow *sharia*, which was the real objective of taking *bai'at* at the hands of a spiritual guide. One had to follow the commandments of Allah whether one stayed at home or travelled, earned a livelihood or spent what has been earned, and slept or was awake. One must live with lawful earnings, offer his prayers, keep the fast, go for pilgrimage to Makkah, and so on. Briefly, his teachings consisted of the teaching of the Qur'an and Sunnah.[53] Ghulam Rasul Mihr has recognized jihad as part of *Rah-e-Suluk-e-Nabuwat*.[54] Apart from Muslims rejecting vices and *bida'at*, Hindus embraced Islam at the hands of Sayyid Ahmad and lived with him for the rest of their lives. Many wanted to keep their Islam secret from their respective families. Sayyid Ahmad provided them clothing, food, kept them with his disciples, and took care of all their material needs. Some Hindus remained his friends till last without converting to Islam. A few joined him and migrated with him to the North-West Frontier after embracing Islam.[55]

A pamphlet circulated among his disciples in which Sayyid Ahmad said:

> The main purpose of becoming a disciple of a mystic guide is to win the pleasure of God and the pleasure of God cannot be had but by following the *Shari'ah* of the Prophet Muhammad (may peace and blessing of Allah be upon him). And the *Shari'ah* of Prophet Muhammad (may peace and blessing of Allah be upon him) is based on two things: first—abstention from polytheism (*shirk*) and second—abstention from sinful innovations (*bid'at*).[56]

With Sayyid Ahmad as a spiritual guide, Shah Ismail as a renowned preacher, and Maulana Abdul Hai as a moderate scholar the movement became popular. From 1810, Shah Ismail had denounced all bad practices done in the name of religion. Sayyid Ahmad himself attracted many to become his disciples, including nobles and scholars. The ideals he set before them included: (a) elimination of *shirk* and *bida'at*, and restoration of pure *tawhid* and *sunnah*; (b) promotion of love for God and a subsequent avoidance of too much involvement in material affairs; and (c) the founding of an Islamic state.[57] Sayyid Ahmad's *Rah-e-Suluk-e-Nabuwat* was different in two aspects from traditional Sufi orders, following Shah Waliullah in one aspect and becoming a pioneer himself in another. First, Sayyid Ahmad asked Muslims not to fully follow the stricter version of the Hanafi School of thought compiled in India during Aurangzeb's time, but to follow the traditions of the Prophet Muhammad (Peace Be Upon Him).[58] Second, Sayyid Ahmad resorted to armed struggle, unique in Sufi orders. One could observe that in later times the resistance movement against colonial authorities in India and Central Asia was taken up by the *Naqashbandiyah* school of Sufi order. Sayyid Ahmad had realized that mere preaching would not influence Sikhs and Christians and so resorted to armed struggle to protect Muslims.[59]

A systematic strategy was thought out by the Movement's leaders to achieve their objectives. His followers invited him to the Doab and he, along with his close disciples, visited the area. The method for travelling and audiences was familiar and traditional in many ways. Sayyid Ahmad accepted *nazar* from his disciples and also their invitations for feasting. Newcomers were given importance, *bai'at* were taken of them, and they were attached to older disciples for spiritual training. This whole process was traditional but there were differences as well. When recommended by Sayyid Ahmad, Shah Ismail and Abdul Hai addressed the gatherings. The Qur'an and *sunnah* were explained and innovations Muslims had assimilated from non-Muslims were denounced.[60]

At the end of the Doab tour, Sayyid Ahmad returned to Delhi and then travelled to Raibaraili in 1819 (A.H. 1234). He returned to his hometown after a decade. His brother Sayyid Ishaq had died in his absence.[61] Sayyid Ahmad stayed in Raibaraili for more than two years. He was accompanied by seventy to eighty disciples, including Shah Ismail and Maulana Abdul Hai. The movement reached a climax and more tours were made to various areas.[62] As stated earlier, Shah Abdul Aziz had allowed Sayyid Ahmad to accept truth seekers as his *murids*. He, however, was more interested in *amal-e-zahiri* than in *batini ashghal*. He conveyed to his disciples that *tariqat* alone was not all encompassing; instead one has to follow *sharia* to please Allah. Once he was asked why he sought *bai'at* in *Chishti, Qadiri* and *Naqashbandi turuq* and then in *Rah-e-Suluk-e-Nabuwat*. He replied:

> The rituals (*ashghal*) of *Chishti, Qadiri, Naqashbandi* and *Mujaddidi turuq* instruct how to perform *darb* (spiritual beating) and what are different *lataif*. And these *turuq* are related to the Prophet esoterically. The disciples of *Tariqah'-i-Muhammadiyah*, he continued, 'are taught in this way: eat for this purpose; dress for this purpose; grow crops for this purpose; marry for this purpose ..., and relation of this *tariqah* to the Prophet is exoteric, that is emphasizing the performance of outward activities in conformity with the *shari'ah*.'[63]

Sayyid Ahmad laid emphasis on teaching of the Qur'an and *sunnah* in the Indian environment, a tradition set by Shah Waliullah. He rejected customs which contradicted the teachings of the Prophet Muhammad (Peace Be Upon Him).[64] His order was simple and he emphasized the practical aspect of religious and moral life more than other Sufi orders. He did not give any written *khilafat nama*, a long prevalent custom among the Sufis.[65] He did not initiate any new rituals or particular oath for *Rah-e-Suluk-e-Nabuwat* and advised his disciples to follow any of the four schools of jurisprudence. They must follow *ahadith* instead of any scholar's legal decision.[66] All sources agree that he helped the needy on many occasions and stressed upon his followers to do the same. There were instances when food was shared with the needy and cash was provided to them. On one such occasion he asked the one seeking help to denounce all innovations and follow the Holy Qur'an and *sunnah* in spirit.[67]

Another aspect of Sayyid Ahmad's movement was the social composition of his following. They represented all segments of society: poor and rich, ignorant and learned. This enabled him to acquire firsthand knowledge of collapsing Indo-Muslim society.[68] *Rah-e-Suluk-e-Nabuwat* also insisted on *ijtehad* and rejected *taqlid*.[69] 'Follow none', he said, 'be he *mujtahid*, Imam, *ghaus, qutb, maulvi, mashaikh*, king, minister, *padri*, or pundit against the authority of the *Qur'an* and the *Hadis*.'[70] There are contradictory views regarding his tours, including that these were undertaken only for the reformation of society or for the preaching of jihad as well. Ubaidullah Sindhi, Hafeez Malik, and Ghulam Rasul Mihr agreed that emphasis was laid on jihad. Sindhi[71] and Hafeez Malik[72] further share the view that he was mobilizing masses for jihad on behalf of Shah Abdul Aziz. Mihr[73] has asserted that though he took *bai'at* for jihad, it was his personal initiative based on his realization that mere Sufism would not reform society in the then prevalent socio-political order. Hedayetullah,[74] however, has argued that his tours were for the reformation of society and did not focus on organizing people for jihad. Pearson said there is no direct evidence that Sayyid Ahmad Barailvi was preaching jihad before his pilgrimage or that any experience in Hijaz inspired him.[75] We assert that though his tours were initially for the reformation of the society according to the traditional Sufi way, later jihad became of foremost importance. The primary sources have recorded that some objected to Sayyid Ahmad's taking arms with him. He replied that Prophet Muhammad (Peace Be Upon Him) had taken arms with him. He ordered his disciples to prepare themselves for the upcoming jihad, and also spend their wealth for the sake of jihad.[76] The preparation for jihad started after his arrival back in Raibaraili, though some of his disciples expressed their reservation through Maulvi Abdul Rahim Kandhlavi. To this, Sayyid Ahmad replied that Sufi practices were activities for peacetime and not for the situation where it was becoming difficult on Indian soil, with each passing day, for Muslims to live peacefully.[77]

Sayyid Ahmad's tours had a significant impact upon the upcoming Jihad Movement as many influential families joined him and offered their homes as sanctuaries.[78] These centres played a vital role in providing money and men to the Mujahidin Movement during and after his life. Initially Sayyid Ahmad's movement received its main support from Delhi, Jajhana, Budhana, Kandhla, Deoband, Rampur, Saharanpur, and Raibaraili. The people of these towns, who joined the movement, were close to Shah Waliullah's family through *piri-muridi*, matrimonial or teacher–student relationships.[79]

One visit to Nasirabad was important due to its sectarian colour. Nasirabad was the abode of Sayyid Ahmad's ancestors and many of his relatives still resided there. The town had a good number of Sunnis alongside Shias. The Shia population of the town, perhaps instigated by Dildar Ali, passed a Muharram procession through a predominantly Sunni area in 1819 (Muharram A.H. 1235).[80] Mihr suggests that the motive behind the decision was to provoke the Sunni population on one hand and demonstrate Shia strength on the other. Also, it is said that Dildar Ali wanted a disturbance in the town as it was in the *jagir* of a person who had developed differences with him. Sunnis sought Sayyid Ahmad's assistance. He rushed to Nasirabad with seventy-five others. He averted a looming clash between the two communities, wanting to protect Sunnis in case of a riot. The Shias did not like Sayyid Ahmad's presence in the town and complained to the ruler of Oudh. Ultimately, the issue was peacefully resolved by the efforts of elders of both communities.[81] Sayyid Ahmad's visit to Nasirabad and subsequently to Lucknow was significant because he developed contacts with Afghans who had settled there and worked in the army of Oudh state. Their neighbourhood was known as the Qandahari cantonment.[82] Sources agree that Sayyid Ahmad frequently visited these soldiers and they visited him when he was in Lucknow.[83]

Another important element of his reform movement was a campaign for the right of widows to remarry. Widow remarriage was not considered honourable among Indian Muslims due to the influence of Hindu tradition. Sayyid Ahmad took the initiative by setting an example in his home. He married the widow of his brother, who had died several years earlier.[84] The remarriage of widows was propagated and Shah Ismail drafted letters that were sent to different cities. The example was followed by many of his disciples. Shah Ismail arranged the remarriage of his widowed sister with Maulana Abdul Hai, though it was said that she was above fifty and not interested in a second marriage.[85]

It was during his tours that Sayyid Ahmad realized that Sufism would not solve all the problems of Muslim society which had become polluted with the passage of time.[86] He put great stress on three major *sunnah* of the Prophet Muhammad (Peace Be Upon Him): widow remarriage, Haj, and jihad. He thought all three had fallen into oblivion in the Indian environment.[87] He thought spiritual preceptors were accessed by a limited segment of the society and their potential was wasted in different vices of the day or in rituals like *qawwali, urs,* dancing, and other un-Islamic activities, instead of any constructive work. Sayyid Ahmad launched the Jihad Movement as he was convinced that once a Muslim was prepared to sacrifice his life in the path of Allah, he would easily leave all his personal interests for the pleasure of Allah. Furthermore, the English expansion in northern India was a major threat to Muslim institutions which could only be restored by jihad.

Performance of Haj and Its Significance for His Future Jihad Movement

While at Raibaraili, Sayyid Ahmad decided to proceed for Haj. The decision was unexpected for many as he had made considerable preparation for migration and jihad. The followers of Sayyid Ahmad have attributed his decision for pilgrimage to a divinely inspired dream.[88] However, one reason for this decision might have been the *fatwa* of Abdullah Sultanpuri against the obligation of Haj for Indian Muslims in the prevalent conditions, found during his stay at Lucknow.[89] Munshi Khair-ud-Din had sent the *fatwa* to Shah Abdul Aziz. Shah Ismail and Abdul Hai had denounced the *fatwa*. Shah Abdul Aziz strongly supported his disciples on the issue.[90] The matter was, however, more important than mere scholastic discussion and Sayyid Ahmad, who was more interested in practice than discussion, announced he would perform Haj. One should not forget that the performance of Haj is obligatory upon those who had finances enough for one's journey and his family back at home during his absence. Sayyid Ahmad and the majority of his followers did not have the required funds, but his role as a reformer demanded more courage and commitment as compared to the common people. Sayyid Ahmad aimed at the revival of Islamic commandments by setting an example, even as the morale of Indian Muslims had fallen so low that they found excuses to avoid religious obligations. The *Waqai* narrated that Sayyid Ahmad ordered his disciples to prepare for Haj and added that there were hidden benefits, including the revival of Islamic injunction.[91] Letters were sent to his disciples in other cities and they were invited to join him for Haj. The content of the letter has been quoted in the *Waqai*:

> We are going to perform Haj and you may bring along with you whoso-ever would like to accompany. But let it be clear to everyone that we have no financial resources. We trust in God, and leave the problems of care to Him who will not disappoint us. On our way, we will seek all sorts of odd jobs to defray our expenses. Aged men and women, who are unable to earn their living and traveling expenses, will perform the useful service of guarding the belongings of our men, while they are out on jobs; and in the expenses, both the earning persons and those sitting at home on guard duty will share equally.[92] (Translation mine)

Sayyid Ahmad's family, aware of the precarious conditions, hesitated to accompany him for Haj. He, however, tried to convince them. A few of his relatives accompanied him.[93] The announcement of his Haj had a profound effect both upon the general public and *ulama*. They flocked to Raibaraili to join him for Haj.

After completing the preparation, including for volunteers from all over the country, the party started its long journey for Haj from Raibaraili on 30 July 1821 (1 Dhul Qa'idah, A.H. 1236). The group of four hundred persons was divided into small *jama'at*.[94] From Raibaraili to Dalmaw the men walked, while women were carried in *palkis*. From Dalmaw the journey was on boats, but the boats could not accommodate all and a few travelled along by foot.[95] Sources agree that Sayyid Ahmad had to arrange boarding and lodging for the caravan but that he had no money to meet expenses. He advised his companions to have faith in God. Indeed, many people provided financial assistance to the pilgrims. Cash was offered, they were invited to feasts, and thus they did not have to cook for themselves.[96] During the Haj journey he encountered the English a few times. Once, an English businessman offered food to the whole caravan.[97] This Englishman was not the Company's employee but was running independent business.[98] The Haj journey became so popular an event that many patiently waited on river banks to receive Sayyid Ahmad and his companions. During every rest stay, brief or long, people flocked to him and took *bai'at* after repentance. Sayyid Ahmad preached everywhere he went, advising people to avoid un-Islamic practices. Sources agree that his preaching had an anti-Shia colour as Muharram rituals were especially condemned and were declared un-Islamic. The general public was advised to stick to the teaching of Islam and avoid innovations.[99]

The caravan stopped at important places and hundreds of people visited to see Sayyid Ahmad. He would also send his disciples to approach the public for preaching. This not only attracted many to join him for Haj but also popularized his reform movement. It was during the Haj journey that he appointed his *khulafa* in different cities who later contributed to the Jihad Movement. In Allahabad, he appointed Sheikh Lal Muhammad, Sheikh Wazir, and others to teach *tauheed*, *sunnah*, and prohibit *shirk* and *bida'at*.[100] The stay at Allahabad was comparatively long and thousands of people took *bai'at* at his hand, including Sheikh Ghulam Ali, a leading noble of the city. Sheikh Ghulam Ali was appointed to preach the tenets of Islam in the city and surrounding villages. He was further asked to demand less than what was due from the tenants so they could listen him attentively. Many of the disciples of the city and surrounding areas presented cash to Sayyid Ahmad for his Haj expenses.[101] At times he left behind Shah Ismail, Abdul Hai, or one of his learned disciples to teach the tenets of Islam to those who had taken *bai'at* after repentance. They were also advised to preach the true nature of *sharia* to them and others since the journey was slow and the caravan was not in a hurry.[102]

The *Waqai* clearly portrays the financial strain involved as at times Sayyid Ahmad's disciples gave a full account of food served to them at each feast.[103] Taking more than one dish at a time was not possible even for Muslims from Bengal, once the richest province of the Mughal Empire.

The policies of the Company had worsened the economy of the country and many Bengalis joined the Jihad Movement in succeeding years.

One significant event of the Haj journey was Sayyid Ahmad's visit to Azeemabad, Patna, where the family of Mazhar Ali, a wealthy noble of the city, took *bai'at* and devoted themselves wholeheartedly to the cause of reform and the Jihad Movement. Mazhar Ali and Shah Muhammad Hussain were appointed *khulafa*,[104] authorized to take *bai'at* on behalf of Sayyid Ahmad, enroll new disciples, and preach in Bihar. No doubt Sayyid Ahmad toured many towns in northern India, but he had never appointed any deputy by virtue of *sanad*. His visit to Patna provided for the systematic organization of the movement and fund collection. The organization continued working for decades after his death.[105]

The stay in Calcutta has been minutely recorded by the *Waqai* and thus many details are available. It has been recorded that the preaching of Shah Ismail, Abdul Hai, and Sayyid Ahmad was so effective that on a daily basis thousands of people repented their past sins, and came forward to take *bai'at* at his hands. He was unable to find time for anything else save prayer and routine human needs. The sons of Tipu Sultan, who were living in Calcutta under English custody, also took *bai'at*.[106]

Since Sayyid Ahmad's Haj journey had become popular among those followers who lived enroute, he was visited by hundreds of people daily during his whole journey. Wherever he stayed, that place played a vital role during the Jihad Movement of the later years. He reached Calcutta in more than three months and the masses flocked to him in such a large number that he was unable to go through the traditional ceremony of initiation, that is, holding the hand of a disciple in his hand. He had to spread his turban to be touched for *bai'at*.[107]

The journey for Haj and his stay in Calcutta for about three months proved important in the history of the eastern subcontinent. The people of the area had an opportunity to meet and take benefit directly from the members of Shah Waliullah's family—Abdul Hai and Shah Ismail and their preceptor. The journey was slow and at times the halt was longer at important places. The preaching of Shah Ismail and Abdul Hai awakened the masses and those who had the potential to become centres of guidance themselves. The three-month stay in Calcutta was spent in preaching and many Muslims from other parts of Bengal, that is, Sylhet, Chatgam, and Nawakhali, visited him and were appointed his deputies after repentance and taking *bai'at*. Those deputies later took his message more vigorously to remote areas of Bengal.[108] One important development was the conversion of many Hindus to Islam at Calcutta. Abdul Hai used to preach twice a week and it was said that ten to fifteen Hindus would convert daily.[109] A few nobles of Calcutta wrote letters to their relatives in Dhaka inviting them to visit Sayyid Ahmad in Calcutta. Accordingly, many people came, and narrated all the evil practices prevalent in eastern Bengal. They asked Sayyid Ahmad to visit their country but he refused politely and instead appointed his deputies, Maulvi Imam-ud-Din and Sufi Noor Muhammad of Sylhet to preach Islam in eastern Bengal. In addition, other educated among them were appointed to teach *sharia* in their respective areas.[110]

It is stated that Titumir was Sayyid Ahmad's disciple.[111] One can guess that he took *bai'at* during Sayyid Ahmad's stay at Calcutta, but the sources consulted have cited nothing about this claim. Bengal played an important role in the Mujahidin Movement due to several factors: they long suffered the bad effects of the Company's economic policies which deprived them of their sources of income; jihad was introduced which was not known to them earlier due to traditional Sufi movements; and many saw a deliverer in Sayyid Ahmad who was addressing their issues.[112] The most important thing, commonly misunderstood by the English writers and administrators of India, was the relationship of *pir-murid*— preceptor and disciple. They assumed that Sayyid Ahmad learnt this sort of organizational method from outside India. In fact, this sort of relation was prevalent in India for centuries and Sayyid Ahmad only changed its mode by utilizing it for Jihad Movement.[113]

After a long stay for more than three months, the caravan, now comprised of about seven hundred and fifty persons was divided into ten units, each under a chief. Each unit boarded a separate ship. The ₹13,000 paid as fare had come from gifts and offerings from various followers and admirers.[114] The pilgrims left Calcutta in February 1822 (*Jumada Al-Awwal* 1237) and arrived in the Hijaz on 20 May 1822 (29 *Sha'aban* 1237). Apart from performing Haj, the *Sirat-e-Mustaqim*[115] was translated by Abdul Hai and Shah Ismail for Sheikh Hassan Effendi, deputy of Ahmad Pasha, Sultan of Egypt. Many scholars of the Hijaz took *bai'at,* including Sheikh Abdullah Siraj, Sayyid Muhammad of North Africa, Sheikh Hamza, Sheikh Ahmad bin Idrees, Muhammad Ali Hindi, Mulla Bukhari, Sheikh Salih Shafi, and Sheikh Ali.[116] One important event of the stay at Mina, in connection with the last rituals of Haj, was the taking of *bai'at* for jihad.[117] The *bai'at* for jihad at the occasion of Haj negates the contention that Sayyid Ahmad started his jihad against the Sikhs with the blessing of the English or at their instigation. This contention was made later by some writers who wished to divert the wrath of English authorities from the

Wahabis and also those who wanted to project Ranjit Singh's reputation as a Punjabi nationalist.[118]

After performing Haj, Sayyid Ahmad returned to India with his companions. He landed at Bombay and after a short stay of a few days came to Calcutta where he arrived in October 1823 (*Safar* 1239). He stayed in Calcutta for over two months. He arrived at his hometown Raibaraili on 28 April 1824 (29 *Sha'aban* 1239). He followed the same pattern of staying at important places, including Monghyr, taking *bai'at,* and appointing deputies in different towns. Guns and pistols were purchased there from a local gun and ammunition manufacturing factory.[119] The whole journey from and to Raibaraili took two years and ten months.[120] The performance of Haj and the journey was the most important part of Sayyid Ahmad's life before migration to the North-West Frontier. The excuse of Indians that sea voyages were dangerous was negated practically and contacts made during this journey proved fruitful in organizing the Jihad Movement. Many of Sayyid Ahmad's adherents who took *bai'at* during this time became leaders of jihad activities during and after his life time, including the Sadiqpur family who took *bai'at* during the Haj journey.

The Doctrine of Jihad

The word jihad is derived from *juhud,* to struggle or to strive, to spend one's whole potential for a cause.[121] The word jihad and its corollaries have been used in the Holy Qur'an in twenty-nine verses of which four are Makkites and twenty-five are Madinites. The Muslims in Makkah were not authorized to use force and thus it denoted the peaceful struggle.[122] The relevant word for fighting for the cause of Islam with arms or armed struggle is *jihad bil saif* or *qital* or *harb.*[123] According to some jurists, jihad was to be waged by the Imam—Muslim ruler once in a year on the enemy territories most dangerous to Muslims,[124] but other jurists did not consider the presence of Imam a prerequisite. The Imam had the right to delay jihad if the Muslims' were weak. The Shiite school, *Isna Asharia* or twelvers, had the same notion but this is subject to the presence of the Imam. However, defensive war or just war could be waged against the enemy in the absence of the Imam.[125]

There is no denying the fact that the jihad of Sayyid Ahmad was inspired by the teaching of the Qur'an and *ahadith*—traditions of the Prophet Muhammad (Peace Be Upon Him). We, however, cannot ignore the political situation of the subcontinent in his time. It was more of a resistance movement against the Sikhs and later the British, not jihad in its pure technical terms. The Muslim world was facing western imperialism for decades and they were upset with their crumbling political and social status and institutions. The colonizers were replacing India's centuries-old institutions with their own.

We might look at resistance in the name of jihad in other Muslim countries including Africa, Middle East, and Central Asia. The situation in India, however, was different from other lands. Indian Muslims were deprived of their previous ruling position by the western colonizers on the one hand and were brought to the status of a minority on the other.[126] The English occupation of Bengal and Mysore, the Company and native states subsidiary alliances, the annexation of Rohilkhand (parts of present Uttar Pradesh), the occupation of Delhi by Gerald Lake in 1803, English overlordship in Marathas territory, and Amir Khan's peace treaty with the Company were several of the factors which strengthened Sayyid Ahmad's belief that simply observing Sufi beliefs and practices alone would not revive Muslim glory in India.

Being a disciple of Shah Abdul Aziz, son and successor of Shah Waliullah, Sayyid Ahmad was trained for quite a long time. His mindset was partially shaped by Waliullah's tradition. Living in Delhi gave him extra insight into the wider existing situation. The spiritual training by Shah Abdul Aziz broadened Sayyid Ahmad's vision. His personal experiences in Amir Khan's army, extensive territorial tours for the reformation of society, and observations of the prevalent socio-political situation of India contributed to the preparing of his plan for jihad.

Shah Abdul Aziz had accused the Sikhs and the Marathas, but did not issue any *fatwa* upon their occupation of Delhi. Still, they and other local non-Muslims forces who sought independence were considered rebels. This, however, did not change the status of *dar-ul-Islam*. But on the English occupation of Delhi, a question was put before Shah Abdul Aziz, 'Could a *dar al-Islam* become a *dar al-harb*?' Shah Abdul Aziz replied:

Reliable works say that a *dar al-Islam* could become a *dar al-harb* in three circumstances. Thus, according to *Durr al-Mukhtar*, a *dar al-Islam* would not be transformed into a *dar al-harb* unless the following three conditions existed:

1. The laws of the *mushriks* (polytheists) were implemented there.
2. The *dar al-Islam* adjoined a *dar al-harb*.

3. Muslims and *dhimmis* (protected subjects) who had earlier been under Muslim protection were no longer safe there.

According to *Kafi*, these territories (*bilad*) where the orders of the Muslims (the imams) were obeyed and which were under their control were called the *dar al-Islam*. In this city (Delhi) the Muslim's Imam (Imam *al-Muslimin*) is unable to enforce his orders; instead the Christian officers' orders are openly carried out. The implementation of the infidels' orders means they are in full control of administrative matters. They govern the people, collect *kharaj* (land tax), *baj* (toll levied by the road patrol), *'ushr* (tithe) on commercial goods, punish thieves and robbers and decide law-suits according to their own regulations. They (the Christian rulers) do not interfere with some Islamic ordinances such as those on Friday prayer, congregational prayers of two *'ids*, *adhan* (calling to prayers) and cow sacrifice only because they do not value the basic principles of these practices to which they are indifferent. They unhesitatingly demolish mosques. No Muslim or *dhimmi* can enter this city or its suburbs without seeking their protection. In their own interests they do not prohibit the entry of common visitors, travellers and merchants, but eminent people such as Shuja al-Mulk and Wilayati Begum cannot enter without their specific permission. Christian rule has been established from here to Calcutta. In some places such as Haiderabad, Lucknow, and Rampur, they have not established direct control for reasons of expediency due to the submission of the rulers. According to the *ahadith*, the precedents of the Prophet's companions and the great caliphs, this situation would transform *dar al-Islam* into a *dar al-harb*....[127]

The *fatwa* of Shah Abdul Aziz was regarded as a very revolutionary document.[128] The Jihad Movement of Sayyid Ahmad was a practical response to the *fatwa* and for that purpose Sayyid Ahmad, at the initial stage of his Jihad Movement, tried to form an alliance of the Indian communities to fight against the East India Company. However, he fought first against the Sikhs due to their proximity to his place of migration and he ultimately was killed in the battle of Balakot in 1831. Hussain Ahmad Madani has asserted that the English felt assured at Sayyid Ahmad's announcement of war against the Sikhs and materially helped in these efforts.[129]

Sayyid Ahmad stayed in his native town Raibaraili for one year and ten months in preparation for jihad. He focused on training and material collection. The aim of Sayyid Ahmad's Jihad Movement is not agreed by writers. Some of his followers and some scholars portray him as being on friendly terms with the English and have emphasized that his Jihad Movement was against the Sikhs only. Others claim that he was against both the English and the Sikhs.

Those who claim that Sayyid Ahmad had friendly relations with the British have no authentic source for their opinion. Some wanted to divert the attention of the British government from the Muslims, especially the 'Wahabis', particularly after the uprising of 1857. Prominent among such writers were Maulvi Muhammad Jaffar Thanesari and Sir Sayyid Ahmad Khan. Thanesari went to the extent of altering the text of Sayyid Ahmad Barailvi's letters. Others of this category based their claim merely on assumption,[130] asserting in support of their contention that Sayyid Ahmad and his associates' preparations for jihad were not questioned by the British authorities. But the British did not notice such movements in their domains unless they were seen as a potential challenge to their writ.[131]

For the Jihad Movement, Sayyid Ahmad tried to enlist the support of Muslims and Hindus alike. The tone and content of his appeal changed only when he wrote to the Barakzai Sardars, emphasizing the establishment of Islamic rule in the subcontinent,[132] and to Hindu Rao, *wazir* of Daulat Rao Sindhia,[133] telling the latter that the princes and nobles had failed to initiate a struggle against the British traders who became rulers of the country. Thus, Sayyid Ahmad and his followers left their homes to expel the foreigners from India and serve the cause of Islam, they did not act from any mundane ambition.[134]

The claim of some writers that Sayyid Ahmad was part of Shah Abdul Aziz's network does not seem sound. He did not go Delhi when the latter died on 5 June 1824, though Shah Ismail and Abdul Hai visited the aggrieved family at Delhi.[135] If he had belonged to that 'network', he would have surely visited Delhi to fill the gap created by the death of the leader of the 'network'. Although he was trained in mysticism by Waliullah's family and was inspired by his teaching, the establishment of a network by Shah Abdul Aziz and the appointment of Shah Ismail and Abdul Hai as members of the network, as Ubaidullah Sindhi has claimed, seems not credible.[136] S. A. A. Rizvi has contended:

There is no historical basis for connecting Jihad Movement of Sayyid Ahmad Shahid with Shah 'Abd al-'Aziz and Shah Wali-Allah. The theories of traditional and modern scholars which transform Shah Wali-Allah and Shah 'Abd al-'Aziz into revolutionaries, is unfortunately undocumented and merely the figment of their imagination.[137]

The argument that the Jihad Movement was Sayyid Ahmad's initiative, though in consultation and with blessings of many learned people of the day, is to be augmented by the fact that the Waliullah's family traditions indicate that only a family member was appointed for a responsibility even if in a very young age.[138] Shah Ismail had always showed great strength and zeal in denouncing the heretic practices prevalent in the then Muslim society. He was physically strong, brave, and a better military commander than Sayyid Ahmad and had the courage to take on any responsibility, assigned to him. He was older than Sayyid Ahmad and the *fatwa* of Shah Abdul Aziz appeared in 1803, so it is strange to believe that Shah Abdul Aziz was waiting for Sayyid Ahmad to be appointed leader of the Jihad Movement at the 'Frontier'. Shah Abdul Aziz could have appointed Shah Ismail instead of Sayyid Ahmad. Furthermore, during their whole careers, neither Shah Waliullah nor Shah Abdul Aziz visited any area for preaching. They always remained in Delhi and people visited them to seek guidance. Moreover, they sent some of their students, after completing their studies, in different directions to settle in a particular area and guide the people to the righteous path. The case of Sayyid Ahmad and his associates was totally different. Sayyid Ahmad always preferred to visit the downtrodden, beyond the elite class. He focused on the general public.

After extensive tours, after spiritual and military training in different places, and after generating support of Muslims of northern India, Sayyid Ahmad prepared to achieve his aim, to wage jihad. In this pursuit, as he organized, he asked his followers to be ready for migration to the North-West Frontier to wage jihad against the Sikhs.

Notes and References

1. The genealogical line of Sayyid Ahmad runs as follows: Sayyid Ahmad s/o Sayyid Muhammad Irfan s/o Sayyid Muhammad Noor s/o Sayyid Muhammad Huda s/o Sayyid Ilmullah s/o Sayyid Muhammad Fuzail s/o Sayyid Muhammad Muazzam s/o Qazi Sayyid Ahmad s/o Qazi Sayyid Mahmud s/o Sayyid Ala-ud-Din s/o Sayyid Qutb-ud-Din Sani s/o Sayyid Sadr-ud-Din Sani s/o Sayyid Zain-ud-Din s/o Sayyid Ahmad s/o Sayyid Ali s/o Sayyid Qiyam-ud-Din s/o Sayyid Sadr-ud-Din s/o Qazi Sayyid Rukn-ud-Din s/o Ameer Sayyid Nizam-ud-Din s/o Ameer Sayyid Qutb-ud-Din Muhammad al-Ghaznavi al-Karavi s/o Sayyid Rashid-ud-Din s/o Sayyid Yusaf s/o Sayyid Essa s/o Sayyid Hassan s/o Sayyid Abu al-Hassan s/o Sayyid Abu Jaffar s/o Sayyid Qasim s/o Sayyid Abu Muhammad Abdullah s/o Sayyid Hassan al-Aw'ar al-Jawad s/o Sayyid Muhammad Sani s/o Sayyid Abu Muhammad Abdullah al-Ashtar s/o Sayyid Muhammad al-Mehdi

Nafs-ul-Zakkiya s/o Sayyid Abdullah al-Mahadi s/o Sayyid Hassan Mathna s/o Hazrat Hassan (R.A) s/o Hazrat Ali (R.A). Mihr, Ghulam Rasul. nd. *Sayyid Ahmad Shahid.* Lahore: Sheikh Ghulam Ali and Sons. p. 33. Henceforth, Mihr, *Sayyid Ahmad.*

2. Nadvi, Sayyid Abul al-Hassan Ali. nd. *Tarikh-e-Dawat wa Azeemat: Seerat-e-Sayyid Ahmad Shahid.* Karachi: Majlis Nashriyat. p. 109. Henceforth, Nadvi, *Seerat-e-Sayyid Ahmad. Chamarkand Colony* S. No. 271, Civil Secretariat, North-West Political Department, Tribal Research Cell, Peshawar, p. 4. Henceforth, *Chamarkand Colony.*

3. A Person appointed by the state to decide the issues related to Islam and statecraft. He was considered the superior authority in such issues.

4. The name of the lady was Fateeha. Mihr, *Sayyid Ahmad*, p. 36. The sources dealing with the reign of Iltutmish are silent over the marriage of the Sultan's daughter to Qaw'am-ud-Din.

5. Mihr, *Sayyid Ahmad*, pp. 37–39.

6. Hedayatullah, Muhammad. nd. *Sayyid Ahmad: A Study of the Religious Reform Movement of Sayyid Ahmad of Ra'e Bareli.* Lahore: Sh. Muhammad Ashraf. p. 45. Henceforth, Hedayatullah, *Sayyid Ahmad.*

7. Nadvi, *Seerat-e-Sayyid Ahmad*, pp. 90–92.

8. Mihr, *Sayyid Ahmad*, pp. 50–57.

9. This was a sort of deviation from the family tradition as they had always served during the Mughal periods but mainly in the capacity of *qazis* or *sheikh-ul-Islam*. Even the elder brother of Sayyid Ahmad served the Amir Khan of Tonk in the capacity of Imam-e-Lashkar, responsible for leading the congregational prayers. Gaining knowledge and an appointment as a *qazi* or some other post was now a less attractive job as Muslims had lost most of their previous domain. It was necessary to look for other sources of livelihood.

10. Nasiri, Alim. 1995. *Shahnama Balakot: Tahrik-e-Jihad ki Manzum Dastan*, vol. I. Lahore: Idara Matbu'at-e-Sulaimani. p. 54. Henceforth, Nasiri, *Shahnama*, vol. I. Another source has contended that he mastered Persian and Arabic and had no problem in understanding the *Mishkat-ul-Masabih*. Thanawi, Ashraf Ali. nd. *Arwah-e-Salasa.* Lahore: Maktaba Rahmaniya. p. 129. Henceforth, Thanawi, *Arwah-e-Salasa.*

11. Nadvi, *Seerat-e-Sayyid Ahmad*, p. 110.

12. Ibid., p. 111.

13. The family might have received some tract of land from the ruler or nobles, something common in medieval and early modern days. We have evidence of such *jagirs* allotted to the saintly families for their livelihood.

14. Hedayatullah, *Sayyid Ahmad*, pp. 51–52; Nadvi, Muhammad Hamza Hasni. 1996. *Tazkira Hazrat Sayyid Ahmad Shahid.* Karachi: Majlis Nashriyat. p. 28. Henceforth, Nadvi, *Tazkira.*

15. Qureshi, Ishtiaq Hussain. nd. *Ulema in Politics.* Karachi: Ma'arif. p. 141. Henceforth, Qureshi, *Ulema in Politics.*

16. Hedayatullah, *Sayyid Ahmad*, pp. 58–59.

17. Ibid., pp. 59–60; Mihr, *Sayyid Ahmad*, pp. 76–77.

18. Nadvi, *Seerat-e-Sayyid Ahmad*, p. 130. Bibi Sara was later on married to Sayyid Ismail s/o Sayyid Ishaq to whom were born Sayyid Ishaq, whose son Maulana Sayyid Noor Ahmad was alive when Mihr was writing his book and had assisted him in his work. Mihr, *Sayyid Ahmad*, p. 14.

19. Ikram, Sheikh Muhammad. 2000. *Mauj-e-Kausar.* Lahore: Idara Saqafat-e-Islamia. p. 15. Henceforth, Ikram, *Mauj-e-Kausar.* He was recognized as Nawab of Tonk by the

English after concluding the peace treaty with them on 9 November 1817. *Chamarkand Colony*, p. 4.

20. Husain, Mahmud. 2008. 'Sayyid Ahmad Shahid (I)', in Mahmud Husain et al. (eds). *A History of Freedom Movement, 1707–1831*, vol. I. Karachi: Royal Book Company. p. 560. Henceforth, Husain, 'Sayyid Ahmad Shahid I'.

21. Khan, Nawab Muhammad Wazir. 2007. *Waqai Sayyid Ahmad Shahid*. Lahore: Sayyid Ahmad Shahid Academy. pp. 62–64. Henceforth, Khan, *Waqai Sayyid Ahmad*. The *Waqai Sayyid Ahmad Shahid* was written by the followers of Sayyid Ahmad in Tonk under the patronage of Nawab Muhammad Wazir Khan (d. 1864).

22. Hardy, Peter. 1972. *The Muslims of British India*. London: Cambridge University Press. p. 51.

23. Khan, *Waqai Sayyid Ahmad*, p. 86.

24. Ibid., p. 85.

25. Nasiri, *Shahnama*. vol. I., p. 78.

26. Ibid., p. 22.

27. Madani, Sayyid Hussain Ahmad. nd. *Naqsh-e-Hayat*. Karachi: Dar-ul-Isha'at. p. 434. Henceforth, Madani, *Naqsh-e-Hayat*.

28. Sindhi, Ubaidullah. nd. *Shah Waliullah aur unki Siyasi Tahrik*. Lahore: Al-Mahmud Academy. p. 73. Henceforth, Sindhi, *Shah Waliullah*.

29. Ibid.; Madani, *Naqsh-e-Hayat*, p. 434.

30. Author of the *Ulama-e-Hind ka Shandar Mazi* and many other works.

31. Mihr, *Sayyid Ahmad*, pp. 92–93.

32. His elder brother had worked in Amir Khan's force but had died before Sayyid Ahmad joined the force.

33. Ghazi, Mahmood. 1993. 'Shah Wali Allah', in Waheed-uz-Zaman and M. Saleem Akhtar (eds). *Islam in South Asia*. Islamabad: National Institute of Historical and Cultural Research. p. 316.

34. Shah Waliullah had relied on the tribal force of Najib-ud-Daula and Ahmad Shah Abdali for the restoration of Muslim Rule in India, which failed though the Marathas were defeated in 1761. Rizvi, Saiyid Athar Abbas. 1982. *Shah 'Abd al-'Aziz: Puritanism, Sectarian Polemic and Jihad*. Canberra: Ma'rifat Publishing House. pp. 531–32. Henceforth, Rizvi, *Shah 'Abd al-'Aziz*.

35. Ahmad, Qeyamuddin. 1979. *The Wahabi Movement in India*. Islamabad: National Book Foundation. p. 25. Farooqi has stated 1807, see Farooqi, N. R. 2006. 'Saiyid Ahmad of Rae Bareli: An Account of His Life and Thought and An Appraisal of His Impact on the Sufi Centres of Awadh and Eastern India', in Saiyid Zaheer Husain Jafri and Helmut Reifeld (eds). *The Islamic Path: Sufism, Politics and Society in India*. Delhi: Rainbow Publishers Limited. p. 295. Henceforth, Farooqi, 'Saiyid Ahmad of Rae Bareli'.

36. Ikram, *Mauj-e-Kausar*, p. 15. One source narrates that Sayyid Ahmad took *bai'at* at Shah Abdul Aziz's hand during his first visit, stayed for six days, and then left. He returned after six months and stayed for six months with Shah Abdul Aziz. Thanawi, *Arwah*, p. 126. Yet another source asserts that he took *bai'at* in all four popular mystic orders of *Qadiriyah*, *Chishtiyah*, *Suhrawardiyah* and *Naqashbandiyah*, see Khan, Muin-ud-Din Ahmad. 1967. 'Tariqah-i-Muhammadiyah Movement: An Analytical Study'. *Islamic Studies*, vol. 6, pp. 375–88. Henceforth, Khan, 'Tariqah-i-Muhammadiya'.

37. Farooqi, 'Saiyid Ahmad of Rae Bareli', p. 295.

38. Khan, 'Tariqah-i-Muhammadiya', pp. 375–88.

39. Usmani, Qamar Ahmad. 1983. *Baraili Sey Balakot: Tazkira Mujahid-e-Kabeer Hazrat Sayyid Ahmad Shahid Barailvi.* Lahore: Idara Islamiyat. p. 27. Henceforth, Usmani, *Bareli Sey Balakot.*
40. Khan, *Waqai Sayyid Ahmad,* p. 86.
41. Mihr, *Sayyid Ahmad,* p. 113. One source said that he returned to Delhi in 1816. Ikram, *Mauj-e-Kausar,* p. 16. However, it does not seem accurate as the *Waqai,* though not mentioning the date of his return, stated that he returned after the Nawab's alliance with the English.
42. Abbot, Freeland. 1968. *Islam and Pakistan.* New York: Cornell University Press. p. 88. Henceforth, Abbott, *Islam and Pakistan.*
43. Khan, 'Tariqah-i-Muhammadiyah', pp. 375–88.
44. Khan, *Waqai Sayyid Ahmad,* p. 13.
45. Jaffar, Ghulam Muhammad. 1995. 'Social Background of the Tariqah-i-Muhammadiyah Movement'. *Journal of the Pakistan Historical Society.* Karachi, vol. 43, no. 4, pp. 363–80. Henceforth, Jaffar, 'Social Background of Tariqah-i-Muhammadiya Movement'.
46. Husain, 'Sayyid Ahmad Shaheed I', p. 562.
47. Hedayatullah, *Sayyid Ahmad,* p. 92. Almost one century later the *Tabligh* Movement, initiated by Maulana Muhammad Ilyas (1885-1944) followed the same path of approaching the people at their door steps. For an earlier academic discussion on Tabligh Movement see Haq, Muhammad Anwarul. 1972. *The Faith Movement of Maulana Muhammad Ilyas.* London: Allen and Unwin.
48. Ahmad, Aziz. 1970. *Studies in Islamic Culture in the Indian Environment.* Karachi: Oxford University Press. p. 211. Henceforth, Ahmad, *Islamic Culture.*
49. Dehlavi, Mirza Hairat. 1976. *Hayat-e-Tayyaba: Sawanih-e-Umri Shah Ismail Shahid.* Lahore: Islamic Academy. p. 64. Henceforth, Dehlavi, *Hayat-e-Tayyaba.*
50. Khan, *Waqai Sayyid Ahmad,* pp. 157–61.
51. Mir Muhammad Ali of Madras questioned the name in 1829 AD. He asserted that Sayyid Ahmad had no right to name his own *Tariqah* as the way of the Prophet. The name might have given rise to the misinterpretation of Sayyid Ahmad as a Prophet by various British authors, including Hunter.
52. Khan, *Tariqah-e-Muhammadiyah,* pp. 375–88.
53. Khan, *Waqai Sayyid Ahmad,* pp. 340–48.
54. Mihr, *Sayyid Ahmad,* p. 131.
55. Khan, *Waqai Sayyid Ahmad,* pp. 351–61.
56. Khan, *Tariqah-e-Muhammadiyah,* pp. 375–88.
57. Bari, M. A. 1965. 'A Nineteenth-Century Muslim Reform Movement in India', in George Makdisi (ed.). *Arabic and Islamic Studies in Honor of Hamilton A. R. Gibb.* Leiden, E. J. Brill, pp. 90–91. Henceforth, Bari, 'A Nineteenth-Century Muslim Reform Movement in India'.
58. Abbott, *Islam and Pakistan,* p. 89. Abbot reference here is to the *Fatawa Alamgiri,* compiled during Aurangzeb's (d. 1707) time.
59. Ibid., p. 91.
60. Mihr, *Sayyid Ahmad,* pp. 128–29.
61. Nasiri, *Shahnama,* vol. I, p. 81; Mihr, *Sayyid Ahmad,* p. 133.
62. Husain, 'Sayyid Ahmad Shaheed I', pp. 562–63.
63. Hedayatullah, *Sayyid Ahmad,* pp. 96–97.
64. Ahmad, *Islamic Culture,* p. 211.
65. Hedayatullah, *Sayyid Ahmad,* p. 99.

66. Jalal, Ayesha. 2008. *Partisans of Allah: Jihad in South Asia*. Massachusetts: Harvard University Press. p. 75. Henceforth, Jalal, *Partisans of Allah*.
67. Khan, *Waqai Sayyid Ahmad*, pp. 340–48.
68. Ahmad, *Islamic Culture*, p. 211.
69. There are four sources of knowledge in Islam: Qur'an, *sunnah/hadith, ijma-e-Sahabah* and *qiyas* or *ijtihad*. The latter is done by a scholar according to the needs of time and place. It is, therefore, not obligatory on the Muslims of other times and places to follow the *ijtihad* of a scholar of distant time and place.
70. Dar, *Religious Thought*, p. 56 as quoted in Abbott, *Islam and Pakistan*, p. 90.
71. Sindhi, *Shah Waliullah aur un ki Siyasi Tahrik*, p. 75.
72. Malik, Hafeez. 1963. *Moslem Nationalism in India and Pakistan*. Washington: Public Affairs Press. p. 161.
73. Mihr, *Sayyid Ahmad*, p. 131.
74. Hedayetullah, *Sayyid Ahmad*, p. 106.
75. Pearson, Harlan O. 2008. *Islamic Reform and Revival in Nineteenth-Century India: The Tariqah-i-Muhammadiyah*. Delhi: Yoda Press. p. 39. Henceforth, Pearson, *Tariqah-i-Muhammadiyah*.
76. Khan, *Waqai Sayyid Ahmad*, pp. 390–94.
77. Mihr, *Sayyid Ahmad*, pp. 141–42.
78. Ahmad, *The Wahabi Movement*, pp. 28–29.
79. Jaffar, 'Social Background of the Tariqah-i-Muhammadiyah Movement', pp. 363–80.
80. Sayyid Dildar Ali (1753–1820) was a Shia scholar of India from Nasirabad, near Raibareli, in Uttar Pradesh, India. His most known work is 'Imad-ul-Islâm', in Arabic, a refutation of the anti-Shia arguments used by Fakhr al-Din al-Razi. He also studied at Mashhad (Iran). Upon his return to Lucknow, he became a Marja' in India, his *fatawa* being regarded as final by the Shia populace. His detailed work in jurisprudence is *Muntahal Afkar*.
81. Mihr, *Sayyid Ahmad*, pp. 149–53; Hedayetullah, *Sayyid Ahmad*, p. 109.
82. Yusaf Khan Qandahari, a commander of Hafiz Rahmat Khan, later joined Shuja-ud-Daula and established his own *Risala* (battalion), the *Qandahariyu ki Chawni*. Mian, Sayyid Muhammad. 1977. *Ulama-e-Hind ka Shandar Mazi*, vol. III. Lahore: Maktaba Mahmudiya. p. 120. Henceforth, Mian *Ulama-e-Hind*.
83. Nadvi, *Seerat-e-Sayyid Ahmad*, pp. 217–33
84. Nasiri, *Shahnama*, vol. I, p. 81.
85. Mihr, *Sayyid Ahmad*, pp. 147–48.
86. The debate of whether sufism is in accordance with Islam or not is not our subject here. There are many books written against the Sufi orders and practices. For an anti-Sufi stand, see Kailani, Abdul Rahman. 2003. *Shariat wa Tariqat*. Lahore: Maktaba al-Salam.
87. N. R. Farooqi, 'Saiyid Ahmad of Rae Bareli', p. 296.
88. Khan, *Waqai Sayyid Ahmad*, p. 560. The followers of Sayyid Ahmad always refer to such dreams in all his major steps whether it was Jihad or Haj. According to the teachings of the Holy Qur'an, dream does not have any validity in matters of *sharia*, though Sufis give it importance. Even Shah Waliullah's writings are full of references to his dreams.
89. Abdullah Sultanpuri was an important person in the time of Humayun, Sher Shah and Akbar. He had issued a *fatwa* declaring Haj non-obligatory upon Indian Muslims due to the hazards of the sea journey. Hedayetullah, *Sayyid Ahmad*, p. 112.
90. Nadvi, *Seerat-e-Sayyid Ahmad*, p. 258.
91. Khan, *Waqai Sayyid*, pp. 560–61.

92. Ibid., pp. 561–62.
93. Nadvi, *Seerat-e-Sayyid Ahmad*, p. 264.
94. Ahmad, *The Wahabi Movement*, p. 30.
95. Nadvi, *Seerat-e-Sayyid Ahmad*, pp. 274–75.
96. Ibid., pp. 268–69.
97. Khan, *Waqai Sayyid*, pp. 606–7. This encounter with Coel, an English businessman, has been narrated by W. Connor in one of his letters to Sir Sayyid Ahmad Khan on 8 July 1872. Connor has written that Sayyid Ahmad Barailvi 'preaching to the Islam is to join their doctrine for the conversion of Sikhs. They did not preach any jihad at all, nor was such thing as jihad known in those days.' Husain, Yusuf. Ed. 1967. *Selected Documents from the Aligarh Archives*. Aligarh: Muslim University Aligarh. p. 157. There are points in Connor's letter which create doubt in the mind of readers. He said that about 50 years back Sayyid Ahmad was going to Lucknow via Farrukhabad. Yet Sayyid Ahmad was going for Haj in 1822, 50 years had passed by 1872. Furthermore, during Sayyid Ahmad Barailvi's Haj journey, he did not preach jihad. He was going to perform Haj and during the whole journey his emphasis remained on reformism and issues related to Haj and their travel.
98. Nadvi, *Seerat-e-Sayyid Ahmad*, p. 278.
99. Ibid., pp. 275–76.
100. Khan, *Waqai Sayyid*, pp. 625–28.
101. Nadvi, *Seerat-e-Sayyid Ahmad*, pp. 283–88.
102. Ibid., p. 294.
103. Khan, *Waqai Sayyid*, pp. 700–722.
104. Ibid., p. 750. The secondary sources have difference of opinion about the taking *bai'at* by the Sadiqpur family, of which Sheikh Muhammad Hussain was a member. This important event, however, took place in Sayyid Ahmad's journey to Haj as Wilayat Ali took *bai'at* in Lucknow and wrote to his family about the proposed visit of Sayyid Ahmad. The *Waqai* has recorded that Maulvi Fateh Ali and Maulvi Illahi Bakhsh were appointed *khulafa*, apart from Shah Muhammad Hussain.
105. Ahamd, *Wahabi Movement*, p. 31.
106. Khan, *Waqai Sayyid*, pp. 814–15, 826–33.
107. Hedayetullah, *Sayyid Ahmad*, p. 114.
108. Ikram, *Mauj-e-Kausar*, pp. 22–23.
109. Nadvi, *Tazkira*, p. 58.
110. Nadvi, *Seerat-e-Sayyid Ahmad*, pp. 333–34.
111. Hedayetullah, *Sayyid Ahmad*, p. 115. The Faraidhi and Wahabi Movement in Eastern and Western Bengal respectively were begun by Shariatullah, Dudu Mian and Titu Mir. Very limited information is available about Shariatullah's early life; that he was born at Faridpur in 1780, left for Haj at the age of eighteen, lived in the Hijaz for twenty years, and started his reform movement upon return to Bengal. 'The first and foremost of their leaders was Shariat-ullah (1781–1840), a man of humble origins in Fardipur district, who founded the sect around 1804. At the age of 18 he went on a pilgrimage to Mecca where his teacher and spiritual guide was Tahir Sombal, chief of Shafi sect.' Chattopadhyay, Dilip Kumar. 1977. 'The Ferazee and Wahabi Movements of Bengal'. *Social Scientist*, vol. 6, no. 2, pp. 42–51. It seems that he left for Makkah in 1799/1800 and returned in 1820. One can assume that the leaders of *Faraidhi* movement may have come in contact with Sayyid Ahmad, but the earlier biographers are silent over the issue.

112. The most important among Sayyid Ahmad's followers in the initial period was Mir Nisar Ali popularly known as Titu Mir. He had become Sayyid Ahmad's disciple when Sayyid Ahmad was going for Haj. Hussain, Sadiq. 2010. *Sayyid Ahmad Shahid aur un ki Tahrik-e-Mujahidin.* Lahore: Al-Meezan. pp. 225–27. Bengal rarely provided leadership to the Mujahidin but many Bengalis joined them on the Frontier and rendered services.

113. The relationship of *piri-muridi* was and is an established phenomenon of the Sufi orders and Sayyid Ahmad himself was the *murid* of Shah Abdul Aziz. The English administrators have usually suggested that Sayyid Ahmad learnt organizational structure from the Wahabis during the Haj but they forget that this sort of organization was neither new nor uncommon in the Indian subcontinent.

114. Ahmad, *Wahabi Movement*, p. 38.

115. The only book attributed to Sayyid Ahmad, compiled by Shah Ismail and Maulana Abdul Hai at his orders.

116. The biographers of Sayyid Ahmad had not given any details of these people except narrating that they were scholars of the time.

117. Nadvi, *Seerat-e-Sayyid Ahmad*, pp. 365–68. The *bai'at* for jihad was taken from his companions at Hudaibiyah when Sayyid Ahmad was proceeding to Makkah for Haj. Nadvi, *Seerat-e-Sayyid Ahmad* as quoted in *Makhzan-e-Ahmadi*, p. 362.

118. Punjabi nationalists have projected Ranjit Singh as a pioneer of Punjabi nationalism and have claimed that Sayyid Ahmad's Jihad Movement was engineered by the English. The only source to support their claim is Maulvi Muhammad Jaffar Thanesari's *Sawanih Ahmadi.* Our findings do not agree, on the basis of official records, sources on the Mujahidin Movement, and different English writers. Ranjit Singh remained an English collaborator from his first treaty with the English and especially after the treaty of Amritsar in 1809. During this period, the territories to the west of the Indus were taken under the terms of the treaty; the Indus was opened for English navigation, and English movement towards Afghanistan which culminated in the First Anglo-Afghan War, 1839–1842. Thanesari's version cannot be accepted as the copies of Sayyid Ahmad's letters, we consulted did not corroborate in some places those published in Thasnesari's work. Thanesari was living in an environment where he wished to divert the attention of the British administrators from the workers of the movement.

119. Ahmad, *Wahabi Movement*, p. 38.

120. Nadvi, *Tazkira*, p. 66.

121. Khan, Waheed-du-Din. 2005. *Din wa Shariat: Din-e-Islam ka aik Fikri Mutali'a.* Lahore: Dar-ul-Tazkeer, 2005. p. 251. Henceforth, Khan, *Din wa Shariat.*

122. Khan, Muhammad Farooq. 2010. *War and Jihad in Islam: Some Important Discourses.* English tr. Muhammad Tahir. Mardan: Awareness for Moderation. p. 2.

123. Jalal, *Partisans of Allah*, p. 7.

124. It is to be noted that the *fiqh* that was codified when the Muslims were politically strong, rarely deals with problems associated with Muslims living in minority.

125. Peter, Rudolf. 1979. *Islam and Colonialism: The Doctrine of Jihad in Modern History.* The Hague: Mountain Publishers. pp. 12–13.

126. Cook, David. 2005. *Understanding Jihad.* Berkeley: University of California Press. pp. 78–79. One may refer to Usman Dan Fodio's Jihad (Sokoto Caliphate) in West Africa, Muhammad bin Abdul Wahab in Arabia, a bit later Imam Shamil's movement against Czarist Russia in Central Asia.

127. Rizvi, *Shah 'Abd al-'Aziz*, pp. 227–28.

128. Rizvi, S. A. A. 1971. 'The Breakdown of the Traditional Society', in P. M. Holt (ed.). *The Cambridge History of Islam*, vol. II. Cambridge: Cambridge University Press. p. 73.

129. Madani, *Naqsh-e-Hayat*, p. 419. Madani's statement about Sayyid Ahmad's material help is not supported by any reliable source. It seems he relied on Thanesari's *Tawarikh-e-Ajeeba*, which itself is not authentic about the *jihad* as it was written in a particular political context.

130. We may put them in the category of 'conspiracy theorists'.

131. The Faraidhi Movement was ignored for a considerable time and the British sent their forces only when it challenged their authority.

132. Nadvi, *Seerat-e-Sayyid Ahmad*, vol. I, pp. 405–6.

133. Daulat Rao Sindhia (1779–1827) was the ruler of Gwalior state in central India from 1794 until his death in 1827.

134. Nadvi, *Seerat-e-Sayyid Ahmad*, vol. I, p. 418.

135. Mihr, *Sayyid Ahmad*, p. 234, note 1.

136. Obaidullah Sindhi actually claimed that his stay in Kabul during and after the First World War was more fruitful as he did not try to assert authority. No doubt, Sindhi did not face the situation the Mujahidin faced, but still his claim is doubtful. The Mujahidin Movement had far reaching effect upon the Pukhtuns and for many decades to come the British worried about their struggle but we do not see such situation in the case of Sindhi.

137. Rizvi, *Shah 'Abd al-'Aziz*, p. 531.

138. Shah Waliullah was appointed at age 17 as principal of Madrassah Rahimmiyah after his father's death. Shah Abdul Aziz was nominated successor of Shah Waliullah after his death at the age of 18.

3

Call for Jihad, Migration to the Frontier, and Declaration of *Imarat*

After his return from the Hijaz, Sayyid Ahmad's whole attention was concentrated upon preparation for jihad. From this point jihad would be the main objective of his life. Although a thorough account of his activities of that time is not available, it seems that he had sent his deputies to different towns for propagating jihad. This is evident from the composition of his followers who hailed from diverse castes and belonged to different areas. According to Ghulam Rasul Mihr, the arrangements for provision of funds, after his departure on the fateful journey, were also made during this time.[1] Sayyid Ahmad was a Sufi, but his call for jihad was against normative Sufi practice, as he preferred jihad over Sufic rituals. He was of the opinion that jihad was the only way out from all the evils prevalent among Indian Muslims. His call for jihad was doubted by some religious scholars, on several grounds, but he did not involve himself in scholastic discussion, and responded pragmatically. Sayyid Ahmad himself visited different places, including Thanesar, and preached the importance of jihad.[2] He sent letters and envoys, including Shah Ismail and Abdul Hai, to preach jihad.[3] Arrangements were made for the most important and crucial phase of his life, migration to North-West Frontier region of the subcontinent.[4] His disciples were trained on both spiritual and physical lines. *Daira* Shah Ilmullah became a centre of all activities. There, military training was imparted along with *dhikr*, and other spiritual knowledge. And the spirit of martyrdom was inculcated in disciples.[5] In response to his call, many people gathered in Raibaraili from other parts of India. In addition to their personal presence, many disciples sent material support in the shape of cloths, arms, money, horses, and utensils.[6] Before starting his journey, Sayyid Ahmad counted the amount in hand, ₹10,000. He gave ₹5,000 to his wives and kept the remaining ₹5,000 for travelling expenses. The amount was put in small bags that were entrusted to five hundred to six hundred different Mujahidin.[7]

Selection and Migration to the Frontier

The North-West Frontier had always played an important role in shaping the history of South Asia and Central Asia. Invaders considered the occupation of this area a key to conquests on either side, especially towards India. Since Sayyid Ahmad's migration, the area has attracted many others,[8] particularly in the name of Islam.[9] The obvious factors that attracted Sayyid Ahmad to the region have been discussed later.

Being a keen observer of the Indian political situation, Sayyid Ahmad was aware of the fate of those princes and adventurers who started militant activities within India. Within no time, the English crippled such activities by constant Imperial politics. Siraj-ud-Daulah of Bengal was defeated by the English in 1757. Tipu Sultan of Mysore suffered defeat in 1799. The Rohilas were subjugated by the English after their defeat and Amir Khan, the Nawab of Tonk, was left with no option but to sign a peace treaty with the English.[10]

Some sources, while writing about the selection of the area, have argued that Sikh rule in the Punjab was more oppressive because they banned the observance of Islamic practices. Sayyid Ahmad had heard stories of Sikh atrocities perpetuated against the Muslims of Punjab while he was on a missionary tour to Rampur, when he met Muslims from Punjab.[11] The Frontier and Punjab were predominantly Muslim areas and their topographical qualities, especially in the Pukhtun areas, could be utilized for the establishment of an independent state.[12] Moreover, Ranjit Singh's rule was not firmly established, particularly in the areas lying to the west of Indus, where the Sikhs could only collect revenue by force.[13]

Like other tribal entities, the Pukhtuns were long known for their egalitarian and brave nature. Moreover, there was a chain of independent Muslim states to the west of India, whose assistance he expected,[14] especially from Central Asia. Finally, being on the periphery and offering safe havean in the mountainous ranges of the region made it very suitable terrain for guerrilla warfare.[15]

Sayyid Ahmad was well aware of the physical strength of the Pukhtuns. They had their colonies in Rohilkhand and had supplied fresh energy to the Mughal empire during its decay. They had played important role in defeating the Marathas in the third battle of Panipat in 1761. The Afghans leading the military of Oudh lived in the Lucknow military cantonment. Many were affiliated to Sayyid Ahmad's family through *piri-muridi* tradition. One of them, Faqir Muhammad Khan, a military officer in Oudh state, was a supporter of Sayyid Ahmad.[16] The Pukhtuns in Raibaralai lived in a separate *muhalla* of their own named Shah Jahan Abad. Though there is no clear evidence that they encouraged him to migrate to the area of their forefathers,[17] many of them accompanied him in his migration.

Sayyid Ahmad did mention in one of his speeches that the Pukhtuns of the North-West Frontier invited him to migrate to their land and wage jihad against the infidels. He said hundreds of thousands would assist him in his struggle against the Sikhs. The inhabitants of the area were unhappy with the oppressive policies of Ranjit Singh. The Sikhs demolished mosques, burnt crops, and looted properties of the people. They also captured Muslim women and children and sold them in Punjab.[18]

It was not prudent or possible for Sayyid Ahmad, to start a militant movement from mainland India in areas governed directly by the English or by princes who were under their suzerainty. The centre of India was a place in occupation, where no help could reach from outside. The English could easily crush the movement in its infancy by enlisting the support of other classes and segments of society.[19] Ranjit Singh was ally of the English and they would not allow activities against him from the territories they governed.[20] A. S. Bazmee Ansari has asserted that Sayyid Ahmad had the advantage of being a descendant of the Prophet Muhammad (Peace Be Upon Him), and expected a warm welcome and support from the Pukhtuns.[21] This is not a weighty argument, because despite their respect for Sayyids, Pukhtuns usually did not accept any outside authority not a stakeholder in Pukhtuns' social structure, unless they urgently need such help.

Sayyid Ahmad had embraced the ideals set by Shah Abdul Aziz. He considered India under British or Sikh domination as a *dar-ul-harb*, where *hijrat* (migration) to *dar-ul-Islam* was obligatory, before the waging of a holy war against the usurpers.[22]

Another factor, inferred from the sources, was that there were hereditary dynasties in India, including those under English protection, and that Sayyid Ahmad knew that these princes would resist his movement when their interests were at stake. The Frontier was different as it was passing through a transitional period. For the last few decades the struggle for Peshawar among various claimants of the Sadduzais, Barakzais and then Sikhs provided an opportunity to exploit the situation for personal, organizational, or religious agendas. The failure of Amir Khan of Tonk to stay independent and the resultant peace treaty (1817) with the English might also have provided food for thought to Sayyid Ahmad to look for new venues. It also is likely that Sayyid Ahmad knew about Sayyid Akbar Shah of Sithana, who had gathered thousands of Pukhtuns, fought against the Sikhs, and was defeated at Pir Sabaq (Nowshera) in 1823.[23]

After arranging the campaign, Sayyid Ahmad left his home-town and started his journey on 17 January 1826.[24] The *Jama'at-e-Khas* or *qalb* was under Muhammad Yusaf Phulti. Sayyid Ahmad himself was part of this *jama'at*. The *Muqadimat-ul-jaish* followed Shah Ismail and led the rest of the Mujahidin during the journey. The *Maisra* was organized by Sayyid Muhammad Yaqub, nephew of Sayyid Ahmad, but since he was left in Tonk, the Sheikh of Badhana was appointed to lead this group. The *Maimana* was under Amjad Khan, a noble of Gatna. *Sa'aqat-ul-jaish*, under Allah Bakhsh Moranvi, was responsible for the supplies. Each *jama'at* was further divided into small groups named *baheelay*.[25] The route adopted for migration to the North-West Frontier was hard and troublesome, covering about two thousand miles. The selection of a long route was due to two factors. First, Sayyid Ahmad could not go to the North-West Frontier through the Punjab because his goal was jihad against the Sikhs of the Punjab. Second, he would be able to spread his message in the territories he would pass through.[26]

The first *jama'at* left Raibaraili in the third week of January 1826. The second followed after a few days interval. The first stop was at Dalmaw. The second was in Fatehpur, where Sheikh Ghulam, Sayyid Ahmad's disciple, came to visit them and made all the necessary arrangements. From Fatehpur they travelled to Bhuwa, Challa Tara Ghat, and finally Jaloon, where the last *jama'at* of Sayyid Abdul Rahman joined them and then the whole body of Mujahidin entered Gwalior, city of Daulat Rao Sindhhia.[27] Sayyid Ahmad stayed in Gwalior for several days. He visited the palace of Daulat Rao Sindhhia to see him because he was sick. Hindu Rao, the brother-in-law of Daulat Rao, ran state affairs during his illness.[28] Daulat Rao and Hindu Rao presented gifts and a handsome amount to the Mujahidin, though none of the sources mention the amount.[29]

Sayyid Ahmad left Gwalior for Tonk after a stay of about two weeks. They halted at Karaoli for a night, followed by Khushal Garh, Dantobi, Tharhi Jhulai (Jaipur) and reached Tonk in six days.[30] Sayyid Ahmad's stay in Tonk was quite long. Nawab Amir Khan, his son Wazir-ud-Daulah, family members and many others, including Abdul Hamid Khan, took the Sayyid's *bai'at*.[31] Sayyid Ahmad sent his nephew Sayyid Muhammad Yaqub and others to bring his family to Tonk.[32] They next stayed at Ajmir, where many from the general public and nobility, including Maulvi Siraj-ud-Din, took *bai'at* at Sayyid Ahmad's hands. They then left for Pali, a business centre in Rajputana.[33] The whole journey from Marwar and Sindh was troubled due to a scarcity of water, the fear of robbers,[34] and misunderstanding by the inhabitants of the area that considered every outsider an agent of the English[35] or Ranjit Singh. Sayyid Ahmad then arrived at Hyderabad, Sindh, then ruled by the Talpurs. Mir Muhammad ruled in collaboration with his uncles Mir Karam Ali and Mir Murad Ali. They were a Baloch family who had taken the government from Kalhora in 1786.[36] Sayyid Ahmad was warmly received by Pir Sibghatullah[37] and the Mirs (rulers) of Sindh, who invited him to the fort for Friday congregation. The Mirs were surprised at the Sayyid's jihad plan. They asked him to keep his family at Hyderabad and stay for some time. He politely refused on the ground that winter would fall soon, which might create difficulties in the journey to the Peshawar Valley. In Hyderabad, many people took *bai'at* at the Sayyid's hand, including some leading members of the Mirs' family.[38]

Sayyid Ahmad sent his messengers in various directions to invite people to join his Jihad Movement.[39] He also invited Bahawal Khan, the ruler of Bahawalpur.[40] Sayyid Ahmad's call for jihad was so popular that Masson, the English agent travelling the area in those days, mentioned that a noble, Rahmat Khan, asked him to join Sayyid Ahmad.[41] Sayyid Ahmad's preaching and invitations from Hyderabad had little productive results and they departed. The Mujahidin were escorted by a brother of Pir Sibghatullah from Ranipur to his native town, Pir Kot,[42] where he himself arrived after three days. The Mujahidin stayed for two weeks in Pir Kot and again many people took *bai'at* at the Sayyid's hand. Pir Sibghatullah intended to join the Mujahidin, but Sayyid Ahmad asked him to stay behind and start jihad against the enemy upon receiving his letter.

The group left Pir Kot and arrived at Shikarpur,[43] after a night stay at Habib Kot. When they arrived at Shikarpur, the governor and inhabitants of the city considered Sayyid Ahmad as an enemy and closed the doors of the city to him. Sayyd Ahmad sent Sayyid Hameed-ud-Din and Sayyid Aulad Hassan Qanuji[44] as his envoy. The doors were opened and Sayyid Ahmad purchased commodities in the city. Many of the inhabitants, including the governor and other nobles, took *bai'at* of repentance at Sayyid Ahmad's hand.[45] They left Shikarpur and stayed at Jagan for four days with Sayyid Anwar Shah.[46] They then entered the territory of Mihrab Khan II, grandson of Naseer Khan Baloch, the ruler of Kalat state. The Mujahidin stayed at Khan Garh,[47] arranged provisions, and left for Shahpur. There Sayyid Ahmad was received warmly by Sayyid Mohsin Shah, the spiritual guide of the Balochs. At Chathar, the next stop, Mulla Muhammad, agent of Mihrab Khan, visited Sayyid Ahmad, took *bai'at*, and accompanied him to the boundary of his domain. Sayyid Ahmad gave Mulla Muhammad a message for Mihrab Khan II in which he asked him to join the jihad and told Mulla Muhammad that he would wait for his ruler's reply.[48]

After short halts of a night or so at several places, Sayyid Ahmad arrived at Bhag, an important town with a considerable population. The same routine followed as *bai'at* was taken from the public and nobles alike. The *wali* invited Sayyid Ahmad and a group of selected companions to a feast. After stops at several more places the Mujahidin arrived at Dhadar, the last town before entering the Bolan Pass. There Sayyid Ahmad stayed for four days. They then entered Quetta[49] after passing Bolan Pass. The governor of the city took *bai'at* and wished to join Sayyid Ahmad but was asked to stay behind.[50] Sayyid Ahmad stayed for some time in Quetta, awaiting arrival of the envoys he had sent to Akhun Fateh Muhammad,[51] the *wazir* of Mihrab Khan II, and Purdil Khan, ruler of Qandahar. Both the envoys returned satisfied by the rulers. From Qandahar came permission to enter the domain and from Mihrab Khan II a message that the matter would be taken properly when the issues with Qandahar were resolved.[52] Upon their arrival in Qandahar, the Mujahidin were welcomed by the ruler, nobles, and the public. Many people took *bai'at* for jihad at Sayyid Ahmad's hand. A good number of them were ready to join the Mujahidin but upon Purdil Khan's insistence, they were not allowed to join them at this stage.[53]

Sayyid Ahmad left Qandahar on the sixth day and camped at Qila Azam Khan. About four hundred people came there to join the Mujahidin. Sayyid Ahmad sent Akhun Zahoorullah to seek Purdil Khan's permission. The latter allowed him to take these people but insisted that the Sayyid's party should leave his domain immediately. Sayyid Ahmad chose two hundred and seventy people from among them and appointed, first, Sayyid Din Muhammad Qandahari and, later, Mulla Lal Muhammad Qandahari as their commander. This was called the Qandahari *jama'at* of the Mujahidin.[54] On the journey to Kabul, the Ghalzai chief sent a messenger and invited Sayyid Ahmad to his area, but he declined on the plea that it would create problems for the forthcoming jihad.[55] Sayyid Ahmad sought transit permission by sending a letter to Mir Muhammad, the ruler of Ghazna, explaining that he intended to go to the Yusafzais of Peshawar Valley and start jihad against the Sikhs. Mir Muhammad permitted their passage and said that every possible help would be extended to the Mujahidin. The next day they arrived at Ghazna and encamped near Mahmud of Ghazna's tomb. Notables, including Mir Muhammad's young son, religious men, and others visited Sayyid Ahmad. The Naib Hakim of Mir Muhammad also visited and arranged provisions for the Mujahidin. Mir Muhammad himself called on the Sayyid in the evening, took *bai'at*, and was followed by the elite and common people. Sayyid Ahmad was known to some nobles of the city, who had already visited Raibaraili and taken *bai'at* at his hand.[56] After a stay for two days in Ghazna, Sayyid Ahmad proceeded to Kabul after receiving permission from Sultan Muhammad Khan, the ruler of Kabul. He was received warmly by Sultan Muhammad Khan in the company of his brothers and nobility, and was led to Fateh Khan's garden which had been chosen for the Mujahidin's stay. Sayyid Ahmad stayed in Kabul for about one and half a months. The time was spent trying to end the differences between the Barakzai brothers and then use their alliance for the jihad cause, but to no avail. Sayyid Ahmad then left Kabul for Peshawar, where he arrived after five days, via Jalalabad, Dakka and Khyber Pass.[57]

The route adopted by Sayyid Ahmad needs proper analysis to clear many misunderstandings found in academic writings. Sayyid Ahmad tried to avoid territory directly ruled by the English. The princely states where Sayyid Ahmad stayed, Gwalior and Tonk, had been recently brought under subsidiary alliance by the English and he might have had a plan to enlist their support, a point supported by the letters of Sayyid Ahmad or his lieutenants to the rulers and nobles of both states. Besides, the rulers of both Gwalior and Tonk were previous allies. Sayyid Ahmad had personally observed their resistance to the English. Moreover, they had not forgotten the bitter taste of their defeat at English hands. The journey via Sindh and Kalat state is also interesting. The Talpurs were apprehensive of the designs of the English and Sikhs. The navigation scheme of the Indus pursued by the English after the treaty of Amritsar (1809) had given an opportunity to Ranjit Singh to expand to the west as he was restricted to the east.[58] Sayyid Ahmad's invitation to Mihrab Khan, the ruler of Kalat, was another example of Sayyid Ahmad's planning. In nutshell, he tried to enlist support of all those rulers who looked at Ranjit Singh and the English with equal suspicion. As stated earlier, this negates any viewpoint that Sayyid Ahmad's Jihad Movement was engineered by the English to engage Ranjit Singh in another direction and leave the field open to them. Ranjit Singh had collaborated with the British since his first treaty in 1803. Both parties protected each other's interests. It is on record that upon Holkar's arrival in Punjab, after the Marathas' defeat by the English, Ranjit Singh asked him to leave his country. He sided with the winning power against the defeated.[59]

Sayyid Ahmad Route of Raibaraili to Peshawar–Hund

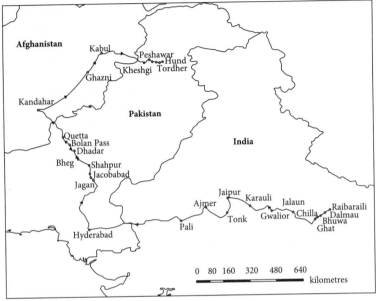

Source: Prepared by Dr Atta ur Rahman and Dr Altaf Qadir.

Sayyid Ahmad's Arrival at Peshawar and Relations with Local Durranis and Other Pukhtuns

Sayyid Ahmad arrived at Peshawar in the third week of November 1826.[60] Yar Muhammad Khan, one of the Barakzai Sardars, ruled Peshawar on behalf of the Sikh *darbar.* Yar Muhammad had twice declared his allegiance to Ranjit Singh[61] and was in no way ready to risk his governorship. He neither extended support to Sayyid Ahmad nor met him upon his arrival. Sayyid Ahmad left the city within a few days.[62] He then moved north towards Hashtnagar,[63] arrived at Charsadda in a night, and stayed outside the town. The Mujahidin had meagre resources left and food was bought on credit from a shopkeeper.[64] The next day, Said Muhammad Khan, the Barakzai governor of the area visited Sayyid Ahmad and took *bai'at,* followed by many others.[65] A general enthusiasm prevailed at Sayyid Ahmad's arrival. Many visited him and offered their allegiance for the upcoming jihad.[66] A main reason for the rising enthusiasm might have been the unrest that existed due to a Sikh garrison under Budh Singh stationed in Attock to maintain law and order, and ensuring flow of tribute from the tribes of the Peshawar Valley.[67] Said Muhammad Khan and others invited the Mujahidin to meals. The Mujahidin not only benefited from the hospitality of local people but had an opportunity to interact with them. They stayed in Charsadda for a couple of weeks. They rallied people for jihad, collected information and consulted about the fast approaching fight against the Sikhs.[68] Despite the local ruler Said Muhammad Khan's taking *bai'at*, he did not help the Mujahidin. The Barakzais were first interested in their rule over the area and were indifferent to the tribes inhabiting the vale. They had remained oblivious to previous anti-Sikh activities. During the battle of Pir Sabaq in 1823, Muhammad Azeem Khan did not help the tribesmen against the Sikhs and waited for the outcome of the battle on the other bank of the Kabul River. Muhammad Azeem Khan had no excuse for keeping aloof from that war. From the southern bank of the river, he could have neutralized the Sikh artillery which destroyed the Pukhtun *lakhkar*.[69] The Barakzai Sardars looked to their own interests. Supporting a resistance movement like that of Sayyid Ahmad did not offer any material gain. Because Sayyid Ahmad was new to the area and had not exhibited strength so far, the Sardars awaited the future course of events.

With Sayyid Ahmad's expectations not fulfilled, he wanted to move in a favourable direction to utilize his support. An opportunity was soon provided by the arrival of units of the Sikh army under Budh Singh at Khairabad. The arrival of the Sikh army was taken as a golden opportunity by Sayyid Ahmad's allies and by his opponents. Amir Khan Khattak of Akora Khattak visited Sayyid Ahmad and invited him to launch his struggle against the Sikhs from his area. Khawas Khan welcomed the Sikh army[70] due to his rivalry with his uncle Amir Khan.[71] After consultations with the locals and his associates, Sayyid Ahmad decided to attack the Sikh army and stop them from crossing the river Kabul. Any crossing could cause panic among the tribesmen and they might flee to the safe places instead of facing the enemy.[72]

The Battle of Akora Khattak

Sayyid Ahmad moved from Charsadda, stayed at Khweshgi for a night, and arrived at Nowshera the next day. The Sikh army was encamped in Akora Khattak,[73] on the southern bank of the river. The Mujahidin were on the other side,[74] at village Misri Banda. Sayyid Ahmad sent a letter to the Lahore *darbar* on 17 December 1826 (18 *Jumada Al-Awwal* 1242), warning:

> Voluntarily embrace Islam which will make you a brother to the rest of Muslim community. Or Surrender and pay *jizya* (poll tax) in order to qualify for our protection. Should none of the above alternative be acceptable to you, get ready to fight, noting the fact that the entire Yaghistan and Hindustan are with us and that we love martyrdom more than you love wine.[75]

Sayyid Ahmad did not wait for the reply, much against the teaching of *sharia*. He planned a night attack upon the Sikh for several reasons. First, the strength of the Sikh army was around seven thousand and was fully equipped, while the Mujahidin were only fifteen hundred, with local tribesmen were not yet tested. They were also ill equipped. Second, Sayyid Ahmad and his associates wanted to make a positive impression in their first encounter because the locals were apprehensive of the outcome of war. A Mujahidin victory would be a boost to the movement. Finally, a night attack was chosen because the Mujahidin wanted to strike at the strength of the enemy with minimum harm to their side.[76]

Physically strong and experienced men were selected from the Mujahidin for the night attack with the consent of the respective *amir* of the *jama'at*.[77] A selected body of nine hundred was sent under the command of Allah Bakhsh Moranvi.[78] The Mujahidin crossed the river, guided by a Pukhtun, and attacked the Sikh force. The attack was not unsuccessful, though the plan of the night attack was not followed. Instead of killing the enemy, the Mujahidin started looting their camp, which was not the objective.[79] Still, a considerable number of the enemy soldiers were killed; five hundred according to one source,[80] seven hundred according to another.[81] The number of Mujahidin killed in the attack were eighty-two, included thirty-six Hindustanis and forty-six Qandaharis.[82] The number of the locals killed in the attack was not known. The selective casualty figure was written in the letters of Sayyid Ahmad to India after the event for the information and condolence of the aggrieved families. The Mujahidin were supplied with men and money from India and recording minute details was considered necessary. Uneducated locals left no record and even literate locals were perhaps too busy fighting to keep details.

Although taking the locals into confidence was necessary for the success of the movement, it may be inferred from the course of events that the locals were not trusted. It has been explicitly written in the *Waqai* that only one person was taken as a guide and the rest were kept behind the

Hindustanis and Qandaharis. As well, the Mujahidin were not organized and were not trained properly in the type of warfare pursued.

In the end, the night attack was more successful than expected. Budh Singh was terrified. He wanted to cross Indus and stay at Attock Fort, but the *qiladar* of the Attock Fort asked him to stay on the western bank, otherwise the whole *sama* would be lost to the enemy and Attock Fort itself would be threatened. Pukhtun tribesmen flocked to Sayyid Ahmad and took *bai'at* for jihad, including Khadi Khan[83] of Hund,[84] the most powerful chief of the Mandanr.[85] Khadi Khan was followed by Ashraf Khan[86] of Zaida, who remained the Sayyid's most trusted associate in the *sama* until his death.

Sayyid Ahmad accepted the invitation of Khadi Khan to establish his centre at Hund as he had yet to select a place for it. Sayyid Ahmad left Misri Banda for Hund. About five thousand people took *bai'at* on his arrival at Bazar,[87] a village near Hund, which sat on the bank of the Indus.[88]

Establishment of Centre at Bazar (Hund) and Declaration of *Imarat*

Though Hund was not a suitable place for a centre of the Mujahidin due to its proximity with the Sikh territory, still Khadi Khan had invited Sayyid Ahmad and such an invitation had not been received from any other chief in the Peshawar Valley. Also, a strong fort[89] was available there that could be utilized for the jihad. Sayyid Ahmad wanted to settle in one place and start organizing the movement on proper lines.[90] Sayyid Ahmad might have thought of needing more recognition from Pukhtun clans and that Khadi Khan's influence in the region would help recruit local chiefs to enlist their support.

After establishing himself at Hund, Sayyid Ahmad sent letters and envoys to the local chiefs, inviting them to join the jihad and liberate their country from the Sikhs. Many chiefs joined Sayyid Ahmad. Three main factors contributed to Sayyid Ahmad's popularity. He was a Sayyid and the Pukhtuns had great respect and veneration for religious people in general and Sayyids in particular. The Pukhtuns were unhappy with the tyranny of the Sikh rule, wanting to take revenge for their defeat at the hands of the Sikhs at Pir Sabaq in 1823 and stop the ongoing Sikh raids for revenue collection. Finally, and probably most importantly, they wanted to follow a person who was not directly interfering in their tribal affairs. Sayyid Ahmad was a non-Pukhtun. He was believed to maintain strict neutrality in resolving tribal feuds and would not side with any faction in the fractious Pukhtun society.

The next major event which shaped the future course of the Jihad Movement was the attack on Hazro. This was a business centre, lying across the Indus in Sikh jurisdiction. The whole scheme was planned and enacted during Sayyid Ahmad's stay in Bazar, Hund. Advocates tried to convince Sayyid Ahmad to attack because the town was a major business centre, but only had a small Sikh contingent and one cannon.[91] Sayyid Ahmad explained that some of his Mujahidin were killed in the battle of Akora Khattak while others were injured and they also did not know the customs of the locals. Non-local sources record that Sayyid Ahmad hesitated to join the raid on Hazro, but when some of the Qandahari Mujahidin wished to join the local Pukhtuns, he reluctantly allowed them.

Sources agree that Sayyid Ahmad considered the raid on Hazro justified and according to the commandments of *sharia* as the Sikhs and the Mujahidin were at war. In retaliation for attacks by the Sikhs, the Mujahidin were warranted to hurt the Sikhs. Ghulam Rasul Mihr believed that Sayyid Ahmad could neither participate in plunder nor was the attack seen as fruitful for his objective—jihad.[92] Sayyid Ahmad advised the group going to raid Hazro that the Muslim population of the town should not be harmed. His advice was based on the Islamic injunction that the Muslims of that town had not yet been invited for jihad.[93] One source relates that the attack was suggested by locals and sanctioned by Sayyid Ahmad. Volunteers for the attack were selected by Shah Ismail with Sayyid Ahmad's approval.[94] It, however, is interesting to note that Sayyid Ahmad in his letter to Indian Muslims, straightforwardly recorded the attack on Hazro. He also wrote that a large amount of booty was captured from Hazro.[95] This suggests that the distancing of Sayyid Ahmad from the attack is a later phenomenon, written by those who wanted to justify the declaration of *imarat*.

Locals and forty Qandaharis crossed the Indus one night and attacked Hazro. The Qandaharis occupied the *garhi*[96] while the locals started plundering the *mandi*.[97] Contemporary sources, written by Sayyid Ahmad's associates, recorded that local Pukhtuns were busy in plundering until the majority of them fled when the Sikhs retaliated and only the Qandaharis stood firm. This resulted in heavy casualties. Fleeing tribesmen were shot dead by the Sikhs. They panicked and many of them drowned in the river while crossing towards Hund. Sayyid Ahmad, however, sent reinforcements and the rest of the Mujahidin were rescued. Among the Hindustani Mujahidin[98] only two were killed.[99]

The attack on Hazro achieved one objective, goods worth an estimated ₹1,500,000.[100] Details of the looted materials are not available, except that a horse that was presented to Sayyid Ahmad. But he did not accept it and returned it to the Mujahid involved. The night attack on the Sikh force in Akora Khattak and the attack on Hazro gave an impression to the Sikhs that the Mujahidin were unable to face them in an open field.[101] The attack on Hazro was described by another source differently. It said that Hazro was besieged by the Mujahidin with the active assistance of Yar Muhammad Khan. The siege continued for two weeks, until the arrival of Budh Singh who forced them to abandon the siege and re-cross the Indus. The town of Hazro was deserted due to the siege and many people left in search of a more peaceful location.[102] In retaliation, the Sikhs attacked the Mujahidin the next day but with no significant gains for either side. Both parties dispersed after a brief skirmish.[103]

Involving a siege or not, the attack on Hazro was taken as justification for the declaration of *imarat*,[104] for all religious and political purposes. It has been narrated by all sources written by Indians that the locals did not act as an organized body.[105] Pukhtuns were not aware of the objectives of Sayyid Ahmad and his associates, and so were not motivated to fight and sacrifice their lives for a cause. Indian authors recorded that the main objective was plunder. Moreover, the local chiefs feuded among themselves and so, inevitably, there was the need for a central, neutral authority who could coordinate and command all the followers. Thus *bai‘at* was taken at Sayyid Ahmad's hand on 10 January 1827 (12 Jumada Al-Thani 1242) and the next day the *khutba* was read in his name in Friday prayers.[106] Importantly in regards to the declaration of *imarat*, the classical literature dealing with the issue of *imarat/khilafat* is very clear. According to the jurists, the establishment of *imarat* is the foremost priority of those at the helm of affairs. Sayyid Abul al-Hassan Ali Nadvi stated that the burial of the Prophet Muhammad (Peace Be Upon Him) was delayed as the companions were busy in resolving the issue of *khilafat*.[107] Sayyid Ahmad, on the other hand, was less aware of the objectives and importance of the establishment of *imarat* and more concerned with the poor leadership of the locals in the attack on Hazro.[108]

Some details of the attack are available in Sayyid Ahamd's letter to India, sent soon after declaration of the *imarat*. The followers of Sayyid Ahmad had tried to disassociate themselves from the attack. The reason was obvious, since the reported mismanagement was taken a major factor for the declaration of the *imarat* and the whole responsibility for the mismanaged raid was laid upon the locals.

There are contradictions among the writers over the nature and objective of the resulting *bai'at*. One source has described it as a complete pledge or oath of allegiance not only for the organization of jihad but for the imposition of *sharia* as well. *Imam* and *sharia* were to be obeyed in letter and spirit; the customs and traditions that were contrary to *sharia* were to be abandoned at once; and all were to prepare for every kind of sacrifice.[109] Another account stated that the *bai'at* did not intend the establishment of *imarat* for the imposition of *sharia*—full political authority over the locals. Rather it was intended to organize the jihad alone. Sayyid Ahmad was made head of the confederacy, in which each local chief had his share and was free to act in his respective domain. Sayyid Ahmad could preach the commandments of *sharia*, could seek assistance for jihad and resolve any dispute among the confederating units but was not authorized to issue orders.[110]

We are convinced that the *bai'at* was meant to collect full political authority beyond just organizing the jihad. Ghulam Rasul Mihr had first suggested that the *bai'at* was for organizing the jihad only,[111] but contradicted his own argument when referring to the third clause of the *bai'at* of Ashraf Khan, Fateh Khan, and Khadi Khan in February 1829. The third clause of the February oath clearly indicated that they had rendered such an oath earlier and they were renewing their previous oath in front of the *ulama*.[112] Second, the Friday *khutba* was read in the name of Sayyid Ahmad, which itself was a sign of political authority.[113] Third, Shah Ismail's *Mansab-e-Imamat* was written in response to the objections of Indian *ulama* after the *bai'at*. Fourth, the letters of Sayyid Ahmad to different princes and local chiefs including Dost Muhammad Khan, ruler of Bokhara, Faizullah Khan of Hazarkhwani and others, after the *bai'at*, were written in the capacity of *Amir-ul-Mominin*.[114] One such letter addressed to his Indian associates said that Sayyid Ahmad's authority was recognized.[115] Fifth, Sayyid Ahmad preferred Panjtar to Khar, where he stayed for quite a long time, due to the oath rendered by its chief, as the chiefs of Swat did not come forward for such an oath.[116] Sixth, Masson's account of the happenings should not be ignored. According to him, the Barakzai Sardars submitted to Sayyid Ahmad because of his unexpected success in the Yusafzai area. Since he was calling them for a religious cause, and though apprehensive of his real designs, they were unable to oppose him.[117] Why did Sayyid Ahmad not implement *sharia* soon after the declaration of his *imarat*? The answer is simple, he went to fight the

Sikhs and was defeated. His lengthy search for a safe place hindered any plan to implement *sharia*.

The declaration of *imarat* was properly circulated; letters were dispatched to different Muslim princes who were invited to assist the Mujahidin in their struggle against the infidels. At his call, many people came to Hund and joined the Mujahidin.[118] Some Yusafzai chiefs including Khadi Khan, Ashraf Khan of Zaida, and Fateh Khan of Panjtar sent letter to the Barakzai chiefs of Peshawar to join Sayyid Ahmad's standard. The main argument they put was the selflessness of Sayyid Ahmad and his spirit for the cause of Islam. They explained that the region had faced Sikh atrocities for the last few years and they could liberate themselves by joining Sayyid Ahmad. Among the Barakzai brothers, Sultan Muhammad Khan and Said Muhammad Khan had previously taken oath at Sayyid Ahmad's hand, while Yar Muhammad Khan and Pir Muhammad Khan assured Sayyid Ahmad, through letters, of their full support for the noble cause of jihad. Yet many tribesmen were apprehensive of the real designs of the Barakzai Sardars and especially Yar Muhammad Khan.[119] The motives of the Barakzai Sardars were not known, but they might have joined Sayyid Ahmad for their vested interests. The Pukhtun tribes of Peshawar Valley were never subdued by the Afghan rulers and even at the time of Ahmad Shah Abdali, they were treated very cordially and taken as friends rather than subordinates. One *farman* issued by Ahmad Shah Abdali to a Yusafzai chief shows that he was addressed as a friend.[120] These tribes and especially the Yusafzais were part of the confederacy and after the overthrowing of the Sadduzais by the Barakzais, they were not on good terms with the latter. They wanted to subdue those tribes and thus strengthen their authority with the support of Sayyid Ahmad. The Barakzai were also aware that by remaining indifferent to the current developments in the area, they might lose their existing authority.[121]

The Battle of Shaidu (Nowshera)

Yar Muahammad Khan along with his brothers left Peshawar leading twenty thousand troops to confront the Sikhs in open field. They informed Sayyid Ahmad of their arrival when they reached Pir Pai, a village located several miles to the west of Nowshera on the southern bank of river Kabul. Sayyid Ahmad, accompanied by Fateh Khan of Panjtar, Ashraf Khan of Zaida, Khadi Khan of Hund, and about five hundred troops came to meet them. The formal oath of allegiance was rendered in the meeting and various matters about the looming battle with the Sikhs were discussed before Sayyid Ahmad's return to Hund.[122] Many Mujahidin were unable to join Sayyid Ahmad. Some were sick due to malnutrition while others had been injured in the battle at Akora Khattak. The sick Mujahidin were sent to Panjtar and the injured were left in Misri Banda as per previous arrangements.[123]

Sayyid Ahmad crossed the Kabul River near Nowshera, it was said, in the company of about eighty thousand tribesmen, and joined the Barakzai brothers encamped on the southern side of the river.[124] The Sikh army under Budh Singh was encamped in Shaidu, a village to the south of Akora.[125] Though Yar Muhammad Khan had pledged to fight against the Sikhs under the leadership of Sayyid Ahmad, the Barakzais subsequently felt threatened as to their existing status. They perhaps felt that Sayyid Ahmad treated them as subordinates instead of allies and they renewed contacts with the Sikhs.[126]

The Mujahidin proceeded to Shaidu and encamped near the Sikh force. The Sikh force, numbering about thirty thousand under Budh Singh, was numerically inferior to the Pukhtuns but superior in training and discipline. Upon the arrival of the Mujahidin, it was decided to attack the Sikh force the following day.[127]

A story relates that Sayyid Ahmad was poisoned[128] before the battle, by Nazar Muhammad, a cook of Yar Muhammad Khan, responsible for providing meals to Sayyid Ahmad.[129] Sayyid Ahmad's own statement reveals that he was given poison on the night before the battle.[130] He fell ill in the night before the battle and was unable to participate, though Shah Ismail seated him on an elephant, and took him to the field. All the Hindustanis remained with Sayyid Ahmad except Shadil Khan Kanjwari who was sent to accompany Fateh Khan of Panjtar. As the battle began, initially the tribesmen and the Mujahidin gained an upper hand and many Sikhs were killed.[131] However, Yar Muhammad Khan reached some compromise with Budh Singh and deserted the Mujahidin without taking part in the battle. This proved fatal for the Sayyid and his allies.[132] The combined force of the Mujahidin was defeated,[133] many were killed in the battlefield, and the rest fled.[134]

The battle of Shaidu was the last fight of the Pukhtuns against the Sikhs in open battlefield.[135] Masson's account does not seem accurate in stating that Budh Singh's force in the *sangar* was besieged by the Mujahidin, the Sikhs starved, and at last Budh Singh decided to attack the besiegers to either survive or perish.[136] Apart from the desertion of the Barakzai chiefs, the absence of Sayyid Ahmad and Shah Ismail also contributed to the defeat. Sayyid Ahmad was seriously sick and Shah Ismail was busy taking care of him.[137] Sayyid Ahmad himself gave a slight hint about the defeat in one of his letters to Shah Yaqeenullah, though without naming any individual responsible for the defeat. He wrote that the Mujahidin suffered a defeat at the hands of the infidels due to the indifference of a few hypocrites.[138]

The defeat of the Mujahidin was a great success for the Sikhs on the Frontier front. The event was celebrated with great pomp. Sohan Lal has written that Maharaja Ranjit Singh ordered the illumination of the whole city of Lahore and the firing of guns upon receiving the victory news.[139] Another contemporary source has recorded that the event was not only celebrated by illuminating Lahore and other cities but a huge amount was distributed among the poor people of the Sikh domain.[140] The defeat at the battle of Shaidu dispersed a large number of people who were gathered against the Sikhs in the Frontier. This proved the last time that such a large number of Muslims mobilized against the Sikhs.[141]

There are different views about the desertion of Yar Muhammad Khan. One is that the Sikh commander Budh Singh threatened him that joining hands with Sayyid Ahmad would be disastrous for him and thus he left the field to change the apparent victory of the Mujahidin into a defeat.[142] Another version suggested that the authoritarian nature of Sayyid Ahmad, treating his allies like subordinates, was the main factor responsible for the desertion of the Barakzai chiefs and especially Yar Muhammad Khan.[143]

The Indian writers do not agree with Masson's opinion and have stated that the *bai'at* of Hund was for waging the jihad only and Sayyid Ahmad did not act like a ruler. Yar Muhammad Khan had joined Sayyid Ahmad after the *bai'at* at Hund and Sayyid Ahmad was *amir-e-jihad* in the battle of Shaidu. Furthermore, Sayyid Ahmad's rule could be better than that of Ranjit Singh which was a bad experience for the people.[144] Olaf Caroe did not agree that Sayyid Ahmad assumed political authority over the tribesmen at this juncture, rather that happened only after he took Peshawar in 1830.[145] A local writer has also suggested that Yar Muhammad Khan was won over by Budh Singh by means of fear or favour and not only deserted the Mujahidin but also spread the news of his flight through his men which changed the victory of the Mujahidin into a disastrous defeat.[146] Whatever the cause or motive, the desertion of the Barakzai chiefs proved disastrous for the Mujahidin. They were defeated on the battlefield and a large number of them killed.[147] The Pukhtuns proved unable to face the Sikhs in open battle in the North-West Frontier after their defeat at Shaidu.[148]

Strangely, none of the narrators, contemporary or latter, has mentioned the exact date of the battle. M. A. Bari said that the battle was fought in March 1827.[149] Ghulam Rasul Mihr has written 14 *Phagan* on the authority of *Umdat-ul-Tawarikh*.[150] We conclude that the battle of Shaidu was fought on 25 February 1827. The date 14 *Phagan* corresponds to 25 February; the *bai'at* of jihad was taken on 10 January and then the Mujahidin would have taken a month or more for preparation. Moreover, the *Waqai Sayyid Ahmad Shahid* has narrated that the defeat was followed by a search for shelter in a season of severe cold and rain.[151] The usual heavy rain falls in February up to recent times. Moreover, Sayyid Ahmad started his preaching tour in April,[152] which corresponds to Ramadhan 1242 A.H., after a stay of about one month in Chinglai. This suggests that he arrived there in the first week of March.[153]

The period after the battle of Shaidu was one of great difficulties for the Mujahidin. There was a shortage of supplies from India in terms of men and money.[154] Sayyid Ahmad had to abandon his previous centre at Hund and search for a safe place. Shah Ismail and Ashraf Khan of Zaida took him across the Kabul River at Sar Ghat, where the river Swat and river Naguman join. They arrived at Babara[155] and left after a night stay there. Sayyid Ahmad was taken to Bagh, via Dakay, Gujar Garhi, Mohib and Surkh Dheri. Bagh is located at the entrance of a Pass, from where they went to Chinglai with the assistance of one Malik Faizullah Khan.[156] The dispersed Mujahidin also gathered at Chinglai, reaching in groups during the next few days. Some stayed in Toru and Panjtar due to their inability to travel. Sayyid Ahmad asked the Mujahidin at Toru and Panjtar to join him at Chinglai after their recovery from sickness.[157] During this period of privation, Sayyid Ahmad, unhappy with the tribal chiefs, decided to start preaching directly among the tribes and get mass support for the Jihad Movement. In this connection, he visited many towns and villages of Swat and Buner, preached jihad and was able to get support from the Pukhtun tribesmen against the Barakzais. This resulted in the battle of Utmanzai. He also looked to prospects in Hazara.

Notes and References

1. Mihr, Ghulam Rasul. nd. *Sayyid Ahmad Shahid*. Lahore: Sheikh Ghulam Ali and Sons. p. 234. Henceforth, Mihr, *Sayyid Ahmad*.
2. Shahjahanpuri, Payam. 1971. *Shahadatgah-e-Balakot*. Lahore: Idara Tarikh wa Tahqiq. pp. 79–80. Henceforth, Shahjahanpuri, *Shahdatgah-e-Balakot*. Husain,

Mahmud. 2008. 'Sayyid Ahmad Shahid (II) Jihad', in Mahmud Husain et al. (eds), *A History of the Freedom Movement, 1707–1831*, vol. I. Karachi: Royal Book Company. p. 581. Henceforth, Husain, 'Sayyid Ahmad (II)'. Dehlavi, Mirza Hairat. 1976. *Hayat-e-Tayyaba: Sawanih-e-Umri Shah Ismail Shahid.* Lahore: Islamic Academy. p. 233. Henceforth, Dehlavi, *Hayat-e-Tayyaba*.

3. Mihr, *Sayyid Ahmad*, p. 234.
4. Ahmad, Qeyamuddin. 1979. *The Wahabi Movement in India*. Islamabad: National Book Foundation. p. 43. Henceforth, Ahmad, *The Wahabi Movement*.
5. Nadvi, Muhammad Hamza Hassan. 1996. *Tazkira Hazrat Sayyid Ahmad Shahid.* Karachi: Majlis Nashriyat. p. 66. Henceforth, Nadvi, *Tazkira*.
6. Nasiri, Alim. 1995. *Shahnama Balakot: Tahrik-e-Jihad ki Manzoom Dastan*, vol. I. Lahore: Idara Matbu'at-e-Sulaimani. pp. 123–25. Henceforth, Nasiri, *Shahnama*, vol. I.
7. Mihr, *Sayyid Ahmad*, pp. 269–70.
8. History shows that during Muslim rule in Central Asia, the Ghaznavids and Hindu Shahis encountered in the region due to the strategic significance of the area. The Mughals and Persians constantly struggled for Herat and Qandahar. Even the British and Russian Empires struggled for upper hand in the area. The Turks and Germans also sent their missions to Afghanistan during the First World War and made contacts with anti-British elements in the tribal belt. In the last decades of twentieth century, same was the case between USA and USSR. This struggle is still going on among China, India, Iran, Pakistan, Russian Federation, and the United States. Examples of those who came to the region in the name of Islam, is Sayyid Ahmad. During the First World War, the Silk Letter Movement, known in history Silk Letter Case, plotted in Deoband and Delhi but Afghanistan became hub of its activities. The activists of the Silk Letter Movement even established a 'Provisional government' in Kabul. The movement, however, failed due to various reasons, mainly due to ill planning and unrealistic expectations of its leaders. For details, see Sindhi, Ubaidullah. nd. *Shah Waliullah aur un ki Siyasi Tahrik.* Lahore: al-Mahmud Academy.
9. Muslims from around the globe were attracted with the assistance of US and other states' intelligence agencies, by various tactics including propagating a *hadith*, which contained different subjects, including a prophecy related to the appearance of an army from *Khurasan* (parts of modern Afghanistan; Khyber Pakhtunkhwa and FATA of Pakistan) to assist the *Mahdi*—the Promised Messiah. This *hadith* is not recorded in the three major books of *ahadith*, i.e. *Muwata Imam Malik, Sahih Bukhari* and *Sahih Muslim*. Many scholars believe that this and many other *ahadith* were fabricated during Abbasid period for political purposes. Muslims attracted to the area in the 20th and 21th centuries mostly believed in this tradition. They propagated it and a majority of the local Muslims also believed in it. Sayyid Ahmad did not claim to the promised Messiah but his adherents later said he was. Momin Khan Momin, a contemporary poet of Sayyid Ahmad and friend of Shah Ismail, wrote a poem on Sayyid Ahmad's migration which contains the word Mahdi. Mihr, *Sayyid Ahmad*, pp. 271–72. See Appendix B for this tradition.
10. Nadvi, Sayyid Abu al-Hassan Ali. nd. *Tarikh-e-Dawat wa Azimat: Sirat-e-Sayyid Ahmad Shahid*, vol. I. Karachi: Majlis Nashriyat. pp. 423–24. Henceforth, Nadvi, *Sirat-e-Sayyid Ahmad*, vol. I.
11. Ghaffar, Abdul. 1983. *Zama Jwand aw Jadojahd*. Kabul: Daulati Matb'a. p. 7; Shahjahanpuri, *Shahadatgah-e-Balakot*, p. 79; Dehlavi, *Hayat-e-Tayyaba*, p. 161.

Dehlavi has mentioned Shah Ismail's visit to Punjab which is not supported by any other source.

12. Husain, 'Sayyid Ahmad (I)', p. 578.
13. Nadvi, *Sirat-e-Sayyid Ahmad*, vol. I, p. 423; Qureshi, Ishtiaq Hussain. nd. *Ulema in Politics.* Karachi: Ma'arif. p. 146. Henceforth, Qureshi, *Ulema in Politics.*
14. Yusafi, Allah Bakhsh. 1973. *Yusafzai Afghan.* Karachi: Sharif Arta Press. p. 451. Henceforth, Yusafi, *Yusafzai.* Khan, Roshan. 1986. *Yusafzai Qaum ki Sarguzasht.* Karachi: Roshan Khan and Co. p. 273. Henceforth, Khan, *Yusafzai Qaum.*
15. Mian, Sayyid Muhammad. 1999. 'Islami Hurriyat ka Alambardar', in Abdullah Butt (ed.). *Shah Ismail Shahid: Majmu'a-e-Maqalat.* Lahore: Makki Dar-ul-Kutub. pp. 29–30.
16. Nadvi, *Tazkira*, pp. 39–40.
17. Nadvi, *Sirat-e-Sayyid Ahmad*, vol. I, pp. 424–25.
18. Khan, Nawab Muhammad Wazir. 2007. *Waqai Sayyid Ahmad Shahid.* Lahore: Sayyid Ahmad Shahid Academy. pp. 1381–82. Henceforth, Khan, *Waqai Sayyid Ahmad.* Sayyid Ahmad referred to the invitation in his speech when Pukhtun opposition began. The invitation from Pukhtuns is not supported by any authentic source.
19. Mihr, *Sayyid Ahmad*, p. 265.
20. Qureshi, *Ulema in Politics*, p. 146. When Holker and Amir Khan went to the Punjab after their defeat by the English and sought Ranjit Singh's support, the latter advised them to avoid further confrontation with the English and sue for peace. Kohli, *Maharaja Ranjit Singh* on the authority of Mian, Sayyid Muhammad. 1977. *Ulema-e-Hind ka Shandar Mazi*, vol. II. Lahore: Maktaba Mahmudiya. p. 131. The sources show Ranjit Singh as an English ally who protected their interests from the Treaty of Sutlej until his death in 1839. The navigation of Indus, no interference in the territories beyond the Sutlej, and the Tripartite Treaty, which culminated in the first Anglo-Afghan war in 1839–42 are evidence.
21. This has been referred to by Sayyid Ahmad in a letter to Dost Muhammad Khan. Sayyid Ahmad wrote to him that one of his ancestors Sayyid Ilmullah or Sayyid 'Alam Allah was a *khalifa* of Shaikh Adam al-Banuri, one of the *khulafa* of Sheikh Ahmad Sirhindi. Ansari, A. S. Bazmee. 1976. 'Sayyid Ahmad Shahid in the Light of his Letter'. *Islamic Studies.* Islamabad, vol. 15, no. 4, pp. 231–45.
22. Khan, Muin-ud-Din Ahmad. nd. *Muslim Struggle for Freedom in Bengal: From Plassey to Pakistan A.D., 1757–1947.* Dacca: Islamic Foundation Bangladesh. p. 22.
23. One should not forget that the family of Sayyid Akbar Shah had lived in the area for generations and this was the *pir khana* of many Pukhtuns of Peshawar Valley, Buner, Swat and Hazara. Furthermore, his family was a stakeholder in the area as he held a large tract of land.
24. Qureshi, *Ulema in Politics*, p. 146.
25. Mihr, *Sayyid Ahmad*, p. 275; Shahjahanpuri, *Shahadatgah-e-Balakot*, p. 80.
26. Husain, 'Sayyid Ahmad (II)', p. 581.
27. Nadvi, *Sirat-e-Sayyid Ahmad*, vol. I, pp. 451–52.
28. Mihr, *Sayyid Ahmad*, pp. 273–75.
29. Nadvi, *Sirat-e-Sayyid Ahmad*, vol. I, pp. 455–57.
30. Mihr, *Sayyid Ahmad*, pp. 275–76.
31. Abdul Hamid Khan of Rampur, a symbol of all the vices of the day, was long employed in Amir Khan's army. He took *bai'at* and accompanied Sayyid Ahmad to the North West Frontier, where he was appointed commander of the Mujahidin during their

sojourn in the Peshawar Valley. He died of a wound received in the battle of Mayar. Mihr, *Sayyid Ahmad*, p. 277; Nadvi, *Sirat-e-Sayyid Ahmad*, vol. I. pp. 460–61.

32. Mihr, *Sayyid Ahmad*, p. 276.
33. Nadvi, *Sirat-e-Sayyid Ahmad*, vol. I, p. 462.
34. Mihr, *Sayyid Ahmad*, pp. 280–94; Nadvi, *Sirat-e-Sayyid Ahmad*, vol. I, pp. 263–71.
35. Mihr, *Sayyid Ahmad*, p. 284.
36. Nadvi, *Sirat-e-Sayyid Ahmad*, vol. I, pp. 469–70.
37. Pir Sibghatullah commonly known as Pir Pagaro, the ancestor of Pir Pagaro of Sindh (d. 2012) was one of the followers of Sayyid Ahmad. No source has mentioned whether he was known to Sayyid Ahmad before his journey to Sindh. Mihr believes that he had taken *bai'at* in the Hijaz during Sayyid Ahmad's Haj. Mihr, *Sayyid Ahmad*, p. 285. Other sources do not agree and assert that they first met when Sayyid Ahmad arrived at Hyderabad, Sindh. Nasiri, *Shahnama*, vol. I, p. 130.
38. Mihr, *Sayyid Ahmad*, pp. 285–86.
39. Ibid., p. 286.
40. The then reigning chief of Bahawalpur was of a Jet family (not to be confused with Jat of the Punjab), called Daudputra. After their expulsion from Shikarpur, they crossed the Indus, possessed various localities, and built their own fortifications. One of them, Bahawal Khan, became powerful after the decline of the Mughal Empire, subdued the neighbouring chiefs, and refused to pay tribute to Taimur Shah, the Sadduzai king of Afghanistan. He was succeeded by his son Sa'adat Khan, who concluded a treaty with both the English and the Sikhs. He was succeeded by his son Bahawal Khan II. Masson, Charles. 1974. *Narrative of Various Journeys in Balochistan, Afghanistan and the Panjab*, vol. I. Karachi: Oxford University Press. pp. 26–27. Henceforth, Masson, *Narrative*, vol. I.
41. Masson, *Narrative*, vol. I, p. 14.
42. Pir Kot is written in Urdu and English, however, its original name in Sindhi is Pir Jo Goth, long the residence of Pir Sibghatullah's family. Sibghatullah was a keen observer and perceived the danger which had arisen for Sindh from the English and the Sikh alliance. Thus he started organizing his disciples, known as Hurs, for the struggle which he considered inevitable with the enemies of the Sindh.
43. British colonial documents of 18th and 19th centuries reveal that it was the major business centre of Sindh. The traders and especially the Hindus of Shikarpur had a chain of enterprises not only in Sindh but also in Central Asia.
44. Father of Nawab Siddiq Hassan, exponent of the Indian Ahl-e-Hadith. Hassan asserts that Sayyid Aulad Hassan accompanied Sayyid Ahmad and later returned to his abode with the latter's permission. He has also mentioned a letter which was sent by Sayyid Ahmad to Sayyid Aulad Hassan from Panjtar. Khan, Sayyid Ali Hassan. 1991. *Ma'aser-e-Siddiqi*. Lahore: Jamiat Ahl-e-Sunnah. pp. 57–58. Henceforth, Khan, *Ma'aser-e-Siddiqi*.
45. Nadvi, *Tazkira*, pp. 73–74.
46. Sayyid Anwar Shah originally belonged to Amritsar, Punjab but migrated to Sindh due to Sikh atrocities. One of the Sikh nobles embraced Islam at his hands and Anwar Shah was tortured and kept under house arrest for two years by the Sikh authorities. Sayyid Ahmad sent Haji Yusaf Kashmiri for the release of Sayyid Anwar Shah. The latter was sent to Sindh after his release where he met Sayyid Ahmad at Jagan. Nadvi, *Sirat-e-Sayyid Ahmad*, vol. I, pp. 483–84; Mihr, *Sayyid Ahmad*, pp. 299–300.

47. Khan Garh does not exist now. At this place General John Jacob, the British commander, established a military post which was developed into a cantonment and subsequently a city, known as Jacobabad. Jacob was buried in the town after his death in 1857.
48. Nadvi, *Sirat-e-Sayyid Ahmad*, vol. I, pp. 484–86.
49. Shal was the previous name of Quetta according to the eighteenth and nineteenth centuries colonial records and vernacular sources. Quetta is official spelling of the city though locally it is called Kaw'ata.
50. There are many instances of officials and governors wishing to join Sayyid Ahmad for jihad but he took none with him. The reason may have been to avoid misunderstanding by some rulers and allow their continued support, deemed vital for the success of the movement. Mihr, *Sayyid Ahmad*, pp. 303–4.
51. Akhun Fateh Muhammad started his career as a soldier in Nadir Shah's army, later on became *wazir* of Naseer Khan Baloch—7th ruler of Qalat state—managed the whole state affairs during his son Mahmud's time and remained *wazir* of Mihrab Khan. Mihr, *Sayyid Ahmad*, p. 306.
52. Mihrab Khan II and the ruler of Qandahar were at war during that time.
53. Nasiri, *Shahnama*, vol. I, pp. 132–33; Mihr, *Sayyid Ahmad*, p. 310.
54. Mihr, *Sayyid Ahmad*, p. 311.
55. The Ghilzai was one of the most powerful tribes of Afghanistan and one of their ancestors Mirwais Hotak ruled part of modern Afghanistan and Persia from 1709 to 1715. A civil war after Mirwais' death among his successors contributed to their defeat at the hands of Nadir Shah (1688–1747) of Persia. After Nadir Shah's assassination, the Sadduzais became master of the country. There was jealousy among the Sadduzais, Barakzais and Ghilzais as each tribe considered itself the legitimate ruler of Afghanistan. Khan-e-Khanan son of Abdul Rahim, a descendent of Shah Hussain, the last Ghilzai ruler of Qandahar wrote to Sayyid Ahmad that he would respond with a march of forty to fifty thousand men at Sayyid Ahmad's call for jihad whenever he receive it. Nadvi, *Sirat-e-Sayyid Ahmad*, vol. I, pp. 505–6.
56. Nadvi, *Sirat-e-Sayyid Ahmad*, vol. I, pp. 507–8.
57. Mihr, *Sayyid Ahmad*, pp. 310–14.
58. For the text of treaty, see Appendix C.
59. Sethi, R. R. 1950. *The Lahore Darbar: Punjab Government Record Office Publications, Monograph No. I*. Delhi: Gulab Chand Kapur and Sons. pp. 1–2. Henceforth, Sethi, *The Lahore Darbar*.
60. Ahmad, *Wahabi Movement*, p. 43.
61. Caroe, Olaf. 1965. *The Pathans, 550 BC–AD 1957*. London: Macmillan & Co Ltd. p. 302. Henceforth, Caroe, *The Pathans*.
62. Bellew, H. W. 2001. *A General Report on the Yusufzais*. Lahore: Sang-e-Meel Publications. p. 86. Henceforth, Bellew, *Report on the Yusufzais*.
63. Hashtnagar, a Persian word used for a cluster of eight towns, but in Pukhtu it is called Ashnaghar. It includes Charsadda, Prang, Rajjar (also Razzar), Umarzai, Utmanzai, Turangzai, Sherpao and Tangi.
64. Khan, *Waqai Sayyid Ahmad*, p. 1095.
65. Mihr, *Sayyid Ahmad*, p. 327; Khan, *Waqai Sayyid Ahmad*, p. 1097.
66. Nasiri, *Shahnama*, vol. I, pp. 136–37.
67. Mihr, *Sayyid Ahmad*, p. 330.
68. Nasiri, *Shahnama*, vol. I, p. 141.

76   *Sayyid Ahmad Barailvi*

69. Caroe, *The Pathans*, p. 297.
70. Khan, *Waqai Sayyid Ahmad*, p. 1103.
71. *Tarburwali*—enmity between cousins had been seen by many as the main reason of Pukhtun socio-political and economic backwardness. Khawas Khan and Amir Khan had a dispute over some issue and since the former had joined the Sikhs, the latter joined Sayyid Ahmad. This was one of the causes of the failure of the movement as Sayyid Ahmad lost support due to siding with one side or another in conflicts.
72. Khan, *Waqai Sayyid Ahmad*, p. 1103; Nasiri, *Shahnama*, vol. I, p. 144.
73. Sikh sources including Kanhiya Lal, *Tarikh-e-Punjab* are silent regarding the battle of Akora. However, *Waqai Sayyid Ahmad* has given a detailed account. See Khan, *Waqai Sayyid Ahmad*. pp. 1108–13.
74. Nasiri, *Shahnama*, vol. I, p. 145,
75. Rizvi, Saiyid Athar Abbas. 1982. *Shah 'Abd al-'Aziz: Puritan, Sectarian Polemics and Jihad*. Canberra: Ma'arifat Publishing House. p. 487. Henceforth, Rizvi, *Shah 'Abd al-'Aziz*.
76. Mihr, *Sayyid Ahmad*, pp. 332–33.
77. Nadvi, *Sirat-e-Sayyid Ahmad*, vol. I, pp. 517–18.
78. Nasiri, *Shahnama*, vol. I, p. 151.
79. Yusafi, *Yusafzai Afghan*, p. 453.
80. Griffin, Lepel Henry. 1892. *Ranjit Singh*. Oxford: Clarendon Press. p. 211.
81. Khan, *Waqai Sayyid Ahmad*, pp. 1114–15.
82. For the names of the Hindustani killed in Akora, see Appendix D.
83. Mihr, *Sayyid Ahmad*, pp. 343–45.
84. Hund, once the summer capital of Hindu Shahi dynasty, had long been a very important place. Before the construction of Attock Fort, it was one of the halts of the caravans moving from India to Kabul and further to Central Asia. Alexander (356–323 BC) and Babar (1483–1530) had crossed the river Indus here during their marches on India.
85. Mandanr, descendents of Mandanr, nephew of Yusaf, is commonly considered a clan of the Yusafzais, as Mandanr was brought up by his uncle Yusaf and was married to his daughter. Numerically it is a major community, inhabiting the present Swabi and Mardan districts of Khyber Pakhtunkhwa, Pakistan. At the time of Sayyid Ahmad's migration to the Frontier, there were two powerful Mandanr chiefs, Khadi Khan of Hund and Muhammad Khan or Ahmad Khan of Hoti.
86. Mihr, *Sayyid Ahmad*, p. 345.
87. Bazar still exists with the same name. It lays in the west of Hund.
88. Khan, *Waqai Sayyid Ahmad*, p. 1117.
89. The external walls of the fort still exist and inside the walls people have constructed their houses. We visited it on 15 November 2011.
90. Mihr, *Sayyid Ahmad*, p. 346.
91. Khan, *Waqai Sayyid Ahmad*, p. 1117.
92. Mihr, *Sayyid Ahmad*, p. 347.
93. Khan, *Waqai Sayyid Ahmad*, p. 1118.
94. Dehlavi, *Hayat-e-Tayyaba*, p. 240. Though Dehlavi has stated that the attack was launched with Sayyid Ahmad's approval, he had also stated that it was not approved by Shah Ismail. He wrote that some Qandaharis participated in the attack but no Hindustani.
95. Thanesari, Muhammad Jaffar. 1969. *Maktubat-e-Sayyid Ahmad Shahid aur Kala Pani*. Lahore: Nafees Academy. p. 62. Henceforth, Thanesari, *Maktubat*.

96. *Garhi* is a name used for military outposts in all the contemporary sources. Though there is a village with the same name, the Mujahidin attacked the military outpost.
97. *Mandi* is in use for the market place until today.
98. It is important to note that the contemporary sources have made this differentiation between Hindustanis and locals and have always considered them different groups despite their having the same cause.
99. Mihr, *Sayyid Ahmad*, pp. 347–49.
100. Rizvi, *Shah 'Abd al-'Aziz*, p. 488.
101. Dehlavi, *Hayat-e-Tayyaba*, p. 241.
102. Lal, Kanhia. 2002. *Tarikh-e-Punjab*. Mirpur, Azad Kashmir: Arsalan Books. pp. 331–32. Henceforth, Lal, *Tarikh-e-Punjab*. Kanhia Lal popularly known as Kanhia Lal Hindi worked in the office of Henry Davies, Lieutenant Governor of the Punjab, and authored several books. The above mentioned event of the siege of the fort at Hazro does not seem authentic for two main reasons. First, if we agree that the town Hazro had a fort, still the Mujahidin did not have adequate resources required for the siege of a fort. Second, the attack on Hazro has been mentioned by many contemporary and secondary sources but none of them have talked about a siege of Hazro. All the sources agree that it was a night attack and a maximum 300 persons carried it out.
103. Mihr, *Sayyid Ahmad*, p. 350.
104. The declaration of *imarat* was made twice, first time on 10 January 1827 immediately after the attack on Hazro. Some believe that it was not for the imposition of *sharia* rather it was for the organization of jihad only. The second time it was declared at Panjtar on 6 February 1829, for the imposition of *sharia* alongside the organization of jihad. S. M. Ikram is of the opinion that it was a full-fledged *imarat* for all religious and political applications. Ikram, S. M. 2000. *Mauj-e-Kausar*. Lahore: Idara Saqafat-e-Islamia. p. 25. Henceforth, Ikram, *Mauj-e-Kausar*. A major section of the *ulama* of the Deoband school of thought in Pakistan took an oath for undertaking jihad at the hands of Masud Azhar in late 1999 in a meeting held in Karachi, soon after his release from an Indian jail. The motives of the present-day jihad phenomenon are doubted by a majority in academia and the general public, but with the exception of one or two groups, all militant organizations working in South Asia claim taking ideological inspiration for their jihadi activities from Sayyid Ahmad. This is found in their literature. These organizations had also named some of their training camps and *madari*s after Sayyid Ahmad and Shah Ismail.
105. In his letter to Indian Muslims soon after the declaration of *imarat* (12 Jamad al-Thani 1242), Sayyid Ahmad had clearly written that the Mujahidin did not act like an organized body and booty was not distributed according to *sharia*. Thanesari, *Maktubat*, p. 62. It is, however, interesting to note that the biographers of Sayyid Ahmad, especially Mihr and Nadvi, have criticized the Pukhtun tribesmen for the mismanagement.
106. Nadvi, *Tazkira*, p. 84. The local sources, i.e. Kakakhel, Yusafi and Roshan Khan have mentioned one *bai'at* of February 1829 and are silent over the 10 January 1827 *bai'at*. Kakakhel, Bahadar Shah Zafar. nd. *Pushtun: Tarikh kay Ayenay main, 550 QM say 1964 tak*. Peshawar: University Book Agency. pp. 691–92. Henceforth, Kakakhel, *Pushtun*; Yusafi, *Yusafzai Afghan*, p. 459; Khan, *Yusafzai Qaum*, p. 279. The *Waqai* has recorded the second *bai'at* as a renewal of the earlier *bai'at*, with the addition that local *ulama* rendered a written *fatwa* that any person not obeying the authority of the *imam* would be considered a rebel. Khan, *Waqai Sayyid Ahmad*, pp. 1378–86.
107. Nadvi, *Sirat-e-Sayyid Ahmad*, vol. I, p. 58.

108. The issue will be dealt somewhere else.
109. Ibid., p. 543.
110. Mihr, *Sayyid Ahmad*, pp. 353–54.
111. Ibid., pp. 352–54.
112. Ibid., p. 464.
113. Thanesari, *Maktubat*, p. 62.
114. Ibid., pp. 58–120.
115. Ibid., p. 119. We understand that Sayyid Ahmad did not consider the Ottoman Caliphate a spiritual entity. Though he never declared it openly, the content of his letters testify to this as 'he invited the general public and Muslim princes of the different regions to submit to his authority and thus avoid the sin of absence of an *imam*' or *caliph*. Thanesri, *Maktubat*, p. 119.
116. A British colonial source has also stated that Sayyid Ahmad assumed political authority in January 1827. Bellew, *A General Report*, p. 86.
117. Masson, Charles. 1974. *Narrative of Various Journeys in Balochistan, Afghanistan and the Panjab*, vol. III. Karachi: Oxford University Press. pp. 75–76. Henceforth, Masson, *Narrative of Journeys* vol. III.
118. Nasiri, *Shahnama*, vol. I, pp. 183–85.
119. Mihr, *Sayyid Ahmad*, p. 360. The Barakzai's had no intimacy with the tribes of the Peshawar Valley due to different factors, including their adoption of the Persian culture and enmity with the Sadduzai, especially Shah Shuja, whose mother was a Yusafzai.
120. *History of the Hoti Family*, p. 19.
121. Nadvi, Sayyid Abu al-Hassan Ali. nd. *Tarikh-e-Dawat wa Azimat: Sirat-e-Sayyid Ahmad*, vol. II. Karachi: Majlis Nashriyat. pp. 3–4. Henceforth, Nadvi, *Sirat-e-Sayyid Ahmad*, vol. II. Sayyid Muhammad Latif wrote that Yar Muhammad Khan formed a coalition with Sayyid Ahmad due to the general attitude of the Yusafzais, the powerful tribe of the area. Latif, Sayyid Muhammad. 1964. *History of the Panjab: From the Remotest Antiquity to the Present Time*. New Delhi: Eurasia Publishing House. p. 439. Henceforth, Latif, *History of the Panjab*.
122. Mihr, *Sayyid Ahmad*, p. 363. The Barakzais have been termed allies and that was one reason that when Sayyid Ahmad tried to treat them his subordinates they renewed their communication with the Sikhs. Masson, *Narrative of Journeys*, vol. III, p. 76.
123. Nadvi, *Sirat-e-Sayyid Ahmad*, vol. II, p. 4.
124. Khan, *Waqai Sayyid Ahmad*, pp. 1123–27. It is noteworthy that the figure is exaggerated as the whole population of the Peshawar vale could not provide that many fighting men. H. W. Bellew has estimated the whole population of Yusafzais and Mandanr of Peshawar and Swat vale was about four lakh (400,000) in 1864. It was also stated that they could bring 73,200 men to field for fighting. The battle of Shaidu was fought 37 years before Bellew wrote his book. See Bellew, *A General Report*, p. 180. Yet another source has recorded that the population of the Peshawar district was 450,099 in 1855. *Gazetteer of the Peshawar District, 1897–98*, p. 92. It is clear that the whole population was not fighting men. The number of troops on Sayyid Ahmad's side could not exceed 30,000. All the sources either written by Sayyid Ahmad's followers or the Sikh writers have exaggerated. The Sikhs wanted to magnify their success, while the Mujahidin wanted to emphasize that Yar Muhammad Khan's desertion resulted in the defeat of such a large force.

125. Shaidu has been destroyed several times due to floods in the Kabul River and the present Shaidu village is not the one where the battle was fought. In personal interviews with locals for this study, they thought that the battle was fought where the old graveyard of the present-day Shaidu is located. The remains of the old Shaidu are visible on the southern bank of the present-day course of the river.

126. Masson, *Narrative of Journeys*, vol. III, p. 76. Masson's account at another place has stated

> In the Mussulman camp all was hope and exultation—numbers, and the presumed favour of heaven, permitted none to doubt of success—and a distribution was already made of the Sikhs towns and villages. The soul of the Saiyad dilated; and in his pride of feeling, he used expression implying that he considered himself the master of Peshawar, and the Sirdars as his vassals. They became suspicious; and their final defection, if not owing to these circumstances entirely, is by some palliated on account of it.

Masson, *Narratives of Journeys*, vol. I, p. 133. There is another account that Yar Muhammad Khan joined Sayyid Ahmad because of his fear that arrival of the Sikh force under Budh Singh would result in increased tribute upon him. Kakakhel, *Pushtun*, p. 691.

127. Mihr, *Sayyid Ahmad*, p. 369; Khan, *Waqai Sayyid Ahmad*, p. 1127.

128. Latif has narrated that Yar Muhammad Khan tried to remove Sayyid Ahmad by poison in 1829. Latif, *History of the Panjab*, p. 441. Latif has committed many mistakes in narrating different events. All local sources are silent over the allegation of poison, though they have condemned Yar Muhammad Khan for his desertion in the battle of Shaidu. All non-local sources have narrated the story of poison on the authority of the *Waqai Sayyid Ahmad*. Sayyid Ahmad himself said in a letter that during the diagnosing of his sickness he was told that he might have been poisoned.

129. Mihr, *Sayyid Ahmad*, pp. 373–74; Khan, *Waqai Sayyid Ahmad*, pp. 1126–27.

130. Thanesari, *Maktubat*, pp. 193–95.

131. Khan, *Waqai Sayyid Ahmad*, pp. 1127–28.

132. Ahmad, *The Wahabi Movement*, p. 49.

133. Lal, *Tarikh-e-Punjab*, pp. 332–33. Another secondary source has also stated that the defeat of the Mujahidin was due to the betrayal of Yar Muhammad Khan, the Peshawar sardar. Hardy, Peter. 1972. *The Muslims of British India*. London: Cambridge University Press. p. 52. Henceforth, Hardy, *The Muslims of India*.

134. Ikram, *Mauj-e-Kausar*, p. 26.

135. One can see that the Sikh government increased the annual tribute upon the Barakzai chiefs. Yar Muhamamd Khan's son was taken as a hostage to the Lahore court. The tribesmen were unable to struggle collectively against the alien power, then or later upon the British occupation of the North-West Frontier. Though British authority was opposed by the tribes separately, collective struggle is only visible during the 1897–98 uprising.

136. Masson, *Narrative of Journeys*, vol. I, pp. 133–34.

137. Nasiri, *Shahnama*, vol. I, pp. 208–9.

138. Thanesri, *Maktubat*, p. 68.

139. Suri, Lala Sohan Lal. 1961. *Umdat-ul-Tawarikh Daftar II*. Delhi: S. Chand and Co. p. 340.

140. Diwan Amar Nath, *Zafar Nama-e-Ranjit Singh*, p. 181 as quoted in Nadvi, *Sirat-e-Sayyid Ahmad*, vol. II, p. 12. Sayyid Muhammad Latif has narrated a slightly different version. As mentioned, his narration is inaccurate in many places related to Sayyid Ahmad and his Mujahidin Movement, committing serious blunders in recording dates, names and events. For details, see Latif, *History of the Panjab*, pp. 437–43.
141. Nadvi, *Sirat-e-Sayyid Ahmad*, vol. II, p. 12.
142. Mihr, *Sayyid Ahmad Shahid*, p. 375.
143. Masson, *Narrative of Journeys*, vol. III, p. 76.
144. Mihr, *Sayyid Ahmad Shahid*, p. 376.
145. Caroe, *The Pathans*, p. 303.
146. Kakakhel, *Pushtun*, p. 691.
147. Dehlavi, *Hayat-e-Tayyaba*, p. 247.
148. They were demoralized to the extent that even during the Sikh's forced march to Afghanistan in 1839, they did not face them and let the force advance towards Kabul. The Sikh force returned via Wakhan.
149. Bari, M. A. 1965. 'A Nineteenth-Century Muslim Reform Movement', in George Makdisi (ed.), *Arabic and Islamic Studies in Honor of Hamilton A.R. Gibb*. Leiden: E. J. Brill. p. 97. Henceforth, Bari, 'A Nineteenth-Century Muslim Reform Movement'. It seems that Peter Hardy's narration is based on M. A. Bari's source. Like the rest of the narration he has also stated that the battle of Shaidu was fought in March 1827. Hardy, *The Muslims of India*, p. 52.
150. Mihr, *Sayyid Ahmad Shahid*, p. 372.
151. Khan, *Waqai Sayyid Ahmad*, pp. 1135–36.
152. Mihr, *Sayyid Ahmad Shahid*, p. 392.
153. Sayyid Ahmad's first *Eid-ul-Fitr* after migration was celebrated between Amar Kot (some people call it Umar Kot) and Pali in Sindh, while the second and first after arrival in North-West Frontier was celebrated on 27 April 1827 (1 *Al-Shawwal* 1242), confirming that the Battle of Shaidu was fought on 25 February 1827.
154. Ahmad, *The Wahabi Movement*, p. 49.
155. Nasiri, *Shahnama*, vol. I, pp. 201–4.
156. Chinglai is situated in the Khudu Khel area of present Buner district of Khyber Pakhtunkhwa, Pakistan. Buner is geographically divided into three regions. Khudu Khel is between district Swabi and the Durmai Pass. After crossing the Durmai Pass, one enters the Chamla Valley. Chamla, at western side, starts from Ambela, the famous pass where the British Indian Army fought the Ambela campaign in 1863. At the eastern end it stretches to Koz Amazai in the Mahabanr where the Mujahidin Colony at Malka was established in 1858. The northern side of the Chamla Valley ends at Baba Ji pass, where one enters the third geographic part of Buner district that includes Takhta Band, Sawarai, Tor Warsak, Juwar, Bajkata and many other large and small villages. It ends on the western side at Karakar, on the eastern side at Chagharzai, and on the northern side at Ilam mountain, north of which is the Swat Valley. The route of Sayyid Ahmad and the Mujahidin to Chinglai is apparent today and we traced it.
157. Mihr, *Sayyid Ahmad Shahid*, p. 381.

4

Transitional Period:
The Search for Headquarters

Teaching of *Sharia* and Jihad among the Pukhtun Tribes

The defeat at the battle of Shaidu (February 1827) shattered the weak organization of the Mujahidin, established a few months earlier. They abandoned their centre at Hund due to its proximity with Sikh territory. Sayyid Ahmad recalled the Mujahidin dispersed at different locations and began a re-organization. His two concerns were recruiting Pukhtuns through preaching to join him and finding a new, secure centre. For this purpose, he started an extended tour into Buner and Swat. He knew that the tribes of these areas were free from both the Barakzais and the Sikhs. He might have also learnt by now that hasty action would not support his objective. Therefore, he concentrated on recruiting the general population, something which might have helped achieve more positive results if done earlier. He was welcomed by the local villagers and many agreed to join his movement.[1]

In April 1827 (Ramadhan 1242 A.H.), Sayyid Ahmad started out from Chinglai and entered the Chamla Valley after crossing the Durmai Kandao (pass). He left Sheikh Wali Muhammad of Phulat with the sick in Chinglai, with instructions to follow when their health recovered.[2] The first village visited was Koga (also Kawga and Kauga). Locals visited and took his *bai'at*.[3] Among others from neighbouring villages, Sayyid Rasul of Nawagai came and offered his allegiance.[4] Pukhtuns, following their tradition, offered them free food and lodging. Everyone would come to Sayyid Ahmad and ask for a specific number of the Mujahidin for whom food was prepared, thus dividing the guests among themselves. Each host would try to offer the best possible meal.[5]

From Koga, Sayyid Ahmad visited a village where Sayyid Mian, a noble of Takhta Band, informed him that he was unable to visit him in Koga due to an old tribal feud.[6] Sayyid Ahmad assured him that he would work for reconciliation among the tribes after his Swat journey. He and the Mujahidin then entered Buner proper[7] and visited Takhta Band. There about three hundred men of Sayyid Mian's clan took *bai'at* at the hands of Sayyid Ahmad to obey the commandments of Allah. Besides, a huge number of people from surrounding villages also visited Sayyid Ahmad and took the oath of allegiance.[8]

Shah Ismail and Shaikh Sa'ad-ud-Din of Phulat were left in Takhta Band due to their sickness. Sayyid Ahmad visited more villages, including Ilai, Tor Warsak, and Juwar. After a brief stay in these villages, Sayyid Ahmad and the Mujahidin crossed Karakar,[9] and entered Bari Kot, avoiding a stay in Nawagai,[10] the first village after entering Swat from Buner side. The sources state that the Khan of Bari Kot welcomed Sayyid Ahmad, who spent a couple of days with him, then left for Thana after leaving behind sick companions, including Haji Waliullah and Haji Rahim Bakhsh.[11] Sayyid Ahmad and the Mujahidin stayed for some time in Thana where familiar preaching was carried out. They then crossed the Swat River and entered Chakdara.

The Sayyids of Ouch sent a delegation and invited Sayyid Ahmad to visit their village. Upon their invitation, he visited the village. He preached the tenets of Islam, arranged a sitting (*mahfil*) of recital of the praise and names of Allah (*dhikr*), and called them for jihad. Sayyid Ahmad usually preferred to visit the Sayyids of an area first and gain their support. He might have intended to build legitimacy among Pukhtuns through his affiliations with local Sayyids. The next halt was Koti Gram, where the new moon was sighted and they celebrated Eid.[12] During their stay in Koti Gram, a caravan of seventy to eighty Mujahidin under Maulvi Qalandar arrived from India. As the number of Mujahidin had increased, they were divided into different groups. It was here that Shah Ismail joined the Mujahidin after his recovery. From Koti Gram, Sayyid Ahmad started his journey for upper Swat and arrived at western Ouch.[13] The Mujahidin were staying in Koti Gram when the ailing Muhammad Yusaf of Phulat died and was buried there.[14] Qazi Ahmadullah of Meerut with sixty to seventy Mujahidin and Abdul Hamid Khan[15] with a number of Mujahidin joined Sayyid Ahmad.[16]

Apart from preaching the tenets of Islam, Sayyid Ahmad tried to reconcile the feuding tribes. It was a major problem of the day. Next,

Sayyid Ahmad halted at Banda,[17] along with his Mujahidin, where another caravan arrived. This consisted of about a hundred Mujahidin under the command of Maulvi Muhammad Ramazan.[18] Then Sayyid Ahmad came to Babuzai area and stayed in Mingora[19] for three days.[20] He was welcomed in the area of the present Swat district by all segments of society including the religious classes. The whole body of Mujahidin was invited for meals by Akhun Mir[21] of Mingora. Swat, then, was religiously under the influence of people who are now called Barailvi.[22] There were instances that the elders came out of their villages several miles to welcome the Mujahidin.[23] The next destinations were Manglawar and Charbagh, respectively, where the Mujahidin stayed for a few days, and the usual preaching of jihad was carried out. Sayyid Ahmad proceeded to Khwaza Khela[24] and stayed there for some time due to the insistence of its residents. From Khwaza Khela, Akhun Faiz Muhammad was sent to Sulaiman Shah[25] of Chitral,[26] to invite him to join the cause of jihad.[27] He was still in Swat when Sulaiman Shah sent his reply, assuring that they would be assisted in every possible way and that he would soon join him via Gilgit.[28]

A village Khonay[29] was visited. The noble of the village was a Sayyid, who offered hospitality to the Mujahidin. On his return journey, Sayyid Ahmad and the Mujahidin came to Asala.[30] The river Swat was crossed near Asala and Durush Khela was visited.[31] Next Sayyid Ahmad visited Shakardara and then Sakhra[32] where Anbalay Khan of Sakhra welcomed him warmly and offered his services for the cause of jihad. Sayyid Ahmad appreciated his spirit and assured him that he would be called in time of need.[33] The visit of another village is mentioned by *Waqai* but the name was not recorded. We assume that it was either Pir Kalay or Ningwalai.[34] Sayyid Ahmad and the Mujahidin crossed river Swat after a night stay in Bara Bandai and entered Charbagh, where Maulvi Abdul Hai also arrived from India and met Sayyid Ahmad.[35] Sayyid Ahmad personally visited villages that were easy of access and also sent associates in different directions to preach jihad. He was usually accompanied by several Mujahidin while visiting a particular village. The many followers were divided into groups and lived in different places.[36] On the return journey Sayyid Ahmad stayed in Charbagh for about eight days. At this time, Akhun Mir of Mingora sent a message that a caravan of Mujahidin has entered lower Swat under the command of Mian Muqeem. Sayyid Ahmad met the newly arrived caravan of Mujahidin, consisted of thirty to forty persons, in Udigram. They had brought cash and arms from India.[37]

After a journey of a few days, Sayyid Ahmad came to Buner and visited the grave of Sayyid Ali Tirmizi, popularly known as Pir Baba. He then came to Panjtar. Fateh Khan of Panjtar welcomed him. Sayyid Ahmad stayed in an orchard selected by Fateh Khan for his stay outside the village.[38]

The impact of his tour was discussed by Sayyid Ahmad himself in a letter to Shah Yaqeenullah. He gave a brief comment on events of the last few months and stated that after the tragic defeat at Shaidu, he visited the Yusafzai area and invited other Pukhtun tribesmen through letters for the cause of jihad. He has further said that all accepted his invitation and within a few days jihad would be declared upon the infidels and those who had diverted from the righteous path.[39] Other sources say that his tour was successful and that he was able to enlist the support of the Pukhtuns. During this time, fresh groups of Mujahidin continued to arrive from India along with funds. Their arrival not only encouraged the Mujahidin but also strengthened them as they included important figures such as Risaldar Abdul Hamid Khan, Qazi Ahmadullah of Meerut, Maulvi Ramazan and Mian Muqeem of Rampur.[40]

The highland tour of Sayyid Ahmad was important. He visited the Yusafzai of Buner and Swat in person and was welcomed wherever he went. His verdict was accepted in many places in adjudicating their internal disputes. Yet, although the Sayyid and his associates claimed that all Pukhtun tribes joined his cause and openly provided full support to the Mujahidin Movement in the area, we did not find any strong evidence to accept this claim. Apart from Anbalay Khan, no prominent tribesman joined the Mujahidin nor did the required leadership support come from any major tribe in the area. Some reasons can be inferred from the sources about the passive attitude of the overall Swat population. The means of communication were meagre and people might have not known about Sayyid Ahmad's recent assault on different enemies in the Peshawar Valley. Even if informed in time, they had little resources to meet the expenditures of a long journey and warfare. They had not experienced direct foreign imperialism or alien aggression in the last few centuries. They did not know about the developments in India and they were little affected by these developments as they were ruled neither by Kabul nor Delhi, but by Pukhtu.[41] A few people from Swat joined a later assault upon the Barakzai in Hashtnagar (Ashnaghar), but that happened during the second stay of Sayyid Ahmad in Khar. Another point worth mentioning regarding Sayyid Ahmad's claims in his letter to Shah Yaqeenullah,[42] is his statement that the Yusafzais of Buner and Swat were reformed, that the spirit of Islam was renewed in them, and thus they resolved their internal disputes. Yet sources suggest that they had neither reformed nor resolved their disputes.[43] Another interesting point found in the *Waqai* is that Sayyid Rasul Mian visited Sayyid Ahmad after the tour of Swat and asked about the people of Swat. Sayyid Ahmad replied that Swatis were kind hearted and had more potential as compared to the Bunerwal, the later he found more sturdy and better in fighting.[44] Yet Sayyid Ahmad was able to attract a single notable individual, that is, Anbalay Khan, who later joined the Mujahidin in the battle of Utmanzai.[45]

Centre at Panjtar and Invitation to the Neighbouring Princes

After his arrival in the Khudu Khel area of the present Buner district, Sayyid Ahmad made Panjtar his new headquarters and started his work with a fresh zeal. Fateh Khan of Panjtar, the chief of the area, had previously invited Sayyid Ahmad to establish his centre there, but earlier Sayyid Ahmad could not accept an invitation that might damage relations with Khadi Khan. The defeat at Shaidu provided a sound reason to leave Hund. The presence of the Sikhs in the plains and the desertion and subsequent opposition of Yar Muhammad Khan made it difficult for the Mujahidin to stay in Hund. The new centre was located in a strategically better place. It was surrounded by mountains and the narrow pass towards it could be better guarded.[46]

Sayyid Ahmad utilized his time in Panjtar for different agendas. He sent letters and envoys to various rulers of neighbouring states and to tribal chiefs in the North-West Frontier and Afghanistan. He wrote letters to many prominent figures,[47] including Dost Muhammad Khan of Kabul; Sultan Muhammad Khan, ruler of Kohat and Bannu; Said Muhammad Khan, ruler of Hashtnagar (Ashnaghar); Shah Mahmud Durrani, ruler of Herat and his heir apparent Shahzada Kamran; Shah Zaman Durrani, the deposed ruler of Afghanistan in exile at Ludhiana; Nasrullah, ruler of Bokhara; Murad Baig of Qunduz, Sikandar Jah Faulad Jang, ruler of Deccan; Ahmad Ali, the prince of Rampur; and Hafiz-ul-Mulk Rukun-ud-Dawla Muhammad Bahawal Khan Abbasi of Bahawalpur.

Beside the princes, all important chiefs of different areas were addressed. The contents of all letters were the same but with slight variations. All were assured that his sole objective was to oust the oppressors and establish the rule of *sharia*.

None of the contemporary princes was a follower of *sharia* in its true spirit. They had imposed heavy taxation, were unable to protect the masses from the high handedness of officers and robbers, and at times failed to provide basic amenities to the people. None of the rulers was either able or willing to assist him in his cause except for two, the ruler of Tonk and Hindu Rao of Gwalior. Even then, their support was limited to assistance for the families of the Mujahidin who were left behind and for those who travelled through their areas to join the Mujahidin in the Frontier.[48]

One aspect of the movement different from previous struggles of Muslims against foreign or internal threats was its appeal to the general populace. In earlier cases, the princes or intelligentsia appealed to outsiders to come forward and espouse their cause.[49] One should not be confused by Sayyid Ahmad's letters and envoys to different rulers as they were not separate entities from the body of Muslims. Still, his appeal to the Muslims of India was a naïve experiment replicated by other such movements in decades to come. Hindu rulers were not ignored in these letters, yet Sayyid Ahmad's appeal was largely aimed at Muslims. Though Hindus were welcomed when they came to join the Mujahidin, none of the emissaries sent to India for preaching, organizing, or fund raising included the name of a single Hindu.[50]

Management of the Mujahidin

It took time to make Panjtar a proper headquarter for the initial Mujahidin number of seven hundred. There was lack of resources and even the mosque was not available to offer prayer five times a day. A place was allocated for prayer, at first with no boundary wall and roof. With the passage of time it was converted into a proper mosque.[51] The Mujahidin also faced problems initially due to lack of money and food. At times they found nothing to eat, however, as the supply of funds regularized they were provided with proper food.[52] With the arrival of new supporters from India, the Mujahidin were regrouped, and a more formal organization was set up. Each group was responsible for cooking their food and handling other related supplies. Sayyid Ahmad himself worked with ordinary Mujahidin. A separate kitchen was maintained for Sayyid Ahmad and guests were fed from his kitchen. Two suits of clothes were provided to each Mujahid per year, plus other items for making a bed such as cloth and cotton. Two bars of soap were given to each on every Thursday and they would go to the nearby stream to wash their clothes.[53] The Mujahidin initially lived in tents, but they faced problems in summer.[54] Sayyid Ahmad began to make a cottage with his own group, an example followed by all the Mujahidin. Within a very short time huts were prepared by all.[55] The strength of the Mujahidin reached one thousand. One Arab named Muhammad had become Sayyid Ahmad's disciple and joined him, came with him to Raibaraili, and then accompanied him to the North-West Frontier. He was assigned the duty of carrying the flag of a group of Mujahidin during the war.[56]

The Mujahidin were not paid a monthly salary, though they were supplied with clothes, food, and other necessities from the money supplied from India. Only once was a body of troopers recruited on a monthly salary after Mahbub Ali and others returned from Panjtar. Their return stopped the recruitment of men and supply of money for some time, though this was finally restarted with the efforts of Shah Muhammad Yaqoob and Shah Muhammad Ishaq.[57]

Funds were sent to the Mujahidin by means of *hundi*,[58] via Peshawar, but when the Durranis and the Mujahidin developed differences, the channel was shifted to Munara.[59] Santo and Moti, two Hindu brothers of Munara, worked as the agents for the transfer of money. They took 12 per cent and in some cases 16 per cent as service charges.[60] The 12 per cent service charges were called interest by Ayesha Jalal. She asserts that Sayyid Ahmad ignored Islamic injunctions and entered into an agreement with the money lenders of Munara.[61] No doubt, the Hindu money lenders of Munara had lent money to the Mujahidin, but Sayyid Ahmad paid no interest on it. Rather money was borrowed and upon the arrival of *hundi*, they deducted the amount lent, as well as service charges for the *hundi*, and paid the rest to the Mujahidin. Whether such service charges are lawful in Islam or not, they prevail in the modern banking system and banks charge for such services that claim to be following Islamic teaching.

Apart from *hundi* sent by Sayyid Ahmad's disciples from India, from time to time he sent envoys to raise money and bring it to the Frontier. The Mujahidin coming to join Sayyid Ahmad in the Frontier also brought money with them.[62]

The Struggle in Hazara

Panjtar became the most important place during Sayyid Ahmad's stay in the region. It attracted many to come and seek his assistance either against the Sikhs or against local opponents. His help was misused at certain times by different people as he was not fully aware of local politics.

It was during Sayyid Ahmad's stay at Panjtar that several chiefs of Hazara, including Sarbuland Khan Tanoli, Habibullah Khan, Nasir Khan of Battagram, Abdul Ghafur of Agror, and Painda Khan Tanoli of Amb asked him for assistance against the Sikhs, to which Sayyid Ahmad agreed.[63] In the meantime, the representatives of Sultan Najaf Khan and Sultan Zabardast Khan of Muzaffarabad came and asked Sayyid Ahmad for assistance. He assured them that he would send Mujahidin and asked that they should assist them with all possible means. The representative of Sultan Najaf Khan assured Sayyid Ahmad that arrangements for jihad would be easily made once the Mujahidin arrived in their area.[64] Sayyid Ahmad, however, was more inclined to favour Painda Khan of Amb due to his previous struggle against the Sikhs. Sayyid Ahmad had admired his courage many times, though other local chiefs did not like Painda Khan.[65] This was a favourable time for the spread of the Jihad Movement. Many caravans of Mujahidin were arriving from India. The local Pukhtun Khans were supporting them. The Hazara chiefs promised their assistance and the Barakzai brothers, except Yar Muhammad Khan, assured Sayyid Ahmad of their support.[66]

For several reasons, Kashmir was the most important place in Sayyid Ahmad's strategy. The majority of the people residing in the area were Muslims. There were multiple resources and it remained an important province of the Mughals, Durranis, and Sikhs. It had natural defence system, protected by mountains, and Sayyid Ahmad might have thought to make it a permanent centre of his activities, a place where he could utilize all possible resources for the future course of jihad.[67] Sulaiman Shah, the ruler of parts of Chitral, had also written to Sayyid Ahmad that he would take his forces to Kashmir against the Sikhs if Sayyid Ahmad proceeded in that direction. Sayyid Ahmad may have thought that the Sikhs could be defeated with the active support of the local chiefs, and thus the conquest of Kashmir possible. A body of one hundred and fifty Mujahidin was sent under Shah Ismail and Sayyid Muahammad Muqeem of Rampur to Pakhali (Hazara). They stayed for three days with Sayyid Akbar Shah of Sithana. Shah Ismail discussed the whole plan with Sayyid Akbar Shah, who informed Shah Ismail that the local chiefs were not trustworthy, except for Kamal Khan, Abdul Ghafur Khan, Amanullah Khan, and his son Nasir Khan. They next went to Amb, where they were well received by Painda Khan, ruler of Amb. Painda Khan sent his brother Amir Khan to accompany the Mujahidin to Pakhali.[68] Ghulam Rasul Mihr, however, has claimed that the body of the Mujahidin crossed the Indus near Chattar Bai and arrived at Agror after a few days. The leading men of the area, including Ahmad Khan of Pakhali, Haider Shah, and Arsala Khan, visited and took *bai'at* of jihad and *imarat* for Sayyid Ahmad at the hands of Shah Ismail. Shah Ismail wished to organize people for jihad during their stay in the area. The first step was taken by establishing themselves in Shamdara (Klakay, Agror).[69] Mulla Shah Said and Akhunzada Mulla Ismail were sent to preach jihad. Shah Ismail realized within a few days that the local chiefs were not willing to join them against the Sikhs unless assured of success.[70]

The letters of Shah Ismail show that Painda Khan was not willing to join the jihad against the Sikhs, though he had appointed Mulla Ismail Akhunzada to accompany the Mujahidin and had written letters to all the people in his domain to provide food to the Mujahidin. The reason for not joining the Mujahidin might have been caution and a fear of losing his power. He was suspicious of the intention of the Mujahidin as many of his opponents had joined them. Though having no good opinion of Painda Khan, Shah Ismail suggested that the Mujahidin should not break with him due to his strength and influence on the people of the area.[71]

Shah Ismail could not simply concentrate on one issue, jihad, against the Sikhs. The chiefs of the area could not be trusted due to their mutual differences, and the unwillingness of locals to join the Mujahidin. Also a factor was the hasty movement of the Mujahidin to the area, without having done their political homework, and the ongoing lack of material resources.[72] Shah Ismail visited many leading men and tried to convince them to form a confederacy for effective strategy against the Sikhs, but they did not resolve their differences. Painda Khan was not liked by other chiefs of Hazara, who condemned him as untrustworthy. They asked Shah Ismail to severe relations with Painda Khan to gain their assistance.[73] This, of course, was difficult for Shah Ismail. Envoys and preachers were sent in various directions to prepare the people for jihad, but to no avail. Local chiefs suggested that more Mujahidin should be called to Hazara, as the inhabitants of the area would join them if their number was increased.[74]

The Mujahidin were in Shamdara, indecisive of their future plan, when Arsala Khan, nephew of Abdul Ghafur Khan of Agror, came with a body of his tribesmen. He told Shah Ismail that he was going to assist

Habibullah Khan and that those having the courage of jihad and the spirit of helping Muslim brothers should join him. He assured that the finances would be his responsibility. Sayyid Muhammad Muqeem and his group aspired to join him and consequently Shah Ismail allowed them, though unwillingly.[75]

There are authentic and reliable sources for several important episodes of the Jihad Movement, especially in regards to the several skirmishes with the Sikhs in Hazara. Sources are silent over the issue of Arsala Khan and his associates who had gone to assist Habibullah Khan, though it has been discussed that after some time Habibullah Khan recovered his abode along with his son who was previously captured by the Sikhs. Ghulam Rasul Mihr has given an account which might be credible, though he perhaps has based it on mere assumption.[76] A local writer, Sher Bahadur Khan Panni, is silent over the issue, though for other cases he has relied on the *Gazetteer of Hazara District 1883–84.* Both of these writers have confused two different events and have presented them as one.[77] The news of Shah Ismail's arrival in Hazara might have alarmed the Sikhs and consequently they called their scattered forces from various places to face the Mujahidin. The concentration of Sikhs at one place led to the release of Habibullah's son and then skirmishes between them and the Mujahidin. Our findings, like the previous studies, confirm that Sayyid Ahmad's interest was in Kashmir for which the presence of Sikhs in Hazara was the major hurdle. Hari Singh, the governor of Hazara, sent Phola Singh with a force of three thousand men to Dumgala. Shah Ismail decided, after consulting his associates, to attack the Sikh force at night. Sayyid Muhammad Muqeem was sent with a few hundred Mujahidin and locals. The night attack was successful. Many Sikhs were killed, though a few Mujahidin also lost their lives.[78] The Sikhs did not pursue the Mujahidin, though some were injured. While a body of the Mujahidin had gone to Dumgala for a night attack, Shah Ismail and his remaining Mujahidin had fought at another place against the Sikhs. A group of Sikhs came out of Shinkiari, apparently not to attack, but Shah Ismail ordered his companions to prepare for war. In the skirmish that followed, some Sikhs were killed and the rest fled. Shah Ismail and some of his people were injured, but they did not leave the place despite their strength being nominal.[79] The night attack and skirmish at Shinkiari had a positive effect upon the people of Hazara. Nasir Khan requested that Shah Ismail stay at Agror and plan future jihad against the Sikhs.

Shah Ismail also thought to establish a centre and start a series of night attacks on the Sikhs. The Mujahidin went to Agror and selected Ogai (also Oghi, Ogi) as their recruitment and training centre. The plan was to expel the Sikhs from the area with the active assistance of the locals. Many locals joined the Mujahidin and their training was started. But the calling back of Shah Ismail to Panjtar led to the abandonment of the entire scheme. The plea for the return of Shah Ismail to Panjtar was that new groups of Mujahidin had arrived and his services were required.[80]

On his return journey, Shah Ismail met Said Amir Akhunzada of Kotah,[81] a renowned scholar. Said Amir Akhunzada assessed Shah Ismail's knowledge by enquiring about selected scholarly questions. He was satisfied by the most appropriate answers. He returned to his village after a night stay with the Mujahidin.[82] He remained one of the most trusted allies of the Mujahidin for the rest of his life.

The motive behind the recall of Shah Ismail to Panjtar was not clear. One source has claimed that it was for dealing first with the Durrani *sardars*,[83] who had created hurdles in the passage of the Mujahidin through their area. The *Waqai* narrated that some of the Mujahidin caravans stayed for two months in Kandao (pass). The name of the pass is not mentioned but probably it was somewhere between Kohat and Ziarat Kaka Sahib. Sayyid Ahmad sent his associates including Din Muhammad[84] to manage their safe passage. Din Muhammad did this with the active support of the inhabitants of Ziarat Kaka Sahib.[85]

Though very little came out of the first expedition of Shah Ismail to Hazara, the Mujahidin established links in the area. We infer that the real motive of the expedition was to scout the prospects of success in Hazara and Kashmir. Shah Ismail realized that active local support was possible only if the Mujahidin could be numerically strengthened. He had acquired considerable influence after the light skirmishes with the Sikhs. The newly established recruitment and training centre at Ogai was abandoned, though it would attract more people from Hassanzai and Mada Khel tribes, the major tribes of the area. Their active anti-imperialist history of struggle would emerge during the decades to come.[86]

The Mujahidin in Peshawar Valley and Khar (Lower Swat)

During Shah Ismail's expedition to Hazara, about fifteen fresh caravans arrived.[87] The arrival of these recruits strengthened the Mujahidin numerically but not ideologically. Among them was Maulvi Mahbub Ali of Delhi, a prominent scholar of the time and a disciple of Shah Abdul Aziz. He objected to Sayyid Ahmad's food and clothes as well as the declaration of the *imarat*.[88] He was of the opinion that Sayyid Ahmad should neither wear fine clothes nor eat good food, as all the Mujahidin were not fed properly. Sayyid Ahmad tried to convince him otherwise, saying that the clothes he used were sent from India by disciples and that the good food was due to guests and that he would certainly not eat it in the absence of guests.[89] Next Mahbub Ali objected to Sayyid Ahmad's relations with the Durrani chiefs. Mahbub Ali wanted Sayyid Ahmad to act against the Durranis, who were creating troubles for the Mujahidin. Sayyid Ahmad wished to resolve the issue, and even provided a precedent from the life of the Prophet Muhammad (Peace Be Upon Him), but Mahbub Ali was not satisfied. It was said that Sayyid Ahmad asked him to accept the responsibility of the *imarat*, but he declined and left the Mujahidin after a few days and returned to Delhi.[90]

Maulvi Mahbub Ali's parting way was not insignificant. All the earlier biographers of Sayyid Ahmad have criticized Maulvi Mahbub Ali for his failure to bear the hardships of jihad.[91] None of these writers have seriously considered his scholarly objections to the Jihad Movement and the declaration of the *imarat*. Maulvi Mahbub Ali was a prominent scholar long active in preaching jihad. He was a personal friend of both Sayyid Ahmad and Shah Ismail and had led a caravan of the Mujahidin to the Frontier. The simple explanation related by Sayyid Ahmad's followers and earlier biographers on this particular issue is not convincing. Perhaps Maulvi Mahbub Ali upon his arrival in the North-West Frontier realized that the ground for jihad was not prepared because of a lack of communication with the people and inadequate resources. He also believed that the struggle initiated in the name of jihad would not alone resolve the problems of decaying Muslim society. He thought a multi-dimensional struggle was needed. This caution is confirmed by Mauvli Mahbub Ali's attitude towards the uprising of 1857 against the English. He did not sign the *fatwa* issued in favour of the 1857 war, though he did not favour the English. After the English victory in 1858, the authorities tried to reward him with a *jagir* of eleven villages, but he declined it.[92] Waheed-ud-Din Khan wrote that Maulvi Mahbub Ali asked Sayyid Ahmad why he had declared jihad against the Sikhs. Sayyid Ahmad replied that it was based on his *kashaf* and dream. To that, Mahbub Ali replied that a declaration of jihad cannot be done on the basis of a dream and *kashaf*. Rather the Holy Qur'an should be followed as it clearly refers to consultation

(Surah al-Shura: 38) in all matters. The Prophet Muhammad (Peace Be Upon Him) always consulted the Muslims. Sayyid Ahmad, however, did not accept his argument and ultimately Mahbub Ali left for Delhi.[93] This argument negates the narration of Sayyid Ahmad's supporters that Mahbub Ali returned to Delhi as he was unfit to bear the hardships of jihad. We conclude that the differences between the two were mainly scholastic rather than personal.

Maulvi Mahbub Ali was followed by many others who returned to their respective towns in India.[94] The return of these people had a negative impact, as upon their arrival the supply of local men and money was stopped. Sayyid Ahmad sent envoys and preachers to India to restore the flow of money and men. Over time this was achieved through the efforts of Shah Muhammad Ishaq[95] and Muhammad Yaqub. During that period, Sayyid Ahmad recruited a few mercenaries. This was not a positive sign for the jihad as mercenaries lacked the ideological commitment necessary for a movement.[96]

Shah Ismail's return from Hazara was followed by a tour to different parts of the Peshawar Valley. This was suggested by Arbab Bahram Khan, a prominent figure of Tahkal, Peshawar, who had taken *bai'at* at the hands of Sayyid Ahmad.[97] Shah Ismail was sent to Hazara as he had acquaintance with the area and its people. The objectives included the reform of society in all aspects social, religious and political, along with the emphasis on jihad. Socially, the Pukhtuns were considered extravagant at times, spending large amounts on marriages and circumcisions.[98] This periodically placed a burden on their meagre resources. Some of the tribesmen used to take money[99] before giving their daughters, and sisters' hand in marriage, a practice described differently by different observers.[100] Whatever the cause, this delayed or prevented many marriages. Arranging a suitable amount at times delayed circumcisions, something necessary at an early age for religious and medical reasons. The most alarming problem for the Jihad Movement was continued factional fighting among Pukhtuns in the region.[101]

After consultation with his associates, Sayyid Ahmad prepared for travel. He left the wounded and sick at Panjtar, and began another tour of preaching. He stopped first at Shawa, where a local chief Anand Khan hosted the Mujahidin. In Shawa, Sayyid Ahmad met Mansur Khan of Chargulai, a notable chief of the Sudham area.[102] He asked Sayyid Ahmad to visit his village. After a night stay at Machi, the majority of the Mujahidin left for Chargulai. Mansur Khan, the chief of the village, and Mahmud Khan of Hashtnagar (then residing in exile due to a Barakzai rivalry) took *bai'at*. These two never opposed the Mujahidin after their first oath of allegiance.[103] Next the Mujahidin visited Amazai (now called Garhi Kapura), Ismaila, Kalu Khan, Turlandai, and Sheikh Jana.[104] The same message was preached in each place, to follow *sharia* in letter and spirit and prepare oneself for jihad. After a two week period, Sayyid Ahmad returned to Panjtar and planned a new tour. This time, he crossed Shawa, Machi, Chargulai and entered the Baizai area of present Mardan district. In Baizai, he visited Katlang, Lund Khwar, and several other places and then went to Shah Kot.[105] Baizai would be the only place in the Frontier where the Mujahidin were not harmed when Pukhtuns turned against them.

The usual preaching of jihad continued in each place visited by Sayyid Ahmad and many people took *bai'at* at his hand. During his stay at Shah Kot, Inayatullah Khan of Ala Dhand visited Sayyid Ahmad and invited him to his home. Their next halt was at Dargai, from where the Mujahidin went to Khar.[106] A few Mujahidin were left in Dargai along with Pir Khan Moranvi, as Dargai had good pasture for the camels of the Mujahidin. The khans and influential figures of the area came to Khar, met with and took the *bai'at* of repentance at the hands of Sayyid Ahmad.[107] It was during the stay at Khar that Maulana Abdul Hai died a natural death on 24 February 1828.[108] He was buried in the south-east of Khar village, now the main graveyard of Khar. It is known as the Muqbara-e-Maulana Abdul Hai Dehlavi and Dullo Baba.[109] The death of Abdul Hai was a great loss for the Mujahidin as they lost a moderate and trusted leader.[110] Maulana Abdul Hai and Shah Ismail were the ones who had the courage and vision to give counsel to Sayyid Ahmad on important matters.[111] Sayyid Ahmad was a great admirer of Maulana Abdul Hai and kept him in high esteem.[112]

Sayyid Ahmad stayed at Khar for about a year (December 1827–December 1828/January 1829). The sources consulted are silent over the selection of Khar as the new centre, except Ghulam Rasul Mihr who has stated that Sayyid Ahmad intended to deal with the Durrani menace first and so Khar was the best option.[113] But, in our view Sayyid Ahmad had not yet decided about a permanent centre for the Mujahidin. He accepted Khadi Khan's invitation to make Hund the centre of the Mujahidin Movement, then the same was done with Fateh Khan's invitation after the defeat in the battle of Shaidu (1827). He had also sent Shah Ismail to look for prospects at Amb, Mansehra, and Kashmir. Sayyid Ahmad stayed in Khar for a year and then returned to Panjtar. All this indicates that he was indecisive about a permanent seat for the movement. This may also be inferred from his restoration of Peshawar to Sultan Muhammad Khan when it was occupied in October 1830. His major interest remained, ever since his arrival at the Frontier, to make Kashmir a permanent base.[114]

During the Mujahidin's stay at Khar, physical exercises were started, including drill and shooting. Mir Abdul Rahman, Hafiz Imam-ud-Din, Haji Abdullah of Rampur, Mir Imam Ali of Azeemabad, and Sheikh Khwahish Ali of Ghazipur were assigned the duties of training the Mujahidin in different methods of warfare. It was a routine that each evening Sayyid Ahmad was briefed about daily activities and he gave instructions as necessary. After the training, Sayyid Ahmad examined their performance and appreciated their efforts.[115] Besides the training, Sayyid Ahmad toured nearby villages preaching the tenets of Islam and organizing people for jihad. For this a few villages have been mentioned, including Dheri and Mian Brangula, though he might have visited other places as well.[116]

The stay at Khar was important for several reasons. It linked the Mujahidin to Swat. An attempt was made in the direction of Peshawar in the battle of Utmanzai. And, last but not least, Sayyid Ahmad married for the third time. The battle of Utmanzai will be discussed in subsequent pages, but here the issue of his third marriage is important. Sources written by the followers of Sayyid Ahmad, both primary and secondary, emphasize that since Sayyid Ahmad was poisoned, there was no other treatment except marriage. It has also been reported that the permission of his previous wives was sought by sending an envoy to Sindh. There is one main objection to his third marriage, it encouraged the Mujahidin to follow his practice and try to marry local women. This proved a major problem later on.

Earlier, Sayyid Ahmad had sent envoys to different chiefs and princes. In response to his envoys, the Sulaiman Shah of Chitral sent presents, including a girl named Fatima. When Sayyid Ahmad intended to get married, his associates started negotiation for that matter in a Sayyid family of Buner. Later, it was suggested that Fatima was the better option for marriage. After investigation it was found that she belonged to a Sayyid family but was an Ismaili. Sayyid Ahmad married the girl and appointed Mian Ghulam Muhammad of Saharanpur to educate her according to the Sunni doctrine. Mihr asserts that she was a minor and had not been educated in her own Ismaili doctrine, thus Sayyid Ahmad was justified in marrying her.[117] Although the Qur'an allowed a Muslim four wives at a time provided he is able to fulfil the prerequisites, the case of Sayyid Ahmad was different. He already had two wives and it was not difficult to arrange their travel to the Frontier. The only consideration was their security which could be easily arranged. Safety was not precarious as the Mujahidin often passed through the area, carrying arms and money, the more important consideration for the tribesmen. Moreover, the area from Sindh to the Frontier was inhabited by Baloch and Pukhtun tribes and their tradition was not to harm the women of the enemy. Perhaps he had not studied tribal custom, otherwise he would have not kept his family away in Sindh due to safety concerns about travel. The leadership qualities of Sayyid Ahmad will be questioned at another place, but here his indecisive nature is evident in two related matters, the selection of a permanent seat for the movement and the failure to call his family to the Frontier.

The Battle of Utmanzai

One of the most important events during the stay at Khar was the battle of Utmanzai. This had many causes. The decision to attack the Barakzai chiefs of Peshawar was a delicate one. Sayyid Ahmad took up arms against those whose support he needed and wanted to 'liberate' from the Sikh domination. The Barakzai chiefs had taken *bai'at*, but had reservations about the legitimacy of the jihad and especially the declaration of *imarat*. The defection of Yar Muhammad Khan at the battle of Shaidu had caused a major loss to the combined force of the Mujahidin and the Pukhtuns.[118] The Barakzais expelled all from their ancestral lands who had supported the Mujahidin or opposed them for any reason. Those expelled by the Barakzai Sardars included Arbab Bahram Khan, Alam Khan of Utmanzai, and Rasul Khan of Jalala.

The Barakzais also created hurdles for fresh Mujahidin coming to the Frontier. The money lenders of Peshawar were ordered not to accept *hundi* instruments coming from India for the Mujahidin.[119] Moreover, a force had been sent to Shah Kot,[120] to stop Sayyid Ahmad's entering Swat months earlier, but he had changed his route and was not restricted.[121] One day, a few of the expelled chiefs came and asked Sayyid Ahmad for assistance. He did not promise help, but after a few days they came again and informed him that the Barakzai chiefs had sent a force to Utmanzai. The force had crossed the Kabul River and might attack the Mujahidin. On learning this, Sayyid Ahmad called Inayatullah Khan of Ala Dhand, Zaidullah Khan of Khar, Mahmud Khan of Garialai, Mansur Khan of Chargulai, Maulvi Muhammad Hubban of Ghurband,[122] Maulvi Abdul Rahman of Toru, and Mulla Kalim Akhunzada of Khar. He informed them about the plans of the Barakzai force and the grievances of the expelled chiefs, and sought their opinion. After a lengthy discussion the unanimous decision about the Barakzai chiefs was that they have betrayed the Mujahidin cause and revolted against Sayyid Ahmad after taking the oath of allegiance.[123]

After securing the *fatwa*, a plan for action was prepared. It was decided to occupy Peshawar and thus eliminate the Barakzai menace, once and for all. For this purpose, Arbab Bahram Khan, his brother Juma Khan, Mazhar Ali Azeemabadi, Sheikh Wali Muhammad of Phulat, Sheikh Ali Muhammad of Deoband, Maulvi Muhammad Hassan of Rampur, and Maulvi Naseeruddin Manglori were sent to Khyber to get the support of the tribesmen residing there and cut the passage of support from Kabul. They conveyed that the tribesmen had agreed to support the Mujahidin.[124] The Mohmand and Khalil tribesmen, and Sa'adat Khan of Lalpura[125] promised to attack the Barakzai Sardars from the western side. With the sick Mujahidin were left in Khar, the rest were led by Sayyid Ahmad, accompanied by Inayatullah Khan, Zaidullah Khan, Rasul Khan and Alam Khan.[126] The Mujahidin halted at Dargai on the first day. The next halt was at Musa Garhi and then they entered Totai.[127] Local Pukhtun chiefs were invited to assist the Mujahidin against the Barakzai chiefs of Peshawar. The local supporters of Sayyid Ahmad joined him including Anbalay Khan from upper Swat.[128]

After a month stay at Totai, in May 1828, the combined force of the Mujahidin and the local Pukhtuns, numbering about one thousand, left for Utmanzai and arrived there after several halts. They were divided into two groups. One under Shah Ismail was to attack the enemy at night. The other group was kept under Sayyid Ahmad himself to block the enemy's entry to the town of Utmanzai after their defeat. In the event, Shah Ismail captured the Barakzai artillery in the first surprise attack. The Barakzai force was defeated in the battle that continued the next day.[129] But the initial defeat did not lead to the occupation of Peshawar. Due to the defection of Alam Khan of Utmanzai and the tribes of Khyber, and Pir Muhammad Khan's timely assistance to his brothers, the Mujahidin adopted a tactical retreat, and returned to Khar after several stages.[130]

The battle of Utmanzai was important in many ways. First, it was the first action against fellow Muslims. All offensives after that were directed against Muslims. Second, Khar was abandoned after this due to its location. It was difficult for the Mujahidin to take the offensive from there. Third, the defection of locals during the fighting created a serious gap between the Mujahidin and the locals. Finally, the inhabitants of the area stirred enough ill feelings against the Mujahidin that Shah Ismail's mission to Dir was not allowed to cross their area after being sent by Sayyid Ahmad[131] at the request of Dir's chief Ghazan Khan.[132]

After the battle of Utmanzai, Sayyid Ahmad stayed for several months in Khar. There he busied himself in resolving various disputes among the locals, mainly over land. However, Sayyid Ahmad had no authority over the people of the area and could only try to convince the locals to settle issues according to the tenets of Islam. At times the local khans did not agree with the verdict of Sayyid Ahmad and many disputes were left unresolved.[133] One important event of the stay at Khar was the recruitment of mercenaries by the Mujahidin. As discussed earlier, after the return of Maulvi Mahbub Ali of Delhi, the arrival of volunteers from the mainland India stopped. Some associates of Sayyid Ahmad requested that mercenaries be recruited to increase the number of the Mujahidin. Sayyid Ahmad agreed and allowed Akhun Zahurullah to enrol two hundred. Newly recruited Muslims from Punjab joined the Mujahidin. After some time the Mujahidin realized that the mercenaries were a burden and disbanding them was proposed. Sayyid Ahmad agreed to the proposal and did so. Some of them joined the Mujahidin as volunteers, while the rest returned to their homes.[134] It is relevant to discuss the recruitment of these mercenaries. Different reasons explain this recruitment from the Punjab. First, the Mujahidin might have wanted to ensure a show of strength. Second, it was already taken for granted that all the Pukhtuns were their allies. Since this time, many militant and other religious organizations have appealed to Pukhtuns on religious grounds as they were thought to be easily enlisted.[135]

After a year's stay, it was realized that Khar was not a suitable place to be kept as the centre for the Mujahidin. They had launched a single offensive and failed to achieve their goal. The khans of lower and upper Swat had not taken the oath of allegiance for jihad and did not consider themselves bound to assist the Mujahidin. The verdicts of Sayyid Ahmad were not accepted in many cases, as they were by Fateh Khan and others in the Peshawar Valley. The people of Swat also had more internal disputes, compared with the people of the Peshawar Valley, due to lack of a central authority. A few of Sayyid Ahmad's associates asked him to go back to Panjtar. They were already invited by both Fateh Khan of Panjtar and Ashraf Khan of Zaida. Upon the chiefs' invitation and his associates' suggestion, Sayyid Ahmad decided to return to Panjtar on the pretext of taking a decisive action against the Barakzai chiefs. The Peshawar Valley and especially the present Khudu Khel and Swabi areas were considered favourable for the growth of the Jihad Movement.[136] Arguably, abandoning Panjtar and staying at Khar was the direct outcome of Mahbub Ali's return to India. As a result, the arrival of new Mujahidin and money from India had stopped. The Mujahidin felt insecure at Panjtar due to its proximity with Peshawar and the Sikh territory and it was imperative they find a suitable centre. It is evident from the preceding events that Sayyid Ahmad started the Swat tour after his defeat in the battle of Shaidu and came to Panjtar after the arrival of volunteers from India. Khar, however, did not prove a fruitful place for the Mujahidin and the invitations of the two chiefs were considered a blessing, which accelerated their decision to go back to Panjtar.

Notes and References

1. Kakakhel, Sayyid Bahadar Shah Zafar. nd. *Pushtun: Tarikh kay Ayenay Mein*. Peshawar: University Book Agency. p. 691. Henceforth, Kakakhel, *Pushtun*.
2. Khan, Nawab Muhammad Wazir. 2007. *Waqai Sayyid Ahmad Shahid*. Lahore: Sayyid Ahmad Shahid Academy. pp. 1145–46. Henceforth, Khan, *Waqai Sayyid Ahmad*.
3. Such oath is common in Sufi orders mainly for repentance of past sins and to pledge to follow *sharia* in the future.
4. Nasiri, Alim. 1995. *Shahnama-e-Balakot: Tahrik-e-Jihad ki Manzoom Dastan*, vol. I. Lahore: Idara Mabu'at-e-Sulaimani. p. 209. Henceforth, Nasiri, *Shahnama*, vol. I.
5. Khan, *Waqai Sayyid Ahmad*, p. 1148.
6. It is evident even today that during tribal feuds, people of conflicting tribes cannot pass the area of the opponent tribe.
7. The present administrative Buner district can be accessed by road from three sides. From south it is accessible from the Swabi-Mardan main road near Salim Khan Lakhtai and one enters Buner after travelling about 12 kilometres northwards. From the southwest it is accessible from the Rustam side in present district Mardan, one enters the Chamla Valley after crossing the Ambela Pass. From the Swat or north-western side one passes Barikot and enters Buner after crossing the Karakar pass.
8. Khan, *Waqai Sayyid Ahmad*, pp. 1149–50.
9. A mountainous range forms the virtual frontier between Buner and Swat.
10. One source has narrated that it was inhabited by Sha'afis without naming the village. Khan, *Waqai Sayyid Ahmad*, p. 1150. Ghulam Rasul Mihr has written the name Nawagai. Mihr, Ghulam Rasul. nd. *Sayyid Ahmad Shahid*. Lahore: Sh. Ghulam Ali. p. 394. Henceforth, Mihr, *Sayyid Ahmad*. In visiting the area we found Nawagai a small village of about 25 households near Bari Kot. It should not be confused with the Nawagai of Buner, which is located in Chamla Valley, and Nawagai of Bajaur Agency.
11. Mihr, *Sayyid Ahmad*, pp. 393–94.
12. Nasiri, *Shahnama*, vol. I, pp. 211–12.

13. Khan, *Waqai Sayyid Ahmad*, pp. 1151–55. Ouch is divided into two parts: eastern—*sharqi* and western—*gharbi*.

14. Sithanavi, Sayyid Abdul Jabbar Shah. 2011. *Kitab-ul-Ibrat: Subah Sarhad wa Afghanistan ki char saw sala Tarikh 1500–1900*, vol. I. Islamabad: Porab Academy. p. 384. Henceforth, Sithanavi, *Kitab-ul-Ibrat*.

15. Abdul Hamid Khan *risaldar*, met Sayyid Ahmad in Tonk and took *bai'at*. He was later appointed commander of troops and was sent in different directions either to punish or pressure the tribesmen in Peshawar Valley.

16. Khan, *Waqai Sayyid Ahmad*, pp. 1153–54; Mihr, *Sayyid Ahmad*, pp. 396–97.

17. Bandai is located in Nipki Khel area on the main road which connects Swat with Peshawar Valley.

18. Khan, *Waqai Sayyid Ahmad*, p. 1155.

19. The main and sister city of Saidu Sharif, headquarters of the present administrative district Swat. Locally it is called Mingawara. The *Waqai* has written the name Magori. Khan, *Waqai Sayyid Ahmad*, p. 1155.

20. Nadvi, Sayyid Abul Hassan Ali. nd. *Tarikh-e-Dawat wa Azeemat: Seerat-e-Sayyid Ahmad Shahid*, vol. II. Karachi: Majlis Nashriyat. pp. 14–15. Henceforth, Nadvi, *Sirat-i-Sayyid Ahmad*.

21. We could not find any more information about the person.

22. The Barailvi movement was started much later by Ahmad Raza Khan (1856–1921).

23. Swat did not have any organized government in those days and all tribes lived independently.

24. The *Waqai* has written it Khaw'aja Khel. Khan, *Waqai Sayyid Ahmad*, p. 1164. We found that some local traditions also refer to Khaw'aja Khela, which later changed to Khwaza Khela.

25. The *Waqai* has named him Shah Kator and referred to his wars against the non-Muslims and Rawafidh—Shias. Khan, *Waqai Sayyid Ahmad*, p. 1164. We consulted local sources for the history of Chitral and found that the Mehtar did not fight any sectarian war as the first sectarian clash in Chitral dates back to the colonial era. Murtaza, Ghulam and Mirza Muhammad Ghufran. 1962. *Nai Tarikh-e-Chitral*. Peshawar: Latif Brothers. Giving sectarian colour to political wars is an Indian phenomenon which the Mujahidin introduced during their stay in the area. Sulaiman Shah was not ruler of Chitral but of a part of it and Chitral proper was ruled by one of his cousins.

26. Kashkar or Qashqar were names used for Chitral by the people of neighbouring Dir, Swat and Nooristan (Afghanistan). Some contemporary people of Sayyid Ahmad have written it Kashghar and people in modern times have confused it with Kashghar/eastern Turkistan in southern China.

27. Khan, *Waqai Sayyid Ahmad*, pp. 1165–66.

28. Mihr, *Sayyid Ahmad*, p. 402.

29. We could not find Khonay or Khoni in the vicinity of Khwaza Khela though there are villages or Muhallahs with similar names in Swat. Some of them are either new developments or were never visited by Sayyid Ahmad.

30. Asala is located at some distance from Khwaza Khela on the Mingora-Kalam road and presently divided in two parts, Bara Asala and Koza Asala.

31. Durush Khela is written Durasht Khel in a contemporary source. Khan, *Waqai Sayyid Ahmad*, p. 1166. Its original name was Darwesh Khela but with the passage of time it changed to Durush Khela.

32. Khan, *Waqai Sayyid Ahmad*, p. 1167. The *Waqai* has recorded Sakhra but we did not find details of the route adopted by the Mujahidin as Sakhra is located far off in a side valley near the border of the present District Upper Dir, Khyber Pakhtunkhwa, Pakistan. There is a Sarkhana, now part of Bara Bandai in Nikpi Khel/Tehsil Kabal, though earlier it was considered a separate entity. Sarkhana is the abode of Sayyids. Mihr has written a name Khanjra which we did not find in that area.

33. Khan, *Waqai Sayyid Ahmad*, p. 1169.

34. Information collected for this study in the field survey.

35. Khan, *Waqai Sayyid Ahmad*, pp. 1166–71; Mihr, *Sayyid Ahmad*, pp. 399–400.

36. Khan, *Waqai Sayyid Ahmad*, p. 1171.

37. Ibid., pp. 1171–72; Mihr, *Sayyid Ahmad*, pp. 399–400.

38. Nadvi, *Sirat-e-Sayyid Ahmad*, vol. II, pp. 16–17.

39. Thanesari, Muhammad Jaffar. 1969. *Maktubat-e-Sayyid Ahmad Shahid aur Kala Pani*. Karachi: Nafees Academy. pp. 68–69. Henceforth, Thanesri, *Maktubat*.

40. Nadvi, *Sirat-e-Sayyid Ahmad*, vol. II, pp. 17–18.

41. For detail, see Sultan-i-Rome. 2008. *Swat State (1915–1969): From Genesis to Merger; An Analysis of Political, Administrative, Socio-Political, and Economic Developments*. Karachi: Oxford University Press.

42. Thanesri, *Maktubat*, pp. 68–69.

43. Sultan-i-Rome. 2009. *Swat: A Critical Analysis*. http://ipcs.org/pdf_file/issue/1542140255RP18-Rome-Swat.pdf (accessed in February 2009). pp. 5–6.

44. Khan, *Waqai Sayyid Ahmad*, p. 1177.

45. It is interesting to note that the majority recruits came from upper Swat in the post 9/11 wave of militancy in Malakand Division.

46. Nadvi, *Sirat-e-Sayyid Ahmad*, vol. II, pp. 19–20.

47. Thanesri, *Maktubat*, pp. 8 ff; Mihr, *Sayyid Ahmad*, pp. 403–6.

48. Mihr, *Sayyid Ahmad*, pp. 405–6.

49. This was practiced in all those lands where Muslims ruled but were in the minority or were at a distance from the centres of other Muslim powers. The Spanish Muslims appealed to the North-African Muslim rulers to assist them against the Christians of Spain and Portugal. The Muslims of the subcontinent appealed to the ruler of Afghanistan to assist them against Maratha or Hindu domination.

50. They resemble with the Tablighi Movement started by Maulvi Muhammad Ilyas (1885–1944) of Delhi and has an extensive network across the world. The workers of the Tablighi Movement also do not preach Islam to the non-Muslims but accept into the fold of Islam if one comes by choice. See Haq, Muhammad Anwarul. 1972. *The Faith Movement of Mawlana Muhammad Ilyas*. London: Allen and Unwin.

51. Mihr, *Sayyid Ahmad*, p. 408.

52. Ibid., p. 407.

53. Khan, *Waqai Sayyid Ahmad*, pp. 1185–87.

54. It was the first summer of the Mujahidin in the North-West Frontier as they had arrived in October 1826 and were not familiar with living in tents.

55. Khan, *Waqai Sayyid Ahmad*, pp. 1191–92.

56. Ibid., p. 1399.

57. Mihr, *Sayyid Ahmad*, pp. 434–35.

58. *Hundi*—letters and credit, one of the oldest forms of money sending in which payment is made to the receiver by showing a receipt only. The modern transaction via banks is the developed form of *hundi* but this involved risk as it could be declined payment.

Such receipts could be lost or damaged in rain and thus there was little chance to recover the amount.

59. Munara, a small village situated on the north-western bank of the Indus is located in present district Swabi, Khyber Pakhtunkhwa. It was a flourishing business centre in those days due to its proximity with Hazro on the south-eastern bank of Indus. Munara was destroyed in a flood in 1841. After the British occupation of the North-West Frontier, colonial authorities developed a rail and road system and thus the old routes and trade centres lost their previous importance.

60. Khan, *Waqai Sayyid Ahmad*, pp. 1115–19.

61. Jalal, Ayesha. 2008. *Partisans of Allah: Jihad in South Asia*. Massachusetts: Harvard University Press. p. 93. Henceforth, Jalal, *Partisans of Allah*.

62. Mihr, *Sayyid Ahmad*, p. 436.

63. Nasiri, *Shahnama*, vol. I, pp. 220–21.

64. Khan, *Waqai Sayyid Ahmad*, pp. 1192–95.

65. Nadvi, *Sirat-e-Sayyid Ahmad*, vol. II, pp. 23–24.

66. Mihr, *Sayyid Ahmad*, p. 414.

67. Ahmad, Qeyamuddin. 1979. *The Wahabi Movement in India*. Islamabad: National Book Foundation. p. 51. Henceforth, Ahmad, *The Wahabi Movement*.

68. Khan, *Waqai Sayyid Ahmad*, pp. 1195–97.

69. Akhunzada Mulla Ismail joined Shah Ismail at Sithana and has been praised by the latter in his letters to Sayyid Ahmad.

70. Mihr, *Sayyid Ahmad*, pp. 419–20.

71. Nadvi, *Sirat-e-Sayyid Ahmad*, vol. II, pp. 38–39.

72. Mihr, *Sayyid Ahmad*, p. 420.

73. Nasiri, *Shahnama*, vol. I, pp. 226–27.

74. Mihr, *Sayyid Ahmad*, p. 420.

75. Nadvi, *Sirat-e-Sayyid Ahmad*, vol. II, pp. 43–44.

76. He has written that the Sikhs became alarmed with the coming of the Mujahidin in the area and in anticipation concentrated in one place to counter them and thus the abode of Habibullah was left and his son was released. Mihr, *Sayyid Ahmad*, p. 424.

77. Panni, Sher Bahadur Khan. 2006. *Tarikh-e-Hazara*. Lahore: Maktaba Jamal. pp. 143–44. Henceforth, Panni, *Tarikh-e-Hazara*.

78. Khan, *Waqai Sayyid Ahmad*, pp. 1198–1200.

79. Mihr, *Sayyid Ahmad*, pp. 426–27.

80. Khan, *Waqai Sayyid Ahmad*, pp. 1202–3.

81. Kotah is located about 16 kilometres to the east of present Swabi town. Said Amir Akhunzada was the ancestor of Sahibzada Abdul Qaiyum, the founder of Islamia College Peshawar. Said Amir Akhunzada remained an active supporter of the Mujahidin Movement throughout his life.

82. Khan, *Waqai Sayyid Ahmad*, pp. 1201–5; Nasiri, *Shahnama*, vol. I, pp. 239–41.

83. Ahmad, *The Wahabi Movement*, pp. 50–51.

84. One of the major contributors to *Waqai Sayyid Ahmad*.

85. Khan, *Waqai Sayyid Ahmad*, pp. 1202–5.

86. From 1852–53 onward, British forces were sent to the area many times. The Hassanzai, Mada Khel, and other tribes offered resistance despite meager resources. The British never fully controlled their area. See Nevill, H. L. 1977. *Campaigns on the North-West Frontier*. Lahore: Sang-e-Meel Publications; Wylly, Harold C. 2003. *From the Black Mountains to Waziristan*. Lahore: Sang-e-Meel Publications.

87. These caravans were led by Sayyid Ahmad Ali, nephew of Sayyid Ahmad, Maulana Inayat Ali Azeemabadi, Maulvi Qamar-ud-Din, Baqir Ali, Usman Ali, Maulana Mazhar Ali Azeemabadi, Maulvi Khurram Ali Balhori, Maulvi Abdul Quddus Kanpuri, Sayyid Muhammad Ali Rampuri, Maulvi Abdullah Amrohi, Hafiz Qutb-ud-Din Phulati, Maulvi Mahbub Ali Dehlavi, Hakim Muhammad Ashraf Dehlavi, Meeran Shah Narnawli and Maulvi Abdul Haq. Nadvi, *Sirat-e-Sayyid Ahmad*, vol. II, p. 52.

88. Mallick, Azizur Rahman. 1977. *British Policy and the Muslims in Bengal, 1757-1856*. Dacca: Bangla Academy. p. 199. Henceforth, Mallick, *British Policy*. Mihr has written on the authority of *Manzurat-ul-Su'ada* that Maulvi Mahbub Ali had objected to Sayyid Ahmad's *imarat*, to which Sayyid Ahmad replied that it was a responsibility laid on him against his wishes. Mihr, *Sayyid Ahmad*, pp. 433–34.

89. Nadvi, *Sirat-e-Sayyid Ahmad*, vol. II, pp. 53–55.

90. Mihr, *Sayyid Ahmad*, pp. 434–35.

91. Khan, *Waqai Sayyid Ahmad*. pp. 1210–15; Mihr, *Sayyid Ahmad*, pp. 434–35; Nasiri, *Shahnama*, vol. I, pp. 243–47; Nadvi, *Sirat-e-Sayyid Ahmad*, vol. II, pp. 55–56.

92. Thanavi, Ashraf Ali. nd. *Arwah-e-Salasa: Yanay Hakayat-e-Awlia, Majmu'a-e-Rasail*. Lahore: Maktaba Rahmania. p. 391. Henceforth, Thanavi, *Arwah-e-Salasa*.

93. Mahbub Ali, *Tarikh-e-Aima Ummat* as quoted in Khan, Waheed-ud-Din. 2005. *Din wa Shariat: Din-e-Islam ka aik Fikri Mutale'a*. Lahore: Dar-ul-Tazkeer. p. 239.

94. Nadvi, *Sirat-e-Sayyid Ahmad*, vol. II, p. 57.

95. Shah Muhammad Ishaq was the student and grandson (daughter's son) of Shah Abdul Aziz. Before his death, Shah Abdul Aziz appointed him Principal of Madrassah Rahimiah. He rendered great services of disseminating and propagating the science of Hadith. He translated the *Mishkatul Masabeeh* into Urdu, which, at his instance, was transformed into a commentary by his student Qutubuddin Khan, and is known as *Mazahir-e Haq*. He migrated to Hijaz in 1841 and died there after a few years.

96. Mihr, *Sayyid Ahmad*, p. 435.

97. Arbab Bahram Khan, of Tahkal (Peshawar), then residing in a village Mir Ali, was the most trusted Pukhtun chief supporting Sayyid Ahmad. He rendered great services for the cause and was killed in 1831 at Balakot with Sayyid Ahmad.

98. Qadir, Altaf. 2006. 'Haji Sahib of Turangzai and his Reform Movement in the North-West Frontier Province'. *Journal of the Pakistan Historical Society*. Karachi, vol. 54, no. 3, pp. 85–95.

99. Called *walwar*, also *da sar rupai*, money taken before the marriage of a daughter or sister. Some people called it the selling of females. This was usually spent on the marriage and related arrangements.

100. According to the Islamists it was *mahar-e-mua'jal*, dowry taken before marriage. Others say that they wanted to know the capacity of the male to be capable to earn enough money to support a family.

101. Nasiri, *Shahnama*, vol. I, p. 250.

102. Sudham falls in the present district Mardan. It includes Rustam, Khairabad, Chargulai and other villages between Shahbazgarhi and Buner in present day Khyber Pakhtunkhwa.

103. Khan, *Waqai Sayyid Ahmad*, pp. 1253–55.

104. Mihr, *Sayyid Ahmad*, p. 439.

105. Shah Kot is to the east of Palai (popular for orange production). Before the construction of the metallic road and rail track by colonial authorities, it was one of the most

important stops in the journey to Swat. It should not be confused with Sakha Kot, situated several kilometres to the south of Dargai.

106. Khar is situated at a distance of 3 kilometres, Dheri 6 kilometres, Jolagram 7.5 kilometres to the west of Batkhela (Malakand Protected Area commonly known as Malakand Agency, Khyber Pakhtunkhwa). Mian Bramgola is 10 kilometres to the north-west, across the river Swat. Many people confused it with Khar, headquarters of Bajawar Agency.

107. Khan, *Waqai Sayyid Ahmad*, pp. 1255–57.

108. Ahmad, *The Wahabi Movement*, p. 51. Mihr, *Sayyid Ahmad*, p. 441.

109. We found it in personal visits to the area.

110. Usmani, Qamar Ahmad. 1983. *Baraili say Balakot: Tazkirah Mujahid-e-Kabir Hazrat Sayyid Ahmad Shahid Barailvi*. Lahore: Idara Islamiyat. p. 196. Henceforth, Usmani, *Baraili say Balakot*.

111. Nasiri, *Shahnama*, vol. I, pp. 256–57.

112. Khan, *Waqai Sayyid Ahmad*, p. 1258.

113. Mihr, *Sayyid Ahmad*, p. 440.

114. Ahmad, *The Wahabi Movement*, p. 53.

115. Khan, *Waqai Sayyid Ahmad*, pp. 1266–68.

116. Ibid., pp. 1256–57; Mihr, *Sayyid Ahmad*, p. 440.

117. Nasiri, *Shahnama*, vol. I, pp. 260–61; Mihr, *Sayyid Ahmad*, pp. 445–46.

118. Ahmad, *The Wahabi Movement*, p. 49.

119. Khan, *Waqai Sayyid Ahmad*, p. 1281.

120. Nadvi has written Shah Kot in the main text but said in a footnote that it might be Sakha Kot. Nadvi, *Sirat-e-Sayyid Ahmad*, vol. II, p. 67. It was Shah Kot as has been clarified earlier, an important place on the old route from the plains to Swat. It still exists but due to the changing routes has lost its previous importance.

121. Mihr, *Sayyid Ahmad*, p. 448.

122. Ghwarband is located in present district Shangla.

123. Khan, *Waqai Sayyid Ahmad*, pp. 1282–83.

124. There is an oral tradition that those tribesmen agreed to support the Mujahidin as the Barakzai chiefs had stopped their *majib*—annual allowance.

125. Sa'adat Khan of Lalpura lived on the western side of the Khyber pass and offered obedience when Sayyid Ahmad was on his way to Peshawar in 1826.

126. Khan, *Waqai Sayyid Ahmad*, pp. 1283–84.

127. Ibid., p. 1284. There is no Musa Garhi in that area. From Dargai, one taking the old route to Bajawar and Dir, first comes Musa Miana at a distance of 3 kilometres on the western side. Upon turning to the north, comes Garhi Usmani Khel at a distance of 7/8 kilometres from Dargai. Further north-west comes Totai Kalay (village). Further in the same direction come Mazaray Baba, a village known by the name of the saint buried there. The old route is still jeepable. During the course of this study we travelled on the same route until Mazaray Baba. Ghulam Rasul Mihr was wrongly informed that Usman Khel did not exist anymore. He has written it Usman Khel but locally it is called Usmani Khel. Mihr, *Sayyid Ahmad*, footnote, p. 450.

128. Khan, *Waqai Sayyid Ahmad*, p. 1284.

129. Nadvi, *Sirat-e-Sayyid Ahmad*, vol. II, pp. 72–78; Ahmad, *The Wahabi Movement*, p. 51.

130. Khan, *Waqai Sayyid Ahmad*, pp. 1300–1303. During the battle of Utmanzai, the episode of Raja Ram has been reported, but has been misunderstood by some, including

Ayesha Jala in her *Partisans of Allah*. Raja Ram, a Rajput of Beswara (Rajputana) had joined the Mujahidin and migrated to the North-West Frontier. Sources are not clear how or why he joined them, but it is evident from his record that he was a reliable person. He was asleep when Sayyid Ahmad retreated and upon awakening he realized that all had left. He fired several shots from the artillery and caused considerable damage to the Barakzai force.

131. Khan, *Waqai Sayyid Ahmad*, pp. 2007–8. Mihr has wrongly written Bajawar. Mihr, *Sayyid Ahmad*, pp. 664–66.

132. Khan, *Waqai Sayyid Ahmad*, pp. 2007–8.

133. Ibid., pp. 1310–13.

134. Mihr, *Sayyid Ahmad*, pp. 456–57; Khan, *Waqai Sayyid Ahmad*, pp. 1316–18; Nadvi, *Sirat-e-Sayyid Ahmad*, vol. II, pp. 80–81.

135. The issue will be discussed further in this study.

136. Nasiri, *Shahnama*, vol. II, pp. 280–81.

5

The Rise of the Mujahidin in the Frontier

Establishment of Headquarters at Panjtar and Renewal of *Bai'at*

Sayyid Ahmad spent about two years (March 1827–January 1829), after his defeat at the battle of Shaidu, in search of a suitable place for a permanent headquarters. During this time, he stayed in Panjtar and in Khar. After studying the situation, he was convinced of the strategic importance of Panjtar and decided to make it his headquarters. It had a strategic location[1] and Sayyid Ahmad also had the support of Fateh Khan, the chief of Panjtar. The second stay in Panjtar witnessed a very important transitional period for the Jihad Movement. It was announced that old social institutions were to be replaced in the name of *sharia*, which created problems for him. Second, important battles were fought with local opponents of the Mujahidin and Sikhs. Panjtar remained the Mujahidin's headquarters for the rest of their stay in the Peshawar Valley. Panjtar served as the Mujahidin headquarters after the 1831 battle of Balakot and the successors of Fateh Khan remained their supporters for a considerable time.

On his return journey from Khar to Panjtar, Sayyid Ahmad was well received by Fateh Khan and the rest of Khudu Khels. This was followed by a series of tours and expeditions in the nearby villages. In some cases the Mujahidin were sent to preach the tenets of Islam along with show of force. Sometimes they were sent to settle disputes among warring factions of the area.[2] After discussions with his associates, including the local *ulama*, *khans*, and other dignitaries, Sayyid Ahmad decided to renew the oath of allegiance from the inhabitants of the area. Such an oath was previously secured by Sayyid Ahmad on 10 January 1827, but his defeat at the battle of Shaidu (February 1827) postponed the imposition of *sharia*.

Sayyid Ahmad and colleagues had considered the issue before his return from Khar, but due to the unsettled environment, it was not implemented.[3]

The narration of *Waqai* reflects that the renewal of the *bai'at* was actually meant to justify action against Khadi Khan for which Sayyid Ahmad needed local support. It was said that Sayyid Ahmad called on Shah Ismail, Sayyid Ahmad Ali, Arbab Bahram Khan, Maulvi Muhammad Hassan and Fateh Khan. He told Fateh Khan that the Mujahidin had come to their country for the purpose of jihad, but that some locals like Yar Muhammad Khan and Khadi Khan were obstructing their way. He sought the advice of all present on the occasion. Fateh Khan suggested that all local *ulama* and *khans* should be called for consultation.

A day was fixed, 6 February 1829, and Fateh Khan invited all dignitaries to Panjtar. It was a *ijtama'a-e-a'am* at Panjtar which was attended by more than thousand local *ulama* and *khans*, including Khadi Khan, Ashraf Khan, and Fateh Khan.[4] After feeding the assembly, Shah Ismail asked them to offer the Friday prayer with the Mujahidin. Sayyid Ahmad delivered a speech after the prayer with the assistance of his translator Kabul Akhunzada.[5] Sayyid Ahmad justified his migration to the North-West Frontier by stating that jihad for the revival of Islam was his only objective and that he was invited by their kith and kin as they were fed up of the Sikhs' atrocities.[6] On their invitation he migrated to their country and they tendered the oath of allegiance.

Sayyid Ahmad stopped his speech at this point and the audience was left to Shah Ismail to further talk about obedience to the *imam*. Verses from the Holy Qur'an were recited to convince them about the importance of obeying the *amir*.[7] A lengthy discussion followed. It was decided that imposition of *sharia* was required. All present offered their allegiance to Sayyid Ahmad. The three leading *khans*, Khadi Khan, Ashraf Khan, and Fateh Khan, submitted a joint oath in written form to the effect that they would replace local traditions with *sharia* in their respective principalities. They would not practice the prevailing evils of alcohol, family feuds, usury, polygamy[8] and the distribution of the widows and children (daughters) of the deceased among brothers.[9] One of the sources stated that Khadi Khan advised Sayyid Ahmad not to take action in haste for implementing *sharia* as the Pukhtuns were not yet ready for a drastic change in a centuries-old social and political fabric. However, Sayyid Ahmad did not pay heed to this advice.[10]

An interesting outcome from this gathering was the securing of a written *fatwa* from local *ulama*[11] regarding the status of a person who would not obey orders of the Amir-ul-Mominin, that is, Sayyid Ahmad.[12]

The *fatwa* was not approved by Khadi Khan and he bluntly told Sayyid Ahmad that he would not follow the verdict of the *mullas*. Both exchanged harsh words, but the *Waqai*'s narration does not reflect that Khadi Khan used derogatory language against Sayyid Ahmad, despite the fact that the Sayyid used very harsh words against him.[13] The *Waqai* has indicated that this *bai'at* was just renewal of the previous one,[14] though some sources have suggested that it was a separate *bai'at* with wider objectives.[15]

Several factors contributed to the imposition of *sharia* and the renewal of the *bai'at*. Sayyid Ahmad and his associates realized that without a paramount authority, the Pukhtuns could not be organized for jihad.[16] It had been proved in the night attack on Akora Khattak, the attack on Hazro, the battle of Shaidu, and the battle of Utmanzai. On all these occasions, the Pukhtuns had acted as an unorganized mass. The factional fighting and mutual enmity could not be stopped within the existing system. There were many instances where local chiefs fought each other that caused heavy losses to each side. Prevailing vices could not be eliminated except in the name of *sharia*, which Sayyid Ahmad thought would be obeyed in the fear of Allah. Yet, though, thousands of people committed in individual capacities to follow *sharia* it could not change the system.[17] Pukhtuns could not be compelled to follow the orders of an individual other than their own chief, unless they could be educated according to the tenets of Islam.[18]

The Imposition of *Sharia* and Local Response

The renewal of *bai'at* was followed by a series of announcements on the replacing of old practices and institutions with new ones framed by *sharia*. A new judicial regime was introduced. The department of justice was to adjudicate cases according to the teaching of *sharia*. The first step saw *quza* appointed in Khudu Khel territory, and then later, as the Mujahidin's rule was extended, judges were appointed in other areas of Peshawar Valley.[19] As *Quza* were appointed in different localities, each was supported by several Mujahidin for adjudicating cases. Maulvi Muhammad Hubban was appointed *qazi-ul-quza*[20] with his seat at Panjtar. He visited areas in the Mujahidin's jurisdiction and checked the performance of his lieutenants. Sayyid Muhammad Mir was appointed *qazi* of Panjtar and its vicinity.[21] Mulla Said Amir was *qazi* of Kotah and the rest of the Utmanzai area. Mulla Safiullah was the *qazi* of Shawa.[22] Pukhtuns were not accustomed to the new judicial mechanism as their disputes had been resolved by their respective village council *jargahs*. Pukhtun chiefs and *khans* were thus deprived of influence and their previous status.

A separate department of accountability was established under Mulla Qutb-ud-Din Ningarhari. He was responsible for ensuring attendance at congregational prayers, protecting public morality, forbidding adultery and ban of alcohol, and any other actions against the tenets of Islam.[23] It was said that the people of respective villages came out and reported that all residents offered prayer five times daily, all observe fasting, there was no adultery practiced, and the like.[24] The imposition of *sharia* abolished the practice of *panah*, one of the major pillars of Pukhtu. People would take shelter in other villages after committing an offence against a strong opponent, and those who provided shelter were responsible for their protection. With the imposition of *sharia*, this practice was altogether abolished with the introduction of the department of accountability.[25] No doubt, the trial of an offender was required, but abolishing a centuries-old institution with a single stroke was not a wise decision.

During the establishment of such new institutions, the incident of Manerai occurred. The residents of Manerai had ousted some of their people and seized their property decades back due to a clan feud. The latter tried to reoccupy their property with the help of supporters but failed, despite the killing of many people from both sides. With the establishment of Sayyid Ahmad's *khilafat*, the aggrieved party approached him for assistance. He called chiefs of the area together, including Fateh Khan, Ashraf Khan, and Khadi Khan. He ordered the return of the property to the rightful owners, but the offenders did not comply. Sayyid Ahmad, therefore, sent a force and, unable to withstand the Mujahidin, the offender vacated the illegal possession.[26] Sources have said that Khadi Khan was not happy with the verdict of Sayyid Ahmad. Khadi Khan wanted to maintain the status quo as the offending possessors were his clients.[27]

In the process of establishing new institutions, a *bait-ul-mal* was established and taxes and fines became sources of income. The payment of *ushar*, a tithe of agricultural production, was made obligatory, with payments going to the *bait-ul-mal*. Earlier there was no concept of *ushar*[28] and people paid a small amount to the ruler through their chiefs. *Tahsildars* were appointed to administer that. Since the Mujahidin knew that it would be difficult to collect *ushar*, a group under Maulvi Muhammad Hubban, accompanied by Shah Ismail and Abdul Hamid Khan, were sent to collect it.[29] The tax paid to earlier rulers was nominal compared to the *ushar*. During Sikhs rule, agricultural land was usually given on lease and hence the government has no concern with the common people unless they declined to pay the tax altogether.[30]

The replacement of these traditional practices with new claims disgusted the Pukhtuns. With the exception of a few, none was ready for such drastic changes in their traditions. The first among them to express his anger was Khadi Khan[31] of Hund. He did not like the interference of the Mujahidin in resolving the dispute in Manerai. Moreover, Sayyid Ahmad's preference for Fateh Khan of Panjtar and Ashraf Khan was disliked by him. All sources agree that Khadi Khan created hurdles for the new Mujahidin coming via Hund, who at times were looted by his men.[32]

The Sikh Attack on Panjtar and the Expansion of the Mujahidin's Rule

The attack on Panjtar by Sikhs under General Ventura[33] was an important episode during the Jihad Movement.[34] Under Sikh rule, the revenue of the areas was usually collected by the leading *khans* from cultivators, but khans were to present a horse, a falcon and hounds as symbol of allegiance to the Lahore *darbar*.[35] General Ventura was sent by the Lahore *darbar* to collect the revenue from the Pukhtun chiefs. Upon his arrival at Hazro, he ordered the chiefs of the Peshawar Valley to pay the tribute. The order was obeyed by Khadi Khan,[36] who also advised Ventura to cross the Indus to subdue the other chiefs of the valley.[37] In the meantime, local inhabitants fled to the hills for the safety of their honour and property. Khadi Khan, upon the arrival of Ventura in his area, declared Muqarrab Khan as *khan* of Zaida. Fateh Khan and Arsala Khan, younger sons of Ashraf Khan, had left the village. However, Muqarrab Khan sent message to Sayyid Ahmad that he had not been willing to become *khan* of Zaida but had accepted the position to avoid faction fighting and bloodshed.[38] The earlier biographers of Sayyid Ahmad relate that Ventura did not proceed until after taking Khadi Khan's brother, Amir Khan, as hostage. Sikh sources did not mention the hostage taking. On behalf of Ventura, Khadi Khan sent a letter to Fateh Khan to pay the tribute but he did not comply.[39] Ventura was informed about Fateh Khan's refusal. Earlier, Fateh Khan's prestige had increased in the area due to the presence of Sayyid Ahmad. Ventura sent a letter to Sayyid Ahmad asking him to explain what he was doing in the territory of Ranjit Singh. Sayyid Ahmad replied that all lands belonged to Allah alone and that the territory where he lived was Muslim territory. He further added that he had come there to wage jihad against the infidels and whosoever could, would possess the area. He invited Ventura to accept Islam and become his brother; being an *ahl-i-kitab*,[40] he could better understand the message. Maulvi Khair-ud-Din Sherkoti was dispatched as an envoy to the commander of the Sikh force, along with a force of three hundred Mujahidin. He left Panjtar and pitched his tents in the plain before going to the camp of Ventura. The bold action of Maulvi Kahir-ud-Din gave confidence to the tribesmen; they left their refuges and returned to their villages. The movement of the locals terrified the Sikh force. Ventura entered Hazro after crossing the Indus out of the fear of a night attack.[41]

The retreat of Ventura without fighting was not accepted by the Lahore *darbar* and the general was blamed for having secret contacts with the Sayyid. To offset the criticism, he reappeared with a fully prepared command of ten thousand troops and planned an attack on Panjtar. Sayyid Ahmad and Fateh Khan asked tribal chiefs to come forward for the defence of Panjtar as it was the gateway to Buner and Swat. A defensive wall was constructed and all entries to the area were guarded by the tribal force and the Mujahidin. The Sikh force entered Khudu Khel, set fire to houses in Totalai, and destroyed a portion of the defensive wall. But the attack was repulsed by the Mujahidin. Ventura once again returned without taking Panjtar or subduing Sayyid Ahmad and his allies.[42]

The second retreat of Ventura strengthened the Mujahidin. Many local chiefs and tribes offered their support for Sayyid Ahmad. Among them, the Ismailzai and Daulatzai tribes of Amazai[43] offered their allegiance and promised that they would follow *sharia* in their public and private lives.[44]

Attempts to Capture the Fort at Attock and an Attack on Tangi

Between the two offences of Ventura, an attempt was made by the Mujahidin to capture the Sikh-manned fort at Attock.[45] The sources have narrated that a man named Khair-ud-Din visited Sayyid Ahmad over several months. Khair-ud-Din was among the nobles of Attock and acquired all the intelligence details needed for an invading force. After consulting other Muslims of the town, it was decided to get the support of Sayyid Ahmad. He asked Sayyid Ahmad to attack the fort and liberate them from tyrannical Sikh rule.[46] The fort was guarded by a Sikh force under Khazana Mal, the *qiladar*. Sikh troops used to stay there between their assaults on the Peshawar Valley and elsewhere. However, the fort did not have a strong force since the defeat of Sayyid Ahmad in the battle of Shaidu (February 1827).[47] Upon the request of Khair-ud-Din, Sayyid Ahmad sent Maulvi Imam-ud-Din with two Mujahidin in disguise to acquire the required information. Imam-ud-Din returned in a few days and reported that Khair-ud-Din spoke the truth. Sayyid Ahmad deputed Khair-ud-Din to capture the fort. After a few days, he informed Sayyid Ahmad that all preparations had been completed and that five hundred Muslim inhabitants of Attock fort were ready to assist the Mujahidin in their assault. He added that on the night, fixed for an attack, his brother and other associates would come out of the fort in the garb of wedding procession and will get in along with the Mujahidin. Thus the Mujahidin and their supporters would capture the fort without much difficulty. Sayyid Ahmad, at this time, was in Amazai. He sent seventy Mujahidin led by Arbab Bahram Khan. The Mujahidin travelled at night and stayed near Jalsai[48] during the day. The travel was resumed the next evening and at their arrival at Jahangira, the Mujahidin were informed by Muhammad Bakhsh that a collaborator has exposed the plot to the Sikh *qiladar* and that the plotters inside the fort were arrested. It was further added that Khadi Khan had sent information to the *qiladar* about the plot. The Mujahidin returned to Amazai after the failed attempt and informed Sayyid Ahmad of what happened.[49] One source said that the plot was exposed by a collaborator for a reward and by Khadi Khan for his vested interests.[50] Abdul Jabbar Shah Sithanavi has narrated that Khadi Khan was informed by Akhun Abdul Ghafur, alias Saidu Baba, and disclosed this information to the Sikhs.[51]

Many sources have blamed a collaborator of the Mujahidin inside the fort for treachery and Khadi Khan for the failure. However, it should not be ignored that the poor planning of the Mujahidin was the major factor. They were unaware of the methods and tools for capturing a fort. They lacked the required skills for a siege or surprise attack. Attock was one of the strongest forts on the Yusafzai and Khattak borders and a small group of soldiers were enough to defend it for a long time. Moreover, relying on people for support who had never opposed Sikh rule was not a prudent decision on the part of Sayyid Ahmad.

Another episode of the Jihad Movement was a surprise attack on Tangi[52] (locally called Tangai). The early decisions of Sayyid Ahmad to resolve differences among the Pukhtun tribes had attracted a large number who sought his assistance. Among others, residents of Tangi visited Sayyid Ahmad at Panjtar. On behalf of Sayyid Ahmad, Maulvi Amir-ud-Din, a local supporter of the Mujahidin, accompanied the people to Tangi for visits. They shared with Sayyid Ahmad news of current conditions, discussed with him ways and means of ending Durrani rule, and sought his help in this. Sayyid Ahmad promised his full support to the people. Furthermore, he considered that the occupation of Tangi offered a gateway to a successful entry into Peshawar. On 17 July 1829 Shah Ismail was sent to Tangi with three hundred Mujahidin. They were accompanied by Arbab Bahram Khan and Maulvi Amir-ud-Din. Upon their arrival at Tangi, their collaborators informed them that they were unable to assist the Mujahidin because of differences among the locals. Some of the Mujahidin were annoyed to the extent that they demanded a harsh punishment for the Tangi people, but Arbab Bahram Khan and Maulvi Amir-ud-Din did not like the idea and the locals were left unharmed. The Mujahidin returned without a fight.[53]

Like the attempt on the fort of Attock, the attack on Tangi was an ill-planned adventure. The Mujahidin had no firsthand information on the area and were hopeful of receiving assistance from the locals. A previous attempt on Utmanzai had also failed. It seems that Sayyid Ahmad was little interested in these attempts. Dispatching untrained and ill-equipped Mujahidin troops numbering only seventy and three hundred to attack Attock fort and to capture Tangi, respectively, perhaps prove Sayyid Ahmad's lack of serious interest in these efforts.

Earlier biographers of Sayyid Ahmad said that the people of Tangi invited the Mujahidin for the implementation of *sharia*. But keeping in view the tribal system and psychology, we see how factional and clan jealousies caused division and violence at times. Besides, there were some who considered themselves deprived in the prevalent setup. Mujahidin support was, therefore, sought perhaps as support in the factional feuds or to pressure opponents, or to receive special attention from the ruling class.

The Mujahidin Differences with Khadi Khan and His Assassination

The expansion of Mujahidin rule was followed by their surprise attack on Hund and the assassination of Khadi Khan. Several reasons explain the enmity. Khadi Khan was the first chief in the Peshawar Valley to offer full support to the Mujahidin to establish their centre. However, the defeat of the Mujahidin at the battle of Shaidu (February 1827) compelled them to search for a more secure headquarters. Abandoning Hund for Panjtar was taken by Khadi Khan as a personal affront. Moreover, Khadi Khan did not like Sayyid Ahmad's attitude that preferred others over him.

When Sayyid Ahmad preferred the company of Fateh Khan of Panjtar and Ashraf Khan of Zaida, he perhaps did not consider greatly how both were traditional rivals of Khadi Khan for ascendancy in the area. This had annoyed Khadi Khan. The Manerai episode after the imposition of *sharia* was another factor which enraged Khadi Khan.[54] When Khadi Khan paid taxes and revenue to the Lahore *darbar*, and helped Ventura during his campaign against the Mujahidin, he created an obvious breach with Sayyid Ahmad. According to a popular perception, Sayyid Ahmad also failed to maintain a balance between the local chiefs and supported his allies against their opponents.

Khadi Khan now sought support against Sayyid Ahmad and his allies. There were constant clashes and skirmishes between Khadi Khan and Ashraf Khan in which Sayyid Ahmad sided with Ashraf Khan.[55] Khadi Khan had a feud with Ashraf Khan over a piece of land near Hund. Ashraf Khan was his father-in-law, while his sister was married to Muqarrab Khan, son of Ashraf Khan. Both sides made considerable preparations for a fight. Ashraf Khan asked Sayyid Ahmad for help. Sayyid Ahmad dispatched Shah Ismail with a force to resolve the issue, but before his arrival, Ashraf Khan's men deterred Khadi Khan's men after a brief skirmish. Ashraf Khan, however, accidentally fell from his horse while on his way back to his village and died.[56] His death was followed by an internal factional struggle between rival groups who preferred either Muqarrab Khan or Fateh Khan, sons of Ashraf Khan, to be designated as the *khan* of Zaida. Sayyid Ahmad preferred Fateh Khan over Muqarrab Khan. Khadi Khan did not like the Mujahidin siding with Fateh Khan of Zaida.[57] Some sources have suggested that Muqarrab Khan was mentally disabled and Ashraf Khan had nominated Fateh Khan as his successor.[58] It is interesting to note that though Muqarrab Khan presented tribute to Francis Ventura upon his arrival, he conveyed secretly to Sayyid Ahmad that he was his follower, and paying tribute to Ventura was due to the pressure of Khadi Khan.[59] It clearly indicates that Muqarrab Khan was alert about his future and was sure that he would not be able to live a peaceful life in the area unless he had good relations with Sayyid Ahmad. A mentally disabled person might not be that much alarmed about his future and career.

Sayyid Ahmad did not involve the local chiefs in resolving the issue when the differences surfaced. Instead he called a *shura*, a consultative body of his associates and Fateh Khan. Subsequently, an *ijtama'a-e-a'am* was called in Panjtar. Many people attended the gathering, including Khadi Khan. The gathering was not aimed at resolving the issue of differences, but seemed rather an attempt to give a religious cover to punishing Khadi Khan for his insolence. Khadi Khan realized that the meeting meant either to bring him to terms or otherwise to seek a *fatwa* against him. Sayyid Ahmad discussed the issue with Khadi Khan on religious grounds, to which Khadi Khan replied that Pukhtuns understand political matters, that they keep the clerics in their right place by not allowing their interference in politics.[60] Khadi Khan did not agree to Sayyid Ahmad's verdict and returned to Hund. After Ventura's second retreat, a meeting between Shah Ismail and Khadi Khan was arranged but the effort to reconcile again failed.[61]

Before taking military action, a *fatwa* of Tamer Lane[62] was invoked. Tamer Lane had sought a statement from his contemporary *ulama* justifying his attacks and massacres in Delhi. Following Tamer Lane, and taking action against Khadi Khan or any local chief, was not religiously justified on the part of Mujahidin. Sayyid Ahmad had claimed himself a reformer, who was working for the restoration of *sharia* in its true spirit. Khadi Khan was declared a rebel and the justification for taking action against him was based on his previous conduct. But the *Waqai* and other sources did not mention the names of any local chiefs, except Fateh Khan, who declared Khadi Khan a rebel. One source said that action against Khadi Khan was provoked by Fateh Khan.[63]

Different sources have explained the action taken against Khadi Khan on different grounds. Some argue that the retreat of Ventura opened the way for the expansion of Mujahidin rule in the valley with but two hurdles remaining. On the western side were the Peshawar chiefs, especially Yar Muhammad Khan, and on the eastern side, Khadi Khan. Sayyid Ahmad had three options. First, fight the Peshawar chiefs with all available resources as they were regarded as the toughest opponent. Second, focus on Khadi Khan and eliminate that threat forever. Or third, leave the Peshawar Valley and search for another centre, perhaps in Pakhali as his new headquarters. Mihr thought that the search for a new centre was not a bad option but that was to leave Sayyid Ahmad's allies at the mercy of his opponents. He further thought that a new centre might have the problem of the same factional politics, and therefore Sayyid Ahmad was justified to fight for his cause.[64]

Sayyid Ahmad planned an attack on Hund when he was in Sudham. The whole scheme was kept secret and only a few of the Mujahidin knew of the intended strike. A force of several hundred under Shah Ismail and Arbab Bahram Khan was sent to attack Hund. They were guided to Hund by Muhammad Baig, a relative of Khadi Khan who had split from him due to a murder. To keep secrecy, they travelled in different directions and met in Lahore. Due to darkness some lost the way, but still groups arrived near the fort of Hund. The fort was attacked when the door was opened early in the morning after the *azan*. Sheikh Wali Muhammad entered the fort along with his men, followed by Shah Ismail and his group. Shah Ismail announced that they were interested only in Khadi Khan and all the other should stay in their homes if wished their safety. Muhammad Baig, accompanied by a group of the Mujahidin, went straight to Khadi Khan's residence. He came out of his house to arrange a defence but was shot dead by an unidentified attacker. He fell from the roof of his house and his dead body was attacked by Muhammad Baig with sword. Apart from Khadi Khan, a farmer was killed outside the gate when he tried to warn the inhabitants of the fort after seeing the Mujahidin outside. Shah Ismail announced that the inhabitants of Hund were safe and need not worry about their future. The elder son of Khadi Khan escaped and fled. A body of the Mujahidin was appointed to guard the residence of Khadi Khan. Amir Khan sent messengers to Shah Ismail to hand over the corpse of Khadi Khan and release his family. Shah Ismail did not release the family, but the dead body was handed over to the messenger. Khadi Khan was buried outside the fort in the ancestral graveyard. His family was shifted to the house of a local *mulla* and what property was left in the house was confiscated by the Mujahidin.[65]

Shah Ismail sent all the details to Sayyid Ahmad. His reply contained directives for future plans and advice to hand over Khadi Khan's family to his relatives. Khadi Khan's family was released.[66] Several of the sources suggest that Sayyid Ahmad released Khadi Khan's family to please Muqarrab Khan, a follower of Sayyid Ahmad and brother in law of Khadi Khan.[67] It should be kept in mind that releasing Khadi Khan's family was delayed due to different reasons and resulted hatred for the Mujahidin.[68] The date of the killing is not recorded, but it might possibly be around the last week of July or first week of August, as Amir Khan had attacked the band of the Mujahidin taking arms to Hund on 14 August 1829.[69]

The occupation of Hund was one of the most important events of the movement. Kakakhel commented that detaining Khadi Khan's family was not a noble act of the Mujahidin.[70] The following points may be worth considering. The fort was attacked suddenly and Khadi Khan was taken by surprise. The sources narrate that he was declared a rebel, by the local *ulama*. Khadi Khan had called for negotiations after the differences developed and he met Shah Ismail in Salim Khan Kalay. Khadi Khan was kept in darkness about his position. Second, except Fateh Khan, none of the local chiefs were taken in confidence about the attack on Hund. The *khans* of Peshawar Valley took it an action of the Mujahidin only and intensified their enmity. Detaining Khadi Khan's family, even for a short time, generated hatred for the Mujahidin because it was regarded as against both Islam and Pukhtu to keep children and women in confinement.

According to war rules codified by the earlier companions of the Prophet Muhammad (Peace Be Upon Him) and jurists, only those present in the battlefield could be imprisoned. Also, according to one directive of Sayyid Ahmad, all arms of the inhabitants of Hund were taken away by the Mujahidin.[71] Sithanvi has narrated that the camels and horses of the inhabitants were confiscated along with arms.[72] According to the canon law, only arms and other belongings could be confiscated from those who have opposed the Muslims in the battlefield. The case of Hund was totally different. None of the inhabitants had opposed the Mujahidin and thus the Mujahidin's action could not be justified on the basis of mere suspicion.

Muhammad Baig's role in the night attack on Hund also warrants some consideration. He had a feud with Khadi Khan over the murder of his relative. He wanted revenge and for that guided the Mujahidin to Hund. He went to the spot where Khadi Khan's dead body was lying and hit it with his sword several times. His action was praised in the annals of the movement.[73] Sayyid Ahmad had previously told Khadi Khan that one morning the management of his fort would be in someone else's hands and that he would be lying like a dead dog.[74] Such derogatory and abusive words were against the tenets of Islam. From these events, the Mujahidin actually became part of the ongoing *tarburwali*, that would contribute to the failure of the Mujahidin Movement in achieving its immediate objectives. They could have taken someone else as a guide, besides Muhammad Baig, but they intensified the faction fighting for their own interests.

The Battle of Zaida

The occupation of Hund was not a minor incident that could be ignored by the local chiefs. Amir Khan, brother of Khadi Khan, and his relatives started persuading the local population to assist them in avenging the death of their brother. Importantly, *badal* had been an integral part of tribal custom and hence Pukthu. The local chiefs did not come forward due to fear of the Mujahidin. Amir Khan and Ghulam Khan[75] approached Yar Muhammad Khan to support them against the Sayyid. A contemporary local poet has described the ensuing battle of Zaida in a *charbitah*.[76] It says that Amir Khan approached Yar Muhammad Khan to assist him in avenging the murder of his brother and taking back their ancestral property now occupied by the Sayyid.[77]

The battle of Zaida was not fought due to the sole reason of avenging Khadi Khan's murder. There were other factors as well. Since the desertion of Yar Muhammad Khan at the time of the battle of Shaidu, Sayyid Ahmad had constantly thought of occupying Peshawar, something referred to in his letters written to different people.[78] On the other hand, Yar Muhammad wanted to get rid of Sayyid Ahmad. Amir Khan's request hastened the process.

Amir Khan collected his clan and threatened the Mujahidin in the fort of Hund. Shah Ismail sent a message to Sayyid Ahmad to send arms to Hund for its protection. A small band of the Mujahidin, taking the arms, was attacked and killed by Amir Khan's men near Hund.[79] Sayyid Ahmad was informed by Gul Badshah, an inhabitant of Peshawar and Sayyid Ahmad's follower, that Yar Muhammad had sent an advance force under Haji Kakar and he would follow in a few days.[80]

Sayyid Ahmad moved to Zaida and stayed with Fateh Khan and Arsala Khan, the sons of Ashraf Khan of Zaida. The advance force of the Barakzais arrived at Haryan.[81] Early skirmishes were without result when Yar Muhammad arrived along with his main force. Meanwhile, Sayyid Ahmad called Shah Ismail from Amb to Zaida. Shah Ismail left behind two hundred Mujahidin under Maulvi Mazhar Ali of Azeemabad and with the rest joined Sayyid Ahmad. Yar Muhammad Khan encamped near the ravine called Badrai, outside Zaida. There were some on both the sides who wished to resolve the issue peacefully, but all attempts failed. While communications to avoid war continued, the Mujahidin made a night attack. It was a sudden attack that killed hundreds of Barakzai troops. The rest of the soldiers fled from the scene. Many were injured, including Yar Muhammad Khan, who later died of his wounds. A large amount of military and other goods were captured from the Barakzai force, including an elephant, seventy camels, about three hundred horses, six cannons, plus other types of arms. On the Mujahidin side, sources claim only two men were killed.[82] The battle of Zaida was fought on 5 September 1829.[83]

Sayyid Ahmad started back for Panjtar and distributed money in the villages along the way. On his entry in Panjtar, cannons were fired, an act of the rulers of the time to mark celebrations. After his arrival, *ghanima* was distributed among the Mujahidin. A few kept it, while others deposited it in the *bait-ul-mal*. It has been noted by all the sources, inspired from the movement of Sayyid Ahmad, that an injured follower of Yar Muhammad was captured. He was treated well and was allowed to go to his home in Peshawar after his recovery.[84] Sultan Muhammad Khan became the ruler of Peshawar after the death of his brother.[85]

One minor note with longer term implications was that Sayyid Ahmad did not stay in Zaida when he sent the Mujahidin for the night attack. After Shah Ismail's departure, Sayyid Ahmad was busy in prayer. Locals came after some time with news of a Mujahidin victory. However, this first news was followed by a rumour that all the Mujahidin sent for the attack had been killed. Sayyid Ahmad was quite surprised. His associates including, Fateh Khan, asked him to leave the place immediately and move to Panjtar. Hesitating at first, Sayyid Ahmad accepted their advice and left Zaida. A messenger from Shah Ismail with the final victory news met Sayyid Ahmad when he had reached Manerai. He returned to Zaida and was well received by the Mujahidin, with twenty-one cannon fired in his honour.[86] Sayyid Ahmad leaving Zaida in flight before confirming the news did not suit the leader of a movement. It gave the impression that he was more concerned about personal safety and perhaps some villagers noted this, and became cautious about the substance of the effort. Moreover, Mujahidin's night attack cannot be justified according to the *sharia* as efforts for peace were still underway between the opposing parties and the Durranis were not expecting such an attack.

The Mujahidin Struggle in Hazara and the Imposition of *Sharia* in Amb

As mentioned, Kashmir was long a preoccupation and an important place in Sayyid Ahmad's strategy for the Jihad Movement. He sent a force under Shah Ismail but was unable to achieve much success there. Soon after the battle of Zaida, he received letters from some chiefs that the military post at Tarbela did not have a strong force. A small group of Mujahidin would be enough to occupy the place.[87] Sayyid Ahmad went personally to Kabal and sent seventy Mujahidin to his ally Khan Zaman Khan. He attacked Tarbela, occupied the area, and besieged the military post with one hundred Sikh soldiers. Hari Singh Nalwa, the Sikh governor of Hazara, was staying at Baharo Kot. He came to the rescue of his troops. Khan Zaman Khan and the Mujahidin, finding it impossible to hold the place, left Tarbela. He sent the Mujahidin back to Kabal and took his men to the mountains. Skirmishes continued for the next several weeks across the Indus, resulting in casualties on both the sides.[88]

From Kabal, Sayyid Ahmad went to Sithana, on the invitation of Sayyid Akbar Shah.[89] Sayyid Ahmad wanted to make an alliance with Painda Khan,[90] ruler of Amb, to open a passage for advancement towards Kashmir. Painda Khan, who previously fought the Sikhs and whose dominion was located in a strategic position, in the meantime, sent a messenger, expressing his wish to meet Sayyid Ahmad. He discussed the matter with Sayyid Akbar Shah, who had reservations, but Sayyid Ahmad did not honour his counsel. The two met at a place outside Ashara, near Amb, but both were suspicious of each other, and had taken safety measures to avoid any mishap. Sayyid Ahmad told Painda Khan that the Mujahidin needed a safe passage through his dominion, in return he would be provided an elephant and cannon.[91] One source said that Sayyid Ahmad also proposed that Painda Khan be appointed as his prime minister.[92]

During Sayyid Ahmad's absence from Panjtar, Sultan Muhammad Khan left Peshawar and attacked Hund. It was said that the motivation came from his mother who wished to avenge the death of her son, Yar Muhammad Khan. There were sixty Mujahidin in the fort under Akhun Zahoorullah and Muhammad Khan. The siege continued for several days. Finally the Mujahidin agreed to hand over the fort to Sultan Muhammad Khan on the guarantee by an officer that they would be spared.[93] Hund was occupied by Sultan Muhammad Khan without any resistance from the Mujahidin. It was said that his next target was Panjtar.[94] But Sultan Muhammad Khan returned to Peshawar and there were no prospects of an attack on Panjtar in the near future.[95]

Sultan Muhammad Khan handed over Hund to Amir Khan, brother of Khadi Khan, before leaving for Peshawar. Amir Khan sought assistance from the Sikhs for protection of the fort. Seven hundred Sikhs were then garrisoned at Hund. The presence of the Sikhs encouraged the chiefs of Peshawar Valley to disobey the orders of Sayyid Ahmad's officers.[96] Painda Khan forbade the Mujahidin's passage through his dominion when Shah Ismail arrived there. To continue with the previous plan of taking Kashmir and making it a permanent base of operation, Sayyid Ahmad dispatched a group of the Mujahidin to Muzaffarabad under Shah Ismail and Maulvi Khair-ud-Din Sherkoti. Shah Ismail informed Painda Khan about his arrival at Sithana and asked for boats. Painda Khan refused passage to Shah Ismail,[97] on the plea that Hari Singh, Sikh governor of Hazara, would not tolerate their passage through his territory.[98] Shah Ismail told Sayyid Ahmad about this unexpected development and Sayyid Ahmad discussed the matter with associates and allies. On Sayyid Ahmad's order, Shah Ismail returned to Panjtar. Sayyid Ahmad wrote to Painda Khan that they wanted a safe passage only for their journey to Kashmir. Painda Khan again refused and Sayyid Ahmad placed the matter before the *ulama* associated with his movement, for their opinion. They declared Painda Khan a rebel and said the Mujahidin could use an iron hand to deal with him. Sayyid Ahmad Ali and Abdul Hamid Khan were ordered to move towards Sithana, along with Pir Khan. Sayyid Ahmad himself advanced via Chanai. Sayyid Ahmad sent all the women and children of the Mujahidin to Dukhara. Sheikh Hassan Ali and other Mujahidin were left for their protection.[99]

Sayyid Ahmad arrived at Chanai[100] with all the Mujahidin and their local allies. Shah Ismail was appointed *amir* and instructions were issued for the upcoming battle. Shah Ismail left Chanai, crossed Gabai, left two hundred Mujahidin at Digara, and himself arrived at Farausa. Sayyid Ahmad Ali was already in Sithana along with artillery. At Madad Khan's suggestion, Shah Ismail ordered a small force to proceed to Ashara via Kanerai.[101] Sayyid Ahmad Ali was also ordered to proceed to Ashara. Informed about Shah Ismail's strategy, Painda Khan sent a letter asking for reconciliation. The letter proved a trick on the part of Painda Khan. In the ensuing battles fought in different places, Painda Khan's forces were defeated. The Mujahidin occupied Ashara, Kotla and Amb. Sayyid Ahmad left Chanai and arrived at Ashara after receiving a letter with news of the victory from Shah Ismail.[102]

After occupying different places, the Mujahidin besieged Chattar Bai, but it was difficult to occupy. Sayyid Ahmad sent Mujahidin to bring cannons from Panjtar. They returned after few days and installed the cannons around Chattar Bai. Sayyid Ahmad personally came to Amb to monitor the fighting. One Abdul Latif led the Mujahidin and attacked the post, but they were repulsed and many were killed or seriously injured.[103] Sayyid Ahmad's presence in Amb and the installation of cannons in front of Chattar Bai forced Painda Khan to sue for peace. It was decided that Painda Khan would vacate Chattar Bai and send his son as a hostage. Later, it revealed that a main objective was to dig out treasure that Painda Khan might have left in Amb.[104]

Sayyid Ahmad dispatched Sayyid Ahmad Ali with a group of Mujahidin to capture Sarikot and Phulra. Sayyid Ahmad Ali crossed the Indus and took Sarikot in a surprise night attack. Painda Khan left Baloti. His people vacated Chattar Bai after losing Sarikot. Painda Khan first fled to Shergarh and then to Agror, to avoid a Mujahidin assault.[105]

Painda Khan sought Hari Singh's assistance to expel the Mujahidin from Amb, which Hari Singh offered with certain conditions. Sayyid Ahmad Ali then occupied Phulra without resistance. He was warned of a surprise attack by the Sikhs but the Mujahidin, relaxed after the passage of two nights, were waiting for the attack. The Sikhs arrived early in the morning. In the ensuing battle, fought in Phulra, many Mujahidin, including Sayyid Ahmad Ali, were killed.[106] The sources had not recorded the exact date of the battle of Phulra. One source has wrongly mentioned it in 1829.[107] Mihr writes that in April 1830 the Mujahidin were sent to Phulra in the last week of Al-Shawwal or first week of Dhul Qa'idah 1245 A.H., which corresponds to April/May 1830.[108] Probably the battle took place in May 1830.

The defeat at Phulra halted the Mujahidin's advance to Kashmir. Sayyid Ahmad called Shah Ismail back to Amb and appointed his officials to administer the area. Hafiz Abdul Latif was appointed *muhtasib*. He was entitled to punish those who did not offer congregational prayers. All acts were prohibited which the Mujahidin considered immoral. *Tahsildars* were appointed to collect *ushar*. It has been recorded that females were punished by Sayyid Ahmad himself, when found guilty of immoral acts.[109]

During Sayyid Ahmad's sojourn in Amb, many local people had left their homes. Sayyid Ahmad ordered the Mujahidin to cultivate their land. The *Waqai* relates that much land was cultivated and the Mujahidin were able to meet their food needs.[110] None of Sayyid Ahmad's biographers have referred to the tithe law of *sharia*[111] in this regard. Moreover, the *Waqai* has narrated that watermelons were eaten by the grower Mujahidin, who also offered them to their friends, but no reference has been made about any payment of related *ushar*. In one instance the Hassanzai tribe requested abolishing *ushar*, which Sayyid Ahmad did accordingly.

At this, Shah Ismail called the tribal chiefs and told them that *imam*, head of the Faithful, did not have the authority to abolish an order of Allah. The *imam* himself had to pay *ushar*, if he grew crops.[112]

During Sayyid Ahmad's stay in Amb, Ranjit Singh sent a force under Sher Singh, Ventura and Allard, which stayed in the vicinity of Nowshera. Ranjit Singh's envoy, Wazir Singh, and Faqir Aziz-ud-Din also accompanied the force. The envoys went and stayed for few days in Amb but no final decision was made. After their return, Sayyid Ahmad sent Maulvi Khair-ud-Din Sherkoti and Haji Bahadar Khan to meet Sher Singh and other generals. The whole discussion was focused on Ranjit Singh's offer of the trans-Indus area to Sayyid Ahmad on the condition that he would give up incursions to the south-east of the river. Some sources have narrated that Ranjit Singh offered to allow Sayyid Ahmad to rule the area on his behalf and pay tax to the Lahore *darbar*. Sayyid Ahmad rejected the offer on the ground that his objective was not collecting tax but the imposition of *sharia*.[113] It has been stated that Ventura crossed the river Kabul (Landai) to attack Panjtar, but Maulvi Khair-ud-Din warned the tribes living on that way and hence Ventura returned due to fear of night attacks.[114]

The Mujahidin Tours, the Battle of Hoti-Mardan, and the Appointment of *Tahsildar*s

The murder of Khadi Khan, the death of Yar Muhammad Khan, and, finally, the occupation of Amb gave an opportunity to the Mujahidin to extend their rule to parts of the Peshawar Valley previously not under their control. Many people from different villages visited Panjtar and congratulated Sayyid Ahmad on his successes.[115] New caravans of the Mujahidin arrived which had been forced to stay at different places due to Durrani opposition. The local chiefs who earlier opposed either repented or left their homes.[116] The *Waqai* said that a few days after the victory against Yar Muhammad Khan, Fateh Khan of Panjtar, and Fateh Khan of Zaida visited Sayyid Ahmad and told him that he should appoint *quza* and *tahsildar*s since he was the unopposed ruler of the area. They wrote to the local chiefs about the matter, with Sayyid Ahmad's consultation. After few days *khan*s started visiting Panjtar. They asked Sayyid Ahmad to appoint Mujahidin to adjudicate cases and collect taxes.[117] One source, however, has told the story in a different way, adding that Sayyid Ahmad himself appointed *quza* and *tahsildar*s for adjudicating cases and collecting *ushar* respectively.[118]

Sayyid Ahmad's absence from Panjtar, Sultan Muhammad Khan's occupation of Hund and its handing over to Amir Khan, and the presence of Sikhs garrison in Hund encouraged tribesmen not to pay *ushar*. Sayyid Ahmad was in Amb when Qazi Muhammad Hubban asked to be sent to the plain to collect the *ushar* dues. He also asked for Shah Ismail's company. Qazi Muhammad Hubban, Shah Ismail, and five hundred and fifty Mujahidin were sent to bring the Peshawar Valley under control. They started from Amb and visited different places, including Gyara Bara, Gandaf, and Pabini. Local people offered hospitality, as well as fodder for all animals of the Mujahidin. They went to Panjtar afterwards and stayed there for some days.

On the first two days, Fateh Khan of Panjtar offered food to all of the Mujahidin, and then the local people were asked to provide food to them. After a few days, Qazi Muhammad Hubban told Fateh Khan of Panjtar that their intention was to 'liberate' some territories which were occupied by the Sikhs during the Mujahidin absence from Panjtar. On the advice of Fateh Khan of Panjtar all those *khan*s were called to Panjtar who had left their home during the Sikhs' assault. These included Fateh Khan of Zaida, Ibrahim Khan and Ismail Khan of Kalabat, Sarfaraz Khan of Marghuz, and others. They assembled at Panjtar and after deliberations decided that all would pay *ushar* after they reoccupied their villages with the Mujahidin's assistance. The *Waqai* wrongly narrated that local *ulama* did not like collection of *ushar* by the Mujahidin as it was their source of income.[119] People were told that *ushar* was to be paid to the *imam* and it was his responsibility to distribute it among the poor and needy.[120]

Qazi Muhammad Hubban was still in Panjtar when Said Amir of Kotah informed him that the people of Kalabat were collecting a *lakhkar* to fight against them. The Mujahidin attacked the village and the *lakhkar* fled. Two local persons were killed while none of Mujahidin died. Ibrahim Khan was appointed *khan* of the village. He had previously left the village due to the Sikh presence in Hund. On the arrival of the Mujahidin at Marghuz, the *khan* fled. Sarfraz Khan was installed to his previous position as *khan* of Marghuz.

They continued their tour of the plain and went to Thandkoi, Kadai and Panjpir. The *khan*s and other notable of these villages visited Qazi Muhammad Hubban and requested pardon. The *qazi* pardoned all and stayed for a night at Zaida. The local people collected food for the Mujahidin and fodder for their animals. From Zaida, Abdul Hamid Khan, *risaldar*, was sent to Hund, accompanied by a force. The Mujahidin went towards Hund and returned after some time. In the morning, it was learnt that Amir Khan and his Sikh allies had left the fort. The next morning the Mujahidin entered Hund, occupied the vacated fort, and managed local affairs. A lot of material was captured by them from the Sikhs who had left in haste.[121] Qazi Muhammad Hubban, Shah Ismail, Fateh Khan of Panjtar, Arsala Khan and Fateh Khan of Zaida, Ismail Khan of Kalabat, and Abdul Hamid Khan decided to demolish the fort of Hund. Several thousand people from surrounding villages were ordered to demolish it. But they failed and the idea was dropped.[122] People of the surrounding villages came to Fateh Khan and told him that they were unable to demolish the fort and had consumed the food stuff they had brought from their homes. Qazi Muhammad Hubban allowed them to return homes.[123] An interesting point, we derive from the narration of the *Waqai*, is that the people, asked to demolish the fort, were neither paid for their labour nor provided with food. It was a sort of *bigar*. If so, it seems that the Mujahidin behaved in no way different from previous rulers, though the earlier rulers did not live among them. The Mujahidin lived in their area and strictly controlled the Pukhtuns.

After a stay of few days in Hund, Qazi Muhammad Hubban told Fateh Khan of Panjtar, Arsala Khan and Fateh Khan of Zaida, and Ismail Khan of Kalabat that he would go to *tapah* Razzar[124] as the people of that area were not paying *ushar*. Qazi Muhammad Hubban, Shah Ismail, and Risaldar Abdul Hamid Khan went to Shawa accompanied by the Mujahidin. Anand Khan and Mushkar Khan, chiefs of Shawa, visited them and said that they would offer food and fodder for the Mujahidin and their animals respectively. The *qazi* asked both the *khan*s to send their messengers to Sheikh Jana and Naway Kalay[125] to meet him. The messenger returned with the message that they were too occupied with their farming season and would not be able to visit him. The *qazi* did not like their reply and sent a messenger to Sayyid Ahmad to send more Mujahidin. Sayyid Ahmad sent one hundred Mujahidin under Maulvi Mazhar Ali Azeemabadi to assist Qazi Muhammad Hubban.[126]

The Mujahidin advanced to Chargulai and met Mansur Khan of Chargulai, Anand Khan and Mushkar Khan of Shawa, Mahmud Khan of Tangi (they were with Mansur Khan), as well as Munir Khan and Mubeen Khan of Sudham. They deliberated strategy regarding *tapah* Razzar. Qazi Muhammad Hubban left for Garyala himself and sent these *khan*s along with fifty Mujahidin to present the *khan*s of Razzar before him. The *khan*s of Abazai area were also called. Qazi Muhammad Hubban told them that they had earlier consented to pay *ushar* and to accept Sayyid Ahmad decrees, but later disobeyed in both the matters. After three days the *khans* replied that they would abide by their promise. Next the Qazi called the *khans* of Katlang, Lund Khwar, Mardan, and Hoti. They came and promised to pay *ushar*, but Ahmad Khan[127] of Hoti did not visit and sent a message that he would come after a few days.[128]

Akhun Khair-ud-Din, a local supporter of the Mujahidin, informed the Qazi that Ahmad Khan of Hoti had appointed Rasul Khan as his lieutenant and gone to Peshawar to get support from the Barakzai chiefs of Peshawar. It was alarming news for the Mujahidin and they decided to attack Hoti before Ahmad Khan's return. The Mujahidin decided on a night attack, as usual, but they did not keep their secrecy. The battle started upon their arrival and culminated in their victory. It was not a total military victory. The locals sought peace from the Mujahidin, which was granted.

After the occupation of Hoti, the Mujahidin attacked Mardan. The battle continued for some time. Four Mujahidin, including Qazi Muhammad Hubban, were killed. Mazhar Ali Azeemabadi was wounded. Peace was also granted there to Rasul Khan and others who sought it. All the belongings of Ahmad Khan were confiscated on the plea that he was a rebel. However, the materials confiscated in Hoti and Mardan by the Mujahidin were returned on the ground that confiscation was not allowed after granting peace, according to the canon law. Some belongings, however, could not be returned as they were kept by the Mujahidin or their local allies. Rasul Khan, Ahmad Khan's brother, was appointed *khan* of Hoti and Mardan. After these arrangements, Shah Ismail left for Amazai along with the Mujahidin.[129] Shah Ismail went to Panjtar via Sudham, Shawa and later from Panjtar went to Amb by Sayyid Ahmad's order.[130]

The tour led by Qazi Muhammad Hubban, culminated with his death in the attack on Hoti, had far reaching impact upon the area and the movement. *Tashildars* were appointed in all those areas visited by the Mujahidin and apparently all these areas came under their strict control. Shah Ismail appointed Haji Bahadar Khan and Haji Mahmud Khan Rampuri *tahsildars* of *tapah* Amazai and Sudham respectively. Ten to fifteen Mujahidin were left with each of them in support. Maulvi Naseer-ud-Din Manglori was appointed *tahsildar* at *tapah* Utmanzai[131] with thirty Mujahidin and Fateh Khan was at Khudu Khel.[132]

Abdul Hamid Khan, *risaldar*, was ordered by Shah Ismail, before leaving for Amb, to continue his tour of the area. He had certain reservations over the tour as no cash was left with him to feed the Mujahidin. He wrote all details to Sayyid Ahmad and sought his advice. He replied to send groups of ten to fifteen Mujahidin to different villages. This was also objectionable to the *risaldar*. He himself decided to visit every village for a day or two, during which time villagers were responsible to feed them and their animals. It should not be forgotten that they totalled five hundred persons. During the tour they visited many villages, including Zaida, Munara, Amazai, Ismaila, Naway Kalay, Yarhussain, Shawa, Chargulai, Sudham, Garyala, Turlandai, Kalu Khan, Salim Khan, Manerai, Swabi and Kala Dara. They stayed for a long time in Kala Dara, asking the inhabitants of the surrounding villages to provide food for them and fodder for their animals.[133]

During the tour some instances regarding the Mujahidin's integrity have been recorded by Sayyid Ahmad's biographers. In some cases they were punished by Risaldar Abdul Hamid Khan for offenses, but villagers were also punished at times. During the visit when they were staying in Dagai, a Mujahid went inside the village, against the instructions of the *risaldar*. He was beaten up by the people when he threatened the villagers after his demand was not met. The *risaldar* was informed of the incident, but none among the villagers handed over the offender. The whole village was punished for this act by staying for two extra days in which food and fodder were provided to the Mujahidin and their animals.[134]

The tour of the Mujahidin was important in several ways. The Mujahidin showed their strength in the absence of Sayyid Ahmad. Second, the locals were overburdened by them in many ways. They had agreed to pay *ushar*, but feeding about five hundred Mujahidin and their animals was a great burden on meagre resources. Third, no doubt *melmastya* was an integral part of Pukhtun culture, but the Mujahidin changed the mode of such hospitality. Traditional hospitality was always offered in the village *hujrah*s. The Mujahidin changed their centuries-old tradition by asking villagers to provide the food in their camp.

Importantly, earlier biographers of Sayyid Ahmad denied any high handedness by the Mujahidin, but the narration of *Waqai* has revealed a different story. One may infer many such instances from the simple narration of the events.[135] Also, they were interfering in local administration, though M. A. Bari has denied it.[136] It was observed that their interference was very visible in local arrangements. They replaced their opponents with their supporters and acted like masters. The locals did not like the Mujahidin presence in their villages, as they were not accustomed to the presence of administrators among themselves. The interference of the Mujahidin in the local scene produced resistance from Pukhtuns.

The battle of Hoti was the second major attack on the traditional chiefs of the area, after Khadi Khan. The Kamalzais were alarmed and they sought once again the support of Sultan Muhammad Khan. The chiefs of the Mandanr and Kamalzais had no means to face the Mujahidin in the open field, especially as they were split over the issue themselves. The result was the battle of Mayar, the capture of Peshawar, and the next chapter in the course of events.

Note and References

1. Nadvi, Sayyid Abu al-Hassan Ali. nd. *Tarikh-e-Dawat wa Azimat: Sirat-e-Sayyid Ahmad Shahid*, vol. II. Karachi: Majlis Nashriyat. pp. 19–20. Henceforth, Nadvi, *Sirat-e-Sayyid Ahmad*, vol. II.

2. Mihr, Ghulam Rasul. nd. *Sayyid Ahmad Shahid*. Lahore: Sheikh Ghulam Ali & Sons. p. 461. Henceforth, Mihr, *Sayyid Ahmad*.

3. Ibid., p. 460.

4. Yet another such gathering was called on 20 February 1829, in which Khudu Khel took oath of allegiance for the implementation of *sharia*. Nadvi, *Sirat-e-Sayyid Ahmad*, vol. II., p. 85.

5. We did not find whether Kabul Akhundzada was his real name or a title.

6. Sayyid Ahmad's claim of invitation is not supported by any source except his own speech at different occasions.

7. Khan, Nawab Muhammad Wazir. 2007. *Waqai Sayyid Ahmad Shahid*. Lahore: Sayyid Ahmad Shahid Academy. pp. 1376–86. Henceforth, Khan, *Waqai Sayyid Ahmad*.

8. It seems strange if Sayyid Ahmad had directed avoiding polygamy as he himself married three women.

9. Ahmad, Qeyamuddin. 1979. *The Wahabi Movement in India*. Islamabad: National Book Foundation. pp. 51–52. Henceforth, Ahmad, *The Wahabi Movement*. Mihr gave further details of the *bai'at* which included, first, they would replace traditions with *sharia*; second, they appointed Sayyid Ahmad their *imam* willingly and rendered their allegiance; third, they may have rendered allegiance previously and were renewing it in the presence of the *ulama* and requesting Sayyid Ahmad to pray for their commitment. Mihr, *Sayyid Ahmad*, p. 464.

10. Khalil, Hamesh. 2008. *Da Charbitay Pakhwani Shairan*. Peshawar: Pukhtu Academy. p. 755.

11. The local *ulama* included: Mulla Niaz Muhammad, Mulla Wali Muhammad, Mulla Muhammad Ismail, Akhundzada Sa'adullah, Mulla Sattar Khan, Sayyid Ali, Akhun Shah Wali Khan, Akhun Muhammad Ghulam, Mulla Muhammad Azeem, Akhun Mukarram, Mulla Ammad, Mulla Sayyid Ahmad, Mulla Muhammad Irfan, Mulla Abdullah, Mulla Pir Muhammad, Akhun Muhammad Ghufran, Akhun Akbar Shah, Akhun Muhammad Wisal, Mulla Abdul Rahman of Toru, Akhun Wali Muhammad, Akhun Abdul Ghafur, Akhundzada Muhammad Gul and Akhund Safiullah. Mihr, *Sayyid Ahmad*, p. 463.

12. Khan, *Waqai Sayyid Ahmad*, pp. 1386–90.
13. Sayyid Ahmad's words with which he warned Khadi Khan were 'one day someone will manage your fort and you will be laying like a dead dog' [trans. Altaf Qadir], Khan, *Waqai Sayyid Ahmad*, pp. 1389–90.
14. Khan, *Waqai Sayyid Ahmad*, pp. 1381–88. Another source had given details of the *bai'at* for the implementation of *sharia* but for a much later time, i.e. after the defeat and death of Yar Muhammad Khan at the battle of Zaida. Kakakhel, Sayyid Bahadar Shah Zafar. nd. *Pushtun: Tarikh kay Ayenay mein, 550 QM sey 1964 tak*. Peshawar: University Book Agency. p. 694. Henceforth, Kakakhel, *Pushtun*.
15. Mihr, *Sayyid Ahmad*, p. 458.
16. Nadvi, *Sirat-e-Sayyid Ahmad*, vol. II, p. 83.
17. Mihr, *Sayyid Ahmad*, p. 460.
18. Nadvi, *Sirat-e-Sayyid Ahmad*, vol. II, p. 83.
19. Almost every author has recorded the declaration of *imarat* at different times. Mihr has written it as being on 6 February 1829. Mihr, *Sayyid Ahmad*, p. 463. Kakakhel has contended it happened after the battle of Zaida in which Yar Muhammad Khan was killed. Kakakhel, *Pushtun*, p. 694. Bellew has stated that it was the first oath of 1827 while at another place he had written that *sharia* was enforced after the murder of Khadi Khan. Bellew, H. W. 2001. *A General Report on the Yusufzais*. Lahore: Sang-e-Meel Publications. pp. 86, 88. Henceforth, Bellew, *A General Report*.
20. Mihr, *Sayyid Ahmad*, p. 463.
21. Nadvi, *Sirat-e-Sayyid Ahmad*, vol. II, p. 87.
22. Mihr, *Sayyid Ahmad*, p. 463, footnote 1.
23. Mihr, *Sayyid Ahmad*, p. 463. We have observed the function of the department of *amar bil maruf wa nahi ani-l munkar* during visits to Afghanistan under the Taliban regime. The officials of the department were assigned exactly the same duties as during the *imarat* of Sayyid Ahmad. We also observed during a visit to Swat in 2008 (after the failure of the second phase of the operation) that the Taliban had also established such a department and their job was almost the same, with more responsibilities, i.e. to ensure no irregularity is done in weighing in the markets, traffic control at times of need, issuing orders to cable operators not to run such channels which harm the religion and culture of the people, forbade construction of gutters in streets, and make sure proper drainage system before constructing houses, etc.
24. Nasiri, Alim. 1995. *Shahnama-e-Balakot: Tahrik-e-Jihad ki Manzoom Dastan*, vol. I. Lahore: Idara Mabu'at-e-Sulaimani. pp. 286–87. Henceforth, Nasiri, *Shahnama*, vol. I. There were similarities between the Mujahidin and Taliban movement. In both cases people made such reports out of fear and used such pretexts to avenge previous grudges.
25. Mihr, *Sayyid Ahmad*, p. 465.
26. Ibid., pp. 465–66. The episode of Manerai is recorded in a bit different way in *Waqai Sayyid Ahmad*. pp. 1352–53.
27. Ahmad, Mohiuddin. 1975. *Saiyid Ahmad Shahid: His Life and Mission*. Lucknow: Academy of Islamic Research and Publications. p. 211. Henceforth, Ahmad, *Saiyid Ahmad*.
28. Different sources, local and others, had narrated that previously *ushar* was paid to *mullas* of the respective clans but it does not seem accurate. The amount of *ushar* was too much and neither were *mullas* of the time wealthy nor was there any precedent in the Shaikh Malli *wesh* system. According to that system, a piece of land called *serai* was allotted to the respective *mulla* or Mian for their livelihood.

29. Mihr, *Sayyid Ahmad*, pp. 586–97.
30. Das, Gopal. 1878. *Tarikh-e-Peshawar*. Lahore: Koh-e-Noor Press. p. 320. Henceforth, Das, *Tarikh-e-Peshawar*.
31. Khadi Khan had invited Sayyid Ahmad to Hund and become his first host. He was son-in-law of Ashraf Khan of Zaida and his sister was married to Muqarrab Khan, son of Ashraf Khan of Zaida.
32. Mihr, *Sayyid Ahmad*, p. 478; Usmani, Qamar Ahmad. 1983. *Baraili Say Balakot: Tazkira Mujahid-e-Kabir Hazrat Sayyid Ahmad Shahid Barailvi*. Lahore: Idara Islamiyat. pp. 204–6. Henceforth, Usmani, *Baraili say Balakot*. Nadvi, *Sirat-e-Sayyid Ahmad*, vol. II, pp. 96–97; Sabir, Muhammad Shafi. 1986. *Tarikh-e-Subah Sarhad*. Peshawar: University Book Agency. p. 447. Henceforth, Sabir, *Tarikh-e-Subah Sarhad*.
33. Francis Ventura was an Italian and had worked under Napoleon Bonaparte for a considerable time. After Napoleon's defeat, he left Europe and after wandering for some time in Egypt and Persia, entered Ranjit Singh's service. He was a professional officer and was considered one of the trusted courtiers. In 1843, four years after the death of Ranjit Singh, he resigned due to palace intrigues and the disaster that he could foresee.
34. The event has been narrated by many sources in different versions. Some have placed it before the battle of Hund while others after it. We agree with Mihr and Mohiuddin Ahmad that the event took place before the battle of Hund.
35. Ahmad, *Saiyid Ahmad*, p. 213.
36. Khan, *Waqai Sayyid Ahmad*, p. 1362.
37. Mihr, *Sayyid Ahmad*, pp. 480–81; Kakakhel, *Pushtun*, p. 692.
38. Khan, *Waqai Sayyid Ahmad*, p. 1363.
39. Ibid., pp. 1362–63.
40. According to the classical Muslim doctrine Jews and Christian are *ahl-e-kitab*, people of the book. Notably, the majority of Muslims today believe that the people of the modern west are not *ahl-e-kitab* as they have deviated from Christianity by adopting secular views.
41. Nasiri, *Shahnama*, vol. I, p. 304; Ahmad, *Saiyid Ahmad*, p. 214; Khan, *Waqai Sayyid Ahmad*, pp. 1363–68.
42. Sikh sources do not mention the Sikh attack on Panjtar. They simply write that General Allard, General Ventura, and Prince Sher Singh were sent against Sayyid Ahmad as Ranjit Singh feared the Mujahidin's assault on Peshawar. Kohli, Sita Ram. 2004. *Maharaja Ranjit Singh*. Lahore: Sang-e-Meel Publications. p. 196. The sources agree that Ventura came twice to subdue Sayyid Ahmad. Mihr, *Sayyid Ahmad*, pp. 493–500; Nadvi, *Sirat-e-Sayyid Ahmad*, vol. II, pp. 116–23; Khan, *Waqai Sayyid Ahmad*, pp. 1391–401.
43. Garhi Amazai/Amazo Garhai/Amazai is comprised of Garhi Ismailzai, Kot Ismailzai, Garhi Daulatzai and Kot Daulatzai. It is located at a distance of 15 kilometres to the east of Mardan, Khyber Pakhtunkhwa, and one enters present day district Swabi if travelling to the east, and across Kandar, Gidar and Gumbat. Gumbat is the last village of district Mardan in that direction. The first village of district Swabi on the road is Dobian. Amazo Garhai is second only to Mardan population-wise, in the whole district. It was a major business centre until the mid-nineteenth century due to its location on the old route. The construction of the fort at Attock and the Ferry Bridge near Khairabad, and then the construction of the metallic road and railway track in the British colonial period changed the route to the present G. T. Road and the old route is rarely known today.

44. Nadvi, *Sirat-e-Sayyid Ahmad*, vol. II, pp. 123–24.

45. The Mujahidin planned to take the fort of Attock with the assistance of Muslim officials in the service of Ranjit Singh. Sayyid Ahmad sent a force under Arbab Bahram Khan, but the campaign failed as the Sikh commander of the fort was informed in time and the Mujahidin returned without fighting. This happened between the two assaults of the Sikhs on Panjtar. Husain, Mahmud. 2008. 'Sayyid Ahmad Shahid (II)' in Mahmud Husain et al. (eds). *A History of the Freedom Movement, 1707–1831*, vol. I. Karachi: Royal Book Company. p. 593.

46. Mihr, *Sayyid Ahmad*, pp. 483–84.

47. Nasiri, *Shahnama*, vol. I, pp. 305–6.

48. Jalsai is located at a distance of 2 kilometres to the north-west of Mankai. Mankai is located at Swabi-Jahangira road, very near to Lahore, district Swabi.

49. Khan, *Waqai Sayyid Ahmad*, pp. 1369–74; Mihr, *Sayyid Ahmad*, pp. 483–85; Nasiri, *Shahnama*, vol. I, pp. 305–7.

50. Nasiri, *Shahnama*, vol. I, p. 307.

51. Sithanavi, Sayyid Abdul Jabbar Shah. 2011. *Kitab-ul-Ibrat: Subah Sarhad wa Afghanistan ki Char Saw Sala Tarikh, 1500–1900*. Islamabad: Porab Academy. pp. 391–92. Henceforth, Sithanavi, *Kitab-ul-Ibrat*.

52. Tangi is located at the extreme north of Charsadda district at a distance of 25 kilometres from Charsadda town, the district headquarters.

53. Mihr, *Sayyid Ahmad*, pp. 503–4; Ahmad, *Saiyid Ahmad*, p. 218; Khan, *Waqai Sayyid Ahmad*, pp. 1409–13.

54. Akhundkhel, Haider Ali. 2008. *Buner Khudu Khel: Tarikhi, Tahqiqi aur Saqafati Jaizah*. Mingora: Graphics World. p. 81. Henceforth, Akhundkhel, *Buner*.

55. Mihr, *Sayyid Ahmad*, p. 479.

56. Khan, *Waqai Sayyid Ahmad*, pp. 1356–57.

57. Ashraf Khan had three sons: Muqarrab Khan, also brother-in-law of Khadi Khan, Fateh Khan and Arsala Khan. Sayyid Ahmad feared that Muqarrab Khan may oppose the former due to the influence of Khadi Khan.

58. Ahmad, *Saiyid Ahmad*, p. 212; Nadvi, *Sirat-e-Sayyid Ahmad*, vol. II, p. 98; Mihr, *Sayyid Ahmad*, p. 480.

59. Khan, *Waqai Sayyid Ahmad*, p. 1363.

60. Khan, Roshan. 1986. *Yusafzai Qaum ki Sarguzasht*. Karachi: Roshan Khan and Company. pp. 280–81. Henceforth, Khan, *Yusafzai Qaum*.

61. Mihr, *Sayyid Ahmad*, pp. 501–2.

62. Tamer Lane's full length *fatwa* is recorded in justification of Mujahidin's action. Thanesari, *Maktubat*, pp. 248–50.

63. *James Settlement Report*. Khyber Pakhtunkhwa Provincial Archives, Peshawar, p. 44.

64. Mihr, *Sayyid Ahmad*, pp. 505–6.

65. Ibid., pp. 507–10.

66. Ibid., pp. 507–11; Khan, *Waqai Sayyid Ahmad*, pp. 1414–24. Mohiuddin Ahmad has stated that Khadi Khan was alone in his house as his family had taken shelter in the house of a Sayyid before the attack (Ahmad, *Saiyid Ahmad*, p. 218). It was a surprise night attack and this version was written only to avoid the blame of confinement.

67. Nadvi, *Sirat-e-Sayyid Ahmad*, vol. II, p. 136; Mihr, *Sayyid Ahmad*, p. 513.

68. Nadvi, *Sirat-e-Sayyid Ahmad*, p. 136.

69. Mihr, *Sayyid Ahmad*, p. 515.

70. Kakakhel, *Pushtun*, p. 692.

71. Khan, *Waqai Sayyid Ahmad*, p. 1424.
72. Sithanavi, *Kitab-ul-Ibrat*, p. 397.
73. Khan, *Waqai Sayyid Ahmad*, p. 1419.
74. Ibid., p. 1390.
75. Some sources have stated that Ghulam Khan was not brother but relative of Khadi Khan.
76. *Charbitah*, a form of Pukhtu poetry, contains four lines in every part and in Pukhtu, is used mainly for narrating stories. The mentioned *charbitah* was written soon after the battle of Zaida as the poet had died in early 1830s.
77. Salarzai, Qazi Abdul Halim Asar Afghani. 2006. *Da Pukhtu Charbitay Bagh wa Bahar.* Peshawar: Pashto Academy. pp. 62–65.
78. Thanesari, *Maktubat*, pp. 285–89.
79. Khan, *Waqai Sayyid Ahmad*, pp. 1425–27; Nadvi, *Sirat-e-Sayyid Ahmad*, vol. II, p. 136.
80. Nadvi, *Sirat-e-Sayyid Ahmad*, vol. II, p. 139.
81. Haryan is located to the south of Lahore at a distance of less than 2 kilometres from the Swabi-Jahangira road, and one had to leave the main road at Zakriya Shakh to reach there. The ravine Badrai falls in the Indus to the south of Haryan, where the advanced detachment of Yar Muhammad Khan stayed. Hund is located in the north-east of Haryan, at a distance of 3 kilometres. Sheikh Dherai is located to the eastern side, at a distance of about 1 kilometre.
82. Khan, *Waqai Sayyid Ahmad*, pp. 1434–50; Mihr, *Sayyid Ahmad*, pp. 524–27.
83. Mihr, *Sayyid Ahmad*, p. 529.
84. Nadvi, *Sirat-e-Sayyid Ahmad*, vol. II, pp. 146–49.
85. Kakakhel, *Puhstun*, p. 692.
86. Khan, *Waqai Sayyid Ahmad*, pp. 1449–50; Mihr, *Sayyid Ahmad*, pp. 528–29.
87. Ahmad, *The Wahabi Movement*, p. 53.
88. Mihr, *Sayyid Ahmad*, pp. 534–35.
89. Sayyid Akbar Shah was amongst the most trusted associates of Sayyid Ahmad. He provided asylum to the Mujahidin after the battle of Balakot (1831). He remained ruler of Swat and Buner from 1850 until he died in May 1857, the day the first news of the Meerut uprising reached Peshawar. His family supported the Mujahidin for decades and the British sacked Sithana twice in retaliation. During Sayyid Ahmad's visit to Hazara, he personally visited Sayyid Ahmad in Kabal and asked to accompany the former to his abode. This was their first meeting. We did not find any reliable source stating that Sayyid Akbar Shah remained treasurer and prime minister of Sayyid Ahmad as has been claimed by few writers, including Plowden, T. J. C. 1932. *Report on the Leading Persons and State of Faction in Swat*. Simla: Government of India Press. Home and Tribal Affairs, Tribal Research Cell, Government of Khyber Pakhtunkhwa. Book No. 515, p. 10; Caroe, Olaf. 1965. *The Pathan 550 BC–AD 1957*. London: Macmillan and Co. Ltd, p. 361; Sultan-i-Rome. 2008. *Swat State (1915–1969): From Genesis to Merger; An Analysis of Political, Administrative, Socio-Political, and Economic Developments.* Karachi: Oxford University Press. p. 38. These sources have referred to his premiership and treasurership during Sayyid Ahmad's possession of Peshawar but we did not find any reliable source about his holding these portfolios. Peshawar was managed for few days by Arbab Juma Khan, brother of Arbab Bahram Khan, and was restored to Sultan Muhammad Khan when Sayyid Ahmad was leaving the city for Panjtar.
90. Painda Khan Tanoli, ruler of Amb, was a formidable enemy of the Sikhs. He fought for many years against them. He, however, did not trust anyone in his life. His area was in a strategic location and Sayyid Ahmad, partly for his past role against the Sikhs

and partly for his strategic location wanted to utilize Painda Khan's resources against the Sikhs and to support the occupation of Kashmir. Mihr, *Sayyid Ahmad*, pp. 539–40; Ahmad, *Wahabi Movement*, p. 54; Khan, *Waqai Sayyid Ahmad*, pp. 1512–21.

91. Khan, *Waqai Sayyid Ahmad*, pp. 1523–29.
92. Hussain, Fida. 1992. *Tarikh-e-Tanawal*. Rawalpindi: Asad Mahmud Printing Press. p. 170. Henceforth, Hussain, *Tarikh-e-Tanawal*. However, it is to be noted that the source cannot be trusted wholly as it has mentioned Painda Khan's *bai'at* at Sayyid Ahmad's hand in Panjtar and contradicts his statement in another place that Sayyid Ahmad was enraged as Painda Khan did not render allegiance.
93. Sultan Muhammad Khan imprisoned them. On the way to Peshawar, the prisoners broke the wall of their prison in Hashtnagar and fled to Panjtar.
94. Mihr, *Sayyid Ahmad*, pp. 546–47; Ahmad, *Saiyid Ahmad*, pp. 227–28.
95. Nadvi, *Sirat-e-Sayyid Ahmad*, vol. II, p. 175.
96. Khan, *Waqai Sayyid Ahmad*, pp. 1555–56.
97. Ahmad, *Saiyid Ahmad*, p. 229.
98. Mihr, *Sayyid Ahmad*, p. 548.
99. Khan, *Waqai Sayyid Ahmad*, pp. 1558–62, 1569–77.
100. Mohiuddin Ahmad has written it as Champai. Ahmad, *Saiyid Ahmad*, p. 229. The exact name is Chanai. One has to adopt the following route from Swabi to arrive there. Main road from Swabi to Topi, turn left before entering Topi town, next comes Gandaf industrial estate, then a police check post near village Ba'da, a turn to east and after about 5 kilometres comes Dalwarai village. After travelling in hills would come Naranj village at top of the hill, then Mangal Chai after further 3 kilometres and Chanai after 2 more kilometres.
101. Some writers had written it Kanirzai while others Kaner zay.
102. Khan, *Waqai Sayyid Ahmad*, pp. 1578–1610.
103. Mihr, *Sayyid Ahmad*, p. 559.
104. Ahmad, *Saiyid Ahmad*, pp. 230–31. Mihr noted a peace treaty between Sayyid Ahmad and Painda Khan. It should not be forgotten that before the peace treaty, Sayyid Ahmad had announced that *jagirs* would be allotted to Painda Khan in Peshawar and Kashmir. Consequently, the peace treaty was signed on 29 Zhul Qa'idah 1245 (21 May 1830). The terms of the treaty were: (1) Painda Khan accepted overlordship of Sayyid Ahmad. (2) He would not side with infidels in the future and would serve Islam. (3) He would deliver to his brother Madad Khan, whatever was due upon him. (4) He would leave Agror. (5) He would not interfere in the territory of Palal Tanoli. (6) He would send one hundred artillery men under his son Jahandad Khan to the Peshawar Valley to assist Sayyid Ahmad. (7) He would send a force of two thousand to Kashmir to assist the Mujahidin. 8. Painda Khan's blood and property could be taken by the Mujahidin if he did not abide by the terms of treaty. Mihr, *Sayyid Ahmad*, pp. 562–63. Mihr has confused certain events while dealing with the Mujahidin's struggle in Hazara. Another source had also confused these events. Either he had relied on Mihr or the source for both is one. Ahmad, *Saiyid Ahmad*, pp. 238–39, dates the mentioned treaty to 19 March 1831, which is totally wrong. The Mujahidin were in Sachchun as they had left the Peshawar Valley after the assassinations of their associates in November 1830.
105. Mihr, *Sayyid Ahmad*, p. 567.
106. Ibid., pp. 569–70.
107. Hussain, *Tarikh-e-Tanawal*, pp. 171–72.

108. Mihr, *Sayyid Ahmad*, p. 565.
109. Ibid., pp. 575–76.
110. Khan, *Waqai Sayyid Ahmad*, pp. 1666–67.
111. We refer to Umar I, the Second Caliph, who ordered that neither would Arabs settle in the conquered areas nor purchase lands there. We are of the opinion that this policy was to avoid conflict with the local population which would react to such acts and consider it as the usurpation of their resources.
112. Mihr, *Sayyid Ahmad*, p. 588.
113. Yusafi, Allah Bakhsh. 1973. *Yusafzai Afghan*. Karachi: Sharif Arta Press. p. 465. Henceforth, Yusafi, *Yusafzai Afghan*; Khan, *Waqai Sayyid Ahmad*, pp. 1645–47; Mihr, *Sayyid Ahmad*, pp. 589–95.
114. Ahmad, *Saiyid Ahmad*, p. 238.
115. Unnamed Persian manuscript, written in 1279 A.H., found in Bazar, Rustam, district Mardan, Khyber Pakhtunkhwa, during the course of this study.
116. Nadvi, *Sirat-e-Sayyid Ahmad*, vol. II, p. 148.
117. Khan, *Waqai Sayyid Ahmad*, pp. 1460–61. The *Waqai* has further explained that Sayyid Ahmad did not appoint tax collectors, rather the local *khans* collected and sent it to Panjtar. The argument of the *Waqai* is, however, not supported by logic as will be discussed in the next chapter.
118. Kakakhel, *Pushtun*, p. 696.
119. Khan, *Waqai Sayyid Ahmad*, pp. 1670–74. There is a misunderstanding among academics that earlier *ushar* was paid to the *ulama*. We have not found any reliable source to confirm that *ushar* was ever paid to *ulama*. There were two means of *ulama's* livelihood: first, the people allotted them a piece of land, called *serai* or they were paid a meager share in crops called *arha*. In fact, *arha* was paid to all *kasabgars*—professionals, including cobblers, barbers, carpenters, potters, etc.
120. Yusafi, *Yusafzai Afghan*, p. 466.
121. Khan, *Waqai Sayyid Ahmad*, pp. 1678–85; Mihr, *Sayyid Ahmad*, pp. 598–600.
122. Mihr, *Sayyid Ahmad*, p. 600.
123. Khan, *Waqai Sayyid Ahmad*, p. 1688.
124. *Tapah* Razzar includes Parmoli (locally called Parmolai), Sheikh Jana, Shawa, Karnal Sher Kalai (previously Naway Kalay), Turlandi (locally known as Tulandai), Tarakai, Dagai, Kalu Khan, Adina, Ismaila, Yarhussain, Sodher, Yaqubai, Sara Cheena, Bazargai and Dobian. The area is home to the Ako Khel clan of the Mandanr tribe. *Tapah* Razzar is *tahsil* of district Swabi. Earlier Parmoli, Sheikh Jana, Karnal Sher Kalai, Shawa, Kalu Khan, Adina, Ismaila, Turlandi and Dagai were part of *tahsil* Swabi while rest of the area was part of *tahsil* Lahor, district Swabi, Khyber Pakhtunkhwa. The inhabitants of Yarhussain claim that they are descendants of Malik Ahmad. There are other ethnically Pukhtun and non-Pukhtun tribes/castes living in the area as well, that is, the Kakakhel, Sayyids, Gujars and Mohmands.
125. Official it was Nawan Kalli and now Karnal Sher Khan Kalli after Capt. Karnal Sher Khan, a resident of the village who was killed in Kargil in 1999.
126. Khan, *Waqai Sayyid Ahmad*, pp. 1690–95.
127. The family history of the Hoti family has narrated that Ahmad Khan was disinherited by his father Lashkar Khan due to his bad character in 1815 and had his name excluded from the list of *khans*. We have certain reservations over the narrative. The Family History was written much latter and in those days any person who had opposed Sayyid Ahmad or the Mujahidin was not considered a good person. This kind of bias

might have affected the history. The family has always been on good terms with the establishment. The family had been granted *jagir* by the Mughals, Durranis, Sikhs and British. They have also remained active in provincial and national politics and bureaucracy after the partition of India.

128. Mihr, *Sayyid Ahmad*, pp. 601–2; Khan, *Waqai Sayyid Ahmad*, pp. 1695–700.
129. Khan, *Waqai Sayyid Ahmad*, pp. 1704–6, 1710–20.
130. Mihr, *Sayyid Ahmad*, p. 608.
131. *Tapah* Utmanzai includes Hund, Munara, Anbar, Kunda, Shah Mansoor, Panjpir, Zaida, Kadai, Marghuz, Kalabat, Pabeni, Baja, Bam Khel, Topi, Mainai and Gandaf.
132. Khan, *Waqai Sayyid Ahmad*, pp. 1724–26.
133. Ibid., pp.1744–46.
134. Ibid., pp. 1731–43.
135. Ibid., pp. 1742–43.
136. Bari, M. A. 1966. 'A Nineteenth Century Muslim Reform Movement in India', in George Makdisi (ed.), *Arabic and Islamic Studies in Honor of Hamilton A. R. Gibb*. Leiden: E. J. Brill. p. 99.

6

Success, Limits, and Failure

The Battle of Mayar and Occupation of Peshawar

As mentioned, Ahmad Khan of Hoti, Mardan had visited Peshawar to seek Sultan Muhammad Khan's help against the Mujahidin. The absence of Sayyid Ahmad and Shah Ismail from the Peshawar Valley along with half of the Mujahidin was a strategic advantage for Sultan Muhammad Khan. Also, the recent tour of the Mujahidin incited locals at different places to take arms against them. The immediate cause of the battle at Mayar was Ahmad Khan's effort to mobilize the Barakzais against Sayyid Ahmad. Other contributing factors included the need to avenge the death of Yar Muhammad Khan at the battle of Zaida. His mother and other family members pressed Sultan Muhammad Khan to take revenge. As well, the chiefs of the Peshawar Valley and Sultan Muhammad Khan feared for their future if Sayyid Ahmad could eliminate local authorities with impunity. Finally, the installation of Rasul Khan as *khan* of Mardan and Hoti enraged Ahmad Khan and a sizeable force of the Barakzai was collected to fight the Mujahidin and restore Barakzai influence.[1]

Risaldar Abdul Hamid Khan was staying in Kala Dara when Haji Bahadar Khan, *tahsildar* of Amazai, sent a letter that the Barakzais were coming to the area, and that the people of Amazai would join them on their arrival. Haji Bahadar Khan asked Abdul Hamid Khan for protection, including for the produce that was collected in *ushar* from the Amazai. The *risaldar* along with his force demonstrated their strength at Amazai and Sudham. After halts at different villages for a day or two, Abdul Hamid Khan went to Panjtar. By this time, the Barakzais were moving from Peshawar to fight the Mujahidin. Sayyid Ahmad was informed about the latest developments through a letter.[2]

Sayyid Ahmad appointed Sheikh Bakht Buland Deobandi and Sayyid Akbar Shah of Sithana to hold the Amb fort. Shah Ismail was made in-charge of the Mujahidin outside the fort of Amb. Maulvi Khair-ud-Din Sherkoti was to guard Chattar Bai. Sayyid Ahmad left Amb and arrived at Panjtar after several days. He ordered the collection of all the *ghalla* received as *ushar* from different villages in Sudham and Gandaf.[3]

Sayyid Ahmad consulted his allies about the movement of the Barakzai force. According to the collective decision, the Mujahidin left Panjtar and advanced to Toru. They were joined by local volunteers and their numbers increased considerably. Maulvi Abdul Rahman of Toru led the envoy to Sultan Muhammad Khan requesting him to avert fighting. Sultan Muhammad Khan, however, was not convinced that Sayyid Ahmad was fighting for the rule of Allah. Shah Ismail was also called by Sayyid Ahmad from Amb, who joined him at Toru after few days.[4] In the meantime, Sultan Muhammad Khan encamped at Hoti. There would be fighting instead of talk.

The battle of Mayar[5] (October 1830) started in the morning and continued for hours. It was for the first time since the battle of Shaidu that the Mujahidin faced their opponent on an open battlefield. The Mujahidin won the battle after severe fighting. The Barakzais were forced to flee. Twenty-eight Mujahidin were killed in Mayar and ten others were killed between Toru and Mayar. The dead included Risaldar Abdul Hamid Khan, Sayyid Musa, son of Sayyid Ahmad Ali, and Sayyid Abu Muhammad Nasirabadi.[6] The Barakzais left eighty dead on the field. They were buried in a collective grave with the help of local villagers.[7] Importantly, none of the local allies of the Mujahidin had deserted them.[8]

Shah Ismail was sent to Hoti (Mardan) to capture the provisions left in the Barakzais camp. An exchange of firing took place, but Shah Ismail's warning to blow up the whole of Hoti with cannon worked. Hoti surrendered. Shah Ismail forbade his men to enter the homes, lest the Mujahidin should lay hands on inhabitants of the town who had supported the Barakzais.[9]

Sayyid Ahmad confirmed Rasul Khan in control at Hoti and Mardan, sent the injured and *ghanima* captured from the Barakzais to Panjtar, and consulted with his allies. Then, accompanied by six to seven thousand tribesmen and Hindustani Mujahidin, he moved towards Peshawar. The major objective was the occupation of the city. They were unable to cross the Kabul River from the Charsadda side as the Barakzais had damaged all boats during their retreat after the battle of Mayar. Consequently, they went to Tangi[10] and crossed the river there. After crossing the river, they arrived at Michini via Shabqadar. They crossed the river Naguman and halted at Regai (also Regi), a village in the vicinity of Peshawar. Arbab Juma Khan informed Sayyid Ahmad that the Barakzais had vacated the city. Arbab Faizullah Khan of Hazarkhwani then visited Sayyid Ahmad and presented Sultan Muhammad Khan's request for peace.[11]

The Mujahidin in Peshawar

Long sessions of negotiations ultimately culminated in a peaceful surrender and Sayyid Ahmad entered Peshawar. Though many options were put to Sayyid Ahmad, he accepted none. Sultan Muhammad Khan was reinstated in Peshawar. Sayyid Ahmad and Sultan Muhammad Khan met near Hazarkhwani, in the suburbs of Peshawar. To justify his opposition to the Mujahidin, Sultan Muhammad Khan presented a document, a declaration addressed to the *khan*s of the Peshawar Valley and signed by numerous heads and mystics of India saying that a man, Sayyid Ahmad by name, had gone to the Frontier with a handful of his followers apparently for waging holy war, but he had denied the essential principles of Islam, downgraded their saints, and endeavoured to enforce a new religion of his own. Some sources further record that he was termed a British agent. Sayyid Ahmad rejected the allegations and passed the declaration to Shah Ismail.[12]

During Sayyid Ahmad's three-week stay in Peshawar, the terms of the peace treaty were finalized. Sultan Muhammad Khan apologized for his past behaviour, took an oath of allegiance to Sayyid Ahmad, and promised to rule according to the doctrine articulated by Sayyid Ahmad. Much against the wishes of his associates, Sayyid Ahmad restored Peshawar to Sultan Muhammad Khan on the condition of paying tribute, and then started back to Panjtar.[13] On their arrival at Charsadda, Sayyid Ahmad appointed Maulvi Mazhar Ali Azeemabadi as the *qazi* for Peshawar. He was sent along with several other Mujahidin to Peshawar and was given the responsibility to adjudicate all cases according to the canon law and to enforce *sharia*.[14]

J. D. Cunningham narrated that Sayyid Ahmad struck coins in his name bearing the inscription 'Ahmad the Just, Defender of the Faith, the glitters of whose sword scattereth destruction among infidels',[15] but we did not find other sources to confirm Cunningham's claim. Circumstantial evidence also does not support the claim as Sayyid Ahmad remained occupied with other business during his three week stay at Peshawar.

The occupation of Peshawar was the hallmark event in the career of Sayyid Ahmad. He became master of the whole Peshawar Valley as well as parts of Hazara and Khudu Khel. None of the local chiefs could dare to challenge his authority.[16] This, however, proved one of the major factors responsible for the ultimate failure of the Mujahidin. The earlier biographers of Sayyid Ahmad and the ideologically inspired writers of the movement have justified Sayyid Ahmad's decision. They thought that since Sayyid Ahmad was fighting for the cause of Islam and had no worldly ambition, it was a right decision to restore Peshawar to the Barakzai chief. Otherwise, the numerous brothers of Sultan Muhammad Khan, who were ruling various principalities in Afghanistan, would have taken up arms against the Sayyid and this would have been resulted in bloodshed of fellow Muslims. There was a chance that the Barakzai brothers might collaborate with the Sikhs against the Mujahidin. Sayyid Ahmad had not gone to North-West Frontier to install new chiefs by removing the previous ones. Otherwise, Sayyid Ahmad could have handed over Peshawar to Arbab Bahram Khan, as he asked, and that would have meant keeping it under his control.[17]

One source has claimed that keeping Peshawar under Sayyid Ahmad's direct control would be contrary to Pukhtu.[18] Ubaidullah Sindhi has observed that Sayyid Ahmad committed a blunder by restoring Peshawar as it incited Pukhtun tribal feelings against the Mujahidin. He should have avoided fighting against them but once defeated, it was necessary to keep the city under his control.[19] We argue here that handing the city back to its previous ruler might have given a message to the Pukhtuns that the Mujahidin were unable to organize a government and hold cities under formal administration.

Since their defeat in the battle of Shaidu, all the offences of the Mujahidin in the Peshawar Valley, and in some cases in Hazara, were directed against local fellow Muslims. It, therefore, made no sense that Sayyid Ahmad simply wanted to avoid fighting against Muslims and so restored Peshawar to Sultan Muhammad Khan. If this was the case, he would have neither invaded Peshawar nor would the Mujahidin have fought battles against Pukhtun Muslims, as detailed in the preceding pages. Another argument of the Sayyid's earlier biographer is that in the case of Sayyid Ahmad holding Peshawar, the Barakzai would have made an alliance with the Sikhs, and thus their energies would be consumed in self-fighting.

It should be underlined that Sayyid Ahmad had declared jihad against the Sikhs, and the Barakzai's alliance with the Sikhs would have provided him the opportunity to fight his real enemy. The Barakzais had no resources and the numerous brothers of Sultan Muhammad Khan were arguing each other. They never came from Afghanistan to avenge the death of their brother Yar Muhammad Khan. Controlling Peshawar would have not offended Pukhtu as the tribes of Peshawar Valley never claimed the Barakzais due to their indifference and Persianized culture. As stated in the previous chapter, the tribes of Peshawar Valley were more inclined to the Sadduzais due to their previous relations.[20]

Sayyid Ahmad had, in fact, removed previous chiefs of different areas and installed new ones. He had installed Ibrahim Khan at Kalabat, Sarfaraz Khan at Marghuz, and Fateh Khan at Zaida. Arbab Bahram Khan's appointment to the governorship of Peshawar, as he had requested, was a good option for several reasons. He was a local, accustomed to the traditions of the people. He had a good number of followers and his brother Arbab Juma Khan held his village despite Barakzai opposition. He had cordial relations with the tribes of Khyber and thus was in a better position to defend the city from the western side. Moreover, he had committed to enlist four thousand troops to support Sayyid Ahmad and meet all their expenses from his pocket.[21]

Importantly, we may infer that local allies of Sayyid Ahmad were offended by not honouring their council to appoint Arbab Bahram Khan. They considered their existence threatened by the restoration of the city to the former ruler. Later events proved that some of Sayyid Ahmad local allies were more enthusiastic in killing Mujahidin so as to prove their loyalty to the Barakzai governor. Yet another factor responsible for handing over Peshawar to its previous ruler was Sayyid Ahmad's interest in Kashmir. Again, since his arrival at the Frontier, he wished to make Kashmir his permanent base.[22] And still, despite his stay of four years in the Frontier, he remained indecisive about a permanent headquarters for the movement.

During his return journey from Peshawar to Panjtar, Sayyid Ahmad stayed in Amazai for quite a long time. This stay was important because of two decisions. First, Maulvi Khair-ud-Din Sherkoti was called from Hazara to be appointed *qazi-ul-quza* as suggested by Shah Ismail. He came, but his appointment did not take place due to his reluctance to accept what he considered a difficult post.[23] Also, having the most serious consequences, Sayyid Ahmad collected all people of the area and asked them to marry their daughters within a specified time frame[24] and without customary *walwar*. Though within few days, many marriages took place,[25] in many cases they were arranged much against the will of the family.

The post of *qazi-ul-quza* had been vacant since the death of Qazi Muhammad Hubban. Sayyid Ahmad appointed Maulvi Muhammad Ramzan to the post after Maulvi Khair-ud-Din Sherkoti's refusal. Maulvi Khair-ud-Din was sent to the Baizai area, Katlang and Lund Khwar, to collect *ushar* and adjudicate cases according to *sharia*.[26] Interestingly, Maulvi Khair-ud-Din Sherkoti imposed *jizyah* on the Hindus of Lund Khwar. Lund Khwar was a major market centre of Baizai and the lower Swat areas. A hundred shops and businesses were owned by Hindus. It was also decided that 25 per cent of the *jizyah* collected would be paid to the local *khans*, who were asked to support the Mujahidin in its collection.[27]

Naseer-ud-Din Manglori was sent to Topi to collect *ushar* as was previously done. Mir Hamid Ali was appointed to Maini with thirty-five Mujahidin to provide flour to the Mujahidin. Hamza Ali Khan, the new *risaldar*, was sent to Shawa with his lieutenants Sheikh Nasar-ud-Din and Sheikh Abdul Rahman. They were accompanied by a major portion of the artillery. Hamza Ali Khan was assigned the duty of appointing Mujahidin to different villages in the numbers necessary for the collection of *ushar*.[28]

At this time, Ghazan Khan, a chief of Dir,[29] sent an envoy to Sayyid Ahmad and asked him to send a mission to Dir. Sayyid Ahmad sent Shah Ismail, who was accompanied by one hundred Mujahidin. But they could not reach Dir due to opposition from the inhabitants of lower Swat.[30] The Swatis objected because of apprehensions that the Mujahidin would enforce *sharia* and would demand *ushar* from them if Ghazan Khan formed an alliance with the Mujahidin.[31]

The Massacre of the Mujahidin in the Peshawar Valley: Myth and Reality[32]

The restoration of Peshawar to Sultan Muhammad Khan and Sayyid Ahmad's return to Panjtar were followed by the worst possible consequences, an organized killing of the Mujahidin left as agents of the movement. The reasons for this violence were many. After Sayyid Ahmad's arrival to the Frontier, local *khans* had divided into two groups. One group supported Sayyid Ahmad, but others, the Barakzai chiefs especially, tried to safeguard their autonomy. The re-installation of Sultan Muhammad Khan at Peshawar by Sayyid Ahmad provided them an opportunity to mobilize and unify a response to the issues of the enforcement of *sharia*, the replacement of old institutions with new practices, and the ongoing threat of the removal or murder of local chiefs.

Frequent visits of local chiefs to Peshawar were reported to Sayyid Ahmad by Maulvi Mazhar Ali.[33] In another letter Arbab Faizullah Khan expressed his apprehensions about Sultan Muhammad's attitude. He wrote that Sultan Muhammad Khan was planning against the Mujahidin. Sayyid Ahmad, in Panjtar, did not realize the nature of the threat and replied to Maulvi Mazhar Ali that the chiefs and Sultan Muhammad Khan had re-established their relations and this was not a cause of alarm.

On 1 November 1830, Sayyid Asghar, a *pesh imam* of a mosque in Dukhara, a village 7 kilometres to the north-east of Panjtar, informed Sheikh Abdul Aziz, who was staying there with other Mujahidin, that the *khans* of the Peshawar Valley were planning to kill all the Mujahidin on an opportune day because of their oppressive attitude. Sheikh Ihsan Ali was dispatched by Sheikh Abdul Aziz to inform Sayyid Ahmad. Sayyid Ahmad did not believe it. He called it a rumour spread to create disunity and misunderstanding between them and local *khans*. Sheikh Ihsan returned to Dukhara and told Sayyid Asghar about Sayyid Ahmad's response to the news. Sayyid Asghar again sent him to Sayyid Ahmad with a proposal to call his Mujahidin from other areas to Panjtar. Sheikh Ihsan again went to Panjtar. He met the Sayyid and tried to convince him, but his efforts were to no avail. None believed the news he brought. Sayyid Asghar was sadden at this, remarking that within a few days they would see if what was reported was true.[34]

After several days, in November 1830, the news reached Sayyid Ahmad that Maulvi Mazhar Ali, his fellow Mujahidin, and Arbab Faizullah Khan had been murdered by Sultan Muhammad Khan. The news was carried by Imam-ud-Din, who had escaped death due to being absent from his residence. Sayyid Ahmad communicated the story to his associates, sending his messengers to the Mujahidin scattered in different villages, including Shawa, Yarhussain, and others, with the call to come forthwith to Panjtar. The message was delivered but without telling the reason. Mujahidin, therefore, stayed for the night in some the villages and some of them were killed. The murder of Maulvi Mazhar Ali and his associates took place two days prior to the planned day, perhaps due to the plot's disclosure to Arbab Faizullah Khan.

Bellew wrote that the signal to attack was 'let every man kill his sacrifice at the hour of evening prayer on—day.'[35] The *Waqai* narrated that the signal was an announcement, 'thrash the maize'. Asking about this, the Mujahidin, stationed in different villages, were told that this meant that

Sayyid Ahmad has demanded *ushar* and they should prepare their maize.[36] Qeyamuddin Ahmad wrote that on the fateful night, suddenly a fire blazed upon the peak of a hill at *isha* prayer time, drums were beaten from house-tops, and Pukhtuns collected in different villages. The confused Mujahidin asked the reason for the tumult, but their curiosity was satisfied when told that maize had to be thrashed—the code word for killing the Mujahidin. Most of the Mujahidin were killed during or even before the *isha* prayers. Haji Bahadar Khan of Rampur, *tahsildar* of Amazai, was in Ismaila on his way to his station. He was invited to dinner by villagers and was killed while offering prayers. Maulvi Ramzan Shah and his companions were killed in Shawa. Only Sayyid Amir Ali escaped alive.

Haji Mahmud Khan was stationed at Sudham with twenty Mujahidin. They were deceived by friendly signs from Mubin Khan of Sudham.[37] Fifteen of them were killed, while four escaped, including Hafiz Ilahi Bakhsh, a boy of fifteen. The boy received a sharp cut on his head after his uncle's murder, but he was saved by a Pukhtun who took him away to his house to be a labourer. He managed to escape from the place and joined Sayyid Ahmad.[38]

The Mujahidin from some areas arrived safely at Panjtar. Maulvi Khair-ud-Din Sherkoti was informed in time about the turbulence. He at once dispatched Mujahidin to demand tribute from local shopkeepers. They arrived with their *khan*s to make a settlement, as expected. He did not allow the *khan*s to leave until they agreed that one of them, Sadr-ud-Din, would remain as a hostage. When armed tribesmen arrived shortly to kill the Mujahidin, they left without harming anyone because of the presence of their chief. The Mujahidin went to Pranghar,[39] stayed with Malak Lal Muhammad Khan, and arrived safely at Panjtar after a month.[40]

Amb had been under Mujahidin control since Painda Khan's defeat. When news of the uprising in Peshawar reached Painda Khan, he collected a force, and asked the Mujahidin to leave his area. Fighting started and continued for a few days and some casualties were reported. The majority of the Mujahidin, with the help of Sayyid Akbar Shah of Sithana, joined Sayyid Ahmad at Bhus Dherai, as the Sayyid was on the way to Nandihar.[41] Mir Hamid Ali Khan, who was at Minai along with thirty-five Mujahidin made it to Panjtar. Maulvi Naseer-ud-Din Manglori, appointed at Topi, and his group also safely retreated to Panjtar. Hafiz Mustafa and his thirty Mujahidin, Sheikh Buland Bakht with sixty to seventy Mujahidin from Amb, and Hafiz Mustafa Hassan and his companions from Chattarbai, all joined Sayyid Ahmad while he was at Bhus Dherai.[42]

The names and numbers of Mujahidin assassinated at different places may be collected from the accounts of those who escaped to tell the story. Those killed included Maulvi Mazhar Ali Azeemabadi and his four companions at Peshawar. Haji Bahadar Khan Rampuri, *tahsildar* of Amazai, died in Ismaila. Maulvi Muhammad Ramzan was killed, most probably with twenty Mujahidin, at Shawa. Four Mujahidin died in Turlandai. The story of Risaldar Hamza Ali Khan was not recorded, but it seems that he was also killed in Yarhussain, along with perhaps thirty-five companions. About thirty Mujahidin stationed at Amazai perished in the violence. It is most probable that all of them were murdered by local villagers. Pir Khan and his twenty-six Mujahidin died in Minai as they were going to Panjtar from Kabal. Din Muhammad, *tahsildar* of Garhi Balochan (Amb), was killed there by local forces.[43]

The assassination of the Mujahidin at the hands of the Pukhtuns merits discussion. Many sources and traditions have exaggerated the number of the Mujahidin killed in this episode. Some sources suggest that the number of the Mujahidin killed ranged from eight hundred[44] to one thousand. One source said their number was in the thousands.[45] However, the number of Mujahidin killed in different villages, as ascertained from different sources, probably did not exceed two hundred. Sources have told of seven hundred Mujahidin in the battle of Balakot. From the migration of Sayyid Ahmad until the battle of Balakot, about eleven hundred Hindustani Mujahidin arrived in the Frontier. Some were killed in earlier battles with the Sikhs and Pukhtuns. Some were sent by Sayyid Ahmad to India to preach and raise funds.

Sources indicate that the number of locals at the side of the Mujahidin in Balakot was not more than one hundred. This means that about six hundred Hindustani Mujahidin were present in Balakot, with two hundred in Kashmir at the time of the battle of Balakot. The small number of the Mujahidin assassinated in November 1830 can also be confirmed from a letter by Sayyid Ahmad to Wazir-ud-Daulah on 13 Dhul Qa'idah 1246. The Sayyid wrote that some Mujahidin were killed by the people of the *samah* but that their main body remained safe, and were ready to fight for the cause of Islam.[46] Still, he has contradicted this statement on another occasion.

It seems strange that Pukhtun tribesmen in general and in *tapah* Razzar in particular rose against the Mujahidin all of a sudden. Several factors generated their rage. The Mujahidin had disregarded their social and political setup. The traditional political order was disturbed by the appointment of foreign *tahsildar*s and *qazi*s. Furthermore, they were forced to marry their daughters and sisters without *walwar*, a specific and customary amount demanded by the girl's family before marriage.[47] In some cases families were forced to marry daughters to the Hindustani Mujahidin. Resentment against this is evident from the *Waqai*, which tells that Azeemullah Khan was butchered by his father-in-law.[48] Azeemullah was the younger brother of Haji Bahadur Khan, the Mujahidin *tahsildar* of Sudham. It seems that he could not accept the betrothal of his daughter by the demand of the *tahsildar* authority.

After the killings, Sayyid Ahmad sent an enquiry commission to *tapah* Razzar. Sayyid Mian of Takhta Band and Kabul Akhundzada of Mangal Thana asked about events. Local Pukhtuns told the commission that their daughters and sisters had been married without their consent. They had been heavily fined, even for petty mistakes. They were severely rebuked for different offenses. They also presented the proclamation of the Indian *ulama* and Sufis that said Sayyid Ahmad was an English agent, who would damage their faith and take their country.[49] Finally, local *ulama* and religious figures, had declared the Mujahidin to be infidels and Wahabis, providing a religious justification for tribesmen already fed up with the Mujahidin.[50]

Migration to Rajdwari and Activities of the Mujahidin

Sayyid Ahmad lost his trust in the people of the plains, especially in *tapah* Razzar. Fateh Khan remained absent from Panjtar for many days during the trouble. He returned with people of his clan and also from Zaida. The Mujahidin fortified their area and prepared for defence. Fateh Khan visited Sayyid Ahmad and said that tribesmen had come to avenge the murder of the Mujahidin. However, Sayyid Ahmad sent them back.[51] He now did not trust Fateh Khan. After crossing Indus near Kabal Gram, his expression showed his thought that Fateh Khan was also responsible for the killings of the Mujahidin.[52]

Sayyid Ahmad, now a broken-hearted leader of the movement, collected his scattered army of the Mujahidin at Panjtar and planned for migration from Peshawar Valley. Some of the allied local tribesmen and a majority of his associates were unhappy with this decision. Arbab Bahram Khan asked Sayyid Ahmad to allow him to take five hundred

Mujahidin and few guns to bring the whole plain under his control. But Sayyid Ahmad did not agree to this on the plea that his objective was never worldly gain.[53]

Sayyid Ahmad decided to migrate to Nandihar, north of the Kaghan Valley. A few chiefs of that area had invited him to relocate there and wage jihad against the Sikhs. They included Zabardast Khan of Khakah Bamba, Nasir Khan Swati, Habibullah Khan of Khel Pakhali and Abdul Ghafur Khan of Agror. They had long asked Sayyid Ahmad to visit their area. With his interest in Kashmir, Sayyid Ahmad honoured their request and the Mujahidin left Panjtar on 29/30 December 1830. They were accompanied by their local associates, including Fateh Khan of Panjtar. They were joined by the Mujahidin who had vacated Amb after Painda Khan's attack. Shahzad Khan of Buner visited him in Bhus Dherai.[54] He had been active in planning to kill the Mujahidin. He sought Sayyid Ahmad's pardon.

They crossed Barandu[55] and stayed for a night beneath Bewan, a mountainous range. It is interesting to note that Sayyid Ahmad rode an elephant captured in the battle of Zaida. The next day they crossed Bewan, and stayed in Karta. Fateh Khan returned from here. From Karta they arrived at Kabal Gram, a village of the Akhun Khel on the bank of the Indus. They crossed the Indus via locally made rafts, *jala*, of *mashk*. All animals including horses, donkeys, camels and elephant were crossed in the same manner. After crossing the Indus, Sayyid Ahmad halted for some time. He remarked that Fateh Khan was responsible for the killing of the Mujahidin. Sayyid Ahmad said this probably from a misunderstanding, because the attitude of Fateh Khan's family did not indicate they opposed the Mujahidin.

They stayed for a day or two in different small villages and then arrived at Thakot, a place in the jurisdiction of Nasir Khan of Battagram. Nasir Khan was one of those who had earlier requested Sayyid Ahmad to migrate to his area. They stayed in Thakot for more than a week. He consulted the leading men of this area and of Nandihar, to select a place for the Mujahidin to stay. Rajdwari was selected, and Sayyid Ahmad and his Mujahidin shifted there. The area was selected due to the hoped availability of supplies and its central location. It was located at the entry of important passes and the valley could be well protected. All the local chiefs shared the place and none would feel jealousy or deprivation.[56] The whole journey from Panjtar to Rajdwari took nineteen or twenty days. They arrived at Rajdwari on 17 January 1831 (4 *Sha'ban* 1246 A.H.).[57]

At the time of the Sayyid's arrival in Hazara, the political situation turned against many local chiefs who had previously opposed the Sikhs.

Najaf Khan had replaced Zabardast Khan at Mauzaffarabad with the help of Sher Singh. Raja Muzaffar Khan, khan of Daraba, and his cousin Najaf Khan Ghoriwala were wandering looking for shelter. Garhi Habibullah had been captured by the Sikhs, and Habibullah Khan had fled to Kaghan Valley.[58] In mid-winter, it was severely cold and the Mujahidin faced a food shortage. Sayyid Ahmad called the local chiefs and sought their advice for commencing jihad. On their proposal, a force of four hundred was dispatched under Shah Ismail and Maulvi Khair-ud-Din Sherkoti to guard all the passes of the valley. This would serve two purposes: the Sikhs would not be able to enter the valley and the Mujahidin would be able to extract resources from the people. Maulvi Khair-ud-Din Sherkoti, with more than three hundred Mujahidin, was dispatched to Bhogarmang, a short distance from Shinkiari, the military post of the Sikhs.

Shah Ismail himself stayed in Sachchun. On their arrival in Sachchun, Hassan Ali Khan, chief of the area, directed the people to pay *ushar* to the Mujahidin. Maulvi Khair-ud-Din started collecting the *ushar* at Bhogarmang from the locals and fed his people. After a month-long stay, Maulvi Khair-ud-Din was transferred to Balakot. He was told by the local chiefs that Muzaffarabad was unguarded, as Sultan Najaf Khan had gone to Peshawar to meet Sher Singh. Attacking and capturing Muazffarabad would further pave the way for taking Kashmir. Maulvi Khair-ud-Din did not agree with their proposal on the ground that the locals would leave the Mujahidin to fight the Sikhs alone.

Shah Ismail also arrived at Balakot on 2 Ramdhan 1246 A.H. Sayyid Ahmad left Rajdwari along with three hundred and fifty Mujahidin and shifted to Sachchun as the previous place was no longer safe. In Sachchun Sayyid Zamin Shah of Kaghan visited Sayyid Ahmad and took *bai'at*. He remained a supporter of the Mujahidin for the rest of his life.[59] The Sikhs now planned to enter the valley on the arrival of spring.[60]

Shah Ismail was now approached by the local chiefs who previously advised Maulvi Khair-ud-Din to attack Muzaffarabad. Shah Ismail agreed immediately.[61] Maulvi Khair-ud-Din opposed Shah Ismail's decision. He told him that taking possession of Muzaffarabad was not possible as their local allies did not have the courage to fight the Sikhs. The Mujahidin, two hundred in number, were sent to Muzaffarabad under the command of Qutb-ud-Din Khan Ningarhari, Mansur Khan Qandahari, and Munshi Ghaus Muhammad of Amazai. Several days later, Maulvi Khair-ud-Din Sherkoti was sent by Sayyid Ahmad after being asked by the local chiefs.[62]

The detachment sent to Muzaffarabad took possession of the city upon their arrival. But the eight hundred Sikhs stationed at Garhi repulsed the

Mujahidin attack on their post. Maulvi Khair-ud-Din and his local ally Zabardast Khan left Muzaffarabad when Sher Singh and Najaf Khan's arrived near Balakot. Maulvi Khair-ud-Din followed a safer route to Balakot, but fell seriously ill and arrived only after the Sayyid's fall in the final battle against the Sikhs.[63]

Sher Singh and Najaf Khan arrived at Garhi Habibullah with a strong contingent of eight hundred men. Sher Singh proceeded to Muzaffarabad, leaving Garhi Habibullah in the charge of Mahan Singh. Shah Ismail planned a night attack on the Sikhs, but Sayyid Ahmad called him to Sachchun. Kashmir, long the preoccupation of Sayyid Ahmad, was once again considered. Kashmiri chiefs arrived in Sachchun and asked the Sayyid to accompany them. Shah Ismail was also approached by the Kashmiris to ask Sayyid Ahmad about this. Sayyid Ahmad wished to accompany them with his entire force, but decided at the request of the local chiefs to first fight the Sikhs with his full force. He, for that reason, called all the Mujahidin to Balakot.[64] One source said that Sayyid Ahmad wished to avoid confronting the Sikhs, but that his local allies wanted to fight.[65] They pleaded with Sayyid Ahmad not to move towards Kashmir before fighting a decisive battle against the Sikhs. They thought that his leaving their area would result in a Sikh incursion because they had sided with the Mujahidin over the last few months. Shah Ismail also wished to move to Kashmir, avoiding the Sikhs to save the Mujahidin's numerical strength. He wished to motivate the Kashmiris against the Sikhs and liberate their country.[66] In the end, the local allies of the Sayyid convinced him to fight the Sikhs in Balakot.

The Battle of Balakot and Its Consequences

Before leaving Sachchun, Sayyid Ahmad called together all the Mujahidin detachments stationed in different locations. They all joined before the final battle at Balakot except Maulvi Khair-ud-Din Sherkoti, who was ill. Shah Ismail was sent ahead to Balakot[67] and Sayyid Ahmad stayed for a night in a village. Sayyid Ahmad wished to call the wives of the Mujahidin to accompany them, but later changed his mind, because they would not be able to protect them in case of a fight against the Sikhs.[68]

Sayyid Ahmad left Sachchun on 17 April 1831 for Balakot. Inhabitants of Jabori provided food and accommodation for a night. The next day they departed. Sayyid Ahmad rode an elephant. When it was not safe to ride it, he walked. After the midday prayer, Shah Ismail was sent to Balakot and Sayyid Ahmad stayed for a night on the top of the hill. The long narration of the *Waqai* has reflected that spending the night changed him completely. He did not take interest in the coming battle and differed with all suggestions put forward by his associates.[69] His lack of interest in war strategy was revealed from another act. The Sikhs had sent a spy to Balakot to collect information about the Mujahidin. He was caught, abused by the Mujahidin, and presented before Sayyid Ahmad. He did not like the spy's insolence and asked him to get all information from Sayyid Ahmad by personally visiting him. He had left every matter to divine Providence.[70] This seemed to show that Sayyid Ahmad was completely disengaged, perhaps a shattered person at that stage. The strategy adopted by the Mujahidin was that of his associates. The next morning, Sayyid Ahmad entered Balakot with the Mujahidin and stayed in the homes vacated by Wasil Khan, chief of the village. A detachment under Lal Muhammad Qandahari was sent to guard the mountainous narrow passage in the south-west of Matikot. For the protection of the southern side, Amanullah Lakhnavi was sent with Mujahidin. Maulvi Naseer-ud-Din was already stationed at the Bhogarmang pass. Mujahidin were dispatched to protect the bridge to the south-east. Small bands of Mujahidin were appointed and sent where thought necessary.[71]

Several days passed between Sayyid Ahmad's arrival at Balakot and the final battle. The Mujahidin had decided that they would fight the Sikhs in a low-lying area between the foot of Matikot hummock and the inhabited portion of Balakot. The low ground was extremely watered and made soggy with the idea of slowing the Sikh advance. However, the Sikhs came from the south-west side where Mulla Lal Muhammad Qandahari was stationed. They overpowered the small detachment of Mujahidin and advanced to the side where main body of the Mujahidin had taken the field. The Mujahidin thus received a strategic blow to their plan. The Sikhs poured over the hill that dominated Balakot.

Sayyid Ahmad ordered his followers to let the Sikhs come down the hill and tramp through the wet fields. The Mujahidin opened fire when the Sikhs came panting up the high ground on which the houses stood. It was not a bad plan under the circumstances. When the Sikhs started coming down the hills the Mujahidin stood firm according to their plan. Suddenly, Sayyid Ahmad personally took the lead, dashed out with some followers towards the foothills. The battle thus started, the Mujahidin split up in small groups and lost coordination with each other. The battle was a pitched one, fought at close quarters. Sayyid Ahmad fell fighting bravely at the foot of the hills. It was Friday, 24 Dhul Qa'idah 1246 A.H., corresponding to 5 May 1831.[72] Sayyid Ahmad's lieutenant, Shah Ismail,[73] was among perhaps six hundred Mujahidin[74] who lost their lives on the battlefield.[75] The *Waqai* detailed that the Mujahidin killed totalled a bit more than three hundred.[76] This seems more accurate than the higher number as many Mujahidin escaped the battlefield or held different stations when the battle commenced.

Shah Isamil and Arbab Bahram Khan were buried in the field of battle. The rest of the Mujahidin were buried in a collective grave in Matikot Nala. Sher Singh, after identifying Sayyid Ahmad's corpse with the help of local people, ordered his burial in Balakot. He also distributed ₹25 alms according to Muslim rituals.[77] After Sher Singh's departure from Balakot, Sikhs dug up Sayyid Ahmad's corpse and threw it in the river. Some believe that his head was later found and buried in Garhi Habibullah, while the rest of his body was buried in Telhata.[78] The burial of Sayyid Ahmad's dead body by Sher Singh's orders and its later exhumation and throwing into the river has been agreed, but the body was never recovered later from the river. The Kunhar there flows too fast. It has been observed in recent times that even vehicles once lost in the river are not found. The battle was fought in May when snow melts at a higher rate to raise the level and speed of the river.

The battle of Balakot was perhaps the most important episode of the Jihad Movement. The death of Sayyid Ahmad became a mystery as none of the surviving Mujahidin had seen his burial or grave. Some believed that he had not been killed, but had gone into hiding in the mountains, and would join them at an opportune time.[79] To augment their belief some wrote pamphlets which were distributed to the adherents of the movement.[80] Many elders of the Deoband school of thought also believed in his reappearance. This actually moulded the entire tone and mood of the Jihad Movement. Sayyid Ahmad and the leaders of the movement had wanted to train movement members to work practically, but many became idle, as in previous mystic orders. Very few tried to keep the spirit of jihad alive. The story of his reappearance might have been created by his followers to maintain the movement. Later, people realized that it was a myth and that Sayyid Ahmad had died with the other Mujahidin at Balakot.[81]

The battle of Balakot shattered the dreams of the Mujahidin. They faced the Sikhs with full might for the first time without the support of the Pukhtuns and were badly defeated. The majority of them were killed. Not a single prominent leader, present on the battlefield, remained alive. The only leader of the movement who remained alive was

Maulvi Khair-ud-Din, who had been seriously ill, and unable to move. Sheikh Wali Muhammad Phulti was elected leader of the surviving Mujahidin. He was incapable of leading such a movement. His sole aim became to protect the widow of Sayyid Ahmad, something he considered a sacred job. He took her to Sindh and later to Tonk, where she lived a peaceful life. Many of the remaining Mujahidin took service at different places. The majority of the survivors settled in Tonk. The remnants of Sayyid Ahmad movement proved incapable of taking any active step against their opponents for a long time.

The defeat at Balakot left the Mujahidin without a leader, a head-quarters, or an organized plan or goal.[82] They wandered in different places for many years and often acted as tools of local chiefs. They were compelled to change their centres from time to time and failed to settle in any one place.

For many years, after the tragedy of Balakot, the remaining Mujahidin did not receive fresh recruits and money from India. The followers of Sayyid Ahmad became hopeless and ended support, considering it waste of their resources.

The Failure of the Mujahidin Movement

The failure of a Jihad Movement was not unusual.[83] The first reason of the failure of Sayyid Ahmad's effort was miscalculation. The Mujahidin wished to set up a government designed for an Arab society dated twelve centuries earlier.[84] Pukhtuns and their society were different from the Arabs of the seventh century. They were living in the nineteenth century, had witnessed major empires, had established dynasties in India, and had proudly fought many invaders. The Arabs of the Prophet Muhammad's (Peace Be Upon Him) time were different. The personality of the Prophet (Peace Be Upon Him) on the one hand and the peculiar socio-political conditions of the Arabs on the other facilitated early Muslim rule. The new arrangement was established by Arabs among Arabs.

But the case of Sayyid Ahmad was totally different. He was neither a Prophet nor a Pukhtun. Expecting the degree of support from Pukhtuns that the Prophet Muhammad (Peace Be Upon Him) received from the Arabs turned into a nightmare.[85] The Mujahidin, no doubt enthusiastic, lacked proper discipline and training required to face a strong, organized Sikh military under Ventura and Sher Singh.[86] They did not have appropriate weapons. When someone pointed this out, Sayyid Ahmad replied that battles were won with the help of Providence rather than weapons and strategy.[87]

The reforms initiated by Sayyid Ahmad to replace the customary tribal setup and family traditions antagonized Pukhtuns.[88] His haste and use of force in imposing alien, rigid ideas on unwilling, proud, and independent people caused its failure.[89] Sayyid Ahmad stayed among Mandanr and Yusafzai communities who were very conservative in their rituals and traditions. They did not marry their daughters to outsiders or without a dowry to their fellow tribesmen.[90] Reportedly, some girls were married to the Mujahidin by force.[91] Marrying daughters to non-Pukhtuns, to so-called *hindki*s, was regarded as a humiliation. The consequences were soon to follow. The policies of Sayyid Ahmad ignited among many Pukhtuns taking recourse in *badal* against the Mujahidin for the dishonour.[92]

Among the Mujahidin there were followers of the strict *Hanafi* school of thought and those who did not follow *Hanafi* law so rigorously. As long as Maulana Abdul Hai lived, a balance was maintained between these factions. But after his death the moderate section gradually weakened. Hardliners antagonized Pukhtuns, the local religious class, the tribal chiefs, and even some of the Mujahidin leaders. The Mujahidin, on their first success against their opponent, miscalculated and too quickly replaced old local institutions with their own. A *qazi* was appointed in each village to adjudicate cases according to *sharia*. But the Pukhtuns had a centuries-old *jargah* system, which decided all cases of mutual interest. The *jargah* also resolved differences between tribesmen, clans, and tribes at large. By abolishing this system, *jargah* members were deprived of their roles, status, and power.[93]

The appointment of *tahsildar*s in different areas offended local *khan*s. Previously, the *khan*s collected the levy from villagers and deposited it in the state exchequer. The amount of the levy was usually not fixed strictly and the *khan*s had to take care of their people. They usually avoided overburdening the people and paid to the state whatever was collected easily. The Mujahidin, on the other hand, strictly collected a fixed rate of tithe on agricultural produce. Moreover, their presence in the area ensured collection of the exact *ushar*. Maulvi Khair-ud-Din, who was appointed at Lund Khwar area, reached Panjtar safely out of the turmoil against the Mujahidin along with all his Mujahidin, in part because he acted differently from other *tahsildar*s. He did not disturb the traditional system and asked the *khan*s to collect the *ushar* on his behalf. Moreover, 25 per cent of the recently imposed *jizyah* on the Hindu population of the area was assigned to them. He also did not strictly impose the orders regarding the marriage of daughters. Rather, he delivered sermons and asked the locals to marry their daughters to a suitable person. Therefore, the concerned *khans* took care that these Mujahidin would not be harmed. Maulvi Khair-ud-Din had recognized the tension and adopted a pragmatic strategy.

Tara Chand asserted that the old religious and political elite were antagonized because the *mullas* were deprived of the tithe they received earlier and the *khans* had selfish motives.[94] It has been stated earlier that the tithe never had been paid to the *mullas*. They were paid a meagre share in the produce, the same as other *kasabgars*; the non-landowners, non-Pukhtuns, and professionals. The political opposition of local chiefs was tackled comparatively easily by the Mujahidin, but the social opposition of the Pukhtuns generated resistance and led to the assassination of the Mujahidin.[95] The drastic changes imposed in the traditions and rituals of the Pukhtuns were not tolerated and led to the failure of a movement which could have achieved great success if the ideological fathers had been accommodative.

Ali Khan Mahsud has given an interesting account of the opposition from the Pukhtuns. He said that the Pukhtuns and especially the Yusafzais welcomed Sayyid Ahmad's call while it was a military campaign, but they opposed it when he interfered in economic affairs. Historically, Pukhtuns do not accept economic aspect of Islam and it was unfortunate for Sayyid Ahmad that he did not recognize and value ground realities.[96] The growing demand of the Mujahidin for payments mobilized the Yusafzais to throw off their yoke.[97] S. M. Ikram also asserted that interference in economic affairs was the major cause of Pukhtun opposition, and so the Sayyid's failure was caused by differences over economic and political matters.[98]

At different times, decisions challenging Pukhtun identity and common practices generated hatred for the Mujahidin and contributed to the failure of the movement. If the occupation of Hund was one of the most important achievements of the movement, it was diminished by the inappropriate holding of the women and minors of Khadi Khan's family, after his death. This created great animosity against the Mujahidin.[99]

Sayyid Ahmad could not maintain a balance among the opposing groups of the Pukhtuns. There were several instances that *tarburwali*—rivalry between cousins—damaged the cause of the jihad. Amir Khan Khattak came to Sayyid Ahmad upon his arrival at Hashtnagar and took *bai'at*. This motivated his nephew Khawas Khan, who opposed his uncle, to join the Sikhs merely to oppose him.[100] Not only was Sayyid Ahmad's attitude unbalanced, but local chiefs also behaved in the same manner as they opposed the Mujahidin so as to oppose their rivals allied with the Sayyid.[101]

Kashmir remained one of the most important places in Sayyid Ahmad strategy, but was never occupied. The chiefs of Hazara were divided in two main groups, each one wished to eliminate the other. On the arrival of the Mujahidin led by Shah Ismail, each group tried to use them against their rivals. Shah Ismail, an able commander and learned scholar, did not fall prey to their schemes, but failed to get active support from any group of the Hazara chiefs.[102]

Shah Ismail was perhaps the only person among the Mujahidin, whose competence could be trusted in military matters. He was called to Panjtar when new caravans of the Mujahidin arrived from India and his services were required to start activities in the Peshawar Valley.[103] The absence of other such clearly competent figures in the Mujahidin leadership caused his removal from Hazara, though he was needed to stay there and continue efforts for the occupation of Kashmir and the Hazara region. His return to Panjtar caused discontent among Hazara chiefs and a sense of insecurity among Mujahidin allies. There was no second- or third-tier leadership among the Mujahidin to the degree required for success. This absence was most felt after the battle of Balakot.

As mentioned, the long tours of large groups of Mujahidin through the countryside also contributed to the failure of the movement in many ways. Besides the economic burden of payment of *ushar* and the provision of food to them and fodder to their animals, the Mujahidin insensitively changed the mode of traditional *melmastiya*. Hospitality had always been offered in the village *hujrah*, but the Mujahidin changed the tradition by asking the people to provide the food in the camp. Rather than being a few guests of a patron khan, the Mujahidin seemed more and more as imposed visitors expecting service in their camps.

Though the earlier biographers of Sayyid Ahmad have denied any Mujahidin high handedness in the villages, the *Waqai* offers such evidences. As well, the Mujahidin interfered in local administration, though some sources deny this.[104] Interference in the existing local setup was apparent. They replaced opponents with their supporters and at times acted like kingmakers. Their interference went beyond administrative affairs. There are instances that they even changed names of individuals, including a blind Hafiz-i-Qur'an, Pasham, who was renamed Resham.[105]

Importantly, during Qazi Muhammad Hubban's visit to restore order in Shawa, he declared in a public gathering that *ahl-e-rusum*, followers of the traditions of their forefathers, against the teaching of *sharia*, were infidels. When a person remarked that the *qazi* was telling a lie, he was presented before the *qazi*, tortured, and forced to recite the *kalima* so as to reconvert to Islam. This type of episode generated discontentment, hatred, and opposition in Razzar area.[106]

The Mujahidin had great expectations of support from local chiefs which was unrealistic. The local village and clan chiefs already had myriad local problems and issues to address. The majority of them did not join Sayyid Ahmad because of the possibility of his defeat by the Sikhs. Unlike the Mujahidin, they could not abandon their homes in case of a loss. They, therefore, kept a balance between the opposing parties as they looked to their future.

A colonial administrator referred to the Pukhtun tribal system when discussing the failure of the Jihad Movement. He compared Sayyid Ahmad with Sher Shah Suri and discussed the strength and weakness of the tribal system. A leader unites them for a common cause and all jealousies are shunned for a while. Enthusiasm makes them ready for a sacrifices and none bothers about the cost.

> [The]...leader gives way to vain-glory, the stimulus which gave unity fails, envy and malice show their heads. The effort, steady and sustained, which is needed to maintain the position won proves to be beyond the tribal reach. The ground won is lost, and the leader forfeits confidence and is discarded.[107]

There were other factors responsible for the collapse of the movement. The indecisive nature of Sayyid Ahmad himself was in large part responsible for the failure. It was beyond doubt that he was a unique thinker and activist. But he lacked the qualities needed to lead a movement claiming the right to mandate broad spiritual, economic, and social changes. He was not a son of the local soil and remained indifferent to the people of the area throughout his stay. He changed his headquarters frequently, first at Hund, later Panjtar, Khar, Panjtar for the second time, Rajdwari, and Balakot. He restored Peshawar to Sultan Muhammad Khan despite the fact that retaining the city would have surely enhanced his prestige and raised the morale of his followers. It would also have firmly established his political rule in the area. He could have made it his headquarters and fought for its defence until the end. Changing headquarters and abandoning one in the case of defeat made the tribesmen indifferent towards the Mujahidin. The perception developed that the Mujahidin were more interested in their personal security and in a crisis would leave the people of an area to the mercy of an invading Sikh force.

Sayyid Ammad had migrated to the Frontier without doing proper study of the environment. He did not understand Pukhtun psychology and he imposed *sharia* without preparing Pukhtuns for the many changes intended. A reformer prepared ground first and then worked for gradual internal change, which sometimes took decades. Sayyid Ahmad made hasty plans and took unconsidered actions, including initiating an offensive within a month of his arrival at the Frontier. Within three months, he had installed himself as *Amir-ul-Mominin*, without understanding how and why the traditional political elites would resist his authority.

Materially, the Mujahidin did not match the Sikh force. The number of the Hindustani Mujahidin never surpassed eleven hundred during their sojourn in the Frontier. The Sikhs under Ranjit Singh had a professional army, trained by veteran European generals. The Mujahidin took for granted that all local people were their allies or subordinates. The Pukhtuns no doubt had an emotional attachment with religion as they appreciated Sayyid Ahmad, but they always had preferred the interpretations of their local clerics in this regard. Sayyid Ahmad's decision to control the people by means of religious decrees suggests that he wished to establish his firm authority over the population. But popular regard for a Sayyid was totally different from accepting his doctrine and authority in its entirety.[108] In the entire history of the Pukhtuns, until Sayyid Ahmad, they had not been ruled by a Sayyid. Later, Sayyid Akbar Shah would rule the Swat Valley from 1850 until 1857.

The Jihad Movement of Sayyid Ahmad, despite its failure and his death, was an important episode in the history of the Pukhtuns. Though the Mujahidin were unable to establish their rule in the Frontier region, their efforts had certain successes and left a legacy that resonated into the twenty-first century.

Notes and References

1. Mihr, Ghulam Rasul. nd. *Sayyid Ahmad Shahid*. Lahore: Sheikh Ghulam Ali. p. 609. Henceforth, Mihr, *Sayyid Ahmad*.
2. Khan, Nawab Muhammad Wazir. 2007. *Waqai Sayyid Ahmad Shahid*. Lahore: Sayyid Ahmad Shahid Academy. pp. 1747–48. Henceforth, Khan, *Waqai Sayyid Ahmad*.
3. Nadvi, Sayyid Abu al-Hassan Ali. nd. *Tarikh-e-Dawat wa Azimat: Sirat-e-Sayyid Ahmad Shahid*, vol. II. Karachi: Majlis Nashriyat. pp. 242–43. Henceforth, Nadvi, *Sirat-e-Sayyid Ahmad*, vol. II. Khan, *Waqai Sayyid Ahmad*. pp. 1778–79.

4. Nasiri, Alim. 1995. *Shahnama-e-Balakot: Tahrik-e-Jihad ki Manzum Dastan*, vol. II. Lahore: Idara Mabu'at-e-Sulaimani. pp. 261–62. Henceforth, Nasiri, *Shahnama*, vol. II.
5. Mayar is located to the south of Hoti (Mardan) at a distance of 5 kilometres.
6. The last two were close relatives of Sayyid Ahmad.
7. Ahmad, Mohiuddin. 1975. *Saiyid Ahmad Shahid: His Life and Mission*. Lucknow: Academy of Islamic Research and Publications. pp. 241–45. Henceforth, Ahmad, *Saiyid Ahmad*. Khan, *Waqai Sayyid Ahmad*, pp. 1813–45.
8. They included Fateh Khan of Panjtar, Mansur Khan of Garyala, Anand Khan and Mushkar Khan of Shawa, Ismail Khan of Kalabat, Sarwar Khan of Amazai, Fateh Khan of Zaida, Shahbaz Khan Khattak and Khawas Khan Khattak of Akora, Dalil Khan of Toru, Nasim Khan of Lund Khawar, Qazi Said Amir of Kotah, Mulla Baha-ud-Din of Topi and Mulla Baqi of Dagai. Mihr, *Sayyid Ahmad*, p. 619.
9. Ahmad, *Saiyid Ahmad*, p. 246.
10. The river is spread over a long area near Tangi and thus easy to cross without boats. It was the winter season which made it easy for the Mujahidin to cross it due to the low flow of water.
11. Mihr, *Sayyid Ahmad*, pp. 644–45.
12. Khan, *Waqai Sayyid Ahmad*, pp. 1987–88; Ahmad, *Saiyid Ahmad*, pp. 250–51; Mihr, *Sayyid Ahmad*, p. 659.
13. Mallick, Azizur Rahman. 1977. *British Policy and the Muslims in Bengal, 1757–1856*. Dacca: Bangla Academy. p. 123. Henceforth, Mallick, *British Policy and the Muslims*.
14. Husain, Mahmud. 2008. 'Sayyid Ahmad Shahid (II)', in Mahud Husain et al. (eds). *A History of Freedom Movement, 1707–1831*, vol. I. Karachi: Royal Book Company. pp. 595–96. Henceforth, Husain, 'Sayyid Ahmad Shahid II'. Mihr, *Sayyid Ahmad*, pp. 659–62.
15. Cunningham, Joseph Davey. 1849. *A History of the Sikhs: From the Origin of the Nation to the Battle of the Sutlej*. London: John Murray. p. 193.
16. Husain, 'Sayyid Ahmad Shahid II', p. 596.
17. Mihr, *Sayyid Ahmad*, pp. 653–54; Ahmad, *Saiyid Ahmad*, pp. 249–50; Khan, *Waqai Sayyid Ahmad*, pp. 1936–42; Sabir, Muhammad Shafi. 1986. *Tarikh-e-Subah Sarhad*. Peshawar: University Book Agency. pp. 451–52. Henceforth, Sabir, *Tarikh-e-Subah Sarhad*.
18. Ahmad, *Saiyid Ahmad*, p. 250.
19. Sindhi, Ubaidullah. nd. *Shah Waliullah ki Siyasi Tahrik Yaniy Hizb-e-Waliullah Delhlavi ki Ijmali Tarikh ka Muqadama*. Lahore: Al-Mahmud Academy. p. 89. Henceforth, Sindhi, *Shah Waliullah*.
20. Ahmad Shah Abdali and Taimur Shah maintained cordial relations with the tribes of the Peshawar Valley and one of the wives of Taimur Shah was Yusafzai.
21. Mihr, *Sayyid Ahmad*, pp. 653–54; Ahmad, *Saiyid Ahmad*, pp. 249–50; Khan, *Waqai Sayyid Ahmad*, pp. 1936–42; Sabir, *Tarikh-e-Subah Sarhad*, pp. 451–52.
22. Ahmad, Qeyamuddin. 1979. *The Wahabi Movement in India*. National Book Foundation. p. 53. Henceforth, Ahmad, *The Wahabi Movement*.
23. Khan, *Waqai Sayyid Ahmad*, p. 2001.
24. According to the *Waqai* narrative, eight days were given to those whose daughter/sister was engaged and their fiancé was living within a few kilometres. One month was given for those whose fiancé was out of the area. Three months were allowed for those whose fiancés were out of the country and they could marry another if he would not

return. Khan, *Waqai Sayyid Ahmad*, pp. 1994–2000. In Pukhtun society, like many others, the marriage of an already engaged female to anyone else remains a rare event even today after 185 years of the Sayyid Ahmad time. One could imagine the resistance from tribesmen of the time.

25. Khan, *Waqai Sayyid Ahmad*, pp. 1994–2000.
26. Mihr, *Sayyid Ahmad*, p. 664.
27. Khan, *Waqai Sayyid Ahmad*, pp. 2074–75.
28. Ibid., pp. 2005–7.
29. Mihr has written Bajawar which does not seem appropriate as Ghazan Khan was the chief of Dir as supported by many contemporary sources. Bajawar could be reached from Mohmand side as well in case of opposition from Swatis.
30. Ahmad Khan of Hoti (Mardan) was son in law of Inayatullah Khan of Ala Dhand, Swat. Plowden, T. J. 1932. *Report on the Leading Persons and State of Factions in Swat.* Simla: Government Press of India. Tribal Research Cell, Government of Khyber Pakhtunkhwa Peshawar, p. 34. Inayatullah Khan was the leader of the opponents of the Mujahidin this time though previously he was on good terms with them but now his son in law had faced the heavy hand of the Mujahidin.
31. Khan, *Waqai Sayyid Ahmad*, pp. 2007–8.
32. We have written the word 'massacre' in the heading. But for the rest of the discussion the word massacre is replaced with the word murder or killing.
33. Maulvi Mazhar Ali Azeemabadi was once called to the court. Sultan Muhammad Khan enquired about the legal status of Yar Muhammad Khan's death at the hands of the Mujahidin. Mazhar Ali sent the question to Shah Ismail at Panjtar and he sent him a long description of religious decrees describing Yar Muhammad Khan as a rebel.
34. Ahmad, *Saiyid Ahmad*, pp. 258–59; Khan, *Waqai Sayyid Ahmad*, pp. 2010–12.
35. Bellew, H. W. 2001. *A General Report on the Yusufzais.* Lahore: Sang-e-Meel Publications. p. 92. Henceforth, Bellew, *A General Report.*
36. Khan, *Waqai Sayyid Ahmad*, p. 2016.
37. Those who actively participated in the killing of the Mujahidin included Ismail Khan of Ismaila, Ma'azullah Khan of Minai, Mubin Khan of Sudham, and Shahzad Khan of Daggar (Buner).
38. Ahmad, *Saiyid Ahmad*, pp. 260–61; Khan, *Waqai Sayyid Ahmad*, pp. 2013–40.
39. Pranghar is located at a distance of six or seven kilometres to the north of Tangi. It can be reached from Dargai, Garhi Usmani Khel side, and is presently part of Mohmand agency, Pakistan.
40. Ahmad, *Saiyid Ahmad*, pp. 261; Khan, *Waqai Sayyid Ahmad*, pp. 2077–98.
41. Khan, *Waqai Sayyid Ahmad*, pp. 2101–2, 2116–42.
42. Ibid.
43. During the assassination of the Mujahidin many individuals and families supported the Mujahidin. They included Sayyid Asghar of Dukhara, Anand Khan and Mushkar Khan of Shawa, Sayyid Mian of Takhta Band, Sayyid Al Rasul and his brother Sayyid Azam of Nawagai, Sayyid Shah Randan and Kabul Akhundzada of Mangal Thana, Sayyid Akbar Shah and his family of Sithana, Said Amir Akhundzada of Kotah, Fateh Khan of Zaida, Ibrahim Khan of Kalabat, Mansur Khan of Garyala, Mahmud Khan of Tangi, Musa Khan of Nagrai and Madad Khan of Degarai. Those who saved them from the tribesmen at the cost of their own lives and honour included a Mulla of Shawa who saved a Mujahid. Different people of Minai saved 15 Mujahidin. Sayyid Mian Muhammad of Minai saved two Mujahidin. Mulla Said Amir of Kotah saved four and also managed

the safe passage of others who had approached him. Malik Lal Muhammad Khan of Pranghar provided safety for one month to Maulvi Khair-ud-Din along with his 80 Mujahidin. Anand Khan and Mushkar Khan of Shawa saved Arbab Bahram Khan's family from the tribesmen. Akhund Gul of Badabher, Peshawar, remained a trusted ally till Sheikh Wali Muhammad's return to India several years after the battle of Balakot. Rasul Khan and Alam Khan of Jalala remained at the Mujahidin's side till Balakot and arranged Maulvi Khair-ud-Din's letter delivery to Sayyid Ahmad when he was going to Pranghar. Sayyid Aurang Shah served several Mujahidin for some days who were unable to accompany Maulvi Khair-ud-Din when he went to Panjtar from Pranghar. An old woman of Suddam saved two companions of Haji Mahmud Khan.

44. Panni, Sher Bahadar Khan. 2006. *Tarikh-e-Hazara*. Lahore: Maktaba Jamal. p. 151. Henceforth, Panni, *Tarikh-e-Hazara*.
45. *James Settlement Report*, p. 46.
46. Nadvi, *Sirat-e-Sayyid Ahmad*. vol. II, pp. 414–15.
47. *Walwar* was not practised by all Pukhtuns but there was a tradition and we have observed that the family of the boy was to provide food stuff and other material which the family of the girl offered to guests. In the case that cash was received, the female's family purchased crockery, bedding, jewelry and other necessities.
48. Khan, *Waqai Sayyid Ahmad*, p. 2101.
49. Ibid., pp. 2061–62.
50. Lal, Kanhia. 2002. *Tarikh-e-Punjab*. Mirpur, Azad Kashmir: Arsalan Books. p. 343. Henceforth, Lal, *Tarikh-e-Punjab*.
51. Ahmad, *Saiyid Ahmad*, p. 262.
52. Khan, *Waqai Sayyid Ahmad*, pp. 2151–52.
53. Ahmad, *Saiyid Ahmad*, pp. 261–62.
54. Mihr has wrongly written the name as Bar Dheri. See Mihr, *Sayyid Ahmad*, p. 712.
55. Barandu is a long ravine that joins the Indus after passing through Buner.
56. Khan, *Waqai Sayyid Ahmad*, pp. 2142–58; Mihr, *Sayyid Ahmad*, p. 714.
57. Mihr, *Sayyid Ahmad*, p. 714.
58. Ahmad, *Saiyid Ahmad*, p. 267.
59. Khan, *Waqai Sayyid Ahmad*, p. 2206.
60. Khan, *Saiyid Ahmad*, p. 269.
61. It has been mentioned earlier that Sayyid Ahmad's main interest was in Kashmir and he was ready to go to any end for that matter. Maulvi Khair-ud-Din was pragmatic and knew the strength of the Mujahidin.
62. Khan, *Waqai Sayyid Ahmad*, pp. 2185–202.
63. Ahmad, *The Wahabi Movement*, p. 57; Ahmad, *Saiyid Ahmad*, pp. 272–73.
64. Ahmad, *Saiyid Ahmad*, pp. 269–70.
65. Lal, *Tarikh-e-Punjab*, p. 344.
66. Nasiri, *Shahnama*, vol. II, pp. 489–91.
67. Balakot stands at the southern tip of the Kaghan Valley, on the right bank of the river Kunhar, but the mountains of Kaghan adjacent to the river on both sides split it from the valley just at the beginning of the town. Thus, the only approach to the town from Mansehra was from the south-west where a road, then a bridle path, entered the slender, zigzag gorges of the Kunhar Valley. Opposite Garhi Habibullah, a corridor split out to cross a bridge leading south-east to Muzaffarabad and Srinagar in Kashmir. Another track followed the western bank of the river northwards to Balakot, which rose to an elevation of 2012 metres. The town was encircled in the north by three rocky knots

which form a natural wall from north-west to north-east. In the South, the Kunhar Valley opened up to allow a vertical but not fully precipitous ascent. In the east a raised mound held a village Kalu Khan. Another mound rose above Matikot village and commanded the town on its western side. A number of *nalas*, ravines, drained the northern hills and protected the town. Barna and Satbana *nalas* joined Kunhar from north-west of the town and Nala Matikot bordered it on the south western side. Mihr, *Sayyid Ahmad*, p. 738; Ahmad, *Saiyid Ahmad*, pp. 274–75. The earthquake of October 2005 changed everything in Balakot and its vicinity. Many villages were destroyed, ravines changed their courses, and some no longer exist.

68. Nadvi, *Sirat-e-Sayyid Ahmad*, vol. II, p. 406.
69. Khan, *Waqai Sayyid Ahmad*, pp. 2247–56.
70. Nadvi, *Sirat-e-Sayyid Ahmad*, vol. II, pp. 415–16.
71. Ibid., pp. 411–13.
72. Ahmad, *The Wahabi Movement*, pp. 64–65. For complete details of the battle and war planning see Khan, *Waqai Sayyid Ahmad*, pp. 2363–2451; Mihr, *Sayyid Ahmad*, pp. 747–86.
73. Husain, 'Sayyid Ahmad Shahid II', pp. 597–98.
74. See Appendix E.
75. Qureshi, Ishtiaq Hussain. nd. *Ulema in Politics*. Karachi: Ma'arif. p. 152. Henceforth, Qureshi, *Ulema in Politics*.
76. Khan, *Waqai Sayyid Ahmad*, p. 2451.
77. Ibid., pp. 2449–50.
78. Nadvi, *Sirat-e-Sayyid Ahmad*, vol. II, pp. 441–49.
79. Bari, M. A. 1965. 'A Nineteenth Century Muslim Reform Movement', in George Makdisi (ed.), *Arabic and Islamic Studies in Honor of Hamilton A. R. Gibb*. Leiden: E. J. Brill. p. 101. Henceforth, Bari, 'A Nineteenth Century Muslim Reform Movement'.
80. Azeemabadi, Wilayat Ali. nd. *Majua'e Rasail-e-Tisa'a*. Delhi: Matba' Farooqi.
81. Nadvi, *Sirat-e-Sayyid Ahmad*, vol. II, pp. 445–46.
82. Bari, 'A Nineteenth Muslim Reform Movement', p. 100.
83. Failure here means a temporary halt in the activities of the Mujahidin. The Jihad Movement continued for decades in one form or the other. It contributed much in different spheres of life. Ubaidullah Sindhi thought that Sayyid Ahmad was not an original thinker and that he was only a soldier of the Shah Waliullah movement. Sindhi thought that halting the activities of the Mujahidin for a time did not mean the failure of the movement as such movements have several phases, may face temporary failures, and ultimately achieve objectives. Sindhi, *Shah Waliullah*, pp. 94–95. Although Shah Waliullah and Abdul Aziz had an impact upon his thoughts, the Jihad Movement was Sayyid Ahmad's personal initiative.
84. Mallick, *British Policy and the Muslims*, pp. 123–24.
85. Many militant organizations active in Pakistan, Afghanistan and other Central Asian countries claim that they are working for the establishment of the *khilafat* of the earliest days of Islam. Apart from such militants, there are some organizations, working on political lines, who also claim that they would establish a *khilafat* as of the earliest time. The latter category includes Hizb-ul-Tahrir and Tanzim-e-Islami.
86. Qureshi, *Ulema in Politics*, p. 153.
87. Khan, *Waqai Sayyid Ahmad*, p. 2214.

88. Chand, Tara. 1967. *History of the Freedom Movement in India*, vol. II. Delhi: Ministry of Information and Broadcasting, Government of India. p. 26. Henceforth, Chand, *History of Freedom Movement*.

89. Mallick, *British Policy and the Muslims*, p. 124.

90. *James Settlement Report*, p. 47.

91. Ali, Shahmat. 2005. *The Sikhs and the Afghanistan Connexion with India and Persia.* New York: Adamant Media Corporation. pp. 273–74.

92. Bari, 'A Nineteenth Century Muslim Reform Movement', p. 99.

93. After 9/11, this happened in the Pukhtun belt, especially the Federally Administered Tribal Areas (FATA) of Pakistan. Both state and non-state actors have killed thousands of *malaks* leaving turmoil in the area. The government has failed to restore peace, while tribesmen are no more bound due to the collapse of their traditional hierarchy. During the last thirty years, different national and international actors have changed their lifestyle. Old institutions, including *hujrah, jumat, jargah*, etc., have been destroyed.

94. Chand, *History of Freedom Movement*, p. 26.

95. Bari, 'A Nineteenth Century Muslim Reform Movement', p. 98.

96. Mahsud, Ali Khan. nd. *La Pir Rukhana tar Bacha Khan Poray: Da Pukhtanu Milli Mubarezay ta Katana.* Peshawar: Danish Khparawanay Tolanay Tekhniki Sanga. p. 224.

97. *James Settlement Report*, p. 46.

98. Ikram, Sheikh Muhammad. 2000. *Mauj-e-Kausar.* Lahore: Idara Saqafat-e-Islamia. p. 30.

99. Kakakhel, *Pushtun*, p. 692.

100. Khan, *Waqai Sayyid Ahmad*, pp. 1235–37.

101. Qureshi, *Ulema in Politics*, p. 149.

102. Mihr, *Sayyid Ahmad*, pp. 420–21.

103. Ibid., p. 427.

104. Bari, 'A Ninteenth Century Muslim Reform Movement', p. 99.

105. Khan, *Waqai Sayyid Ahmad*, p. 2083.

106. Ibid., pp. 1693–95.

107. Caroe, Olaf. 1965. *The Pathans, 550 BC–AD 1957.* London: Macmillan and Co. Ltd. pp. 305–6.

108. Bari, 'A Nineteenth Century Muslim Reform Movement', p. 99.

7

Impact of the Movement upon the Frontier

The Jihad Movement of Sayyid Ahmad was a new experience in the history of South Asian Muslims. An ordinary person, having mystic training, organized a movement in the name of Islam. He was an original thinker and initiated a reform movement to purify the society from *bida'at*. He endeavoured to purify the 'popular Islam' according to his interpretation of 'reformist Islam'. He aimed at establishing a *khilafat* on the ideals of the early days of Islam. The movement left multi-dimensional impacts upon Indian Muslims and the Pukhtuns of the North-West Frontier.

Much has been written on the offshoots of the movement and their impact on Bengal, Deccan, and parts of northern India.[1] The impact of the Jihad Movement on the political, socio-economic, and religious life of Pukhtuns of today's Khyber Pakhtunkhwa and adjacent areas has not been examined. With partial and incomplete sources, the saying, 'history is the reconstruction of past on the basis of partially known facts' must apply here. This chapter, therefore, is based on disjointed information, derived from scattered sources, and previous chapters. An attempt is made to interpret and apply this information to the Pukhtun region.[2] Anthropologically considered dynamics of the social structure have also been considered.

Political and Religious Impacts

The first major political impact of the failure of this first phase of the Mujahidin Movement was the occupation of the Peshawar Valley by the Sikhs. Though the Barakzai governors of Peshawar, Bannu and Derajat, paid tribute to the Lahore *darbar*, the Sikhs had failed in attempts to physically occupy Peshawar Valley. A year after the battle of Pir Sabaq

(Nowshera), the tribesmen rose against the Sikhs and Ranjit Singh failed to maintain order in the cis-Indus districts.[3] After Sayyid Ahmad arrived at Peshawar along his Mujahidin, Ventura (d. 1858) attacked Panjtar twice, but failed to either oust the Mujahidin or occupy the village.[4] The Sikhs as well as the Barakzais were relieved at the defeat of the Mujahidin in the battle of Balakot (1831), but this did not benefit the Barakzai *sardar* of Peshawar. The Sikh army entered Peshawar on the pretext of Prince Naunihal Singh's wish to see the city. The inhabitants of the city resisted, but were defeated by the Sikhs. Following the example of their elder brother Muhammad Azim Khan,[5] Sultan Muhammad Khan and his brothers did not resist; they fled. They took shelter in Sheikhan, a village in suburb of Peshawar, and then went to Kabul via Jalalabad. Thus in 1834 was Peshawar finally annexed by the Sikhs.[6]

The Balakot episode (1831) did not end the Jihad Movement. It continued in variant legacies for more than a century, experiencing many ups and downs during the colonial period. The emergence of Pakistan in 1947 halted such activities for the time being, but did not end such mindsets and spirits. In recent decades, such outlooks were strengthened and radicalized anew by many state and non-state actors.[7]

The Jihad Movement of Sayyid Ahmad changed the outlook of Indian Muslims. It may be considered the beginning of mass mobilization along the religious lines for the reformation of society. Instead of looking to the rulers, elites, and outsiders to save them from foreign rule and internal decay, Sayyid Ahmad internally re-organized Muslims and initiated a process to unify the Muslim community.[8] The practice of the Jihad Movement, building a movement through the organization of the general public, was followed by Muslim leadership in the decades to come.

The impact on the North-West Frontier was different in nature. Politically speaking, Sayyid Ahmad's Jihad Movement affected the people of the area to a great extent. The North-West Frontier had not been accustomed to strict political administration in the centuries before Sayyid Ahmad's sojourn in the region. The authority of various empires who tried to control Pukhtunkhwa extended control only over the plains and, partially, one or two passes through the mountains. The earlier Mughals (1526–1707) had failed in efforts to bring the Pukhtun tribes under strict administration. The tribes often resisted the passing of Imperial forces through main routes in the mountains. They were not accustomed to being ruled by any external power, a freedom symbolized by the government failure to receive any tax.[9] The area was typically supervised by a local administration and previous rulers avoided interference in the internal affairs of the tribes, including their village administration. Pukhtuns paid a nominal tax to the public exchequer and that too was collected only through their traditional chiefs.[10]

After taking the second oath of allegiance from the Pukhtuns in Panjtar on 6 February 1829; Sayyid Ahmad firmly established his authority in their midst. His administration was different from that of previous rulers, when local administration was run by traditional chiefs and the heads of the clans. Sayyid Ahmad appointed his Hindustani associates as *quza*[11] and as *tahsildar*s in the parts of the Peshawar Valley under his jurisdiction. The *qazi* system was a completely new experience for Pukhtuns. It deprived their traditional *khan*s of their previous status and eclipsed the traditional *jargah*. The Sikhs and the English followed the same policies of bringing the Pukhtuns under close rule after their annexations of Peshawar in 1834 and 1849, respectively. Sayyid Ahmad removed a number of the traditional chiefs from their positions and appointed others. As mentioned earlier, the *khan*s of Kalabat, Marghuz and Thand Koi were replaced with his choices.[12] This was a policy later pursued by colonial authorities to bring 'turbulent' Pukhtuns under control. British colonial authorities also replaced the traditional *jargah* with their own officially appointed version of the institution.[13] Sayyid Ahmad's policy of 'Islamization' was later followed in Pukhtunkhwa by other religiously defined movements. This resulted in the creation of two opposing camps among Pukhtuns, 'religious ideologues' and 'liberals'. Moderates were often eliminated in the process, a problem that blocked evolutionary processes of modernization and curtailed political debate.

Though Sayyid Ahmad and his successors failed to establish an 'Islamic state' on the lines of earlier Muslims, their remaining adherents regrouped and fought British colonial authorities for decades.[14] This fighting and opposition in the name of Islam gradually changed the mindset of Pukhtuns. Pukhtuns, despite their emotional attachment to Islam, typically fought for tribal honour and political interests. Pragmatically, they were not religious ideologues. The Jihad Movement brought about changes in the thinking of many about their identities. Though it took decades rather more than a century, the Jihad Movement left a template for ongoing religious fervour among many Pukhtuns.[15]

After the decline of Mughal rule, the North-West Frontier was constantly fought over by different claimants for power. Inhabitants were compelled to support one party or the other. The tribes of the Peshawar Valley had mainly associated with the Afghan Sadduzais. One reason for many joining the Jihad Movement was their dislike for the Barakzais.

They hoped that Sayyid Ahmad would redress their grievances. Their expectation, however, proved futile. Though conflict between various claimants for the area continued for several decades, the tribes took up arms only a few times, at long intervals. The Mujahidin on the other hand exhorted them to be prepared for jihad at all times.

During the four years of the Mujahidin efforts to establish their ascendency in parts of the Peshawar Valley and the Khudu Khel area, Pukhtuns fought and witnessed eight battles as well as the wider Mujahidin offensive against their opponents. Successive events showed that the Mujahidin presence weakened Pukhtun military unity. The Mujahidin removed by force several of their Pukhtun political opponents, Khadi Khan of Hund, Ahmad Khan of Hoti, and others, which demoralized many Pukhtuns.[16] The case of Khadi Khan was especially alarming for local people. In their long history of warfare, the Pukhtuns avoided seizing the women of the enemy, though it had happened to followers of Bayazid Ansari.[17] The Mujahidin held the family of Khadi Khan for two weeks.[18] This, captivity, as human shields or hostages, was a rare instance of its kind in the area and not authorized by the Qur'an and *sunnah*. There is evidence that those claiming ideological inspiration from Sayyid Ahmad and Shah Ismail, considered it lawful to turn the women folk of defeated infidels or 'rebels' into concubines.[19]

Sayyid Ahmad's policy demanding Pukhtuns to either obey his command or face the consequences compelled some chiefs, including Painda Khan and the Barakzais, to seek assistance from the Sikhs[20] or flee before them, though the former had fought the Sikhs previously a number of times.[21] As his policy weakened Pukhtun social and political relations, it paved the way for the direct occupation and control by the Sikhs of the trans-Indus Pukhtun-settled plains.[22]

The policy of eliminating traditional leadership in the tribal areas was a policy initiated in the late twentieth century by the Musharraf regime to bring tribesmen under mainstream government control. It was the same policy pursued by the Taliban.[23] Both replicated the policy of Sayyid Ahmad and the Mujahidin. Such a policy was also followed at times by the British and Pakistan after 1947. The process accelerated after 11 September 2001 when both Pakistan state authorities and militants intervened in the tribal belt. *Malak*s and tribal chiefs were not just individuals, but institutions in one person.[24] The resulting killing, some say 'genocide', of tribal chiefs brought a huge administrative gap and each side interfered as it wished. Though every successive state policy was not directly inspired by the Mujahidin, the tactic they pursued was first adopted by the Mujahidin.

The Mujahidin also adopted the policy of replacing opponents with supporters. The replacement of Ahmad Khan, with his brother Rasul Khan of Hoti (Mardan), the *khan*s of Kalabat, Marghuz, and few others are evidence. This policy brought the Sikhs to the heartland of the Yusafzais and Mandanr, because to maintain their position or regain the lost status, the opponents of the Mujahidin sought Sikh assistance. The presence of such persons in the Peshawar Valley gave the Sikhs an opportunity to occupy the area and appoint governors in Peshawar and Hazara on behalf of the Lahore *darbar*. Sikh direct contact with Pukhtuns revealed their weaknesses to the Sikhs.[25] Pukhtuns of the Peshawar Valley were weakened in the struggle between the Sikhs and the Mujahidin, but also as the Pukhtuns struggled with claims to authority by the Mujahidin.

The Jihad Movement had a visible impact on the region as well as on Muslims of other areas. Mujahidin migrated in to wage jihad against the Sikhs, a new phenomenon for the people of the area. The North-West Frontier had been a highway for invaders for centuries. Some of the invaders recruited Pukhtuns, who joined the invading armies, usually towards India, and returned with spoils. Though tribesmen settled in parts of northern India, the invaders usually avoided settling in the North-West Frontier. Sayyid Ahmad and his Mujahidin did not come to the region as invaders, but as immigrants, for waging jihad against the Sikhs. The Mujahidin made the area the hub of their activities. However, waging jihad for such a long period, with their local resources and in their own area, was a totally new experience for Pukhtuns.[26]

Resistance movements often flourished in remote areas where state control was weak. But the people of such areas often extracted concessions from state authorities. It was not necessary that resistance should be based on religion. The grounds could be ethnic, economic, social, political, or religious. Another major difference was the background of the fighters against the outside imperialists. In many such cases the movements have been initiated by locals acting on their own. Michael Adas had nicely described such movements. The major difference between the movements Adas has described and the Mujahidin Movement is that those movements were typically initiated by local leaders mobilizing their communities against the Imperial authorities.[27] But the Jihad Movement of Sayyid Ahmad first opposed the 'usurpers' and then turned against its earlier supporters in the North-West Frontier. Many Pukhtuns, therefore, finally considered Sayyid Ahmad and his Mujahidin to also represent alien or Imperial power. Due to his 'oppressive policies', they turned against him. He had migrated from the princely state of Oudh, from a totally different social background, and a different religious orientation. The orientation of their religious doctrine was visible from the *Waqai* and other books written by the followers of Sayyid Ahmad. They cast a sectarian colour on the opposition of the Barakzai brothers.[28] The sources do not prove that Shia–Sunni differences had ever led to violence at any stage before that time. In fact, the people of the Peshawar Valley often followed some Shia rituals in Muharram.[29] That the only bond between the Mujahidin and Pukhtuns was religion, hints that religion was not enough to keep the heterogeneous groups united as social, political and economic grievances emerged.[30]

The episode of the Jihad Movement changed the outlook of the people of the region. Sayyid Ahmad had been followed by many to the North-West Frontier in the name of religion. Maulvi Naseer-ud-Din Dehlavi,[31] Mir Aulad Ali, Maulvi Inayat Ali, and Wilayat Ali migrated to the North-West Frontier and created troubles for the colonialists for a long period.[32] Pukhtun religious practices conform to certain rituals and they follow Pukhtu, the Pukhtun code of conduct, in cases when this code is contradicted by *sharia*. Pukhtun emotional attachment to religion did not broaden their vision, restricted to following certain rituals only,[33] when challenged and appealed to by Sayyid Ahmad.

In the history of Indian Muslims, the *ulama* had supported and opposed the ruling elite at different times for obvious reasons. They were appointed to high posts during the Sultanate period and during Mughal rule. At different times some revolted against rulers when they deemed it necessary. It was, however, a new experience for Indian Muslims to be led by religious people and *ulama* in a struggle against foreign imperialists and 'infidels'. Muhammad Tayyab contended that the Jihad Movement gave a message to the people that *ulama-e-haq* could sacrifice their lives but would not bow before the infidels.[34] The precedent of Sayyid Ahmad was followed by many other *ulama* as they led religious, social and political movements. The 1820s was actually the first experience along a trail. They observed that it had not been fruitless.

The mobilization of mass followings by the religious class gave a message of self-reliance. Previously, Indian Muslims always looked to outside rulers for help. However, it might also badly affect Muslims. Foreign rulers had at least some organization and usually either returned to their native lands when the situation demanded or established their rule. Mass mobilizations, on the other hand, when religiously motivated, were difficult to manage properly. Such unfocused activity resulted in later 'jihad enterprise' and the 'privatization of jihad', a phenomenon which badly affected the social fabric of Pukhtuns.[35]

In the recent decades, 'reformist Islamic movements' and their militant offshoots in Pakistan, Afghanistan, and Kashmir have linked themselves ideologically with Sayyid Ahmad's jihad. The Deoband School of thought in Khyber Pakhtunkhwa developed hundreds of institutions, but Dar-ul-Ulum Haqqania Akora Khattak was the pioneer in the province. They have taken inspiration from Sayyid Ahmad and his Jihad Movement. The graduates of Haqqania participated in the war against the USSR in Afghanistan and continued their support for the Mujahidin and Taliban later on. Many graduates of the *Dar-ul-Ulum* were appointed to high posts in Afghanistan during the Taliban rule.[36] For them, the Taliban struggle and their occupation of Kabul was a step forward in the long struggle for the implementation of Islam in the whole world, the establishment of an Islamic Caliphate, based on the lines of the early days of Islam.[37] They thought that Kabul would become the centre of the Islamic Caliphate. Pakistani supporters of the Taliban idealized that the slogan of *Allah-o-Akbar* would soon be heard in Moscow and Leningrad and that the 'Islamic system' would be established over the whole earth.[38]

These ideological links were established not only by 'independent religious organizations' but also by the Pakistan government. All Pakistan studies and social studies text books, prepared by the Text Book Boards of different provinces and approved by the review committee of Curriculum Wing of the Ministry of Education, Islamabad,[39] refer to the Mujahidin Movement in the same manner. Interestingly, the words 'revolt' and 'betrayal' are used to describe Pukhtun resistance against the Mujahidin of Sayyid Ahmad. This planned effort was to mould the mindset of youth to a specific ideology. The Pakistani establishment disregarded the socio-economic forces affecting the state almost in the same manner as the Mujahidin. Apart from the text books, a majority of the elites of the state establishment also linked the 1980s Afghan War to the legacies of Shah Waliullah (d. 1763), Sayyid Ahmad (d. 1831), and Haji Sahib Turangzai (d. 1937).[40]

Sayyid Ahmad was followed by many twentieth-century militant organizations who established training camps in Mansehra and Kashmir. Hizb-ul-Mujahidin, Jaish-e-Muhammad, Harkat-ul-Ansar, Lashkar-e-Tayyiba, and many others had camps in different areas.[41] Such information was to be widely found in print and electronic media.[42] On the example of Sayyid Ahmad, the Jaish-e-Muhammad had a training camp in Mansehra, near Jabba Mor, named *Madrassah Sayyid Ahmad Shahid*.[43]

Masud Azhar, leader of the former Jaish-e-Muhammad used to visit the training camp fortnightly. He delivered very emotional speeches on the need for jihad and about the atrocities of the 'enemies of Islam'. Many references were made to the Jihad Movement of Sayyid Ahmad and Shah Ismail during these speeches. Their camp was visited by *ulama* who delivered speeches on the need of jihad on such occasions. [44]

Different centres of the Mujahidin have been a place of inspiration for religious figures whether or not they participated in armed struggle. We observed during the 1990s that leaders of the Tableeghi Jama'at from India and Pakistan visited Panjtar. The descendants of Fateh Khan showed them parts of the destroyed defence wall, constructed by the Mujahidin on the eve of Sikh attack on Panjtar and a few graves of the Mujahidin.

The Jihad Movement of Sayyid Ahmad had long-lived impacts, both positive and negative, on the religious life of the people of the Frontier. In a personal interview, Muhammad Tayyab referred to the identification of the *ulama-e-haq* and *ulama-e-su*.[45] *Ulama-e-haq* supported Sayyid Ahmad, and the others opposed him. In the same way, Pukhtun chiefs were divided into two groups. The 'good character' chiefs and *khans* joined Sayyid Ahmad. The 'bad character' ones opposed him. He also said that the people of North-West Frontier were involved in different kinds of *bida'at* and created troubles for Sayyid Ahmad and his Mujahidin. The source of income of the *ulama-e-su* had been greatly affected by the teaching of Sayyid Ahmad. They, therefore, issued *fatawa*,[46] and accused him of being an English agent, a heretic, and an infidel. He said this was not based on concrete evidence or religious grounds but to protect their interest in the area.[47]

The current *madrassah* network in Khyber Pakhtunkhwa may be seen as a major legacy of Sayyid Ahmad's Jihad Movement. At least one place, Akora Khattak, where Sayyid Ahmad fought against the Sikhs, now has a major religious institution.[48] During the field work for this study, we found that the management of the Dar-ul-Ulum Haqqania has named a hostel 'Ismailia', after Shah Ismail. We were told that the skirmish as a result of the night attack took place near there.[49]

With the migration of Sayyid Ahmad, and especially after the second *bai'at* at Panjtar on 6 February 1829, a *'fatwa* culture' was revived which had been popular a couple of centuries earlier and which had almost ceased to exist by then.[50] We did not find many references to the different ideologies and their struggle for supremacy in the two centuries preceding Sayyid Ahmad's migration to the area. The situation changed drastically with his migration and the renewal of *bai'at* at Panjtar. This was in the shape of a *fatwa* that Sayyid Ahmad took in writing from the local *ulama* about the status of a person who would not obey orders of the *amir-ul-mominin*.[51] The *fatwa* was used to assassinate Khadi Khan and it paved the way for *fatawa* and counter *fatawa*.

To oppose, then kill the Mujahidin, required a number of factors, but the emotions of the people rose on the basis of a *fatwa* issued by some *ulama* against the Mujahidin. The *fatawa* culture did not stop after the death of Sayyid Ahmad. The sources speak of around twenty *fatawa* issued against Sayyid Ahmad, Shah Ismail and the Mujahidin at different times.[52] Interestingly, some of the *fatawa* were extremely biased, calling Sayyid Ahmad and Shah Ismail infidels and English's agents. Even many years after Sayyid Ahmad's death, *fatawa* were issued against Mulla Said Amir of Kotah, a close associate of Sayyid Ahmad. Many of the allegations were not sound, the outcome of differences between two groups, supporters of Sayyid Ahmad and his opponents. The *fatwa* culture prevails today in the shape of *fatawa* issued by either side in a dispute.[53] The religious intolerance that started with Sayyid Ahmad and his Mujahidin or his opponents increased over time. Some people were killed by opponents due to minor difference of opinion about religious matters.[54] Such differences were not about the fundamentals of Islam, but were over minor issues, which often made little sense.[55]

One of the most important impacts of the Jihad Movement on the North-West Frontier was the realization of the need to understand religious scripture directly instead of through *shuruh*.[56] The '*isnad* paradigm'[57] was seldom known to the people in the North-West Frontier and they relied on a few tertiary books about religion. Referring to the original sources, Qur'an and *ahadith*, started with Shah Waliullah in Delhi and spread to other cities within several decades. The case of the North-West Frontier was quite different in this regard. The major sources of religious knowledge were several specific books, *khulasa, munyat ul mussali, quduri*, and other books of jurisprudence. During their sojourn in the North-West Frontier, the leaders of the Jihad Movement started teaching the Qur'an[58] and *ahadith*. It is recorded that many *ulama* attended such circles. With the passage of time, many local *ulama* started teaching the Qur'an and *ahadith*.[59] One such example was Maulana Said Amir of Kotah, a *qazi* of his area, appointed by Sayyid Ahmad. Said Amir continued supporting the Mujahidin even after the Balakot battle (1831) until his death. He started a campaign of teaching Qur'an and *ahadith* to the Pukthuns of his area and faced severe criticism from many local *ulama*. He was declared an infidel by some.[60]

This tradition of teaching the Qur'an was followed by Muhammad Tahir (1913–87) of Panjpir, a student of Maulvi Nasir-ud-Din Ghurghushtvi, Maulana Hussain Ali (Mianwali), and Maulana Aizaz Ali of Deoband. Muhammad Tahir's main emphasis remained on teaching the Qur'an. He also faced criticism from different people, including his own teacher Maulana Nasir-ud-Din Ghurghushtvi. He, however, did not change his mission until his death. His mission was continued by his students and son.[61]

Besides the Jama'at Isha'at Tawhid wa Sunnah, many other *ulama* have been busy in teaching the Qur'an and *sunnah*. This teaching of the basic sources of Islam has had a positive impact upon the people as they have access to the original sources and at times reject the traditional approach.[62]

The teaching of the Qur'an and *ahadith* helped the Pukhtuns of the North-West Frontier to understand Islam beyond peculiar tribal lines. Understanding Islam from the original sources with its proper context brought a major change in the mentality of many Pukhtuns. They started learning the Qur'an and *ahadith* directly instead of through secondary and tertiary sources. However, polarization by religious ideologues badly affected the populace. Learning Qur'an and *ahadith* was not in the capacity of everyone as it required degrees of specialization. Any individual hardly finds time for the proper study and understanding of the Qur'an and *ahadith* which often makes understanding superficial. The danger has been with the self-righteous attitude of those hardly acquainted with the Qur'an, who have issued decrees after merely listening to a few lectures from scholars and learning a few verses of the Qur'an without its proper context.[63]

The leaders of the first phase of the Jihad Movement, and especially Shah Ismail, rejected authority and emphasized scriptural interpretation, *ijtehad*.[64] This trend continued among the followers of Sayyid Ahmad as well as of the *Ahl-e-Hadith* movement of the Indian subcontinent, though their relation with the Mujahidin was always 'self-proclaimed'. Maulvi Nazir Hussain was inspired by a public speech of Sayyid Ahmad and went to Delhi. He taught *ahadith* for fifty years in Delhi, and was imprisoned in the Anbala conspiracy case.[65] Years later colonial authorities freed him and gave him the title of *shams-ul-ulama*.[66] Another prominent *Ahl-e-Hadith* of the Punjab, Muhammad Hussain Batalvi wrote a treatise, *Al-Iqtesad fi Masail al-Jihad*. He dedicated its English translation to the governor of the Punjab and declared jihad an outlawed practice, at least against colonial authorities. The government allotted him a holding in Montgomery (Faisalabad).[67]

The *ijtehad* trend was followed by many scholars before and after the partition of India. One may refer to Khalifa Abdul Hakim (1896–1959), Fazl-ur-Rahman (1919–88), Sayyid Abul Ala Maududi (1903–79), Amin Ahsan Islahi (1904–97), Ghulam Ahmad Parvez (1903–85), Israr Ahmad (1932–2010), Javed Ahmad Ghamidi (b. 1951), and many others. Importantly, Waheed-ud-Din Khan (b. 1925) of Delhi continued this tradition. Whether they have taken inspiration from the Jihad Movement or not, they exhibited a continuation of the same practice. Two important figures in the North-West Frontier were Muhammad Tahir (1913–87) of Panjpir, Swabi, and Abdul Salam (b. 1938) of Rustam, Mardan. In a personal interview, Abdul Salam asserted that his struggle was the continuation of the mission of Sayyid Ahmad and Shah Ismail.[68]

The Socio-Economic Impact

Sayyid Ahmad emphasized the revival of three *sunnah* of the Prophet Muhammad (Peace Be Upon Him), widow remarriage, Haj, and jihad. The remarriage of widows had become forbidden among Indian Muslims and some *fatawa* were issued for this. Sayyid Ahmad not only insisted upon widow remarriage, but personally set an example by marrying his elder brother's widow. This resulted in the desired effect and soon a majority followed his practice. Not only Muslims, but also Hindus were inspired. Ishwar Chandra Vidayasagar (1820–91) started an agitation in the 1850s for the proper legislation of Hindu widows' remarriage.[69] In the Pukhtun areas, this *sunnah* of the Prophet Muhammad (Peace Be Upon Him), remarriage of widows, was not uncommon, which is evident from the narration of the *Waqai*.[70] The other two, Haj and jihad, were not common. Only in rare cases did a few performed Haj or waged jihad. Sayyid Ahmad and his Mujahidin did not emphasize performing Haj after their migration to the North-West Frontier, but emphasized jihad. This legacy was continued by all organizations operating in the area. Their main emphasize remained on jihad. All such groups assured that the only solution to all problems lay in jihad.[71] One may find such essays in *Suragh-e-Haqiqat* written by Muhammad Masud Azhar. Interestingly enough, many of the essays are speeches which delivered at different places in the North-West Frontier.

The Mujahidin established a new economic institution *bait-ul-mal*, having permanent sources of income from *ushar* and fines. *Ushar*, the tithe of agricultural produce, was made obligatory. Earlier there had been no formal payment of *ushar* to the state,[72] only an amount paid to the ruler through chiefs. The Mujahidin appointed *tahsildars* for the collection of *ushar*. Since the Mujahidin knew that it was difficult to collect *ushar*, a group of them under Maulvi Muhammad Hubban, accompanied by Shah Ismail and Abdul Hamid Khan, were sent to collect it.[73] The establishment of the *bait-ul-mal* and the imposition of *ushar* were totally new concepts among Pukhtuns. Later, Sayyid Akbar Shah, a close associate of the Mujahidin and later ruler of Swat (1850–57), also collected *ushar* from the people of Swat to meet the expenditure of war.[74] As well, the Mujahidin collected *ushar* from the people of Nandihar after the battle of Balakot.[75] The same collection was followed by Sayyid Abdul Jabbar Shah during his rule in Swat (1915–17) and then under the Mianguls (1917–69).[76]

We come across no reliable source confirming that Pukhtuns were accustomed to the payment of *ushar* before the time of Sayyid Ahmad. As discussed in the previous chapter, the collection of *ushar* was one of the major factors causing the fall of the Mujahidin. The resistance of the people to the collection of *ushar* was mainly due to two factors. First, previously fiscal matters were managed by the *khans* who belonged to the area and had acquaintance with the people. The Hindustani Mujahidin who were sent for the collection of *ushar* neither knew the local traditions nor were acquainted with the people. They used force in collecting *ushar*, which the local people resented. They resisted at the opportune time. Second, the *ushar* rate was higher than the tax previously collected by the state authorities through local leaders. Before Sayyid Ahmad's arrival in the area, the Sikhs collected nominal taxes from the tribal chiefs, a symbolic tribute of eagles and horses.[77] The same legacy appeared during the Taliban ascendency in Swat. They collected *ushar* for the winter/autumn harvest (*kharif*) of 2008 in some areas of Swat. The objectives were to assert authority and to meet financial needs. Villagers had no choice but to pay to the Taliban.[78] They also collected *ushar* for the spring/summer harvest (*rabi*) in Koza Bandai, Bara Bandai, Ningwalai, and Dewlai during the military operation (May–June 2009) in the area.[79]

Contribution of the Jihad Movement to Literature

The leaders of the Jihad Movement were not only political activists. Some were great scholars who produced scholarly works before and after their migration to the area. Keeping in view the scope of this study we focused on the literature produced by those leaders of the Mujahidin who were actively involved in the movement during the life time of Sayyid Ahmad. Shah Ismail, a prolific writer, contributed much. His *Taqwiyat-ul-Iman* and *Sirat al-Mustaqim* were the first two religious treatises in the Urdu language.[80] The production of religious works in popular language not only spread their message but also promoted the language itself.

One of the major contributions by the leader of the Jihad Movement, *Sirat al-Mustaqim*, was dictated by Sayyid Ahmad, then edited by Shah Ismail and Abdul Hai.[81] The content of the book discussed *iman* (faith), Sufism, and the different stages of the Sufi life, ways to avoid *bida'at*, and the right way of *ibada* and, especially, prayer, fasting, payment of *zakat*, and Haj.[82] Chapter 2 of the *Sirat al-Mustaqim* was most important in the context of Sayyid Ahmad's socio-religious reform movement. *Bida'at* were discussed in detail and how it had polluted Muslim lives. The text attacked popular practices of atheists and polytheists in the garb of Sufis, the issue of *wahdat-ul-wujud*, and the visits of people to the tombs of popular religious saints.[83]

The most important literary contribution of the Jihad Movement was Shah Ismail's *Taqwiyat-ul-Iman*, written in Urdu at a time when the language was not yet popular. The book was not just a service to religion, but also contributed to the promotion of the language.[84] The book was divided into two chapters. The first chapter had five parts, with second chapter in seven parts. It was written against all the *bida'at* found among Indian Muslims. Shah Ismail not only listed such innovations, but also suggested remedies. The answers included the purification of the beliefs of Muslims, to have firm belief in the oneness of Allah, to refer every problem to Allah for solution and to follow the path of the Prophet Muhammad (Peace Be Upon Him).

The *Taqwiyat-ul-Iman* has remained the most popular book from that time. Many treatises have been written in its opposition and support. The first objection came from Maulana Fazli Haq Khairabadi in his treatise *Imtena'a-ul-Nazeer* and later in a book, *Tahqiq-ul-Fatawa fi Abtal-ul-Saghawa*.[85] Fazli Rasul Badauni wrote five books rejecting the *Taqwiyat-ul-Iman*. The followers of Shah Ismail then wrote books refuting all of Badauni's works. Ahmad Raza Barailvi wrote about a dozen books against the *Taqwiyat-ul-Iman* and the people who followed it. Naeem-ud-Din Muradabadi wrote *al-Tayyab-ul-Bayan* in rejection of *Taqwiyat-ul-Iman*. Aziz-ud-Din of Muradabad, a follower of Maulana Sanaullah of Amritsar, wrote *Akmal-ul-Bayan fi Tayid-e-Taqwiyat-ul-Iman*.[86] The publication of *Taqwiyat-ul-Iman* contributed greatly to the religious literature of the nineteenth and twentieth centuries.

Another important work of Shah Ismail was *'Abqat.* In this he discussed monotheism, the stages of Sufism, and different aspects of Sufism. It is an important work because people often considered the leaders of the Jihad Movement, and especially Shah Ismail, as being against Sufi practices. The publication of *'Abqat* proved otherwise. The leaders of the Jihad Movement wished to reform prevalent practices of Sufism thought against the true spirit of Islam. The book was written in an unusual way, and is difficult to understand by the common reader. The audiences of the book are typically related to Sufi orders.[87] This book is not usually mentioned by members of the Jama'at al-Dawah and Ahl-e-Hadith as it illustrates the difference between them and the leaders of the Mujahidin Movement. The former have completely outlawed Sufism while the Mujahidin leaders wanted to reform existing Sufi orders.

Another important work of Shah Ismail was *Mansab-e-Imamat,* written in Persian. The book was for *ulama* who had objected to the declaration of *imarat* by Sayyid Ahmad. The book is divided into two chapters. The first chapter dealt with the status of the Prophets (Peace Be Upon Them), the status of the believers and saints, and different kinds of politics. The author discussed in the second chapter various kinds of *imamat,* types of Khilafat-e-Rashida and the relations of *imam* and the public.[88] The book was well written in a place where Shah Ismail had little opportunity to collect references. It showed his extensive knowledge and memory.

Another important work of Shah Ismail was *Idhah al-Haq al-Sarih,* written in rejection of innovations and related issues. The book was divided into two *fasals.* We consulted its Urdu translation by Miraj Muhammad Bariq.[89]

Shah Ismail wrote other books including *Imdad-ul-Fattah fi Tawdhih al-Idha, Tanwir-ul-Aynain fi Ithbat Rafa' al-Yadain,* and *Usul al-Fiqah.* We could not read *Imdad.* The *Tanwir* was written in support of *rafa' al yadain* and the *Usul* discussed the principals of jurisprudence and the issue of *ijtihad.*[90]

Maulana Wilayat Ali[91] wrote a *qasida* in Persian to reject *shirk,* idolatry. It is said he wrote this during visits to Kabul when he was sent by Sayyid Ahmad to persuade the Afghan ruler to join the Jihad Movement.[92] Wilayat Ali also wrote a *risala,* a treatise on the issue of *imamat.* It was translated into the Sindhi language and was spread in Sindh as well as in the original Persian in Kabul and Qandahar.[93]

Khurram Ali Belhuri wrote a booklet, *Nasihat-ul-Muslimin*. It is divided into five chapters. The content deals with the rejection of idolatry as it existed, whether in major or minor form among Indian Muslims.[94]

The list of the treatises, *rasail*, and books given here is of titles that have not been mentioned in the previous pages. All of these were written by opponents of Sayyid Ahmad and Shah Ismail, either in India or in the North-West Frontier, who rejected the ideology and practices of the Mujahidin. These included *Risala Muhammad Hassan Daraz, Risala fi Haiat-ul-Nabi* by Muhammad Abid Sindhi, *Risala Gulzar-e-Hidayat Sibghatullah, Risala Hujjat-ul-a'amal* by Maulvi Muhammad Musa, *Risala Tukhfat-ul-Miskin* by Maulvi Abdullah, *Risala Rasm-ul-Kherat* and *Risala Tahlil ma Ahlullah fi Tafseer ma Ahlu be Gherillah* by Maulvi Khalil, *Hidayat-ul-Ahmadia* and many others.[95] Ahmad Ali, a follower of Akhun Abdul Ghafur of Swat collected different *fatawa* and published them in the shape of *Burhan-ul-Mominin*.[96] It was written to refute the views of Mulla Said Amir of Kotah, the close associate of Sayyid Ahmad. Mulla Said Amir remained a supporter of the Mujahidin till his death. The Akhun of Swat did not like his increasing influence in Buner and Swat and declared him an infidel. Abdul Rauf, a son of Said Amir, wrote *Shahab al-Saqib li Rajm-il-Qazi a'l al-Ghaib* in opposition to the objections raised by Abdul Ghafur and his followers about his father.[97]

The publication of such literature brought clarity to the minds of some, but intensified the differences among the many schools of thoughts. Another aspect of such writings was visible in the fanaticism exhibited on either side. Moreover, the *ulama* emphasized the rejection of opposing ideologies, instead of affirming positive contributions to society. Previous resources were expended in such polemics which otherwise could have been utilized for educating and reforming the society to bring the desired revolution. Scholastic differences did not remain within limits. The polarization of such views among the general public badly affected social dynamics and generated hatreds derived from minor issues.

Notes and References

1. See Ahmad, Qeyamuddin. 1979. *The Wahabi Movement in India*. Islamabad: National Book Foundation; Husain, Mahmud et al. (eds). 2008, *A History of the Freedom Movement, 1707–1831*, vol. I. Karachi: Royal Book Company; Qureshi, Ishtiaq Hussain. nd. *Ulema in Politics*. Karachi: Al-Ma'arif; Butt, Zahoor-ud-Din. *Shah Waliullah ka*

Qafila. Lahore: Idara Adab-e-Atfal; Chattopadhyay, Dilip Kumar. 1977. 'The Ferazee and Wahabi Movements of Bengal'. *Social Scientist*, vol. 6, no. 2; Khan, Muin-ud-Din Ahmad. 1967. 'Tariqah-i-Muhammadiya Movement: An Analytical Study'. *Islamic Studies*, vol. VI; Hedayatullah, Muhammad. nd. *Sayyid Ahmad: A Study of the Religious Reform Movement of Sayyid Ahmad of Ra'e Bareli*. Lahore: Sh. Muhammad Ashraf.

2. We have focused on the movement's influence on the North-West Frontier, now Khyber Pakhtunkhwa Province of Pakistan.

3. Caroe, Olaf. 1965. *The Pathans, 500 BC–AD 1957*. London: Macmillan & Co. Ltd. pp. 298–99. Henceforth, Caroe, *The Pathans*.

4. Sindhi, Ubaidullah. nd. *Shah Waliullah aur un ki Siyasi Tahrik: Yaniy Hizb-e-Waliullah Delhlavi ki Ijmali Tarikh ka Muqadama*. Lahore: Al-Mahmud Academy. pp. 87–88. Henceforth, Sindhi, *Shah Waliullah*.

5. Muhammad Azim Khan had also not taken part in the battle of Pir Sabaq (1823) and watched the Pukhtun tribesmen fall in the battle.

6. Sabir, Muhammad Shafi. 1986. *Tarikh-e-Subah Sarhad*. Peshawar: University Book Agency. pp. 505–8. Henceforth, Sabir, *Tarikh-e-Subah Sarhad*. Mahsud, Ali Khan. nd. *La Pir Rokhana tar Bacha Khan Porey: Da Pukhtanu Milli Mubarezey ta Katana*. Peshawar: Danish Khparawanay Tolanay Tekhniki Sanga. pp. 216–17. Henceforth, Mahsud, *La Pir Rokhana tar Bacha Khan*. Dost Muhammad Khan prepared a force to retake Peshawar from the Sikhs. He failed mainly due to the desertion of Sultan Muhammad Khan. Sultan Muhammad Khan hoped that Ranjit Singh would appoint him governor of Peshawar once again, but his hopes were not fulfilled, instead a small fief was allotted to him.

7. Different scholars have different views about the radicalization of the Pukhtun belt. For Robert Nichols it is a traditional phenomenon, visible in the area since Bayazid Ansari (1525–82). Sana Haroon argues that religious figures were used by different state actors for strengthening their authority since the days of Mughals but their prestige and influence increased with the formation of tribal areas where they have open field to exercise it. For details, see Haroon, Sana. 2011. *Frontier of Faith: A History of Religious Mobilization in the Pakhtun Tribal Areas c. 1890–1950*. Karachi: Oxford University Press. Henceforth, Haroon, *Frontier of Faith*. Haroon's argument may be partly accepted. Afghan rulers used *pirs* either for mediation between different tribes or at times to mobilize them against alien authorities.

8. Hardy, Peter. 1972. *The Muslims of British India*. Cambridge: Cambridge University Press. p. 58. Henceforth, Hardy, *The Muslims of British India*.

9. Haq, Noor ul. Rashid Ahmed Khan and Maqsudul Hasan Nuri. 2005. *Federally Administered Tribal Areas of Pakistan*. Islamabad: Asia Printers. http://ipripak.org/papers/federally.shtml (accessed on 29 January 2011). In Swat, Akbar, the Mughal Emperor, had sent a strong force to capture the valley but this was defeated with heavy losses, including Raja Birbal. Sultan-i-Rome. 2002. 'Mughuls and Swat'. *Journal of the Pakistan Historical Society*. Karachi, vol. 50, no. 4, pp. 41–42.

10. Amir Dost Muhammad Khan paid allowances to the Afridis and tribesmen of the Peshawar Valley. Haroon, *Frontier of Faith*, p. 36. Amir Dost Muhammad Khan was unable to bring Peshawar Valley under his rule. It was ruled by his brothers as Ranjit Singh's tributaries and he failed to retake Peshawar from the Sikhs in 1835/1836 when he faced defeat at Jamrud. For the Mughals, allowances to tribes of Khyber, see Qadir, Altaf and Zakir Minhas. 2013. 'Khyber Pass in Imperial Politics of the Mughals, 1519–1707'. *Journal of the Research Society of Pakistan*. Lahore, vol. 50, no. 2, pp. 41–59.

11. Mihr, Ghulam Rasul. nd. *Sayyid Ahmad Shahid*. Lahore: Sheikh Ghulam Ali and sons. p. 463. Henceforth, Mihr, *Sayyid Ahmad*.

12. Khan, Nawab Muhammad Wazir. 2007. *Waqai Sayyid Ahmad Shahid*. Lahore: Sayyid Ahmad Shahid Academy. pp. 1676–80. Henceforth, Khan, *Waqai Sayyid Ahmad*.

13. Khan, Mir Abdul Samad. nd. *Loe Pukhtun*. Peshawar: University Book Agency. p. 54.

14. Abbot, Freeland. 1962. 'The Jihad of Sayyid Ahmad Shahid'. *The Muslim World*. vol. 52, no. 3, pp. 216–22.

15. This is evident from the periodicals, newspapers and religious literature of the present day Mujahidin and Taliban.

16. We are not including the name of Yar Muhammad Khan as he never fought for tribal prestige and had no association with the tribesmen of the Peshawar Valley. Muhammad Azim Khan did not participate in the battle of Pir Sabaq (1823), though his artillery could have neutralized the Sikh artillery. The same was the case with Sultan Muhammad Khan, who saved his family and treasury during the Sikh entry into Peshawar in 1834.

17. Many Rushanites were made captive, kept in their homes by the victors of the battle of Bara, and then later released by the orders of Akbar, the Mughal Emperor. For details, see Yusafzai, Jamil. 'Deh Ghulaman'. *Pakistan Journal of History and Culture*. Islamabad, pp. 39–64.

18. Khan, *Waqai Sayyid Ahmad*, pp. 1414–24.

19. During field work, a Taliban commander, on the condition of anonymity, told me that they had made many concubines from the 'infidel Shias' captured from Parachinar. Another one expressed his desire to capture Katrina Kaif, after the conquest of India, to make her his concubine. This actually portrays the knowledge of their perception of religious scripture. They do according to the medieval jurisprudence, though their claim is that of 'reformist Islam'. Some scholars of the Qur'an contend that making concubines is not legal if one looks at the spirit of the Qur'an. They base their argument on verse 3 of Surah 4 (Al- Nisa), al-Qur'an.

20. Mihr, *Sayyid Ahmad*, pp. 569–70.

21. Revolutions cannot sustain original forms as the vanguards do not fully instil cultural change in the population. Islam, a major revolution in history also could not stand firm in its original ideology as the vanguards either died or retired from practical life when the revolution was achieved. Moreover, the Caliphate established by the immediate successors of the Prophet Muhammad (Peace Be Upon Him) was peculiar to the prevailing Arab tribal structure. This could not be practiced for long as Muslims interacted with the developed and sedentary societies of Persia and Syria. Mawdudi is of the opinion that the major reason for the failure of Sayyid Ahmad was calling for jihad and the imposition of *sharia* without mentally preparing the Pukhtuns for the cause. Maududi, Sayyid Abul Ala. 1977. *Tajdeed wa Ahya-e-Din*. Lahore: Islamic Publications. pp. 119–23.

22. Hussain, Sadiq. 2010. *Sayyid Ahmad Shahid aur un ki Tahrik-e-Mujahidin*. Lahore: Al-Meezan. p. 218. Henceforth, Hussain, *Sayyid Ahmad*. Khan, Taj Muhammad. *Uruj-e-Afghan*. Peshawar: Manzoor Aam Press. p. 148. Henceforth, Khan, *Uruj-e-Afghan*. Sultan-i-Rome. 2008. *Swat State (1915–1969): From Genesis to Merger; An Analysis of Political, Administrative, Socio-Political, and Economic Developments*. Karachi: Oxford University Press. p. 38. Henceforth, Rome, *Swat State*.

23. A majority believe that the Taliban are financed, harboured, and supported by authorities. Those who try to bring the connections between state and militants are mysteriously assassinated by the 'unidentified' assassins. According to one report

forty-eight journalists have been assassinated with no culprit caught yet. An example is the murder of Salim Shehzad, a reporter who was abducted and shot dead in May 2011. http://news.oneindia.in/2011/05/31/pak-abducted-journalist-body-found-isi-salim-shehzad-aid0101.html (accessed on 22 June 2011).

24. *Mad Mullahs, Opportunists, and Family Connections: The Violent Pashtun Cycle.* http://www.tribalanalysiscenter.com/PDF-TAC/Mad%20Mullahs.pdf (accessed on 5 January 2010).

25. Caroe, *The Pathans*, pp. 312–16.

26. The rare instances may be their struggle against the Mughals in the sixteenth and seventeenth centuries, the wars between Bayazid Ansari and his opponents in the sixteenth century, and the tribes fighting against the Sikhs at Pir Sabaq in 1823.

27. Such movements have been given different names by scholars; 'nativistic', 'millennial', 'messianic', 'nostalgic', 'sectarian', and 'revivalist'. For detailed study of such movements, see Adas, Michael. 1979. *Prophets of Rebellions: Millenarian Protest Movements against the European Colonial Order.* Chapel Hill: University of North Carolina Press. A very glaring example is that of Che Guevara, unable to attract inhabitants of the local area to join his militia during the eleven months he attempted recruitment as he had been known for confrontation instead of compromise. See Wright, Thomas C. 2000. *Latin America in the Era of the Cuban Revolution.* London: Praeger. p. 86.

28. Giving sectarian colour to the events is visible in Khan's *Waqai Sayyid Ahmad* and Dehlavi's *Hayyat-e-Tayyaba.*

29. For details of different rituals practiced in the area see, Ghaffar, Abdul. 1983. *Zama Jwand aw Jadojahad.* Kabul: Daulati Matb'a. For details of Abdul Ghaffar Khan's movement see, Shah, Sayed Wiqar Ali. 1999. *Ethnicity, Islam and Nationalism: Muslim Politics in the North-West Frontier 1937–47.* Karachi: Oxford University Press; Easwaran, Eknat. 1984. *A Man to Match His Mountains.* California: Nilgiri Press. We remember that during Muharram, in the first 10 days and especially on 8th, 9th, and 10th people used to offer locally made cold drinks to wayfarers. Later on, due to the preaching of some 'reformist' clerics especially, Panjpiris, the practice was altogether abandoned in Swabi.

30. An evident example is Pakistan, apparently created in the name of Islam but the grievances of eastern wing were not addressed and the ultimate result was the creation of Bangladesh.

31. Naseer-ud-Din was the son of Ummatullah, daughter of Shah Rafi-ud-Din. He had migrated to North-West Frontier four years after Sayyid Ahmad's death. Mihr, Ghulam Rasul. nd. *Sarguzasht-e-Mujahidin.* Lahore: Sheikh Ghulam Ali and Sons. p. 134. Henceforth, Mihr, *Sarguzasht-e-Mujahidin.*

32. Bellew, *A General Report*, pp. 95–96.

33. Chakesari, Saif-ul-Haq. 2010. *Islam ka Tasawuar-e-Jihad aur Alqaeda.* Mingora: Shoaib Sons. p. 361. Henceforth, Chakesari, *Islam ka Tasawuar-e-Jihad.*

34. Personal interview with Muhammad Tayyab Tahiri, Amir Isha'at Tawhid wa Sunnah, at Panjpir, Swabi, 26 December 2010.

35. See Chakesari, *Islam ka Tasawuar-e-Jihad.* Many people have written on the issue from their own perspectives. The Western academia and media called it a religious cause for the security of the 'Free World'. Hollywood produced movies on the Afghan War dedicated to the 'egalitarian' people of Afghanistan when the Afghans were fighting against the 'enemy' of the 'Free World'. However, the same Hollywood later produced movies accusing the Afghan people.

36. Apart from written material in books and newspapers, we, during our personal visits to Afghanistan during Taliban regime, met many officials who had graduated from Haqqania.
37. Haq, Rashidul. 1996. 'Naqsh-e-Aghaz'. *Monthly Al-Haq*. Dar-ul-Ulum Haqqania Akora Khattak, vol. 32, no. 1, pp. 9–10. This extract is actually taken from Sami-ul-Haq's essay written as an editorial for *Al-Haq* in 1981 or 1982. We could not find the original issue in the collection at Dar-ul-Ulum Akora Khattak.
38. Haq, Samiul. 1996. 'Naqsh-e-Aghaz'. *Monthly Al-Haq*. Dar-ul-Ulum Haqqania Akora Khattak, vol. 32, no. 1, pp. 2–8.
39. According to 1973 Constitution of the Islamic Republic of Pakistan education is a provincial subject but approval of text books is centralized. In this process the text of the manuscripts are greatly modified and altered so as to be in line with government policy. When books are published they are different from the original text written by the author(s). This alteration policy is mainly applied in case of books related to social sciences. For a detailed study on the distortion of facts in textbooks in Pakistan, see Aziz, K. K. 1995. *The Murder of History: A Critique of History Textbooks used in Pakistan*. Lahore: Vanguard. Under the 18th Constitutional Amendment, the preparation of text books is purely a provincial matter but different state and non-state actors use different lobbies not to let the academia write the objective essays.
40. See extract from the speech of Lt. General Fazli Haq, 27 September 1981, in Haq, Samiul. 'Naqsh-e-Aghaz', pp. 9–10.
41. Ayesha Jalal has referred to the running of militant organizations' camps only. Jalal, *Partisans of Allah*, p. 61. But we, during our study survey, have found that different organizations have named their training camps after the leaders of the Jihad Movement.
42. For details, see different articles and editorials in *Washington Post, New York Times, Los Angeles Times*, the *Tribune, London Times*, and the *Hindu* after 9/11 and periodicals of such organization who have reported their camp activities in details.
43. We are not sure whether it is still functional as we had visited in summer 2001.
44. We have personally heard his speeches, back in July–August 2001 during our field survey for the proposed study on Militancy in Pakistan which could not be completed for obvious reasons. Masud Azhar started serial publication of *Waqai Sayyid Ahmad Shahid* in his *Zarb-e-Momin*.
45. *Ulama* on the right path and *ulama* on the wrong path, were the technical terms used in religious tradition since the early days of Islam. It is interesting to note that every opposing group of the *ulama* is named *ulama-e-su* by its opponents and *ulama-e-haq* is used for themselves.
46. *Fatawa* is plural, while *fatwa* is singular.
47. Personal interview with Muhammad Tayyab, Amir Isha'at Tawhid wa Sunnah at Panjpir, Swabi, 26 December 2010.
48. Personal interview with Muhammad Sa'id, Jama'at-i-Islami activist and former Senator, at Hayatabad, Peshawar, 28 July 2005.
49. We are thankful to Hilal Ahmad, teacher and librarian at Dar-ul-Ulum Haqqania, Akora Khattak for his assistance in locating several places and providing access to the library.
50. Akhun Darwizah used the words *malaun* (cursed) and *mulhid* (heretic) for Bayazid Ansari. See Darwizah, Akhun. 1987. *Makhzan*. Peshawar: Pashto Academy. pp. 1–2, 122–36. In another place he used the above words as well as *kufar* (infidels), *ahl-e-inkar* (the ones who denies the right), and *Pir-e-Tarik* (guide to darkness). See Darwizah, Akhun. nd. *Tazkirat-ul-Abrare wal Ashrar*. Peshawar: Islami Kutub Khana. pp. 136–40.

51. Khan, *Waqai Sayyid Ahmad*, pp. 1386–90.

52. Tahir, Muhammad. nd. *Al-Intesar Li Sunnat-e-Sayid-al-Abrar*. Panjpir: Maktaba al-Yaman. pp. 18–21. Henceforth, Tahir, *Al-Intesar*.

53. The major groups of the *ulama* in present day Swabi district, Khyber Pakhtunkhwa, where Sayyid Ahmad ruled for some time from Panjtar and where he had supporters and opponents alike, are locally known as Panjpirian and Shah Mansurian. The names reflect the living places of the leaders of the respective groups. They have differences over certain issues, neither of the two differed on the fundamentals of Islam. Interestingly, both claim that they follow the Deoband School of thought.

54. One may refer to the assassination of Salman Taseer (1944–2011), the governor of the Punjab, gunned down by his official bodyguard on 4 January 2011 at Islamabad. The initial statement of the assassin was that he took the action as the governor had spoken against the Blasphemy Act. Not analyzing the Act, many intellectuals are not against the Blasphemy Law but the procedure adopted for the Blasphemy Act, introduced by the Military regime of Zia. In many cases people act in individual capacity instead of state institutions.

55. For instance *dua*—prays after *faraz* or *sunnah* prayers, different rituals on the occasion of death, colour of the turban etc.

56. Among Muslims, all the works of religious scholars have been interpreted by later generations. With the passage of time the majority of people relied on the *sharha* (sing.)—interpretation, *shuruh* (plural) instead of the original source.

57. Graham, William A. 1993. 'Traditionalism in Islam: An Essay in Interpretation'. *Journal of Interdisciplinary History*, vol. 18, no. 3, pp. 495–522.

58. One of the major objections to Sayyid Ahmad and Shah Ismail was their teaching the Qur'an to the public. Tahir, *Al-Intesar*, p. 19.

59. For the revivalist spirit of South Asian Muslims, see Robinson, Francis. 2008. 'Islamic Reform and Modernities in South Asia'. *Modern Asian Studies*, vol. 42, no. 2/3, pp. 259–81. Henceforth, Robinson 'Islamic Reform and Modernities in South Asia'.

60. Ghafur, Abdul. nd. *Burhan-ul-Mominin*. NP. The mentioned *fatwa* is a collection of twenty decrees, issued by different *ulama* of the North-West Frontier. We acknowledge the cooperation of Muhammad Tayyab, Amir Isha'at Tawhid wa Sunnah, for providing a copy as well as translation of its parts.

61. Gul, Momen. *Jama'at-e-Isha'at-e-Tauhid wa Sunnah* (manuscript). Momen Gul was the Provincial General Secretary, JITS, NWFP, Pakistan in 2005. Personal interview with Muhammad Tayyab, Amir Isha'at Tawhid wa Sunnah at Panjpir, Swabi, 26 December 2010.

62. We learnt Qur'an while very young, a tradition which was unknown to our grandparents.

63. One may find instances in academic circles, TV programmes, political gathering and social gatherings. The special victims of these pseudo intellectuals are mainly science graduates, who have a lesser understanding of the social issues.

64. Khan, Abdullah. 1984. 'The Religious Thought of Shah Ismail Dihlawi', MA thesis, Institute of Islamic Studies, McGill University Montreal, pp. 90–109.

65. The Anbala Trial started with the arrest of Muhammad Jaffar, a *lambardar* of Thanesar, district Anbala in December 1863, immediately after the Ambela campaign of October 1863. The trial continued for a long time against persons charged in waging war against the Queen. They included Yahya Ali of Sadiqpur, Muhammad Jaffar of Thanesar, Abdul Rahim of Sadiqpur, Muhammad Shafi, Abdul Karim, Abdul Ghaffar, Qazi Mian

Jan of Commercolly, district Pubna, Abdul Ghafur of Hazaribagh, Hussaini of Patna, Hussaini of Thanesar, Elahi Bux of Patna. The Anbala trial preceded the subsequent trials of 'Wahabis' in coming years. See Ahmad, *The Wahabi Movement*, pp. 232–68.

66. Ikram, Sheikh Muhammad. 2000. *Mauj-e-Kausar*. Lahore: Institute of Islamic Culture. pp. 68–69. Hereafter Ikram, *Mauj-e-Kausar*.

67. Shakir, Amjad Ali. 2010. 'Hazrat Sayyid Ahmad Shahid aur Jama'at-e-Mujahidin', in Sadiq Hussain, *Sayyid Ahmad Shahid aur un ki Tehrik-e-Mujahidin*. Lahore: Al-Meezan. pp. 11–12.

68. Personal interview with Abdul Salam at his residence in Peshawar city, 22 October, 2007. Abdul Salam was a close associate of Muhammad Tahir and developed differences with his son Muhammad Tayyab in early 1990s. Due to this, he was expelled from Jama'at Isha'at-e-Tawhid wa Sunnah. Abdul Salam is now running a seminary in Peshawar and is closely associated with Jama'at al-Dawah.

69. Farooqi, N. R. 2006. 'Saiyid Ahmad of Rae Bareli: An Account of His Life and Thought and An Appraisal of His Impact on the Sufi Centres of Awadh and Eastern India', in Saiyid Zaheer Husain Jafri and Helmut Reifeld, *The Islamic Path: Sufism, Politics and Society in India*. Delhi: Rainbow Publishers Limited. pp. 296–97. Henceforth, Farooqi, 'Saiyid Ahmad of Rae Bareli'.

70. Khan, *Waqai Sayyid Ahmad*, p. 2075.

71. One may refer to different essays, published in newspapers and periodicals of these organizations, later compiled in book form by the author himself. Azhar, Muhammad Masud. 2007. *Suragh-e-Haqiqat*. Karachi: Maktaba Hassan.

72. As also mentioned earlier different sources, including local and others, have said that previously *ushar* was given to *mulla*s of the respective clans. But this does not seem accurate as the amount of *ushar* was too much and neither were contemporary *mulla*s wealthy nor was there any precedent in the Shaikh Malli *wesh* system. According to the *wesh* system, a piece of land called *serai* was allotted to the respective *mulla* or Mian for their livelihood.

73. Mihr, *Sayyid Ahmad*, pp. 586–97.

74. Sultan-i-Rome. 2008. *Swat State (1915–1969): From Genesis to Merger; An Analysis of Political, Administrative, Socio-Political, and Economic Developments*. Karachi: Oxford University Press. p. 38. Henceforth, Rome, *Swat State*.

75. Mihr, *Sarguzasht-e-Mujahidin*, p. 29.

76. For a detailed study of the revenue sources and administration of the Swat State, see Rome, *Swat State*, pp. 190–95.

77. Muhammad, Fazal. 2009. *Safah-e-Alam par Tarikhi Nuqush*. Lahore: Al-Mashal. p. 201. Henceforth, Muhammad, *Tarikhi Nuqush*.

78. Sultan-i-Rome. 2009. 'Swat: A Critical Analysis'. *IPCS18 Research Papers*. http://ipcs. org/pdf_file/issue/1542140255RP18-Rome-Swat.pdf (accessed on 2 February 2009).

79. Personal interviews with different people of the area in summer 2010.

80. Robinson, 'Islamic Reform and Modernities in South Asia', pp. 259–81.

81. Ikram, *Mauj-e-Kausar*, p. 33.

82. See Ahmad, Sayyid Ahmad and Shah Ismail. nd. *Sirat-e-Mustaqim*. Lahore: Islami Academy.

83. Haq, S. Moinul. 1979. *Islamic Thought and Movements in the Subcontinent (1711–1947)*. Karachi: Pakistan Historical Society. p. 443.

84. Ikram, *Mauj-e-Kausar*, pp. 38–39.

85. Qureshi, Afzal Haq. 1992. *Maulana Fazli Haq Khairabadi: Aik Tahqiqi Mutali'a*. Lahore: Al-Faisal. pp. 26–27. Fazli Haq Khairabadi abandoned his previous opinion about Sayyid Ahmad and used to say that Shah Ismail was right while he (Khairabadi) was wrong. Jabbari, Muhammad Salim. 2005. 'Shah Ismail Shahid aur Taqwiyyat-ul-Iman', in Shah Ismail, *Taqwiyyat-ul-Iman*. Faisalabad: Tariq Academy. pp. 23–24. Henceforth, Jabbari, 'Shah Ismail aur Taqwiyyat-ul-Iman'.

86. Jabbari. 'Shah Ismail Shahid aur Taqwiyyat-ul-Iman'. pp. 16–26.

87. We read Ismail, Shah. 1988. *'Abqat*, Urdu tr. Manazar Ahsan Gilani. Lahore: Maqbool Academy.

88. Ismail, Shah. 1994. *Mansab-e-Imamat*, Urdu tr. Hakeem Muhammad Hussain Alavi. Lahore: Makki Dar-ul-Kutub.

89. Ibid. nd. *Idhah al-Haq al-Sarih: Bida'at ki Haqiqat aur us key Ahkam*. Karachi: Qadimi Kutub Khana.

90. Ibid. nd. *Usul al-Fiqah*. Delhi: Matba'a Mujtaba'i.

91. Wilayat Ali remained with Sayyid Ahmad in the North-West Frontier for some time but was later sent to India for preaching jihad and fund raising.

92. Hussain, Sadiq. 2010. *Sayyid Ahmad Shahid aur un ki Tahrik-e-Mujahidin*. Lahore: Al-Meezan. pp. 240–41. Henceforth, Hussain, *Sayyid Ahmad*.

93. Hussain, *Sayyid Ahmad*, p. 241.

94. Chishti, Abdul Halim. (ed.). 1976. *Taqwiyat-ul-Iman ma'a Tazkir-ul-Ikhwan wa Nasihat-ul-Muslimin*. Karachi: Noor Muhammad Karkhana Tijarat-e-Kutub. p. 242.

95. Tahir, *Al-Intesar*, pp. 18–19.

96. We are thankful to Muhammad Tayyab, Amir Isha'at Tawhid wa Sunnah for providing a copy and translation of its parts. The copy does not have details of publication.

97. Rauf, Abdul. nd. *Shahab al-Saqib li Rajm-il-Qazi a'l al-Ghaib*. Peshawar: NP. Details of publication are not available but it seems to has been published around 1910.

Conclusion

The Jihad Movement of Sayyid Ahmad in the nineteenth century was a transformation of the outlook of the Muslim religious elite. During the long Muslim rule in northern India, the religious class was on the whole highly respected and were appointed to high posts, on the basis of their academic qualification and, of course, at times for supporting the rulers. The weakening of Muslim central authority in northern India and Bengal alarmed both the Muslim elite and general public. Besides local forces of disruption, western colonizers were the major threat as they had developed economies, were well equipped, and were highly skilled in diplomacy.

Among the internal threats, the Marathas were the most dangerous. They engaged Aurangzeb for years until his death in 1707. He did not succeed in destroying them. His death accelerated a process of the decline of Mughal authority. Several of the Muslim aristocracy along with Shah Waliullah, a Muslim scholar of the eighteenth century, asked Ahmad Shah Abdali, the Afghan ruler, to intervene and save Muslim India from complete devastation. The defeat of the Marathas at the battle of Panipat in 1761 did not stop the Mughal political decline. The rise of Sikhs in the Punjab and of the English in the south and east of India were not checked as the Muslim political elites were unable to adequately respond. The turn of the nineteenth century further alarmed Muslims when the forces of the East India Company entered Delhi in 1803 and Shah Alam II, the Mughal Emperor, became a Company pensioner. The status of India was debated by the *ulama* in India, but no practical steps were taken.

Sayyid Ahmad emerged on the horizon in the second decade of the nineteenth century. Belonging to a middle-class family, he had widely travelled and knew the grievances of the Indian masses and the nobility alike. He stepped forward and organized the Jihad Movement on religious grounds. His initial activities touring different areas to preach character-ized the innovative nature of his movement. Unlike traditional Sufis, he never waited for people to visit him at his home for guidance, though like traditional Sufis he never forgot the goal of spiritual attainment, which was an essential part of *piri-muridi* relationship. After some initial success, he diverted his attention to organizing armed struggle against the 'infidels'.

His performance of Haj with several hundred followers was itself a new experience. It also implanted the seed of a jihad spirit in Bengal, which provided recruits to the Mujahidin for the North-West Frontier region during coming decades.

Sayyid Ahmad proved different from the contemporary Muslim religious elite as none of them declared jihad against the infidels. All of them, including Shah Waliullah, looked to the Muslim nobility and sought assistance from outsiders to stop the political decline of the Muslim establishment. Sayyid Ahmad initiated mass mobilization not only to reform the society but also to pursue armed struggle against the Sikhs and English. Though a few writers have claimed that he was a creature of the English deployed against the Sikhs of the Punjab, no serious sources support this claim. The most authentic sources regarding the objectives of his struggle are his own letters written to different people before and after his migration to the North-West Frontier. Instead of relying on the nobility, which was partially responsible for the decay, he led the movement in person and assumed religious as well as political authority soon after his arrival in the Mandanr area.

The selection of the North-West Frontier was one of the most important decisions of the movement. Sayyid Ahmad remained part of Amir Khan's (d. 1834) force for seven years and knew military strategy as well as his strength. He could not initiate his Jihad Movement in northern India in the presence of hereditary principalities and the English forces. The geo-strategic location of the North-West Frontier was promising as previous invaders from the north were always joined by the inhabitants of the area. The egalitarian nature of its inhabitants was also known. They rarely accepted central authority and preferred to remain independent in resolving internal matters. Previous attempts of the Mughals to dominate them had failed. The Sikhs of the Punjab had compelled the Barakzai *sardar*s of Peshawar to pay homage and tribute to Lahore, but the majority of the people in the countryside were not subjugated. Sayyid Ahmad had also in view the independent rulers of principalities around the North-West Frontier. His sending envoys and letters to them and seeking their assistance against the 'infidels' are a testament to his wider perspective.

Sayyid Ahmad's declaration of *imarat* was the turning point for the Jihad Movement. The 'reformer' who claimed to be the 'saviour' of the Muslims of the area assumed political authority. The initial tribal enthusiasm at his arrival was taken for granted as indicating their willingness to accept his authority. The declaration of *imarat* created two major problems: some of the tribal chiefs viewed it as an attempt to subordinate them by replacing the traditional political institutions, and some of the *ulama* took it as an act that was illegal according to *sharia*. Prominent among the latter was Maulvi Mahbub Ali (d. 1864), who returned to Delhi as did others soon after arriving at Panjtar.

One possible way acceptable to the people and their 'tribal' outlook might have been to avoid political claims and act in a religious capacity only. Sayyid Ahmad and Shah Ismail wrote many letters, including a treatise by the latter, entitled *mansab-e-imamat*, to convince Muslims of India and Pukhtuns that his *imamat* was legitimately authorized. One can easily see the legacies of Sayyid Ahmad's *imamat*, especially among followers of the Deoband school of thought and the Ahl-e-Hadith. Many of them came forward to take private initiative to 'wage jihad' against the 'infidels' and opponents alike. Many among these two groups have claimed to be ideologically inspired. Masud Azhar (b. 1968) of Bahawalpur and Hafiz Muhammad Saeed (b. 1950, at Sargodha) of Lahore are two examples. The periodicals of both portray their thoughts. Many of the *ulama* of the Deoband school of thought took the *bai'at* of jihad at the hand of Masud Azhar after his release from an Indian jail in December 1999, in exchange for the passengers of IC 814.

The different stages of the Jihad Movement revealed Sayyid Ahmad to be indecisive on occasions. One example was his never settled search for a centre for jihad activities. Initially, he settled in Hund, but abandoned that after his defeat at the battle of Shaidu in 1827. He wandered in Buner, Swat, and the Khudu Khel areas. He remained at Khar for one year and returned to Panjtar. The year spent in Khar could have been utilized for preaching among the Pukthuns. The restoration of Peshawar to Sultan Muhammad Khan was not taken as a correct decision by some. Many tribesmen were opposed to the rule of the Barakzai *sardars*. Arbab Bahram Khan asked that Peshawar be handed over to him. This might have been a stabilizing decision as the Arbab possessed political strength and Sayyid Ahmad would have had no worries about the city ruler. Arbab Bahram Khan further assured Sayyid Ahmad that a force of four thousand would accompany Sayyid Ahmad in his future endeavours and that he would pay their expenses. Many also opposed abandoning Panjtar after the assassination of the Mujahidin in parts of the Peshawar Valley. But again Sayyid Ahmad paid no heed and moved on.

The numbers of Mujahidin claimed to have been assassinated in the dramatic reaction by Pukhtuns are not supported by relevant sources. Sayyid Ahmad's statements about the number of assassinated Mujahidin are contradictory. In one letter he stated that several were killed.

In another statement he said that thousands of Mujahidin had been 'massacred'. From the migration of Sayyid Ahmad to the Indus region until the battle of Balakot in 1831, around eleven hundred Mujahidin may be estimated to have migrated to the North-West Frontier. This includes two hundred and seventy from Qandahar and several from Sindh. There were never enough Mujahidin recruits to make the assassination of thousands of Mujahidin a credible possibility.

Though many writers thought that his tours in the Peshawar Valley and Swat were for preaching only, these were different events from his tours in northern India. No doubt he was accompanied by many disciples during his tours in northern India and he also sent envoys for preaching. But he never sent missionaries in the North-West Frontier and wherever he went he was accompanied by his armed Mujahidin. Apart from personal visits, whenever he sent others on such tours these also were accompanied by a significant number of Mujahidin. Examples of such tours were those of Qazi Muhammad Hubban and Abdul Hamid Khan, when both were accompanied by a huge force of Mujahidin. And the locals were responsible to provide food not only for the Mujahidin but also for their horses.

The assassination of Khadi Khan of Hund might have been justified for obvious reasons, but detaining his family in confinement, including women and children, was neither justified according to local traditions nor to the tenets of Islam. *Sharia* clearly said that only people taken part in the battle could be held. Khadi Khan was killed in a surprise attack. His family women and children were not combatants. Pukhtuns, notorious for *tarburwali*, enmity between cousins and related bloodshed, were not accustomed to women being held captive, even for a short time. This act of the Mujahidin alienated many Pukhtuns, who from then viewed Sayyid Ahmad as a usurper and turned against the Mujahidin.

The failure of the Mujahidin to establish an 'Islamic State' along the lines found in the early days of Islam has been discussed by many writers. Many attributed the 'failure' to the nature of the Pukhtuns who 'betrayed' Sayyid Ahmad. This has been written widely in textbooks and is believed by many, perhaps a majority, in the region. Among those ideologically inspired by the Jihad Movement, the analysis of Sheikh Muhammad Ikram is the most balanced. The failure did not have single factor. Sayyid Ahmad's high expectations were one of the major problems. He relied on a population who had a set socio-cultural tradition and initiated dramatic changes in practices without first introducing and legitimating innovations, or 'reforming' established manners and thinking.

All his actions were taken in haste, and the pace itself often alienated the local population. He declared jihad on the Sikhs without doing proper tactical or strategic homework and faced severe defeat in his first encounter in the open field. The declaration of *imarat* alienated local chiefs, who viewed him a competitor, similar to previous invaders. His indecisive nature and apparent flight for personal safety in the face of defeat further added to local feelings of alienation from the Mujahidin. Sayyid Ahmad did not have adequate weaponry and strength to face skilled and organized Sikh infantry and artillery. He also became involved, intentionally or not, in *tarburwali* matters which only increased his problems, especially as some opponents sought assistance from the Sikhs.

Many of the *khan*s were replaced with the 'favourites' of Sayyid Ahmad, including the *khan*s of Marguz, Kalabat, Hoti, and others. Also, his role in the turmoil after the death of Ashraf Khan of Zaida was debatable. The replacement of traditional Pukhtun institutions with his own 'Islamic' ones was another major factor which weakened his legitimacy. He alternatively could have delayed replacing old institutions to focus all energies on his main objective, ousting the Sikhs from Muslim lands and the English from India, especially in a situation when he was mainly dependent upon the Pukhtuns for his whole struggle.

The strategy adopted by Sayyid Ahmad was also debated afterwards and a school of thought has criticized it. Prominent among this school was Waheed-ud-Din Khan of Delhi who discussed Sayyid Ahmad's Jihad Movement in his book.[1] He contended that Sayyid Ahmad's movement was not a legitimate jihad in the absence of an *amir-ul-mominin* and because his *imarat* was self-proclaimed, something opposed by many. Observers further argued that it was actually a resistance movement that took revenge for the miseries of Muslims. This school thought that waging jihad with inadequate material support in a Muslim minority country to establish an 'Islamic State' was against the life pattern of the Prophet Muhammad (Peace Be Upon Him), who did not establish an Islamic State in Makkah. He only did it when Muslims were in the majority in Madinah.

Some believed Sayyid Ahmad could have restricted himself to reforming Muslim society and preaching Islam. This school believed that Muslims were wasting their energies in useless struggle and hatred against western powers for the last two hundred and fifty years instead of mending the ways of fellow Muslims and preaching to the colonizers. We agree with the view to some extent as the Jihad Movement waged by Sayyid Ahmad, or later by others, took a sectarian colour very soon as their endeavours were diverted to declaring opponents 'heretics' and 'infidels'. The major target of all such groups has usually been the Shia community.

We argue that though waging jihad in private capacity without inadequate resource is not legitimate according to *sharia*. At the same time we cannot justify state oppression as resistance to alien or even own state is unavoidable if the state managers opt for oppression. Human race cannot be restricted through legislation or laws if state becomes an oppressive tool in the hands of a class/institution and serve the interests of selected few in any shape.[2]

The Jihad Movement left both positive and negative cultural and religious impacts. One of the positive impacts was the initiation of the teaching of the Qur'an and *ahadith* in the North-West Frontier. Earlier religious figures of the area did not emphasize such teaching and were more inclined to teach books of jurisprudence of the *Hanafi* school of thought. The leaders of the Jihad Movement, especially Shah Ismail, continued a series of lectures during his stay in the North-West Frontier. Consulting the secondary or tertiary sources of jurisprudence had limited the vision and knowledge of local *ulama*. First among the locals to follow the footsteps of the leaders of the Jihad Movement was Said Amir of Kotah. He began teaching the Qur'an and *ahadith* in his village and was followed by others. He faced severe criticism and was declared a 'heretic' and 'infidel' by his opponents for teaching the Qur'an and *ahadith*. His opponents wished to maintain their monopoly over religious matters and did not want interference from the public in their domain.

The most evident example of the new teaching was Muhammad Tahir (1913–87) who taught the Qur'an in the present districts of Swabi and Mardan. He was known as the founder of the *Jama'at al-Isha'at Tawheed wa Sunnah*, locally known as Panjpiri school of thought. This school claimed itself to be 'real' followers of the Deoband school of thought. The Panjpiris were spread across parts of Khyber Pakhtunkhwa and the Punjab, and are commonly known for their uncompromising attitude towards people of opposing ideologies. Beside Panjpiris, there are others who emphasized the teaching of the Qur'an. Some among the activists of Jama'at-e-Islami Pakistan think that the spread of the contemporary *madrassah* network is one of the legacies of the Jihad Movement.

Of the negative impacts of the Jihad Movement, the most important is the polarization of religious ideologues. Organizations and individuals who claim that they are ideologically inspired by the Movement narrate stories of Mujahidin successes against their opponents in public gatherings intended to arouse partisan sentiments in the general public. The public, typically having little knowledge of the historical facts, believe exaggerated and fabricated versions of such stories and many join these organizations. The most important of such organizations have been Jama'at-e-Dawah, the former Jaish-e-Muhammad, and Harkat-ul-Mujahidin. The training camps of Jaish-e-Muhammad and Harkat-ul-Mujahidin were named after Sayyid Ahmad and Shah Ismail and training units of the new recruits after the leaders of the Jihad Movement. Masud Azhar, one of their leaders, has contributed hundreds of essays on jihad and the Mujahidin Movement in Urdu newspapers, besides his books on the same topic.

The recent wave of militancy may not be directly attributed to Sayyid Ahmad and his Jihad Movement. Many factors have combined over recent decades include state and non-state actors. Pakistan, United States, and Middle-East countries during the Soviet Union intervention in Afghanistan and after are all responsible for elements of recent turmoil. However, all the organizations involved in the armed struggle in Afghanistan and Kashmir attract the general public by narrating stories of the Mujahidin of Sayyid Ahmad in their speeches. They have established a network of Urdu newspapers to reach the majority portion of the Pakistan population. They have started a programme in a popular seminary in Karachi, to train youth in the art of 'Islamic journalism'. All such activities are continued with the active support of different state and non-state actors for different agendas. While dealing with the impact of the Jihad Movement, we have attributed many things to the legacy of Sayyid Ahmad, but may simply point out the common nature of claims made by those involved in current armed struggle that they are ideologically inspired by the Jihad Movement.

The Jihad Movement of Sayyid Ahmad and his associates was a new experience in the history of the subcontinent. He established an impressive network of disciples to recruit and fund-raising, a network which functioned for many decades after his death. It might have brought positive changes in the Muslims in South Asian society if he had limited his efforts to the reformation of society. The *Rah-e-Suluk-e-Nabuwat* could have worked for preaching about Islam, reforming Muslim beliefs, and striving for the social and economic uplift of the people, if it avoided the armed struggle. Initiating a jihad in the absence of an *amir-ul-mominin* or without the support of a head of a Muslim political state actually exposed the Muslims to major threats. Jihad in such 'private capacity' has often led to destruction and sectarianism. Not to doubt the credibility of the participants in the jihad and not to deny their sacrifices might still allow the comment that the wrong strategy was adopted. Statistics are not available but much has been expended in this regard since Muslim lands were colonized by western powers as many perished with more negative and less positive impact.

The Jihad Movement and its offspring have had a limited vision in action and strategy. There are differences between the Jihad Movement of Sayyid Ahmad and present-day militant organizations, but many today claim to embody the legacy of the Mujahidin. Today, they are resistance movements in nature and aspire to resolve problems of Muslims, but they are less aware than they need to be of the social and political dynamics involved. They need to rethink their strategy if they really wish to work for the uplift of Muslims. Political organization, economic uplift, educational planning, and social revolution are options.

Note and Reference

1. Waheed-ud-Din Khan. 2005. *Din wa Shariat: Din-e-Islam ka aik Fikri Mutale'a*. Lahore: Dar-ul-Tazkeer.
2. With the exception of few, the modern states are oppressive in one way or the other and serve the interests of 'corporate sector' at the cost of common taxpayers. The human race needs to formulate a new social contract and thus suggests some remedy though baptism of Marxism is not suggested.

Glossary

Ahadith	Saying/traditions of the Prophet Muhammad (Peace Be Upon Him)
Ahl-e-Hadith	Those who claim that they follow none of the schools of *fiqah* but *ahadith*
Ahl-e-Rusum	Those who follow the rituals of their forefathers, usually contrary to the teaching of *sharia*
Akhun	Preceptor; instructor; teacher
Alim	Religious scholar; scholar of religious education
Amal-e-zahiri	External deeds; engagements seen by others
Amir	Head; leader
Amir-ul-Mominin	Head/ruler of the Muslims
Azan	Call for prayer
Badal	Revenge
Bai'at	Oath of allegiance
Bait-ul-mal	Public treasury
Bida'at	Innovations in religious affairs; the deeds considered Islamic but in fact not authorized by Islam
Bigar	Forced labour
Batini	Intrinsic; internal; hidden; related to inner of the man
Batini ashghal	Intrinsic occupation; esoteric experiences; the inner engagement of a man
Charbitah	A genre of the Pukhtu poetry in which four stanzas complete an expression and in which usually historical events are narrated though not necessarily
Dargah	The shrine or tomb of a saint in South Asia

Dar-ul-Harb	A land or country where Muslims could not follow all Islamic injunctions freely and hence living there for the Muslims is not authorized by Islamic law; a country of infidels where war can be waged, according to Islamic law
Dar-ul-Islam	A country where the Muslims could follow Islamic injunctions without any obstacle and hindrance
Dharb	Spiritual beating
Diwani	Revenue collection
Dua	Prayer; invocation
Fatwa (plural: *fatawa*)	Religious decree; a judicial decree; verdict
Ghalla	Corn; grain
Ghanima	War booty
Ghaus	A title of Muslim saints who spend most of their time in Allah's worship and it is commonly believed that they are so engrossed in worship that their heads and limbs fall asunder
Haj	Pilgrimage to Makkah. Haj is obligatory upon those Muslims who have enough financial resources to fulfil the needs of the performer of Haj and his family back at home during his absence.
Hindki (plural: *Hindkian*)	A name given by the Pukhtuns to the people from the down country; Hindku-speaking people
Hijrat	Migration for Islamic cause
Hujrah	Jointly or communally owned house type building which not only serves as a guest house but also as a focal point for community actions and opinions, a place for sleeping for unmarried men and so forth. It serves as multipurpose community centre.
Ibada	Divine worship; adoration like prayer, fasting, payment of *zakat* and *haj*

Ijtehad	Analogical inference from Qur'an and *ahadith*; interpretation or re-interpretation of Islamic law and injunctions
Ijtema'-e-'Aam	General gathering; general meeting
Ijtema'-e-Khas	Meeting of selected person; special meeting
Imam	Head of the Faithfuls; spiritual or religious leader of the Muslims; *Amir-ul-Mominin*
Iman	Faith; belief
Jagir	Estate; a piece of land granted by the ruler/ state to an individual
Jala	Local made ferry, made of hide and wood
Jama'at	Group
Jama'at-e-Khas	Special group or segment of the Mujahidin (followers of Sayyid Ahmad Barailvi)
Jargah	Council of elders; consultative forum; meeting
Jihad	Struggle or striving in the way of Allah; spending one's potential for a cause; war waged for the cause of Allah
Jizyah	Poll tax
Jumat	Mosque
Kalima	The Muslim confession of faith
Kandao	Hill pass
Kasabgars	The non-land owing ethnic groups associated with different professions; professionals
Kashaf	Revelation; a divine inspiration
Khalifa (plural: *khulafa*)	Deputy
Khan	A title for a Pukhtun chief
Khilafat Nama	Insignia
Khulasa	An elementary book of Hanafi *fiqah*; summary; abridgement
Khutba	Sermon; oration
Lashkar/Lakhkar	A tribal force taking the field under the tribal banner at the time of need without any payment, at their own cost, arms, and ammunition
Madrassah (plural: *Madaris*)	School for religious education; seminary

Mahfil	Setting; congregation; assembly
Maimana	Left wing or the portion of the force stationed at the left in a battlefield
Maisra	Right wing or the portion of the force stationed at the right in a battlefield
Malak	A title for a Pukhtun or/and Punjabi chief; also title of a person who is appointed by the government for revenue collection at local level on a per cent of the collected amount instead of fixed salary
Mashk	The pot used for water carrying; it is also used for the substance got from deer and used in perfume
Melmastya	Hospitality
Mishkat-ul-Masabih	A book of the collection of the saying/traditions of the Prophet Muhammad (Peace Be Upon Him)
Muhtasib	Ombudsman; superintendent of weights, measures, provisions, and public morals
Mujtahid	One who qualify for or do *ijtehad*; a supervisor or superintendent in religious matters
Mashaikh	Holy persons; hermits
Mulla, Maulvi	One who performs religious ceremonies as profession, for example, leading the prayers in the mosques, teaching the Holy Qur'an, *ahadith* and *fiqah*, and so-forth
Munyatul Mussali	An elementary book of Hanafi *fiqah*
Murid	Disciple
Muqadimat-ul-jaish	Vanguard of the army
Nala	Ravine
Na'at	A form of poetry which discusses the life and achievements of Prophet Muhammad (Peace Be Upon Him)
Nazar	An offering; donation
Nazim	Governor
Nikah	Contract for marriage according to Islam
Padri	Christian priest

Palki	A kind of litter or sedan; a palanquin
Panah	Giving asylum, one of the major pillars of Pukhtu or Pukhtunwali
Pundit	A learned Brahman; a learned or wise man
Pesh imam	A person who lead the congregational prayers
Pir	Preceptor; a spiritual guide
Pukhtu/Pukhtunwali	The Pukhtun code of conduct; the norms, rules and traditions, etc., that govern the lives of the Pukhtuns
Qalb	The portion of the forces stationed at the centre in the battlefield
Qasida	An ode; laudatory poem; encomium
Qawwali	A style of Sufi devotional music by rhythmic improvisatory repetition of a short phrase, intended to rouse participants to a state of mystical ecstasy
Qazi	Judge
Qazi-ul-Quza	Chief justice
Qiladar	The governor of a fort; commandant of a garrison in a fort
Qutb	A title or degree of rank among religious mendicants
Rafaʿ al yadain	Rising hands to the shoulders in the prayers
Rah-e-Suluk-Nabuwat	Path/order of the Prophetic Enlightment, the name given to the order of Sayyid Ahmad Barailvi in *Sirat-e-Mustaqim*.
Risala	Treatise; also a group of troops
Risaldar	Commander of the troops
Samah	Plain
Saʿaqat-ul-jaish	The persons or group responsible for supplies and left-over things of the camp
Sharia	Islamic law
Sharha (plural: *shuruh*)	Commentary; explanation; annotation
Serai	The land allotted to religious figures, like Sayyids, Mians, and *mulla*s, and institutions like mosques

Shirk	Polytheism; idolatry
Shura	Consultative body; consultation
Tahsildar	Administrative officer and tax collector
Talib (plural: *Taliban*)	A seeker of Islamic education
Tapah	A genre of Pukhtu folk verse that no individual can claim as his creation and which, it is believed, is generally said by women
Taqlid	Following the centuries-old interpretation of the earlier jurists
Tarburwali	Rivalry between paternal cousins; cousinhood
Tariqah	Order; path
Tariqah-e-Muhammadiyah	Path/order of Prophet Muhammad (Peace Be Upon Him); one of the names given to the order of Sayyid Ahmad Barailvi
Tasawwur-e-Sheikh	To contemplate the personality of one's spiritual preceptor or guide and focus attention on him as the highest object of love
Tariqat	Mysticism
Tawajuh	Spiritual attention
Urs	Literally means wedding, is the death anniversary of a Sufi saint in South Asia, usually held at the saint's shrine/tomb
Ushar	Tithe of the agricultural production
Wahdat-ul-wujud	The belief of *la maujud-u-illa Allah*, that is, nothing exist save Allah; or the belief of *hamahust*, that is, all that is present/exist is but Allah
Wali	Governor
Walwar	The sum received by the family of the bride from the family of the bridegroom, which they generally expend on the marriage of the bride
Wazir	Minister; premier
Wizarat	Premier-ship; minister-ship; ministry
Quduri	A preliminary book of Hanafi *fiqah*
Zahiri	External deeds
Zikar	Remembrance of Allah; reading the Qur'an and recital of the praise and names of Allah

Appendix A: English Translation of the *Farman* of King Ahmad Shah Abdali, Durr-i-Durran, King of Kabul (Afghanistan)

Be it known to our sincere and faithful friend Fateh Khan Hoti who should be rightfully proud of the honour we are bestowing upon him that our Imperial Majesty is graciously pleased with your good services, first in the conquer of Kandahar and Khurrasan after the death of King Nadir Shah of Iran and second in the third battle of Panipat and especially for the conspicuous act of killing the Baho, the Commander-in-Chief of the Maratha Forces; in recognition of these services we are bestowing upon you, our sincere and faithful friend, the yearly Mujib of ₹12,000 in the shape of estate consisting of the villages, namely, Kheshki, Nassata (*sic.*) Kot, Shahi, Tarnab, Chena, Garhi Dildar, Tangi, and Dargai in Illaqa Hashtnagar, which shall remain as a Perpetual Jagir in your family. In return of this Jagir you will have to support us with a battery of six cannons and guns and a cavalry of eight hundred Sawars together with two thousand trained military subordinates besides a contingent of twenty thousand Yusafzai Ghazies for the help of Imperial forces. This Jagir of ten villages of Hashtnagar is in addition to the land revenue of Yusafzai already granted to your ancestors by His Imperial Majesty Akbar dated the 12th Zilhuj 996 A.H.

Source: History of the Hoti Family, pp. 13, 20, 21.

Appendix B: *Hadith* Related to Mujahidin of Khorasan and Mahdi

Thoban R. A. (Companion of the Holy Prophet Peace Be Upon Him) reported that the Messenger of Allah said, when you see that black flags have appeared from Khorasan, go to (join) them, as the Caliph of Allah Mahdi will be among them.

Sources: Abu Abdullah Ahmad bin Muhammad bin Hanbal. 1998. *Musnad-e-Ahmad,* vol. 5, Hadith No. 22441. Beirut: Alam-ul-Kutub. p. 277.

Abu Abdullah Muhammad bin Abdullah al-Hakim. 1990. *Mustadrak Hakim,* vol. 4, Hadith 8531. Beirut: Dar-ul-Kutub al-Ala'mia. p. 547.

Appendix C: Treaty between the British Government and the Raja of Lahore (Dated 25 April 1809)

Whereas certain differences which had arisen between the British Government and the Raja of Lahore have been happily and amicably adjusted; and both parties being anxious to maintain relations of perfect amity and concord, the following articles of treaty, which shall be binding on the heirs and successors of the two parties, have been concluded by the Raja Ranjit Singh in person, and by the agency of C. T. Metcalfe, Esquire, on the part of the British government.

Article 1: Perpetual friendship shall submit between the British government and the State of Lahore: the latter shall be considered, with respect to the former, to be on the footing of the most favoured powers, and the British government will have no concern with the territories and subjects of the Raja to the northwards of the river Sutlej.

Article 2: The Raja will never maintain in the territory which he occupies on the left bank of the river Sutlej more troops than are necessary for the internal duties of that territory, nor commit or suffer any encroachments on the possession or rights of the chiefs in its vicinity.

Article 3: In the event of a violation of any of the preceding articles, or of a departure from the rules of friendship, this treaty shall be considered null and void.

Article 4: This treaty, consisting of four articles, having been settled and concluded at Amritsar, on the 25th day of April, 1809, Mr C. T. Metcalfe has delivered to the Raja of Lahore a copy of the same in English and Persian, under his seal and signature; and the Raja has delivered another copy of the same under his seal and signature, and Mr C. T. Metcalfe engages to procure within the space of two months a copy of the same, duly ratified by the Right Honourable the General in Council, on the receipt of which by the Raja, the present treaty shall be deemed complete and binding on both parties, and the copy of it now delivered to the Raja shall be returned.

Source: Cunningham, J. D. 1955. *History of Sikhs*, reprint Delhi: S. Chand and Co. pp. 406–7.

Appendix D: Names of the Hindustani Mujahidin Killed in the Battle of Akora Khattak (1826)

S. No.	Names	Residence
1	Allah Bakhsh Khan	Moorain, Anao, UP
2	Shamsher Khan	Moorain, Anao, UP
3	Sheikh Ramzani	Moorain, Anao, UP
4	Abdul Jabbar Khan	Moorain, Anao, UP
5	Abdul Majid Khan Afridi	Jahanabad, Raibaraili, UP
6	Sheikh Hamdani	Khalispur, Malihabad, UP
7	Ghulam Haidar Khan	Khalispur, Malihabad, UP
8	Ghulam Rasul Khan	Khalispur, Malihabad, UP
9	Akbar Khan	Khalispur, Malihabad, UP
10	Munawwar Khan	Khalispur, Malihabad, UP
11	Ali Hassan Khan	Gatna, Pratapgarh, UP
12	Sheikh Muazzam	Jagdeshpur, Pratapgarh, UP
13	Karim Bakhsh	Barhana, Muzaffarnagar, UP
14	Mianji Ihsanullah	Barhana, Muzaffarnagar, UP
15	Fahim Khan	Hussainpur, Muzaffarnagar, UP
16	Sayyid Muhammad	Lahari, Muzaffarnagar, UP
17	Abdul Rahman	Siamali, Muzaffarnagar, UP
18	Shadal Khan	Khairabad, Sitapur, UP
19	Imam Khan	Khairabad, Sitapur, UP
20	Din Muhammad	Korharstana, Sitapur, UP
21	Ibadullah	Meo, Jhansi, UP
22	Aulad Ali	Madh, Hamirpur, UP
23	Mirza Humayun Baig	Lucknow
24	Jawahir Khan	Lucknow

contd...

contd...

S. No.	Names	Residence
25	Abdul Razzaq	Deoband, Saharanpur, UP
26	Imam-ul-Din	Rampur, Saharanpur, UP
27	Muhammad Kamal	Khurrampur, Saharanpur, UP
28	Sheikh Budhan	Most probably UP
29	Khuda Bakhsh	Most probably UP
30	Qazi Tayyab	Most probably UP
31	Ghulam Nabi	Gwalior
32	Sheikh Makhdum	Fatehpur Masjid, Delhi
33	Karim Bakhsh	Fatehpur Masjid, Delhi
34	Sheikh Baqir Ali	Sadiqpur, Azeemabad, Bihar
35	Sayyid Abdul Rahman	Sindh
36	Hassan Khan	Sindh

Source: Mihr, Ghulam Rasul. nd. *Sayyid Ahmad Shahid.* Lahore: Sheikh Ghulam and sons. pp. 340–41.

Appendix E: List of Mujahidin Killed in Balakot (1831)

S. No	Names	Residence
1	Sayyid Ahmad Barailvi	Raibaraili, Lucknow
2	Shah Ismail	Delhi
3	Mirza Muhammad Baig	Unknown (sic.): Punjab: author
4	Abdullah	Delhi
5	Abul Hassan	Nasirabad, Lucknow
6	Ubaidullah (New Muslim)	Unknown
7	Sayyid Amir Ali	Jaysi
8	Sheikh Abdul Rauf	Phulat
9	Sheikh Zia-ud-Din	Phulat
10	Hakim Qamar-ud-Din	Phulat
11	Sheikh Bahadar Ali	Phulat
12	Sheikh Hammad	Phulat
13	Sheikh Tawwakul	Phulat
14	Nabi Hussain	Azeemabad
15	Rahat Hussain	Phulat
16	Allah Bakhsh	Phulat
17	Allah Dad	Phulat
18	Muhammad Masum	Phulat
19	Ashraf Khan	Gurakhpur
20	Haji Barkat	Azeemabad
21	Alim-ud-Din	Bengal
22	Faiz-ud-Din	Bengal
23	Lutfullah	Bengal
24	Munshi Muhammadi Ansari	Unknown
25	Sharf-ud-Din	Bengal

contd...

contd...

S. No	Names	Residence
26	Sayyid Muzaffar Hussain	Bengal
27	Munawwar	Lucknow
28	Karim Bakhsh	Lucknow
29	Mirza Murtaza Baig	Lucknow
30	Noor Ali	Lucknow
31	Hafiz Abdul Wahab	Lucknow
32	Khuda Bakhsh	Lucknow
33	Mahmud Khan	Lucknow
34	Sheikh Amjad Ali	Ghazipur
35	Sheikh Muhammad Ali	Ghazipur
36	Sheikh Asghar Ali	Ghazipur
37	Sheikh Dargahi	Ghazipur
38	Khuda Bakhsh s/o Sheikh Dargahi	Ghazipur
39	Abdul Qadir	Ghazipur
40	Abdul Manan	Binaras
41	Hassan Khan	Binaras
42	Mianji Chishti	Barhana
43	Hayat Khan	Khairabad
44	Noor Bakhsh	Shamli
45	Sheikh Shuja'at Ali	Faizabad, Lucknow
46	Hafiz Amir-ud-Din	Garh Makteshari
47	Bakhshullah	Khairabad
48	Imam-ud-Din	Bombay
49	Sayyid Noor Ahmad	Nagram
50	Chand Khan	Nagor
51	Noor Muhammad	Nagor
52	Mianji Abdul Karim	Ameetha
53	Abdul Jabbar Khan	Shahjahanpur
54	Abdul Qadir	Jhanjhana
55	Hafiz Mustafa	Jhanjhana
56	Hassan Khan	Zamania
57	Ahmadullah (cousin of Maulvi Abdul Hai)	Nagpur

contd...

contd...

S. No	Names	Residence
58	Abdul Rahman	Nagpur
59	Nawab Khan	Gatna
60	Qalandar Khan	Qandahar
61	Badal Khan	Bans Baraili, Lucknow
62	Ghulam Muhammad	Panipat
63	Muhammad Hassan s/o Ghulam Muhammad	Panipat
64	Mirza Hussain Baig	Bans Baraili, Lucknow
65	Sheikh Nusrat	Bans Baraili, Lucknow
66	Mir Amanat Ali	Sadhora
67	Karim Bakhsh	Sadhora
68	Rahimullah	Saharanpur
69	Farjam	Saharanpur
70	Ali Khan	Saharanpur
71	Munshi Khwaja Muhammad	Hassanpur
72	Qazi Ahmadullah	Meerut
73	Sheikh Buland Bakht	Deoband
74	Abdul Aziz	Deoband
75	Sallo Khan	Deoband
76	Daud Khan	Khorja
77	Wali Dad Khan	Khorja
78	Murad Khan	Khorja
79	Sheikh Nasrullah	Khorja
80	Mawla Bakhsh	Mewat
81	Wazir Khan	Mewat
82	Qadir Bakhsh	Kanjpur
83	Nathay Khan	Hazara
84	Sayyid Chiragh Ali	Patiala
85	Azimullah Khan	Akora Khattak, Nowshera
86	Arbab Bahram Khan	Tahkal, Peshawar
87	Sheikh Muhammad Raza	Meerut
88	Qadir Bakhsh	Lehari
89	Hafiz Ilahi Bakhsh	Kerana

contd...

contd...

S. No	Names	Residence
90	Sar Andaz Khan	Pakhli, Mansehra
91	Sheikh Muhammad Ishaq	Gurakhpur
92	Dilawar Khan	Gurakhpur
93	Abdul Subhan Khan	Gurakhpur
94	Mansur Khan	Gurakhpur
95	Abdullah Khan	Gurakhpur
95	Musharaf Khan	Gurakhpur
96	Roshan Saqqa	Kotal
97	Sakhawat	Rampur
98	Khairullah	Amroha
99	Father of Khairullah (name could not known)	Amroha
100	Mirza Jan	Chanai (Swabi)
101	Son of Mirza Jan (name could not known)	Chanai (Swabi)
102	Hafiz Abdul Qadir	Doab
103	Allah Bakhsh	Anbala
104	Bakhshullah	Bahadur Garhi
105	Lal Muhammad Muhajir	Pranghar
106	Sheikh Imam Ali	Alahabad
107	Allah Bakhsh	Baghalpat
108	Qazi Ala-ud-Din	Baghra
109	Sayyid Amir-ud-Din	Baghra
110	Rahim Bakhsh	Alahabad
111	Bheekan	Shahpur
112	Shamsh-ud-Din	Haryana
113	Sayyid Mardan Ali	Miranpur
114	Muhammad	Arabia
115	Faizullah	Shaidi
116	Allah Dad	Unknown
117	Qadir Bakhsh	Unknown
118	Abdul Qadir	Unknown
119	Raja Ram	Probably Raibaraili (Beswara, Raibaraili: author)

contd...

contd...

S. No	Names	Residence
120	Sayyid Zain-ul-Abidin	Peshawar
121	A Pukhtun (name could not determined)	Peshawar
122	A Pukhtun (name could not determined)	Peshawar
123	Sayyid Imam Ali	Alahabad
124	Mirza Ahmad Baig	Punjab
125	Sher Jang Khan	Khalispur
126	Faizullah	Takht, Hazara
127	Bakhshullah Khan	Bara Basti
128	Hafiz Mustafa	Kandhalah
129	Name could not determined	Panipat
130	Mehruban Khan	Mewat
131	Bakhshullah	Unknown
132	Mehdi Shah	Shah Maidan, Batgram
133	Habib Khan Jachcha	Bhogarmang
134	Muhammad Halim	Shagai, Balakot
135	Mirza Jan Khan	Dodhial, Pakhli
136	Ghazi Shah	Temri, Pakhli
137	Nawab Khan	Bhgarmang, Mansehra
138	Unknown	Balakot
139	Hamza Khan	Sufaida, Mansehra
140	Mian Khan Swati	Jabori
141	Muhammad Usman Swati (brother of 140)	Jabori
142	Muhammad Ubaid	Mangal
143	Sandal Khan	Punjab
144	Bakhshullah	Anbala

Sources: Khan, Nawab Muhammad Wazir. 2007. *Waqai Sayyid Ahmad Shahid.* Lahore: Sayyid Ahmad Shahid Academy. pp. 2451–54; Mihr, Ghulam Rasul. nd. *Sayyid Ahmad Shahid.* Lahore: Sheikh Ghulam Ali & Sons. pp. 800–801; Khan, Khawas. 1983. *Roedad-e-Mujahidin-e-Hind.* Lahore: Maktaba Rashidia. pp. 138–50.

Bibliography

Personal Collection/Libraries (Manuscript)

Gul, Momin. *Jamaat-e-Isha'at-e-Tauhid wa Sunnah* (my copy).

History of the Hoti Family. Hoti Family Collection, Mardan (my copy).

Makatib-e-Sayyid Ahmad Shahid. British Libraries London.

Naqvi, Sayyid Jaffar Ali. *Manzurat-ul-Su'da fi Ahwal-e-Ghuzat-e-wal Shuhada.* Punjab University Library.

Unnamed Persian manuscript written in 1279 A.H (my copy).

Sithanavi, Sayyid Abdul Jabbar Shah, *Shahadat-ul-Saqlain.* Family Collection of Sithana Sayyids.

Khyber Pakhtunkhwa Provincial Archives, Peshawar

Chamarkand Colony. Serial No. 271, Civil Secretariat, North-West Frontier Political Department, Tribal Research Cell, Peshawar.

Emigrants and Indians Abroad: Mujahideen 1939. Serial No. 408, Bundle No. 27, Special Branch Police, List-I.

Fazal Rabbi, Maulvi, AF 11, CID NWFP.

Frontier Policy of the Punjab. Serial No. 34, Bundle No. 5, Foreign Frontier Department, Printed Files.

Hindustani Colony, Ambela Sittana Sayyads. Serial No. 612, Bundle No. 18.

Hindustani Fanatics A-F-17. Special Branch Police NWFP.

Imperial Gazetteer Hazara District Gazeteer. Serial No. 1200, Bundle No. 43.

James Settlement Report 1865.

Movements of the Hindustani Fanatics Colony. Foreign Frontier Political Department, Part-A, Serial No. 514, Bundle No. 31.

Mutiny Reports from Punjab & N.W.F.P, vol. II. nd. Reprint; Lahore: Al-Biruni.

Plowden, 1932. T. J. C. *Report on the Leading Persons and State of Factions in Swat.* Simla: Government Press of India.

Saiyid Abdul Jabbar Shah of Sitana. Serial No. 1028, Bundle 37.

Settlement of the Hindustani Fanatics in the Amazai Country. Serial No. 127, Bundle No. 10.

English Sources

Abbot, Freeland. 1968. *Islam and Pakistan*. New York: Cornell University Press.

———. 1962. 'The Jihad of Sayyid Ahmad Shahid'. *The Muslim World*, vol. 52, no. 3, pp. 216–22.

Adas, Michael. 1979. *Prophets of Rebellions: Millenarian Protest Movements against the European Colonial Order*. New York: Cambridge University Press.

Ahmad, Aziz. 1968. 'An Eighteenth-Century Theory of the Caliphate'. *Studia Islamica*, vol. 28. pp. 135–44. http://www.jstor.org/stable/1595266 (accessed on 24 March 2009).

———. 1970. *Studies in Islamic Culture in the Indian Environment*. Karachi: Oxford University Press.

Ahmad, Manzooruddin. 1967. 'The Political Role of the "Ulama" in the Indo-Pakistan Sub-Continent'. *Islamic Studies*, vol. 6, no. 4, pp. 327–54.

Ahmad, Mohiuddin. 1975. *Saiyid Ahmad Shahid: His Life and Mission*. Lucknow: Academy of Islamic Research and Publications.

Ahmad, Qeyamuddin. 1979. *The Wahabi Movement in India*. Reprint; Islamabad: National Book Foundation.

Ahmed, Nazir. 1988. 'Shah Wali Allah and His Literary Works'. *The Dhaka University Studies*, vol. 45, no. 1, pp. 61–78.

———. 1989. 'Shah Wali Allah and the Contemporary Political Scene'. *The Dhaka University Studies*, vol. 46, no. 2, pp. 205–16.

Ali, M. Athar. 1975. 'The Passing of Empire: The Mughal Case'. *Modern Asian Studies*, vol. 9, no. 3, pp. 385–96. http://www.jstor.org/stable/311728 (accessed on 9 March 2009).

Ali, Md. Mohar. 1971. 'The Bengal Muslims' Repudiation of the Concept of British India as Darul Harb'. *The Dacca University Studies*, vol. 19, no. 1, pp. 47–68.

Ali, Mubarak. 2005. *Ulema, Sufis and Intellectuals*. Lahore: Fiction House.

Ali, Shahamat. 1985. *An Expedition to Kabul: Immediately Before & After the Death of Maharaja Ranjit Singh*. Reprint; Delhi: Amar Prakash.

———. 2005. *The Sikhs and the Afghans in Connexion with India and Persia*. Reprint; New York: Adamant Media Corporation.

Ali, Shaukat. 1993. *Millenarian and Messianic Tendencies in Islamic History*. Lahore: Publisher United.

Allan, Charles. 2007. *God's Terrorists: The Wahabi Cult and the Hidden Roots of Modern Jihad*. Massachusetts: Da Capo Press.

Ansari, A. S. Bazmee. 1976. 'Sayyid Ahmad Shahid in the Light of His Letter'. *Islamic Studies*, vol. 15, no. 4, pp. 231–45.

Awan, Samina. 2009. 'Redefinition of Identities, Subaltern and Political Islam: A Case of Majlis i Ahrar in Punjab'. *Journal of Research Society of Pakistan*, vol. 46, no. 2, pp. 157–90.

Aziz, A. 1964. *Discovery of Pakistan*. Reprint; Lahore: Sh. Ghulam Ali & Sons.

Aziz, K. K. 1995. *The Murder of History: A Critique of History Textbooks Used in Pakistan*. Lahore: Vanguard.

Baha, Lal. 1978. *N.W.F.P. Administration under British Rule, 1901–19*. Islamabad: National Commission on Historical and Cultural Research.

———. 1979. 'The Activities of Mujahidin 1900–1936'. *Islamic Studies*, vol. 18, pp. 97–168.

210   Sayyid Ahmad Barailvi

Bari, M. A. 1966. 'A Nineteenth Century Muslim Reform Movement in India', in George Makdisi (ed.), *Arabic and Islamic Studies in Honor of Hamilton A. R. Gibb.* Leiden: E. J. Brill.

Bellew, H. W. 1977. *From the Indus to the Tigris: A Narrative of a Journey Through the Countries of Balochistan, Afghanistan, Khorasan and Iran,* 1872. Reprint; Karachi: Royal Book Company.

———. 2001. *A General Report on the Yusufzais.* Reprint; Lahore: Sang-e-Meel Publications.

———. nd. *The Races of Afghanistan.* Reprint; Lahore: Sang-e-Meel Publications.

Bingley, A. H. 1984. *Sikhs: Their Origin, History, Religion, Customs, Fairs and Festivals.* New Delhi: Sumit Publications.

Bokawee, Mohammad Afzaul Shah. 2006. *The Pukhtoons.* Rawalpindi: Pap-Board Printers Pvt. Ltd.

Bonner, Michael. 2006. *Jihad in Islamic History: Doctrine and Practice.* Princeton, New Jersey: Princeton University Press.

Buckler, F. W. 1922. 'The Political Theory of the India Mutiny'. *Transactions of the Royal Historical Society.* Fourth Series, vol. 5, pp. 71–100. http://www.jstor.org/stable/3678458 (accessed on 9 March 2009).

Caroe, Olaf. 1965. *The Pathans, 550 B.C.–A.D. 1957.* London: Macmillan & Co. Ltd.

Chand, Tara. 1967. *History of the Freedom Movement in India.* Vol. II. Delhi: Ministry of Information and Broadcasting, Government of India.

Chattopadhyay, Dilip Kumar. 1977. 'The Ferazee and Wahabi Movements of Bengal'. *Social Scientist,* vol. 6, no. 2, pp. 42–51. http://www.jstor.org/stable/3516683 (accessed on 24 March 2009).

Cunningham, Joseph Davey. 1849. *A History of the Sikhs: From the Origin of the Nation to the Battle of the Sutlej.* London: John Murray.

Dallal, Ahmad. 1993. 'The Origins and Objectives of the Islamic Revivalist Thought, 1750–1850'. *Journal of the American Oriental Society,* vol. 113, no. 3. pp. 341–59. http://www.jstor.org/stable/605385 (accessed on 17 April 2008).

Dani, Ahmad Hassan. 2002. *Peshawar: Historic City of the Frontier.* 2nd edition; Lahore: Sang-e-Meel Publications.

De, Amalendu. 1995. 'The Social Thought and Consciousness of the Bengali Muslims in the Colonial Period'. *Social Scientist,* vol. 23, nos. 4/6. pp. 16–37. http://www.jstor.org/stable/3520213 (accessed on 24 March 2009).

Dodwell, H. H. 1929. *The Cambridge History of India: British India 1497–1858.* Chapel Hill: Cambridge University Press.

Douie, James. nd. *The Panjab, North-West Frontier Province and Kashmir.* Reprint; Lahore: Book Traders.

Edwardes, Michael. 1968. *Glorious Sahibs: The Romantic as Empire Builders 1799–1838.* London: Eyre & Spottiswoode.

Elliot, J. G. 1968. *The Frontier 1839–1947: The Story of the North-West Frontier of India.* London: Cassell.

Elphinstone, Mountstuart. 1990. *An Account of the Kingdom of Caubul.* Vols. I & II. Reprint; Quetta: Gosha-e-Adab.

Esposito, John L. and John O. Voll. 2001. *Makers of Contemporary Islam.* New York: Oxford University Press.

Ewans, Martin. 2001. *Afghanistan: A New History.* London: Curzon Press.

Fatima, Altaf. 2008. 'The Role of Popular Muslim Movements in the Indian Freedom Struggle'. *The American Journal of Islamic Social Sciences*, vol. 25, no. 2, pp. 141–52.

Firestone, Reuven. 1999. *Jihad: The Origin of Holy War in Islam*. New York: Oxford University Press.

Gaborieau, Marc. 2000. *The Mahdi forgotten British India: Sayyid Ahmad Barelvi (1786–1831), His Followers, His Opponents*. http://remmm.revues.org/index259.html (accessed on 1 July 2010).

Gazetteer of the Amritsar District 1892–93. 1893. Lahore: Government of the Punjab.

Gazetteer of Hazara District 1883–84. 2000. Reprint; Lahore: Sang-e-Meel Publications.

Gazetteer of the Punjab: Provincial Column 1888–89. 1889. Lahore: Government of the Punjab.

Gazetteer of the Peshawar District 1897–98. 1989. Reprint; Lahore: Sang-e-Meel Publications.

Gazetteer of the Lahore District 1883–4. 1989. Reprint; Lahore: Sang-e-Meel Publications.

Gazetteer of the Bannu District 1883–4. 1884. Lahore: Government of the Punjab.

Gazetteer of the Dera Ismail Khan District 1883–84. 1884. Lahore: ARYA Press.

Gazetteer of the Mooltan District 1883–84. 1884. Lahore: ARYA Press.

Gazetteer of the Gujrat District 1883–84. 1884. Lahore: ARYA Press.

Gazetteer of the Gujranwala District 1883–84. 1884. Lahore: Government of the Punjab.

Ghamidi, Javed Ahmad. nd. *The Penal Shari'ah*. Translated by Shehzad Saleem. Lahore: Al Mawrid.

Gopal, Ram. nd. *How the British Occupied Bengal: A Corrected Account of the 1756–1765 Events*. Reprint; Lahore: Book Traders.

Graham, William A. 1993. 'Traditionalism in Islam: An Essay in Interpretation'. *Journal of the Interdisciplinary History*, vol. 18, no. 3, pp. 495–522.

Grewal, J. S. 2002. *The New Cambridge History of India: The Sikhs of the Punjab*. Revised edition; New Delhi: Foundation Books.

Griffin, Lepel Henry. 1892. *Ranjit Singh*. Oxford: Clarendon Press.

———. 1976. *The History of the Principal States of the Punjab and their Political Relations with the British Government (The Rajas of the Punjab)*. Reprint; Lahore: Sheikh Mubarak Ali.

Gupta, Hari Ram. 1944. *History of the Sikhs: Trans-Sutlej Sikhs 1769–1799*. Lahore: The Minerva Book Shop.

Habib, Irfan. 2001. *Confronting Colonialism: Resistance and Modernization under Haidar Ali and Tipu Sultan*. Delhi: Manohar.

———. 2002. *State and Diplomacy Under Tipu Sultan: Documents and Essays*. Delhi: Manohar.

Haq, Noor ul, Rashid Ahmed Khan and Maqsudul Hasan Nuri. 2005. *Federally Administered Tribal Areas of Pakistan*. http://ipripak.org/papers/federally.shtml (accessed on 29 January 2011).

Hardy, Peter. 1972. *The Muslims of British India*. London: Cambridge University Press.

Haroon, Sana. 2011a. *Frontier of Faith: A History of Religious Mobilisation in the Pakhtun Tribal Areas c. 1890–1950*. Karachi: Oxford University Press.

———. 2011b. 'Reformism and Orthodox Practice in Early Nineteenth Century Muslim North India: Sayyid Ahmed Shaheed Reconsidered'. *Journal of the Royal Asiatic Society*. Series 3, vol. 21, no. 2. pp. 171–198.

———. 2008. 'The Rise of Deobandi Islam in the North-West Frontier Province and Its Implications in Colonial India and Pakistan 1914-1996'. *Journal of the Royal Asiatic Society*. Series 3, vol. 18, no. 1, pp. 47–70.

Hashmi, N. A. Tajul Islam. 1976. 'Maulana Karamat Ali and the Muslims of Bengal 1820–1873'. *The Dacca University Studies.* Part A, vol. 24, pp. 123–36.

Haq, S. Moinul. 1968. *The Great Revolution of 1857.* Karachi: Pakistan Historical Society.

———. nd. *Ideological Basis of Pakistan: In Historical Perspective (711–1940).* Karachi: Pakistan Historical Society.

Hedayatullah, Muhammad. nd. *Sayyid Ahmad: A Study of the Religious Reform Movement of Sayyid Ahmad of Ra'e Bareli.* Lahore: Sh. Muhammad Ashraf.

Holman, Dennis. 1961. *Sikander Sahib: The Life of Colonel James Skinner 1778–1841.* London: Heinemann.

Honigberger, John Martin. 2006. *Thirty-Five Years in the East Relating to the Punjab and Cashmere.* Reprint; Lahore: Sang-e-Meel Publications.

Husain, Delawar. 1989. 'Nineteenth Century Indian Historical Writings: An overview of the trends and assumptions with reference to the works of W. W. Hunter, H. Beveridge and H. F. Blochman'. *The Dhaka University Studies.* Part A, vol. 46, no. 1, pp. 103–15.

Husain, Mahmud et al. (eds). 2008. *A History of the Freedom Movement 1707–1831.* Vol. I. Reprint; Karachi: Royal Book Company.

Hutchison, J. and S.E. J. Vogel. 1933. *History of the Punjab Hill States.* Lahore: Government Printing Press.

Ibbeston, Denzil. 1993. *Punjab Castes.* Reprint; Delhi: Low Price Publications.

Innes, Arthur D. 1985. *A Short History of the British in India.* Reprint; Delhi: Inter-India Publications.

Iqbal, Javed. 2003. *Islam and Pakistan's Identity.* Lahore: Iqbal Academy.

Iqbal, Muhammad. 2007. *The Reconstruction of Religious Thought in Islam.* Edited and Annotated by M. Saeed Sheikh. 7th edition, Lahore: Institute of Islamic Culture.

Irvine, William. 2007. *Later Mughals, 1707–1739.* Reprint; Lahore: Sang-e-Meel Publications.

Islam, M. Mufakharul. 1981. 'Laissez Faire or Selective Interaction? (Government Policy in the Nineteenth Century India)', in S. A. Akanda (ed.), *Studies in Modern Bengal.* Rajshahi: Institute of Bangladesh Studies.

Islahi, Amin Ahsan. 2009. *Fundamentals of Hadith Interpretation.* Translated by Tariq Mahmud Hashmi. Lahore: Al-Mawrid.

Jaffar, Ghulam Muhammad. 1991. 'Nawwab Mubariz Al-Dawlah and Activities in Hyderabad (Dn)'. *Journal of the Pakistan Historical Society.* Part III, vol. 39, pp. 299–306.

———. 1994. 'Mawlawi Nasir Al-Din's Jihad Activities After the Death of Sayyid Ahmad Shahid'. *Journal of the Pakistan Historical Society.* Part II, vol. 42, pp. 173–80.

———. 1995. 'Social Background of the Tariqah-i-Muhammadiyah Movement'. *Journal of the Pakistan Historical Society.* Part IV, vol. 43, pp. 363–380.

Jafri, Saiyid Zaheer Husain and Helmut Reifeld. 2006. *The Islamic Path: Sufism, Politics and Society in India.* Delhi: Rainbow Publishers Limited.

Jalal, Ayesha. 2008. *Partisans of Allah: Jihad in South Asia.* Massachusetts: Harvard University Press.

Karim, Abdul. 1963. *Murshid Quli Khan and His Times.* Dacca: Asiatic Society of Pakistan.

Karim, Nehal. 1992–93. 'Sepoy Mutiny and Social Mutation'. *The Dhaka University Studies Journal of the Faculty of Arts.* vol. 48, no. 2; Vol. 49, Nos. 1 and 2; Vol. 50, No. 1, pp. 107–14.

Keddie, Nikki R. 1994. 'The Revolt of Islam, 1700–1993: Comparative Consideration and Relations to Imperialism'. *Comparative Studies in Society and History,* vol. 36, no. 3, pp. 463–87. http://www.jstor.org/stable/179293 (accessed on 17 April 2008).

Keene, Henry George. 1999. *The Moghul Empire: From the death of Aurungzeb to the overthrow of the Mahratta power.* Reprint; Lahore: Sang-e-Meel Publications.

Khalil, Jehanzeb. 2000. *Mujahideen Movement in Malaknad and Mohmand Agencies (1900–1940).* Ed. M. Y. Effendi. Peshawar: Area Study Centre.

Khan, Abdullah. 1984. *The Religious Thought of Shah Ismail Dihlawi.* Master Thesis, Institute of Islamic Studies, McGill University, Montreal.

———. 2011. 'Sayyid Ahmad Shahid's Role in Islamic Revivalism: A Critique'. *Al-Idah.* (*Biannual Research Journal*, Shaykh Zayed Islamic Centre, University of Peshawar), no. 22.

Khan, Muhammad Hashim Khafi. 1952. *The Later Moghuls.* Ed. John Dowson, Calcutta: Susil Gupta.

Khan, Muhammad Nawaz. 2004. *Peshawar: The Unwritten History.* Shahbaz Garhi: Gandhara Markaz.

Khan, Muin-ud-Din Ahmad. 1967. 'Economic Conditions of the Muslims of Bengal Under the East India Company 1937–1860'. *Islamic Studies*, vol. 6, no. 3, pp. 277–315.

———. 1967. 'Tariqah-i-Muhammadiyah Movement: An Analytical Study'. *Islamic Studies*, vol. 6, no. 4, pp. 375–88.

———. nd. *Muslim Struggle for Freedom in Bengal: From Plassey to Pakistan A.D. 1757–1947.* Dacca: Islamic Foundation Bangladesh.

Khan, Seid Gholam Hossein. 1975. *The Seir-Mutaqherin.* Vols. I-IV; Reprint; Lahore: Sheikh Mubarak.

Khosla, K. R. (ed.). nd. *The States and Estates and Who's Who in India & Burma.* Lahore: The Imperial Publishing Co.

Khurana, G. 1985. *British Historiography on the Sikh Power in the Punjab.* London: Mansell Publications Limited.

Kohli, S. R. 2004. *Maharaja Ranjit Singh.* Reprint; Lahore: Sang-e-Meel Publications.

Latif, Syed Muhammad. 1964. *History of the Panjab: From the Remotest Antiquity to the Present Time.* Reprint; Delhi: Eurasia Publishing House.

———. 1981. *Lahore: Its History, Architectural Remains and Antiquities with an Account of its Modern Institutions, Inhabitants, Their Trade, Customs, & c.* Reprint; Lahore: Oriental Publishers.

Leonard, Karen. 1979. 'The "Great Firm" Theory of the Decline of the Mughal Empire'. *Comparative Studies in Society and History*, vol. 21, no. 2, pp. 151–67. http://www. jstor.org/stable/178414 (accessed on 9 March 2009).

Levy, Reuben. 1957. *The Social Structure of Islam.* Cambridge: The University Press.

Macmunn, George Fletcher. 1977. *Afghanistan: From Darius to Amanullah.* Quetta: Gosha Adab.

———. 1977. *The Martial Races of India.* Reprint; Quetta: Gosha-e-Adab.

Malik, Ikram Ali. 1985. *A Book of Reading on the History of the Punjab 1799–1947.* 2nd Impression; Lahore: Research Society of Pakistan.

Malik, Salahuddin. 1976. 'The Punjab and the Indian "Mutiny": A Reassessment'. *Islamic Studies*, vol. 15, no. 2, pp. 81–110.

Mallick, Azizur Rahman. 1977. *British Policy and the Muslims in Bengal 1757–1856.* Dacca: Bangla Academy.

Marc Gaborieau and Zillur R. Khan. 1985. 'Islam and Bengali Nationalism'. *Asian Survey*, vol. 25, no. 8, pp. 834–51. http://www.jstor.org/stable/2644113 (accessed on 17 April 2008).

Masson, Charles. 1974. *Narrative of Various Journeys in Balochistan, Afghanistan and the Panjab.* Vols. I-III. Reprint; Karachi: Oxford University Press.

214 *Sayyid Ahmad Barailvi*

Marshal, P. J. 1985. 'Early British Imperialism in India'. *Past and Present*, no. 106, pp. 164–169. http://www.jstor.org/stable/650642 (accessed on 17 April 2008).

McLeod, W. H. 1992. 'The Sikh Struggle in the Eighteenth Century and its Relevance for Today'. *History of Religions*, vol. 31, no. 4, pp. 344–62. http://www.jstor.org/stable/1062799 (accessed on 8 May 2008).

Maiello, Amedeo. 2004. '*HAGG, GIHAD* AND *TASAWWUF*: The Interpretation of Sayyid Ahmad Shahid's Movement in Nineteenth Century Tonk Part I'. *ARCHAEVS, Studies in the History of Religions*, no. 4 (1–4), pp. 109–78.

Mukherjee, Rudrangshu. 1982. 'Trade and Empire in Awadh 1765–1804'. *Past and Present*, no. 94, pp. 85–102. http://www.jstor.org/stable/65049 (accessed on 17 April 2008).

———. 1985. 'Early British Imperialism in India: A Rejoinder'. *Past and Present*, no. 106, pp. 169–73. http://www.jstor.org/stable/650643 (accessed on 17 April 2008).

Mad Mullahs, Opportunists, and Family Connections: The Violent Pashtun Cycle. www.tribalanalysiscenter.com (accessed on 05 January 2010).

Naqvi, Ali Raza. 1974. 'Laws of War in Islam'. *Islamic Studies*, vol. 13, no. 1, pp. 25–43.

Narang, Gokul Chand. nd. *Transformation of Sikhism*. New Delhi: New Book Society of India.

Nevill, H. L. 1977. *Campaigns on the North West Frontier*. Reprint; Lahore: Sang-e-Meel Publications.

Nichols, Robert. 2001. *Settling the Frontier: Land, Law, and Society in the Peshawar Valley, 1500–1900*. Karachi: Oxford University Press.

Noelle, Christine. 1997. *State and Tribe in Nineteenth-Century Afghanistan: The Reign of Amir Dost Muhammad Khan (1826–1863)*. London: Curzon Press.

North, Douglass C. 1990. *Institutions, Institutional Change and Economic Performance*. New York: Cambridge University Press.

Obhrai, Dewan Chand. 1983. *The Evolution of North West Frontier Province: Being a Survey of the History and Constitutional Development of N. W. F. Province, in India*. Reprint; Peshawar: Saeed Book Bank.

Oliver-Dee, Sean. 2009. *The Caliphate Question: The British Government and Islamic Governance*. Plymouth: Lexington.

Osborne, W. C. 1973. *The Court and Camp of Ranjit Singh*. Karachi: Oxford University Press.

Pearson, Harlon O. 2008. *Islamic Reform and Revival in Nineteenth Century India: The Tariqah-i-Muhammadiyah*. Delhi: YODA PRESS.

Pearson, M. N. 1976. 'Shivaji and the Decline of the Mughal Empire'. *The Journal of Asian Studies*, vol. 35, no. 2, pp. 221–35. http://www.jstor.org/stable/2053980 (accessed on 9 March 2009).

Pottinger, Henry. 1976. *Travels in Beloochistan and Sinde; Accompanied by A Geographical and Historical Account of those Countries, with a map*. Reprint; Karachi: Indus Publications.

Qadir, Altaf. 2006. 'Haji Sahib of Turangzai and His Reform Movement in the North-West Frontier Province'. *Journal of the Pakistan Historical Society*, vol. 54, no. 3, pp. 85–95.

———. 2008. 'Anti-Colonial Movement: The Struggle of Haji Sahib Turangzai' to Do Away with the Authority of the British *Raj*'. *Journal of the Pakistan Historical Society*, vol. 56, no. 2, pp. 111–23.

Qanungo, K. R. 1960. *Historical Essays*. Agra: Shiva Lal Agarwala & Co.

Qureshi, Ishtiaq Hussain. nd. *Ulema in Politics*. Karachi: Al-Ma'arif.

Rashid, Haroon. 2002. *History of the Pathans Vol. I. The Sarabani Pathans*. Islamabad: Author.

Rashid, Sheikh Abdul. 1975. *History of the Muslims of Indo-Pakistan Subcontinent 1707–1806*. Vol. I. Lahore: Research Society of Pakistan.

Rawlinson, H. G. 1948. *The British Achievement in India: A Survey*. London: William Hodge & Company.

Rizvi, Saiyid Athar Abbas. 1982. *Shah 'Abdul 'Aziz: Puritanism, Sectarian Polemics and Jihad*. Canberra: Ma'arifat Publishing House.

Roberts, P. E. 2006. *British Rule in India: Rule of East India Company 1600–1857*. Dehradun: Reprint Publications.

Robinson, Francis. 2008. 'Islamic Reform and Modernities in South Asia'. *Modern Asian Studies*, vol. 42, nos. 2/3, pp. 259–81.

Rose, H. A. nd. *A Glossary of the Tribes and Castes of the Punjab and North-West Frontier*. Reprint; Lahore: Aziz Publishers.

Salim, Ahmad (ed). 2008. *Peshawar: City on the Frontier*. Karachi: Oxford University Press.

Sanyal, Usha. 2005. *Ahmad Riza Khan Barelwi: In the Path of the Prophet*. Oxford: Oneworld.

Sardesai, G. S. nd. *Shivaji Souvenir*. Bombay: Keshav Bhikaji Dhawale.

Sarkar, Jadu Nath. 1949. *Fall of the Mughal Empire, 1739–1754*. Calcutta: M. C. Sarkar & Sons Ltd.

Sarkar, S. C. and K. K. Datta. 1959. *Modern Indian History*. Vols. I–II. Allahabad: The Indian Press.

Sethi, R. R. 1950. *The Lahore Darbar: Punjab Government Record Office Publications Monograph No. 1*. Delhi: Gulab Chand Kapur and Sons.

Singh, Ganda. 1977. *Ahmad Shah Durrani: Father of Modern Afghanistan*. Reprint; Quetta: Gosha-e-Adab.

Singh, Harbans. 1964. *The Heritage of the Sikhs*. Bombay: Asia Publishing House.

Singh, Khushwant. 1953. *The Sikhs*. London: George Allen & Unwin Ltd.

Shah, Ibrahim. 1998. 'Governors of Peshawar: Post-Mughul Period (1738–1997)'. *Journal of the Pakistan Historical Society*, vol. 46, no. 3, pp. 81–87.

Shah, Sayed Wiqar Ali. 1999. *Ethnicity, Islam and Nationalism: Muslim Politics in the North-West Frontier, 1937–47*. Karachi: Oxford University Press.

Sharma, L. P. 1987. *History of Modern India*. Delhi: Konark Publishers.

Sharma, S. K. 1981. *History of India*. Calcutta: Royal Publications.

Smyth, G. Carmichael. 1961. *A History of the Reigning Family of Lahore with an Account of the Jamoo Rajas: The Sikh Soldiers and their Sirdars*. Reprint; Lahore: Ferozsons Ltd.

Spain, James W. 1985. *The Pathan Borderland*. Reprint; Karachi: Indus Publications.

Spear, Percival. 1965. *The Oxford History of Modern India, 1740–1947*. London: Oxford at the Clarendon Press.

Steinbach. 1982. *Punjab*. Delhi: Sumit Publications.

Stokes, Eric. 1970. 'Traditional Resistance Movements and Afro-Asian Nationalism: The Context of the 1857 Mutiny Rebellion in India'. *Past and Present*, no. 48, pp. 100–118. http://www.jstor.org/stable/650482 (accessed on 17 April 2008).

Sultan-i-Rome. 1992. 'Abdul Ghaffur (Akhund) Saidu Baba of Swat: Life, Career and Role'. *Journal of the Pakistan Historical Society*. Part III, vol. 40, pp. 299–308.

———. 2002. 'Mughuls and Swat'. *Journal of the Pakistan Historical Society* (Karachi), vol. 50, no. 4 (October–December), pp. 39–50.

———. 2004. *Forestry in the Princely State of Swat and Kalam (North West Pakistan: A Historical Perspective on Norms and Practices)*. IP6 Working Paper No. 6, p. 18. www.nccr-north-south.unibe.ch (accessed on 29 September 2014).

Sultan-i-Rome. 2006. 'Geography of the North-West Frontier Province'. *Pakistan Perspectives*, vol. 11, no. 1, pp. 113–32.

———. 2006. 'Pukhtu'. *Pakistan Vision*, vol. 7, no. 2 (December), pp. 1–30.

———. 2008. *Swat State (1915–1969): From Genesis to Merger; An Analysis of Political, Administrative, Socio-Political, and Economic Developments*. Karachi: Oxford University Press.

———. 2009. 'Swat: A Critical Analysis'. *IPCS Research Papers*. http://ipcs.org/pdf_file/issue/1542140255RP18-Rome Swat.pdf.

Suri, Lala Sohan Lal. 1961. *Umdat-ul-Tawarikh Daftar*. I–III Parts I–V. Translated by V. S. Suri. Delhi: S. Chand and Co.

Swinson, Arthur. 1967. *North-West Frontier: People and Events, 1839–1947*. London: Hutchinson & Co.

Tanner, Stephen. 2002. *Afghanistan: A Military History from Alexander the Great to the Fall of the Taliban*. Karachi: Oxford University Press.

Torrens, W. M. 1938. *Empires in Asia: How We Came by It: A Book of Confessions*. Calcutta: Lakshami Narayan Nath.

Trotter, James. 1917. *History of India*. London: William Clowes and Sons Ltd.

Vigne, G. T. 1982. *A Personal Narrative of a Visit to Ghuzni, Kabul, and Afghanistan, and of a Residence at the Court of Dost Muhammad Khan with Notices of Runjit Sing, Khiva, and the Russian Expedition*. Reprint; Lahore: Sang-e-Meel Publications.

Waheeduddin, Fakir Syed. 1965. *The Real Ranjit Singh*. Karachi: Lion Art Press.

Wallace, F. C. 1956. 'Revitalization Movements'. *American Anthropologist*. New Series, vol. 58, no. 2, pp. 264–81. http://www.jstor.org/stable/665488 (accessed on 17 April 2008).

Wylly, H. C. 2003. *From Black Mountains to Waziristan*. Reprint; Lahore: Sang-e-Meel Publications.

Yunas, S. Fida. nd. *Afghanistan: Jirgahs and Loya Jirgahs, The Afghan Tradition (977 A.D. to 1992 A.D.)* Peshawar: Area Study Centre, University of Peshawar.

Yousafzai, Hassan M. and Ali Gohar. 2005. *Towards Understanding Pukhtoon Jirga: An Indigenous way of Peace building and more...* Peshawar: Just Peace International.

Zaman, Muhammad Qasim. 1999. 'Commentaries, Print and Patronage: "Hadith" and the Madrassa in Modern South Asia'. *Bulletin of the School of Oriental and African Studies*, vol. 62, no. 1, pp. 60–81.

Arabic Book

Abd-ul-Gahfur. nd. *Burhan-ul-Mominin*. NP.

Persian Books

Azeemabadi, Wilayat Ali. nd. *Majmua'a Rasail-e-Tisa'a*. Delhi: Matba'a Farooqi.

Darwizah, Akhun. nd. *Tazkirat-ul-Abrar-e wal Ashrar*. Peshawar: Islami Kutub Khana.

Urdu Sources

Akbarabadi, Saeed Ahmad. 2007. *Hind Pakistan ki Tahrik-e-Azadi aur Ulama-e-Haq ka Siyasi Mowaqaf.* Lahore: Jamiat Publications.

Akhund Khel, Haider Ali. 2008. *Buner Khudu Khel: Tarikhi, Tahqiqi aur Saqafati Jaizah.* Mingora, Swat: Graphics World.

Akram, Nighat. 2007. *Islami Tasawwar-e-Jihad aur A'ahd-e-Hazir Ki Aham Jangain: Aik Tajziyati Mut'ale'a.* Ph.D. Dissertation, Department of Qur'an and Sunnah, Karachi University.

Ali, Mubarak. nd. *Tarikh aur Mazhabi Tahrikain.* Lahore: Fiction House.

Amjad, Mu'ezz. 2010. *Iltezam-e-Jama'at aur Jihad.* Lahore: Al-Mawrid.

Amritsari, Abu al Aman. 1958. *Sikh Muslim Tarikh: Haqiqat kay Ayenay Main.* Lahore: Idara Saqafat-e-Islamia.

Azhar, Muhammad Masud. 2007. *Suragh-e-Haqiqat.* Reprint; Karachi: Maktaba Hassan.

Babar, Zaheer-ud-Din Muhammad. 2007. *Waqai Babar.* Translated by Yunas Jaffari. UK: Shahar Bano Publishers.

Bari. 1976. *Company ki Hukumat.* Lahore: National Book Foundation.

Bukhari, Sayyid Mir Badshah. 1992. *Tahrik-e-Mujahidin: Jang-e-Balakot kay ba'd.* Peshawar: Taj Kutub Khana.

Butt, Abdullah. 1999. *Shah Ismail Shahid: Majmu'a-e-Maqalat.* Lahore: Makki Dar-ul-Kutub.

Butt, Zahur-ud-Din. nd. *Shah Waliullah ka Qafila.* Lahore: Idara Adab-e Atfal.

Chakesari, Saif-ul-Haq. 2010. *Islam ka Tasawwar-e-Jihad aur Al-Qaeda.* Mingora: Shoaib Sons Publishers and Booksellers.

Das, Gopal. 1878. *Tarikh-e-Peshawar.* Lahore: Koh-e-Noor.

Dehlavi, Mirza Hairat. 1976. *Hayat-e-Tayyaba: Sawanih-e-Umri Shah Ismail Shahid.* Reprint; Lahore: Islamic Academy.

Durrani, Ashiq Muhammad Khan. 2007. *Tarikh-e-Afghanistan ba Hawala Tarikh-e-Saduzai.* Multan: Bazm-e-Saqafat.

Ghamidi, Javed Ahmad. 2009. *Burhan.* Lahore: Al-Mawrid.

Hakim, Khalifa Abdul. 2007. *Islam ka Nazria-e-Hayat.* Translated by Qutb-ud-Din Ahmad. Lahore: Idara Saqafat-e-Islamia.

Hameedullah, Muhammad. 2009. *'Ahd-e-Nabavi Mein Nizam-e Hukamrani.* Reprint; Lahore: Nigarishat.

Haq, Syed Moinul. 1962. *Akhbar-e-Rangeen: Shah Alam aur Akbar Sani ka Dehli.* Karachi: Pakistan Historical Society.

Hazarvi, Ghulam Ghuas. 2006. *Jang: Sirat-e-Nabavi ki Roshni Main.* Reprint; Lahore: Jamiat Publications.

Hussain, Fida. 1992. *Tarikh-e-Tanawal.* Rawalpindi: Asad Mahmud Printing Press.

Ikram, Sheikh Muhammad. 2000. *Mauj-e-Kausar.* Reprint; Lahore: Idara Saqafat-e-Islamia.

Kakakhel, Sayyid Bahadar Shah Zafar. nd. *Pushtun: Tarikh kay Ayenay Main, 550 BC–1964 AD.* Translated by Sayyid Anwar-ul-Haq Jilani. Peshawar: University Book Agency.

Khan, Khawas. 1983. *Roidad-e-Mujahidin-e-Hind.* Lahore: Maktaba Rashidia.

Khan, Mir Abdul Samad. nd. *Loi Pukhtun.* Peshawar: University Book Agency.

Khan, Muhammad Asif. 1958. *Tarikh Riyasat-e-Swat wa Sawanih Hayat Bani Riyasat-e-Swat Hazrat Miangul Shahzada Abdul Wadud Khan Bacha Sahib.* NP.

Khan, Muhammad Ayub. 1985. *Afaghina Hoshiyarpur.* Lahore: Faran Publications.

Khan, Nawab Muhammad Wazir. 2007. *Waqai Sayyid Ahmad Shahid.* Lahore: Sayyid Ahmad Shahid Academy.

Khan, Roshan. 1986. *Yusafzai Qaum ki Sarguzasht.* Karachi: Roshan Khan and Co.

Khan, Waheed-du-Din. 2005. *Din wa Shariat: Din-e-Islam ka Aik Fikri Mutale'a.* Lahore: Dar-ul-Tazkir.

Kohli, Sita Ram. 2004. *Maharaja Ranjit Singh.* Reprint; Lahore: Sang-e-Meel Publications.

Lahori, Muhammad Qasim Ibrat. 1977. *Ibrat Nama.* Edited by Zahur-ud-Din Ahmad. Lahore: Research Society of Pakistan.

Lal, Kanhia. 2002. *Tarikh-e-Punjab.* Mirpur, Azad Kashmir: Arsalan Books.

Ludhianvi, Sheikh Bashir Ahmad. nd. *Imam Waliullah Dehlavi aur un ka Falsafa-e-Imraniyat wa Ma'ashiyat.* Lahore: Maktaba Bait-ul-Hikmat.

Madani, Hussain Ahmad. nd. *Naqsh-e-Hayat.* Reprint; Karachi: Dar-ul Isha'at.

Malik, Ikram Ali. 1990. *Tarikh-e-Punjab: Qadeem Zamana ta 1857.* Lahore: Salman Matbu'at.

Maududi, Sayyid Abu al Ala. 1976. *Tajdid wa Ahya-e-Din,* 21st ed. Lahore: Islamic Publications.

———. 2001. *Al-Jihad fil Islam.* Reprint; Lahore: Idara Tarjuman-ul-Quran.

Mian, Sayyid Muhammad. 1977. *Ulama-e-Hind ka Shandar Mazi,* vol. III. Reprint; Lahore: Maktaba Mahmudiyah.

———. 2002. *Jihad-e-Islami aur Dawr-e-Hazir ki Jang: Aik Taqabali Jaizah.* Reprint; Lahore: Jamiat Publications.

Mihr, Ghulam Rasul. nd. *Sayyid Ahmad Shahid.* Reprint; Lahore: Sheikh Ghulam Ali & Sons.

———. nd. *Sarguzasht-e-Mujahidin.* Reprint; Lahore: Sheikh Ghulam Ali & Sons.

Monthly *Al-A'zam,* Hafizabad, July 1993.

Monthly *Al-Da'wa.* Lahore, vol. 4, no. 6, June 1993.

Monthly *Al-Da'wa.* Lahore, vol. 4, no. 10, October 1993.

Monthly *Al-Haq.* Darul ulum Haqqania Akora Khattak, vol. 32, no. 1, October 1996.

Monthly *Al-Tawhid wa Al-Sunnah.* Dar-ul-Qur'an Panjpir, Swabi, vol. 2, no. 12, July 1993.

Muhammad, Fazal. 2009. *Safah-e-Alam par Tarikhi Nuqush.* Lahore: Al Mashal.

Murtaza, Ghulam and Mirza Ghufran. 1962. *Nai Tarikh-e-Chitral.* Peshawar: Latif Brothers.

Nadvi, Masud Alam. 1979. *Hindustan ki Pehli Islami Tahrik.* Reprint; Lahore: Idara Matbu'at-e-Sulaimani.

———. nd. *Muhammad bin Abdul Wahab: Aik Mazlum aur Badnam Muslih.* Reprint; Lahore: Al-Hilal Publications.

Nadvi, Muhammad Hamza. 1996. *Tazkira Hazrat Sayyid Ahmad Shahid.* Karachi: Majlas Nashriyat.

Nadvi, Sayyid Abu al-Hassan Ali. nd. *Tarikh-e-Dawat wa Azimat: Sirat-e-Sayyid Ahmad,* vols. I & II. Reprint; Karachi: Majlas Nashriyat.

———. nd. *Jab Iman ki Bahar Ayi.* Karachi: Majlas Nashriyat.

Nadvi, Sayyid Sulaiman. nd. *Seer-e-Afghanistan.* Karachi: Majlas Nashriyat.

Nasiri, Alim. 1995. *Shahnama Balakot: Tahrik-e-Jihad ki Manzum Dastan,* vols. I & II. 2nd Revised edition; Lahore: Idara Matbu'at-e-Sulaimani.

Nizami, Khaliq Ahmad. 1978. *Shah Waliullah kay Siyasi Maktubat.* Reprint; Lahore: Idara Islamiyat.

Panni, Sher Bahadar Khan. 2006. *Tarikh-e-Hazara.* Lahore: Maktaba Jamal.

Quddusi, Ijaz-ul-Haq. 1966. *Tazkirah Sufiya-e-Sarhad.* Lahore: Markazi Urdu Board.

Sabir, Muhammad Shafi. 1986. *Tarikh-e-Subah Sarhad.* Peshawar: University Book Agency.

Sabir, Muhammad Shafi. nd. *Tazkirah Sarfaroshan-e-Sarhad*. Peshawar: University Book Agency.

Sindhi, Ubaidullah. nd. *Shah Waliullah aur un ki Siyasi Tahrik: Yani Hizb-e-Waliullah Dehlavi ki Ijmali Tarikh ka Muqadama*. Lahore: Al Mahmud Academy.

Sithanavi, Sayyid Abdul Jabbar Shah. 2011. *Kitab-ul-Ibrat: Subah Sarhad wa Afghanistan ki Char sau Sala Tarikh 1500–1900*, vol. I. Islamabad: Porab Academy, 2011.

Shahjahanpuri, Abu Salman. 1977. *Tahrik-e-Nazm-e-Jama'at*. Lahore: Altaf Rahim.

Shahjahanpuri, Payam. 1971. *Shahdatgah-e-Balakot*. Lahore: Idara Tarikh wa Tahqiq.

Shahpuri, Abad. 1981. *Sayyid Badshah ka Qafila*. Lahore: Al-Badar Publications.

Suri, Lala Sohan Lal. 1961. *Umdat-ul-Tawarikh Daftar II*. Delhi: S. Chand and Co.

Tahir, Muhammad. nd. *Al-Intesar li Sunnat-e-Sayyid-ul-Abrar*. Panjpir, Swabi: Maktaba al-Yaman.

Tashna, Nazir Ahmad. 2006. *Tarikh-e-Kashmir, 1324–2005*. Lahore: Al Faisal Nashiran.

Thanavi, Ashraf Ali. nd. *Arwah-e-Salasa: Yani Hakayat-e-Awlia, Majmu'a-e-Rasail*. Reprint; Lahore: Maktaba Rahmaniyah.

Thanesari, Muhammad Jaffar. 1969. *Maktubat-e-Sayyid Ahmad Shahid aur Kala Pani*. Reprint; Lahore: Nafees Academy.

Usmani, Qamar Ahmad. 1983. *Baraili say Balakot: Tazkirah Mujahid-e-Kabir Hazrat Sayyid Ahmad Shahid Barailvi*. Lahore: Idara Islamiyat.

Waliullah, Shah. 2003. *Hujjat-ul-Allah-e-Baligha*. Translated by Abdul Rahim. Lahore: Al-Faisal Nashiran.

Yusafi, Allah Bakhsh. 1973. *Yusafzai Afghan*. Karachi: Sharif Arta Press.

Yusafzai, Jamil. 2009. 'Deh Ghulaman'. *Pakistan Journal of History and Culture*, April–September, pp. 39–64.

Zaheer, Muhammad. 2006. *Alamgir aur Sultanat-e-Mughlia ka Zawal*. Karachi: Educational Press.

Pukhtu Sources

Darwizah, Akhun. 1987. *Makhzan*. 2nd edition; Peshawar: Pukhtu Academy.

Ghaffar, Abdul. 1983. *Zama Jwand aw Jadojahd*. Kabul: Daulati Matba'.

Khalil, Hamesh. 2008. *Da Charbitay Pakhwani Shairan*. Peshawar: Pukhtu Academy.

Khan, Muhammad Asif. nd. *Tarikh Riyasate-Swat wa Sawanih Hayat Bani Riyasat-e-Swat Hazrat Miangul Gul Shahzada Abdul Wadud Khan Bacha Sahib*. NP.

Khan, Muhammad Nawaz. 2004. *Tarikhi Tapay*. Peshawar: University Book Agency.

Khan, Taj Muhammad. nd. *Uruj-e-Afghan*. Peshawar: Manzoor-e-Aam Press.

Mahsud, Ali Khan. nd. *La Pir Rokhana tar Bacha Khan Puray: Da Pukhtanu Milli Mubarizay ta Katana*. Peshawar: Danish Khparawanay Tolanay Tekhniki Sanga.

Salarzai, Qazi Abdul Halim Asar Afghani. 2006. *Da Pukhtu Charbetay Bagh wa Bahar*. Reprint; Peshawar: Pashto Academy.

Shaheen, Salma. 1994. *Rohi Sandaray: Tapay*, vol. II. Peshawar: Pukhtu Academy.

Sultan-e-Rome. 1997. 'Da Saidu Babaji na tar Wali Swat Puray: Yawa Tanqidi Jaizah'. *Pukhtu*, vol. 29, no. 11–12, pp. 12–23.

———. 1998. 'Da Swat Gharuna aw ka dh Azadai da Tarikh Babuna: Yawa Tajziyah'. *Pukhtu*, vol. 30, no. 11–12, pp. 44–57.

Personal Interviews

Dr Inayatullah Baloch, at South Asia Institute Heidelberg, Germany, May–June 2008.

Dr Sultan-i-Rome, at his residence in Hazara, Swat, June–July 2007.

Maulana Abdul Salam, at his residence in Peshawar city, 22 October 2007.

Maulana Muhammad Tayyab, Amir Isha'at Tawhid wa Sunnah at Panjpir, Swabi, 26 December 2010.

Dr Muhammad Sa'id, Jama'at-i-Islami activist and former Senator) at Hayatabad Peshawar, 28 July 2005.

Index

About the Author

Altaf Qadir is Assistant Professor, Department of History, University of Peshawar, where he joined as a lecturer. He is a Life Member of the Pakistan Historical Society. Qadir served as Lecturer in history for about three years in the Department of Higher Education (Colleges), Government of former North-West Frontier Province.